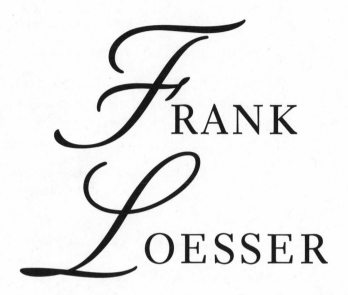

FRANK LOESSER

THOMAS L. RIIS

With a Foreword by Geoffrey Block, General Editor

YALE UNIVERSITY PRESS NEW HAVEN & LONDON

Set in Electra type by Tseng Information Systems, Inc.
Printed in the United States of America.

Library of Congress Cataloging-in-Publication Data

Riis, Thomas Laurence.

Frank Loesser / Thomas L. Riis ; with a foreword by Geoffrey Block.

p. cm. — (Yale Broadway masters)

Includes bibliographical references (p.), discographical references (p.), and indexes.

ISBN 978-0-300-11051-7 (cloth : alk. paper)

1. Loesser, Frank, 1910–1969. 2. Composers—United States—Biography. I. Title.

ML410.L7984R55 2008

782.1′4092—dc22

[B]   2007014702

A catalogue record for this book is available from the British Library.

The paper in this book meets the guidelines for permanence and durability of the Committee on Production Guidelines for Book Longevity of the Council on Library Resources.

10 9 8 7 6 5 4 3 2 1

Frontispiece: Pvt. Frank Loesser at work with pen and pipe, 1945. Frank Loesser Enterprises.

For Ruth, Charlie, and Jamy,
and in memory of Larry

Contents

Foreword

THE ACTOR (PERHAPS EDMUND GWENN) WHO ON HIS DEATHBED allegedly quipped, "Dying is easy, comedy is difficult," got it dead wrong when it came to the work of Frank Loesser. Loesser's death from lung cancer at the age of fifty-nine in 1969 was extraordinarily difficult; on the other hand, throughout his time in Hollywood and his relatively short but amazingly productive and successful period on the Broadway stage, comedy seemed to flow from him effortlessly on a staggering array of topics. Whether depicting a woman confronting the psychosomatic symptoms of a perpetual cold in response to a fourteen-year engagement in "Adelaide's Lament" from *Guys and Dolls* (1950) or capturing the agony of office workers unable to survive without the taste of cardboard between their lips in "Coffee Break" from *How to Succeed in Business Without Really Trying* (1961), Loesser rarely failed to capture human foibles and aspirations in a timelessly clever song. In *The Most Happy Fella* (1956) he also made us cry, and since comedy was easy, this accomplishment meant even more to him.

Thomas L. Riis's *Frank Loesser* is the first book to comprehensively examine the work of this important lyricist, composer, and, in the case of *Fella*, librettist, including Loesser's prolific Hollywood career, with its roughly one hundred films and nearly as many collaborators. Loesser's work in Hollywood, first as a lyricist and then as a composer-lyricist, is best remembered today for the words he wrote to complement Hoagy Carmichael's melodies "Two Sleepy People" and "Heart and Soul," and for a song he wrote and then sang for years at parties with his first wife before it won an Academy Award — "Baby, It's Cold Outside." The latter revealed Loesser's ability to transform a song into a conversational mini-scene (with overlapping and occasionally simultaneous musical lines), a harbinger of the Broadway work to follow.

Although Riis naturally emphasizes the major trilogy (*Guys and Dolls*, *Fella*, *How to Succeed*), he displays the full catalog of Loesser's accomplishments, including the films of the late 1930s and 1940s; the wartime stage dramas called "Blueprint Specials" that Loesser put together while serving in the army; the first Broadway hit, *Where's Charley?* (1948); and the one Broadway disappointment, *Greenwillow* (1960). Riis even touches on the little-known commercial and creative dead ends that followed the Pulitzer Prize–winning and long-running *How to Succeed*, mainly *Pleasures and Palaces* (directed by Bob Fosse), which closed out of town, and *Señor Discretion Himself*, a show that Loesser abandoned after several years of intense work and left incomplete at the time of his death.

Riis also relates how Loesser succeeded in the business side of Broadway. Together with George Abbott, who wrote the libretto for and directed *Where's Charley?* and who helped Loesser develop his idiosyncratic Broadway talents, Loesser encouraged and nurtured luminous fellow composer-lyricists, from experienced professionals Robert Wright and George Forrest (*Kismet*) to the untested Richard Adler and Jerry Ross (*Pajama Game* and *Damn Yankees*) and Meredith Willson (*The Music Man*). In an interview section included with the DVD version of a 2006 PBS documentary on Loesser's career called *Heart & Soul: The Life and Music of Frank Loesser* (Final Cut Productions), Adler, the lone survivor of this group, credited Loesser as "professionally the most important human being in my life." In another interview from the documentary, Jerry Herman, the composer-lyricist of *Hello, Dolly!*, *Mame*, and *La Cage aux Folles*, praised Loesser's absence of waste, as well as the surprises in his songs, and repeated a story about the day in his youth when Loesser took the time to listen to his work. He recalled vividly how Loesser drew a picture of a train to explain how a good song contains a locomotive that drives the song and ends with a caboose to finish with a twist, and expressed his gratitude to Loesser for encouraging an aspiring unknown composer-lyricist. In addition, Stephen Schwartz, from a later generation, revealed in the program that Loesser's "Adelaide's Lament" inspired Schwartz's "Popular" from *Wicked*.

For most of the world, the identity of the man who composed such wonderful screen and stage songs as "Spring Will Be a Little Late This Year," "On a Slow Boat to China," "Once in Love with Amy," "Inch Worm," "Sit Down, You're Rockin' the Boat," "Standing on the Corner," and "I Believe in You" remains anonymous. While many people can hum these songs, I would wager that few people know they were all created by the subject of this volume or that several served interesting dramatic situations. In any event, the two classic Broadway musical comedy perennials that everyone knows, *Guys and Dolls* and *How to Succeed*, stand in the spotlight of Loesser's legacy. These timeless shows persist in making audiences laugh while connoisseurs marvel at their imagination and art, thanks in large part to Loesser's words and music. In addition, the underappreciated *Most Happy Fella*, the "opera" that Frank Loesser, the man who made musical comedy look deceptively easy, preferred to describe as a "musical with a lot of music," continues to gain new converts and make them cry.

GEOFFREY BLOCK
General Editor

Preface

FRANK LOESSER WROTE THE WORDS AND MUSIC FOR DOZENS OF songs still cherished by generations of Americans who would be hard-pressed to identify their creator. "Two Sleepy People," "Praise the Lord and Pass the Ammunition," "Baby, It's Cold Outside," "On a Slow Boat to China," "Once in Love with Amy," "Luck Be a Lady," "I've Never Been in Love Before," "Sit Down, You're Rockin' the Boat," "The Inch Worm," "Thumbelina," "Wonderful Copenhagen," "The Ugly Duckling," "I Believe in You," and many others, some 700 lyrics all told, make up the impressive catalog. Loesser wrote four hit musicals in the period from 1948 to 1961, the greatest of which, *Guys and Dolls* (1950), appears on virtually all top-favorites lists. He also composed both words and music for a handful of failed but interesting musical comedies whose fitness for Broadway is still occasionally discussed. Beyond his immense individual productivity during a multifaceted career cut short by lung cancer in his fifty-ninth year (1969), Loesser's personal magnetism, business acumen, and mentoring skills inspired dozens of assistants, protégés, young songwriters, novice singer-actors, and aspiring producers. His generosity, sense of humor, steel-trap musical memory, and volatile temper were celebrated by those who knew him well.

Frank Loesser was a major player and, briefly, even something of a household name during an epoch dominated by the team of Richard Rodgers and Oscar Hammerstein II (from 1943 until 1960). Furthermore, his career as a highly successful lyricist in Hollywood (1936–42) is virtually unknown even among fans of his later work. During the war years, Loesser composed musical revues made to order for performance and consumption by U.S. troops

stationed abroad. Heretofore, these have escaped scholarly attention altogether. He enjoyed a string of hit parade successes (records by popular singers and sheet music sales) immediately after the war and appeared on the
occasional radio and television program in cameo interviews.

Because Loesser lived so close to the center of things throughout his
career and made such a massive contribution to both Hollywood film music (especially in the medley of songs for Samuel Goldwyn's *Hans Christian Andersen*, 1952) and Broadway musical theater through the 1950s, it is
something of a scandal that no serious study of his work—besides an excellent biography by his daughter—has been written to date. The sheer size of
his accomplishment has at least begun to be addressed in the recently published *Complete Lyrics of Frank Loesser* (2003). But much more remains to
be said.

A New York native, Loesser grew up in a household where both his father
and his much older half-brother had made substantial careers in classical
piano teaching and performance, although apparently young Frank never
studied more than tonal basics at home and pursued other nonmusical interests intensively. Yet he loved New York and could not escape the allure
of Tin Pan Alley and Broadway during his teen years (1923–29), among the
most exciting periods in the city's entertainment history. The story behind
the story of Loesser's career path lies in viewing him as part of a larger phenomenon, writing his great shows in the second half of what Mark N. Grant
has called the "high-water period" of great Broadway shows lasting from 1927
to 1966 (in *The Rise and Fall of the Broadway Musical*, 5). Grant accepts as
given "that the American musical peaked as an art form during a forty-year
golden age . . . that ended almost forty years ago." The top shows of this era,
he writes, "coalesced and integrated the complementary theatrical arts—
playwriting, music, design, dance, movement, truthful acting—in a way that
differentiates them from and raises them above all other light music theater
genres of the world, past and present. . . . The Broadway musical at its height
was a vernacular version of Wagnerian *Gesamtkunstwerk*: a total art form for
the masses." How Loesser learned music and found his place in this "golden
age" are among the issues I hope to raise and at least partially resolve in this
account.

Other questions and issues we will encounter relate to the dramatic and
musical contents of his major Broadway vehicles: the familiar conventions
and the surprising novelties. If we can understand more closely what exactly
inspired Loesser's creative attention, then perhaps we can more precisely

assess his lasting contributions. Unlike the other immortals of Broadway song—Jerome Kern (1885–1945), Irving Berlin (1888–1989), Cole Porter (1891–1964), George Gershwin (1898–1937), and Richard Rodgers (1902–1979) come to mind—few aficionados today even know the outlines of his life and career or have an inkling of his personality. These will be the subjects of the biographical introduction and chapter 1.

Loesser was both beloved and notoriously difficult. Thus, at least a brief examination of the education, background, and experience that formed his mercurial and challenging character is in order. He faced personal and occupational hurdles as a teenager. What opportunities appeared for a bright, young New Yorker just prior to the Great Depression? What can be learned about his relationship to the modern media developing in his day: movies, radio, recording technology, and television? His interest in the music business was extensive, and it forms a persistent theme throughout his career. Is there more to be found with closer inspection of these many layers of activity?

Younger than some of his illustrious contemporaries of the post–World War II era, such as Arthur Schwartz (1900–1984), Harold Arlen (1905–1986), and Marc Blitzstein (1905–1964), Frank Loesser (1910–1969) lived in an era in which vernacular music—specifically popular songs about topical, comic, and romantic subjects (allied to both Hollywood and Broadway)—rose to inhabit a dominant place on the cultural menu of a majority of Americans. During the 1950s, both diehard classical music aficionados and the hippest jazz artists professed to enjoy and appreciate the best that Broadway had to offer. The cultural cutting-edge role of Broadway would decline fairly precipitously by the end of the 1960s, in the wake of the rock revolution and tumultuous social upheaval. Yet its earlier impact should not be forgotten.

Loesser's life ran coterminously with this arc of history. Born in 1910, the last year of the Edwardian period, less than a decade after the Wright brothers' famous first flight (1903) and Ford's Model T went into production, he matured in an era that saw economic catastrophe, worldwide military conflict, the rise of Communist superpowers, the Korean War, and the doubling of the country's overall population (from 92 million to roughly 200 million).

During the 1940s and '50s, Loesser and his peers took part in the largest military mobilization up to that time in American history, followed by unprecedented growth in industrial power and economic productivity. The attitudes and insights that grew out of the challenges of war and postwar life experiences shaped American expectations in the entertainment industry as well as in all other pursuits. A spirit of confidence combined with ready money aided producers in taking live theater and the movies in new directions. Loesser's personal experiences as yeoman lyricist, citizen soldier, and Hollywood insider enabled him to note and respond to the latest trends. His lack of interest in rock 'n' roll did not prevent a willingness to boost the fortunes of young composers during the last decades of his life. He passed on when the Vietnam War was raging, in the same summer as the Woodstock Music and Art Festival and the Apollo 11 moon landing. It may have seemed to him that the world was turning upside down as he lay dying of lung cancer in 1969, but his works live on in frequent revivals and tributes.

Whatever one's perspective on Frank Loesser, his fellow songwriters, and other musical theater denizens of the middle third of the twentieth century, historians are finally getting around to paying heed. Several new books covering the general territory are included in the list of works cited here. Adding to the many finely detailed chronicles of Gerald Bordman from the last quarter of the twentieth century is the compendious three-volume set A Chronology of American Musical Theater by Richard C. Norton (2002). Even more recently, Raymond Knapp's The American Musical and the Formation of National Identity (2005) examines American musicals "according to their treatment of themes," such as race, war, exoticism, and identity. It provides several insights and illustrative musical examples. Mark N. Grant's book of 2004, cited above, offers a provocative, up-to-date, and bold assessment of the form. It is a rare example of a musically detailed book that will not lose a nonspecialist's attention. The only two books devoted exclusively to the accomplishments of Frank Loesser are the biography by Susan Loesser mentioned above (reprinted by Hal Leonard in 2000) and The Complete Lyrics of Frank Loesser (2003). Robert Kimball, distinguished author and editor of several books on musical theater, and Steve Nelson, professor of musical theater at New York University and producer of the Songwriter Series for the Library of Congress, coedited this useful volume. It contains far more than a mere list of lyrics, also supplying a timeline, much publication information, and a brief summary of Loesser's life and accomplishments. These books, especially the latter two, have been indispensable for my work. I have also benefited from the generosity of Joseph Weiss at Frank Loesser Enterprises, whose offices in midtown Manhattan contain much unique material pertaining to the life and work of Loesser.

After the biographical summary contained in the introduction, chapter 1

discusses Loesser's development as a writer and musician and his early experiences, working relationships, and accomplishments in the Hollywood
studio system at an early apex. It then follows Pfc. Frank Loesser's active career as he created best-selling songs while serving in the U.S. military during
the Second World War. Chapter 2 takes up Loesser's postwar songs and first
Broadway success, *Where's Charley?*

Chapters 3–5 set out to be analytical chronicles of Loesser's three greatest shows after *Where's Charley?*—*Guys and Dolls* (1950), *The Most Happy
Fella* (1956), and *How to Succeed in Business Without Really Trying* (1961).
These three have enjoyed regular revivals and strong critical acclaim to the
present day but have not as yet been fully treated by musical scholars (although several excellent chapters and articles have appeared in books by
Geoffrey Block and Joseph Swain, cited in the bibliography). Chapter 6
takes up the shows of Loesser that have enjoyed less fame and fewer performances. Some familiar materials are restated for contextual understanding,
but most of the discussion in these chapters focuses on the untold parts of
the story and exploring the shows' dramatic dimensions. Observations about
the musical and textual elements of the Broadway shows, especially those
that seem especially indicative of Loesser's distinctive gifts and style, receive
the most attention. Finally, chapter 7 describes and comments on Loesser's
penchant for the music business, his institutional work to preserve his songs
and shows, and his role as coach, mentor, and agent for young talent.

Each chapter bears an excerpt from a Loesser lyric as an epigraph. The
bibliography includes the works cited, as well as a note about unpublished
material and useful general histories of Broadway, Hollywood, and Tin Pan
Alley songs. Three chronological lists of Loesser song lyrics and a brief dis-
cography accompanying the basic production data of his live stage shows
complete the appendixes.

Acknowledgments

ALMOST EVERY PERSON TO WHOM I HAVE MENTIONED MY INTEREST in Frank Loesser over the last few years has responded in one of three ways: by making a pun on his last name, by confusing him with Alan J. Lerner and Frederick Loewe (the guys who wrote *Brigadoon*, *My Fair Lady*, and *Camelot*), or by singing back to me the opening words of "Fugue for Tinhorns" ("I've got the horse right here. His name is Paul Revere. . . . Can do.") So my first thanks go to friends, family members, colleagues, and acquaintances who have kept my focus steady by reminding me of a single dynamic image: Frank Loesser working his lyrical and musical magic on Broadway at a time when many others were similarly employed, but making his most indelible mark with *Guys and Dolls: A Musical Fable of Broadway* (which features "Fugue for Tinhorns"), a show of craft and wit and a resonant icon of New York City itself. Frank Loesser and *Guys and Dolls* form a grand metaphor for all that is "fabulous" and exciting about musical comedy across the land—or at least as it used to be. Loesser's lessons will, I predict, have a greater and not a lesser impact in the twenty-first century.

It was Geoffrey Block who first invited me to submit a proposal for the Yale Broadway Masters series, and it was he who stimulated my first analytical thinking on the subject of Loesser's songs and shows. Jeannie G. Poole, Eldridge Walker, and Gregory Rice guided me through the wonders of Paramount's music building. George Boziwick and his staff opened the door—or rather the boxes—to the Loesser materials at the New York Public Library for the Performing Arts at Lincoln Center, and Joseph Weiss has continually and generously offered useful guidance at Frank Loesser Enterprises, as have

Luke Dennis at the Harvard Theater Collection and Mark Eden Horowitz at the Music Division of the Library of Congress. Peter Silvestri and David Bogart gave helpful advice about the Frank Music Corporation archives. Miles Krueger shared his voluminous memories and personal collection of musical theater artifacts. Stuart Ostrow likewise turned over a part of his own book in progress for my reference. Their recollections of the New York scene and its main characters in Loesser's day enhanced my perspective, as did Gregor Benko's e-mails and telephone calls. My former student David Schiller introduced me to Jeffrey Tucker, who led me to Loesser's army shows. Richard Crawford's comments and questions gave shape and coherence to an early draft of this manuscript. Steven Ledbetter, Steve Swayne, James Leve, Adrienne Fried Block, J. T. LaSaine, Susan Loesser, and Abba Bogin shared their ideas freely. Geoffrey Block and the anonymous readers for Yale University Press also improved many aspects of the book. Michael Buchler came to my rescue with answers to analytical questions and called my attention to sources that would otherwise have lain neglected. Katie Dishman scoured the archives of General Mills in search of ancient commercial recordings. Because of the care of these and others, I was saved from putting too many more errors into print than I already have.

So many dear friends have played host or sounding board, or dropped hints and suggestions, or loaned recordings that led to good results that I will probably fail to include someone, but thank you all: John Bisceglia, Michael Buck, Ian Burke, Peter Caughey, David Chevan, Bud Coleman, Brad Conner, Paul Floyd, Karl Gert zur Heide, Tomás Hernández, Stewart Hoover, William Kearns, Stephen Luttmann, Kellie Masterson, Greg Norton, Eric Petersen, Joe Portanova, Keith Reas, Ben Saypol, Ben Sears, Judith Tick, Judy Tsou, Cassandra Volpe, Barbara Zarlengo, and Richard Zimdars. Caring attention has been showered on me all along the way in extrascholarly forms as well: my deepest appreciation goes to Bob Henson; Rhonda and Ole Fadum; Steve Frye, Julie Graf, and their children, Genevieve and Charlie; and Jim Magee, Mary McMillan, and their son, Jamy. As always my parents, Ruth and Larry Riis, never failed to lend unstinting support. Dad passed away in May 2003, just as this project was getting off the ground; I will miss being able to share the results with him.

My colleagues at the University of Colorado at Boulder, especially the Music Library staff there and its director Laurie Sampsel, and Carola Schormann and Christian Biellefeld at the University of Lüneburg, Germany, frequently broadened my thinking or pointed me in helpful directions. The dean of the University of Colorado, Boulder, College of Music, Daniel Sher, and the university's Graduate Committee on the Arts and Humanities helped to provide financial assistance for my research trips. Keith Condon, Jessie Hunnicutt, and Duke Johns carefully oversaw my work at Yale University Press. Mary Newberry made the index. I am grateful to Charles Manley for granting permission to publish parts of his father's letter about *Guys and Dolls* sent to the Production Code Administration office in 1955. Finally, Jo Sullivan Loesser, still actively involved in her husband's music, encouraged me at a time when I needed a boost.

Biographical Introduction

FRANK LOESSER WAS BORN IN NEW YORK CITY ON JUNE 29, 1910, THE second child of his father Henry's second wife, Julia Ehrlich Loesser. Henry's first marriage, to Bertha Ehrlich (Julia's older sister, who died in 1907), had produced one offspring, Arthur, born in 1898. Henry and Julia's first child, Grace, came along in 1907. The family was close and nurturing; by all accounts, its members were devoted to one another and intensely cultured. Henry was a renowned piano teacher and accompanist. Arthur, the favorite son, was recognized as a musical prodigy. Frank's sister, Grace, later a talented writer, also studied music, and young Frank naturally followed in his family's footsteps. He resisted taking piano lessons and indeed formal music instruction of any sort, but he seemed able to assimilate practically everything he heard by ear. Early on he rebelled against strict by-the-book teaching but absorbed knowledge and skills in spite of himself in an environment that encouraged his independence. His mother, Julia, held her children to high standards. She read widely and later gave paid lectures on contemporary literature.[1]

Though precociously bright, Frank behaved disruptively at school. He was admitted to high school at Townsend Harris Hall, PS 165, a school for exceptionally gifted students whose alumni included "Yip" Harburg and Ira Gershwin, before reaching age thirteen, but his pranks got him expelled before graduation.[2] Henry Loesser's sudden death, less than a month after Frank's sixteenth birthday, devastated his family and forced Frank into a series of odd jobs. Besides these miscellaneous money-raising efforts, he began to write lyrics for songs by his musical friends during his teen years. The

Sister Grace and young Frank in traditional German costume, 1914.
Frank Loesser Enterprises.

Arthur, Grace, and Frank Loesser, ca. 1920. Frank Loesser Enterprises.

first of these verses to have escaped destruction, for which his pal Carl Rice had written the music, were registered for copyright in 1929. In 1930 he collaborated on an operetta with another neighborhood friend, but the show remained incomplete. Billy Schuman (later known as William Schuman, distinguished composer and musical administrator at the Juilliard School and Lincoln Center for the Performing Arts) wrote the music. His first published lyric, also with Schuman's music (though not part of the operetta), is entitled "In Love with a Memory of You" (1931).

In a veritable torrent of verbal creativity, Loesser provided lyrics for a long list of aspiring tunesmiths between 1931 and 1936, many of whom eventually achieved a degree of notoriety with one or more songs written with other lyricists. Their names include Percy Wenrich (1887–1952), Jean Herbert (b. 1905), Charles Tobias (1898–1970), Bob Emmerich (1904–1988), Samuel Pokrass (ca. 1893–1939), Dailey Paskman (1897–1979), Ernest Breuer (1886–1981), and Joseph Meyer (1894–1987).[3] Once Loesser had declared his ambition to break into the songwriting business, nothing held him back, an impulse he communicated eloquently in a letter to his brother in 1933:

I have gone back to the song business. Although I have been writing them five years or more, I have never stuck to a trade for more than a year at a time. Not because I got tired of it, but every once in a while some "money-making" idea comes up (process-serving, for example) which takes me off the track, in the hope that I can make a better living in it than with music. But in every month *off* Broadway, I lose a *year's* trade. I said "trade." It is no *art*. I found that out. It is all contact, salesmanship, handshaking, etc. — not a bit different from cloaks and suits or any other industry. This time I am a salesman and a handshaker (still a little genteel for Broadway but going Broadway fast). This will bring success. I know it, and I am going to stick to it.[4]

One of his early goals was to work in the Brill Building, on Forty-ninth Street, the home to various publisher-songwriters of near legendary fame: T. B. Harms, the Witmark brothers (Isidore, Julius, and Jay), Paul Dresser (brother of Theodore Dreiser), and many others. Fascinated with the business of song making, Frank soon found his niche as a popular song lyricist and aspiring "song plugger." Pluggers were business insiders whose job it was to play and sing the songs produced by nonperforming composers. They worked out of publishers' offices, advertising by word of mouth and through demonstration in clubs, cabarets, radio stations, and stores. Such a job was made to order for a young comer like Loesser. A decade earlier, Irving Berlin, George Gershwin, and Jerome Kern, among other notable songwriters, had received similar practical training in this capacity. It seems that Loesser never quite acquired the pianistic skills and vocal endurance to make the grade, but he continued to perform his and his friends' songs and to write new ones in a steady stream.

Allied with a cabaret performing partner, Irving Actman, Loesser found employment in a small downtown night club, the Back Drop, in 1935. Together the two young men wrote six sets of lyrics and tunes that were picked up for a Broadway revue in January 1936. *The Illustrators' Show* opened at the Forty-eighth Street Theatre and, though it closed after five performances, gave them encouragement to strive for bigger things.[5] Loesser journeyed to Hollywood to seek his fortune later that year and married Lynn Garland (née Mary Alice Blankenbaker, a singer from Indiana he had met at the Back Drop) a few months afterward. After writing a string of individual song lyrics for various studios, he signed a long-term contract with Paramount in October 1937.

Loesser's first film songs, collaborations with Manning Sherwin, Hoagy Carmichael, and Burton Lane, began to appear in 1938. His personal for-

Songwriting partners Frank Loesser and Irving Actman, ca. 1938. Frank Loesser Enterprises.

tunes improved considerably, and his work became popular enough to register on the *Your Hit Parade* radio broadcasts (which had begun in 1935) no
fewer than eight times during 1937 and 1938, including "Heart and Soul,"
"Two Sleepy People," and "Says My Heart" (the first to reach the number
one position). Although he missed New York, the glamorous and sunny am-
bience of Hollywood agreed with Loesser. By 1939 he was using dollar signs
to spell his name, had hired servants for his home, and had bought his wife
a mink coat. Growing accustomed to a life of luxury, he swam, rode horse-
back, and partied frequently, while still managing to maintain a steady work
schedule.

Producer Ernest Martin recalled Loesser's "strange work habits" from a
later day, but his patterns likely were set during his Hollywood years. "He'd
be up at four-thirty or five a.m., have a martini, and to work between five and
eight in the morning. He wasn't a boozer, he merely oiled up. Then after he
wrote, he'd go to sleep, get up later, work some more. Napped during the day,
for maybe three or four hours."[6] His seemingly constant flow of energy during waking hours also led him to take up bird-watching and cabinetry and
to pursue a fascination with sailing ships in the decades to come. True to his
city upbringing, Loesser never learned to drive a car.[7]

In 1939 the title song for Paramount's movie *Seventeen* contained for the
first time both the music and lyrics of Frank Loesser. In 1941 his song "Dolores" (with music by Louis Alter), sung by Frank Sinatra in the film *Las Vegas
Nights*, reached the top spot on sales charts and received an Academy Award
nomination.

Going to War

Loesser was inspired and energized by the country's move to war in December 1941. In "Praise the Lord and Pass the Ammunition," he secured
both fame and fortune for the duration. Some 750,000 pieces of sheet music and over two million vinyl recordings flew off the shelves once radio stations picked it up.[8] The dummy melody that Loesser had used to gain a sense
of the flow and rhythm of the words for "Praise the Lord"—attributed, so
the story goes, to a doughty military chaplain at Pearl Harbor (and eventually claimed by the navy for Chaplain Howell E. Forgy)—somehow fit better than he imagined it could with the simple, clenched-teeth hook line.
Friends urged him to keep his own tune. Its "infectious folk song quality," in

David Ewen's words, led to a surge in profits like nothing Loesser had ever experienced with a single song.[9] Understanding that a more complicated melody would have spoiled its direct appeal imprinted an important lesson. The success of "Praise the Lord," only the second full song for which he had provided text and tune complete, gave him confidence to write more music along with his words.

In the fall of 1942 Loesser enlisted in the army in order to work with the military's Radio Productions Unit in Santa Ana, California, whose task it was to produce two recruiting shows a day without having to operate through the regular commercial networks. The unit had its own eighty-piece orchestra and a battery of writers, performers, and producers with Hollywood experience. An elite crowd filled with top talent, it included, among many competent writers, Milton DeLugg, who became Loesser's first musical amanuensis. Loesser did not at this stage write notes on paper with much ease or fluency, and he found in DeLugg an understanding collaborator. With this crucial assistant in place, Loesser was poised to expand his creative horizons.[10]

Another wartime hit, intended as a tribute to fallen GIs and a morale booster for the folks back home, was written—rather coolly in Loesser's guilty recollection—on commission. "Rodger Young" (often referred to as "The Ballad of Rodger Young") celebrates the dedication of a single soldier who died in the Pacific theater. Though Young had received the Congressional Medal of Honor for his bravery, his name was chosen from a long list merely because it scanned well for the songwriter. The army musicians loved the song, however, so Loesser colluded in supplying a largely fictitious background story about Young's musical experience. "Rodger Young" was introduced on Meredith Willson's radio program in early 1945 and subsequently was recorded by Burl Ives, Nelson Eddy, and John Charles Thomas, among others.[11]

In 1943 Loesser was transferred to New York, where he was assigned to write a series of shows called "Blueprint Specials" (so named because they used a copying process resembling architectural blueprints). These modest musical revues—skits with songs, rather than full-fledged book shows (see chapter 1)—were to be complete in all details, to allow for ready production by soldier entertainers overseas, "whether professionals or the most inexperienced amateurs."[12] Even as he was writing these army shows from 1942 to 1945, Loesser completed songs, usually just the lyrics but sometimes both words and music, for about twenty motion pictures, mostly at Paramount but also for RKO (Radio-Keith-Orpheum), MGM (Metro-Goldwyn-Mayer), Warner Brothers, Universal, Columbia, and Republic.[13]

Loesser never aspired to rise above the rank of private, because he liked what he did and actively avoided additional responsibilities that would surely have come with promotion. He also liked the idea of imitating Irving Berlin, who had remained a private during World War I despite his achievements. Now a wealthy man, Loesser was able to keep suites for himself and his family during the war at New York City's Navarro Hotel, to which, without the knowledge of his superior officers, he escaped to take his midday naps. He served past V-E Day, was discharged in June 1945, and returned to Hollywood, attracted chiefly by an extremely generous new contract from Paramount.

On to Broadway

Loesser's songs received two nominations for Academy Awards in 1943 and 1947, but not until 1949 did one finally come his way. A song originally presented at parties year after year by Loesser and his wife, "Baby, It's Cold Outside," was included in *Neptune's Daughter*, a film starring Esther Williams and Ricardo Montalban. The movie had a mildly risqué screenplay and featured the comic antics of Red Skelton and the comic voice of Mel Blanc, along with Xavier Cugat and His Orchestra to provide the rumbas. The song, performed as a double duet by Williams, Montalban, Skelton, and Betty Garrett, was an instant success and recorded immediately by Dinah Shore with Buddy Clark and by Ella Fitzgerald with Louis Jordan, among many other teams.[14]

Although making a steady income from his Hollywood work, Loesser still lacked real control over his songs once they left his desk. Undoubtedly he had begun to taste the satisfaction of seeing a complete show that he had helped create come to the boards, and he wanted more. So the time was right when a call came from Cy Feuer and Ernest Martin, who had partnered in hopes of producing a musical version of the classic English farce *Charley's Aunt*. Loesser had known Cy Feuer from 1941, when Feuer was heading the music department for a low-budget film company, Republic Pictures, where Loesser had done a bit of work—the lyrics for seven songs with melodies by Jule Styne—for *Sis Hopkins*.[15]

At first Feuer and Martin had hoped to secure the music from Harold

Arlen and only the lyrics from Loesser. Fortunately for Loesser, Arlen was unavailable, and Loesser eagerly agreed to take on the tune-writing duties as well. With the engaging and light-footed Ray Bolger in the title role, *Where's Charley?* gained mixed reviews and made a profit, carrying on for nearly eight hundred performances. For the first time a major Broadway vehicle appeared with both words and music by Loesser (see chapter 2).[16]

Making Classics: *Guys and Dolls* . . . and More

Loesser reached a pinnacle with *Guys and Dolls*, which premiered on November 24, 1950, at the Forty-sixth Street Theatre. Hailed by all the leading critics, *Guys and Dolls* managed to sustain and balance both comic and romantic themes in comfortable harmony. It was acclaimed a nonpareil and has not lost its status over the years.

Cy Feuer and Ernest Martin repeated as originating producers, bringing in Loesser to write the songs from the beginning—that is, after permission to use Damon Runyon's stories was secured. (Unusually for Broadway, most of the songs in *Guys and Dolls* were completed before the book was written.) Because of his musical expertise and the speed at which he worked, Loesser's presence was probably more strongly felt here than in *Where's Charley?* Choreographer Michael Kidd was brought on board, and the veteran director George S. Kaufman mentored the team. After many false starts on the book—the original book by Jo Swerling was found to be unworkable— Abe Burrows was called in. Already a friend of Loesser and a popular radio personality, Burrows became the perfect collaborator with the demanding Kaufman. He molded his libretto tightly around Loesser's songs.

Loesser was now at the top of his game, working in the city he most loved, with all the resources at his disposal that he could ask for. To secure his future financial security, and following in the steps of his idol Irving Berlin, Loesser determined to publish his music himself, founding the Frank Music Corporation in 1950 (built on the earlier Susan Publications of 1948). He later went on to add other composers to his list, enriching himself as well as lending assistance to many young talents. This plan worked so well that in 1953 he acquired and developed Music Theatre International, an organization whose goal was to purchase rights to Broadway shows and then lease them for later productions outside New York. Finally, Loesser set up Frank Productions in 1960 so that he could produce his future shows. He ran all three businesses from one office in midtown Manhattan.[17] A deal maker by nature,

Loesser proved to be an effective businessman, and his companies, during his lifetime and afterward, had a supportive hand in a long line of successful shows, including *The Pajama Game* (1954), *Damn Yankees* (1955), *The Music Man* (1957), *The Fantasticks* (1960), *A Funny Thing Happened on the Way to the Forum* (1962), and *Fiddler on the Roof* (1964).

His first two children, Susan (born in 1944) and John (born in 1950), were being raised in California with the help of a full-time nanny, since neither Frank nor Lynn were much inclined to parenting. The children came to New York often enough to gain a sense of their father's fame, but Loesser's personal life was complicated by his frequent traveling between the East and West coasts and his wife's fluctuating health and vitality.

With the success of *Guys and Dolls*, Loesser was still receiving offers from Hollywood that were hard to resist. In 1952, on Moss Hart's recommendation, Loesser was tapped to write the songs for Samuel Goldwyn's movie musical *Hans Christian Andersen*. It resulted in another popular triumph and became a substantial profit maker for the creative team (see chapter 4).[18]

Loesser found his next vehicle for a Broadway show in the 1924 Pulitzer Prize–winning play *They Knew What They Wanted* by Sidney Howard. Set in the Napa Valley of California, it tells the story of an aging winemaker and his young mail-order wife. A tale of infidelity and reconciliation, with exuberant characters that Howard had apparently drawn from his experience as a Napa Valley worker, the play had picked up awards for its first cast and made a marked impression in New York. Revivals in the 1930s and '40s had been less well received by critics, but Loesser nevertheless liked the "youthful, jaunty" play and thought it could be refashioned as a musical drama.[19] Encouraged by his Hollywood friend Samuel Taylor, Loesser decided that he himself would take on the challenge of reworking the dialogue rather than farm it out to someone with experience in book writing. The show, *The Most Happy Fella*, coproduced by Kermit Bloomgarden and Lynn Loesser (who had found her calling as a casting agent and talent scout), became Loesser's proudest achievement.[20]

The result was far vaster than anyone had originally imagined. With only his own taste to answer to—and all the technical assistance his wealth and fame could summon—Loesser spent over five years constructing the show. He added characters and modified and updated virtually every scene in the play, extending or clarifying the dramatic conflicts (see chapter 4). He included dancers and sought an enlarged orchestra to play a lavish score,

Shamus Locke and Lynn Loesser, Broadway coproducers, 1957. Billy Rose
Theatre Division, The New York Public Library for the Performing Arts, Astor,
Lenox and Tilden Foundations.

Frank Loesser, Jo Sullivan Loesser, and Frank's mother, Julia, ca. 1960. Frank
Loesser Enterprises.

which finally contained over thirty full numbers. Many critics saw it as too
much of a good thing, but the general reception was positive. To fend off any
suspicions that he was foisting anything as pretentious as opera on the public, Loesser insisted that *The Most Happy Fella* (1956) was merely a "musical
with a lot of music," nothing more.[21] The critics mostly took him at his word.
Its longevity onstage (some 676 performances in the first Broadway run)
compares favorably with that of other famous "operatic" shows on Broadway,
such as Gershwin's *Porgy and Bess* (1935) or Kurt Weill's *Street Scene* (1947),
but *The Most Happy Fella*'s length and large amount of uncuttable music
have worked against revivals.[22]

   Despite his continued professional success, Loesser's marriage to Lynn,
subjected to years of stress, finally disintegrated, and they divorced in 1957.
Loesser began dating Jo Sullivan, another singer and the original Rosabella
in *The Most Happy Fella*. They married in 1959 and eventually had two
daughters: Hannah, born in 1962, and Emily, in 1965.

In 1960 Loesser created a show that remained a personal favorite of his but enjoyed only a short run. *Greenwillow* was a folksy, pastoral show, but unfortunately it had little dramatic staying power. It has been unsuccessful in revival, but the original cast recording (reissued in compact disc format) still allows it to be heard. *Greenwillow* has many attractive songs.

The breadth of Loesser's imagination was revealed again in his next Broadway outing, a biting satire of the corporate world, *How to Succeed in Business Without Really Trying* (1961). It provided Loesser with his longest single Broadway run (1,417 performances), his greatest international exposure to date, and kudos all around. *How to Succeed*, with Burrows again the book writer, became only the fourth Broadway musical to win the Pulitzer Prize for drama. It was his last hit.

The Final Years

Loesser's final completed score aimed at a Broadway audience, *Pleasures and Palaces*, closed out of town in 1965, after two years of preparation. The ill-favored play by Sam Spewack that served as its basis was a semihistorical romance set in eighteenth-century Russia; it included among its characters the Empress Catherine the Great and America's first naval hero, John Paul Jones, who in this story had been hired to fight the Turks that were threatening Russia at the time. Loesser and director-choreographer Bob Fosse conceived of it as a lavish spectacle and hired top set and costume designers to work the visual magic. But the show was plagued by problems at every turn. The preferred leading man, Richard Harris, rejected the part, and his substitute failed to carry it off. Songs fell flat. Orchestrations were deemed weak. Revision after revision proved unappealing. (Loesser wrote nearly twice as much music as was ever used for any one version of the show.) After *Pleasures and Palaces* played for six unhappy weeks in Detroit, garnering uniformly negative reviews, Loesser made the decision to cut his losses.[23]

Loesser's last show, left incomplete at his death in 1969, was called *Señor Discretion Himself.* The story by Budd Schulberg, which he first read in 1965, concerns a middle-aged Mexican widower with marriageable daughters and a failing business. Loesser was immediately taken with the colorful plot and rich cast of characters. He worked out an arrangement with Schulberg to develop the show, dove completely into fleshing out the book, and created a substantial body of music, some two dozen songs altogether. Prospects seemed good, but after two years of work, Loesser felt stymied by a va-

Frank Loesser, sporting a goatee, at his Long Island home in Remsenburg, near Westhampton, 1963. Photograph by John Loesser. Frank Loesser Enterprises.

riety of twists and turns in the plot that he could not reconcile, and he finally ended work on it in March 1968. As his daughter succinctly put it, "My father did not write from that time on, . . . no music, no lyrics, no books."[24]

Other clouds arose on the horizon. His first real artistic collaborator and lifelong friend Irving Actman died suddenly at the age of sixty in the autumn of 1967. Loesser, already plagued with emphysema, was suffering from other unidentified aches and pains and was briefly hospitalized in the fall of 1968 for tests. What was eventually determined to be lung cancer would spread to the rest of his body before a firm diagnosis could be made in June 1969.

His good friend John Steinbeck died in December 1968, and his half brother Arthur passed away in January 1969. Saddened by the deaths of those close to him, the national anxieties related to the war in Vietnam, and domestic social ills, Loesser was also alienated from his beloved Broadway (where *Hair*, the counterculture hit of 1968, was flourishing). An enthusiastic patriot during the Second World War, he was out of sympathy with the rebellious sixties: "Young people were smoking pot and raising hell and singing songs [he] refused to understand or even listen to."[25] His health continued to decline as the cancer spread. Family and friends gathered round, and Frank Loesser died quietly "early [in the] morning, his time of day," according to his daughter, on July 26, 1969. He had directed that his body be cremated, that the ashes be scattered, and that no services or ceremonies be observed.[26]

CHAPTER 1

Juvenile Poet, Hollywood Lyricist, Wartime Songwriter

I'm a gentleman, a scholar
And a versatile young lad.
I'm a painter and a poet
And I'm not half bad.
I'm an author and a writer
And a most accomplished gent—
Why you ought to see the fairy tales
That I invent.

—FRANK LOESSER, UNPUBLISHED LYRICS, CA. 1933

The Family

SUSAN LOESSER ONCE DESCRIBED HER FATHER AS A "GREAT FIERY comet," and it seems fair to state that Frank Loesser was often seen and felt by his family and friends as a force of nature not subject to normal controls. His prodigious energy was turned in dozens of directions over the years, but those who benefited most were the natives and newcomers to the worlds known as Hollywood and Broadway. The Frank Loesser they saw and came to idolize or fear (or admire through his songs) had many layers and facets. He was formed from a congeries of conditions in an intoxicating urban setting.[1]

Loesser was reared within a respectable German immigrant family, whose members cultivated and honored their intellectual and artistic heritage from nineteenth-century Europe. Germans had been bringing both public and home-centered styles of music making to the New World since the American Revolution, encouraging the foundation of bands, orchestras, choral societies, and chamber music clubs in dozens of cities and towns across the country.[2]

Though ethnically Jewish, neither of Loesser's parents was notably religious, and like many German Jews of their time and professional class—his family were bankers—they had largely assimilated the secular Prussian culture in which they had been raised. Frank Loesser's forebears on both sides—the Loesser and Ehrlich families—valued art, literature, philosophy, and the musical achievements of the Austro-German tradition, all the more so for having to preserve them far away from the home country. His daughter wrote that "my father grew up in a house . . . seething with intellects. . . . It was Goethe his mother read him at bedtime, not Sholom Aleichem."[3]

Frank's father, Henry Loesser, came to the United States during the 1880s to avoid military conscription and a seemingly inevitable career in the family business.[4] His was part of a familiar American immigrant experience, seeking fresh opportunities in the New World. He met his future wife, Bertha Ehrlich, in the boarding house where they both lived in Yorkville, Manhattan. Bertha kept the books at a drug company, and Henry made a living in the grocery business, but he aspired to a musical career and she supported him. Both Henry and Bertha were pianists. At the time of their marriage in 1892, they moved uptown to West 107th Street, and Henry took the plunge into full-time piano teaching. Along with maintaining a studio of pupils, he reportedly accompanied the renowned Wagnerian soprano Lilli Lehmann during her time in New York.[5] He appears to have succeeded well enough, since all evidence confirms that Frank Loesser grew up in a comfortable home filled with music, mostly by European classical masters.

Henry and Bertha's only child, Arthur, was born in 1894. This son, sixteen years older than Frank, was a model music student and the apple of his parents' eyes. Arthur Loesser (1894–1969) made his European performing debut in 1913 and became a successful and widely traveled concert pianist during the following decades (including tours of Australia, China, Singapore, Japan, and Indonesia). He authored numerous articles as well as sets of program notes for the Cleveland Orchestra (1927–42), and two books, *Humor in American Song* (1943) and *Men, Women, and Pianos: A Social History* (1954), a classic work. He ended his career as a renowned teacher and administrator at the Cleveland Institute of Music.[6]

A rebel from the start, Frank was still doted upon by his parents. His musicality, his stubbornness, and his temper were recognized from an early age. Claiming to have noticed the proverbial gift of a good ear in a four-year-old prodigy, Henry wrote to Arthur in 1914 that his infant half brother was "developing more and more into a musical genius. He plays any tune he's heard and can spend an enormous amount of time at the piano. Always he wants attention and an audience." While such comments bear the whiff of proud parental prejudice, they are hardly surprising in light of Frank Loesser's eventual accomplishments. Frank always sought attention and an audience.[7] A bit later Arthur declared, "When he was about six he improvised at the piano, aiding it with his own voice, something he called 'The May Party.' (Those decorative children's processions were often seen in Central Park.) It was a strain of onomatopoetic program music, allied in spirit to the 'Storm' and 'Battle' pieces of the 19th century. I recall there was a lot of drum in it. In his early teens he began to pick out current popular tunes on the keyboard, harmonies and all. In his early phases, Frank's position at the piano was simple and natural. Later on he acquired a habit of letting his torso go into light spiral tantrums while playing. I understand that this type of bodily symbolism used to be quite *de rigueur* in representative boogie-woogie circles."[8]

Despite the condescending tone, Arthur's portrayal tells much about Frank's abilities and aptitude for assimilating musical styles. Arthur's recollection about Frank's early dalliance with music corrects a misimpression implied in many accounts of Loesser's career to the effect that, since he never "seriously studied" piano at home with his talented father or brother, he then must have been entirely untouched by the music around him until much later in life. Clearly this was not the case. Frank Loesser's musicality simply emerged in unsuspected places. While reading notes on a page was never his forte, his musical ear missed little. His fundamental performing skills, as singer and pianist, were demonstrated often over the years.

The common assertion that Loesser was "self-taught" fails to account for the level of musical creativity that he eventually achieved, nor does it help to explain his personal tastes as a composer, much less his aspirations for his Broadway shows. Further details of his early life are relevant to his later career, however. He was surrounded by music from birth and learned to sight-sing (that is, to use sol-fa syllables for practicing melodies). All later evidence confirms that he possessed an outstanding memory for tunes, chord qualities, and lyrics.[9] Second, he was attentive to the doings around him, especially the musical activities among friends and family. In 1948 he recalled for Vincent Persichetti the experience of hearing his pal William Schuman play the piano and the violin (poorly) at Schuman's family home, as well as "having been hustled off all through my youth to hear recitals by various wunderkinder."[10] Abba Bogin later recounted Frank's boyhood recollections about hiding behind a parlor sofa so as to overhear his brother's chamber music sessions with friends. He simply absorbed everything, according to Bogin, and like any curious child would ask from time to time what was being played. Years later, when encountering a Haydn quartet or Bach suite, Loesser's recall of exact titles and tunes struck Bogin as virtually perfect.[11]

As Arthur somewhat grandly suggests above ("bodily symbolism . . . quite *de rigueur* in . . . boogie-woogie circles"), Frank could mimic other performers precisely. His taste for socializing, combined with a well-tuned ear and observant eye (the latter expressed in a profusion of sketches and doodles), point directly to a lively personality, someone with an independent creative flair, a willing partner or leader in dramatic escapades. His crowd of friends always loved movies and theatricals.[12]

Frank's rebelliousness extended to a lack of sympathy with his parents' native language and especially its literary associations. He refused to speak German as a young child, and he was never comfortable, even as an adult, in speaking his parents' mother tongue. Despite Henry's early predictions, apparently Frank neither took up the formal study of piano with anyone outside the family, nor did he learn to read or write music for many years. While he may well have practiced on the sly or studied informally with talented friends, the evidence is unrecorded. His family's undisguised, indeed vehement, hostility to popular music, plus a certain generational dissonance, affected Frank deeply. He relished filling the role of the impish younger son who, while talented and clever with words and music, was bored with school and impatient with cultural products that seemed alien to his New York home. Whatever was happening in Manhattan, however, was another story.

In 1949 Arthur Loesser recalled one of Frank's early musical triumphs: "For a time Frank forsook the piano and took up the mouth organ. He did rather well at it, without however reaching into the higher ether of the art. He entered a Greater New York harmonica contest, the final play-offs of which were in Central Park. . . . Frank won third prize, which turned out to be nothing but another assortment of harmonicas. The two boys who had bested him were from Brooklyn and the Bronx, and thus Frank proudly styled himself 'Champion of Manhattan.'"[13] As Frank entered adolescence, the world outside of his home neighborhood (the Upper West Side) provided all sorts of additional stimulation.

New York, New York!

A rage for modernist artistic activity was sweeping New York in the 1920s. Even the staid classical music circles in which Loesser's family moved were not unaffected. Arthur played in a world premiere of the second violin sonata (*Fantasia quasi una sonata*, op. 18) by the American modernist composer Marion Bauer, on a League of Composers program in 1925, when Frank would have been fifteen years old. (Bauer was an especially active member of a group that Carol Oja refers to as "the forgotten vanguard" of musical modernism in the twenties.) But this single event for Arthur Loesser was hardly an isolated one in the New York concert world. Igor Stravinsky's celebrated *Sacre du printemps* (1913) and Arnold Schoenberg's almost equally influential *Pierrot lunaire* (1912) were first presented in New York in 1922 and 1923, respectively, to standing-room-only audiences.[14]

Whereas before World War I, visual art exhibitions like the famous Armory Show of 1913, which included new works by Picasso, Toulouse-Lautrec, John Marin, and Marsden Hartley, among others, had been viewed with suspicion if not downright hostility, similarly shocking musical phenomena, heard in performances of works by Henry Cowell and George Antheil, had become somewhat more fashionable by the mid-twenties and the advent of the Dada movement.[15] And artistic brashness was by no means limited to a small, elite class of professionals. George Gershwin's *Rhapsody in Blue* formed the centerpiece for Paul Whiteman's 1924 Aeolian Hall event, called "An Experiment in Modern Music." Of Whiteman's impact, Oja has commented that "he was arguably one of the most important figures in the United States challenging the barriers between high and low art."[16]

The point is not to allege a specific debt owed by Loesser to the highbrow modernists of his youth or to popular/classical crossover figures like Whiteman and Gershwin, but to underline the artistic zeitgeist that flavored the city in which he was raised and which he always loved more than any other. A quick-witted adolescent in the 1920s, young Frank was, if not fully caught up in, at least susceptible to its influences and would remain so for life.

In Loesser's seventeenth year, 1927, Broadway enjoyed its most productive season ever, including premieres of hit musicals by Vincent Youmans, Leo Robin, and Clifford Grey (*Hit the Deck!*), Rodgers and Hart (*A Connect-*

icut Yankee), George and Ira Gershwin (*Funny Face*), and most famously, Jerome Kern and Oscar Hammerstein II (*Show Boat*). It is hard to believe that a bright and curious teenager like Frank Loesser would have ignored the presence of these shows along with the attendant critical hoopla in the press. He was already writing comic verse for fun and would soon be writing stories for a local newspaper.[17]

The Birth of a Lyricist

The art of writing lyrics is a rare skill, not widely understood by poets, musicians, or the listening public. Commonly viewed as a secondary art at best—a matter merely of taking a beautiful but undressed melody and adding rhyming or at least sensible words—the process is only rarely discussed apart from tunes. Philip Furia, with his many books on the subject, is one of few modern writers who have made an important contribution to our understanding of Tin Pan Alley classics and the great lyrics of Broadway between 1920 and 1950. He notes that successful wordsmiths themselves have tended to embrace an overly modest view of their efforts: "Even the lyricists who did publish their lyrics separately made sure no one would accuse them of impersonating a poet. Ira Gershwin entitled his collection, with mock-pomposity, *Lyrics on Several Occasions by Ira Gershwin, Gent.*, adding a disclaimer as forbidding as Mark Twain's 'Warning' to readers looking for a motive, moral, or plot in *Huckleberry Finn*: 'Since most of the lyrics in this lodgment were arrived at by fitting words mosaically to music already composed, any resemblance to actual poetry, living or dead, is highly improbable.'"[18]

Frank Loesser was born at the tag end of the ragtime boom, a period that signaled to many Americans that a vital and novel *musical* idiom could spring from native soil. Why not a new verbal style to match the catchy cakewalk rhythms? Ragtime songs were nothing if not colloquial. Yet many, especially those that exploited African American stereotypes (a subset sometimes referred to as "coon songs") were often hobbled by an overtly racial dialect that struck most people then and now as baldly insulting. By the 1910s, however, with the swinging syncopations of ragtime and protojazz integrated within a large swath of popular song melodies, Americans, without realizing it, had also begun to adopt a less racist and more direct approach to lyrics, the special creation of one man in particular: Irving Berlin.

True, the urban farces of Harrigan and Hart and the remarkable razzle-dazzle of George M. Cohan's songs had anticipated Berlin's fervid Americanness in their slangy lyrics, but Berlin, by a persistent dedication to short, clear, and simple word combinations, established a baseline that others would soon be taking for granted. The rhythmically charged rags could satisfy with an easy text, but Berlin applied his minimalist principles to nonragtime songs as well — and created classics. "Blue Skies" (1927) is a later example, but it marks the culmination of this early trend:

> Blue skies
> Smiling at me,
> Nothing but blue skies
> Do I see.
>
> Bluebirds
> Singing a song,
> Nothing but bluebirds
> All day long.

Generally providing one line of text to four measures (or sixteen beats' worth) of music, the phrases seem harmless enough on the page, but the persistent rhymes, open vowels, and the redundancy of things *blue* — suggesting both happiness and sadness simultaneously — matched to a perky melody, are vintage Berlin.

Other members of the Berlin generation, which included P. G. Wodehouse, Joe Young, Gus Kahn, and Noble Sissle, spread the gospel of simplicity and syncopation, but slightly younger comers, such as Cole Porter, E. Y. Harburg, Lorenz Hart, and Ira Gershwin, pushed the envelope even further. These men were influenced also by the playful and clever quality of light poetry, so-called society verse, which in the 1920s was allied with the fresh tunes of their musician partners. Many lyrics now strove for an independence that created a more equal relationship with their tunes. Neither tunes nor texts dominated, but neither was placed entirely in the shadow of the other. As a result of this heightened sensibility, dozens of aspiring lyricists generated hundreds of songs between 1925 and 1950, a period Allen Forte has dubbed "the golden era of American vernacular music."[19] "A new era of wit began [in the 1920s]," writes Philip Furia, "an era when, for the first time in American popular song, people began *listening* to the lyric."[20] Frank Loesser could not have joined the business at a better time.

While Frank's sociability, energy, and feeling for the vibrant life around him were never in doubt, he was also a reader and a thinker, ever the keen observer. It is Arthur Loesser again who names a specific inspiration for Frank's love of words and wordplay, and who in his 1949 account of the matter repeatedly stresses Frank's intellectual prowess: "There was . . . one well-known author in whom Frank [as an adolescent] delighted. I can still remember the high gusts of glee that came from him when we first read aloud the *Nonsense Novels* of Stephen Leacock. He became a Leacock enthusiast for months; I believe that was when he first appreciated the power and pleasure that comes from *well-chosen words* [emphasis added]. It was precisely in this period that Frank's own verbal genius began to be evident."[21]

Loesser's unorthodox intelligence, transmitted through ludicrous jokes and wordplay, has a clear parallel in Leacock's writing career. Stephen Leacock (1869–1944) was a heavily credentialed Canadian scholar who died a professor emeritus of economics at McGill University, but who also excoriated dry academicism and delighted a generation of fans with irreverent essays entitled "Too Much College: or, Education Eating Up Life" and "What Good Is Latin?" His *Nonsense Novels* are parodies in short-story form of overripe, quaintly romantic situations or Victorian authors such as Arthur Conan Doyle. They still impress with their appealing silliness. Chapter titles like "Maddened by Mystery: or, The Defective Detective," "Q: A Psychic Pstory of the Psupernatural," and "Hannah of the Highlands: or, The Laird of Loch Aucherlocherty" suggest his inveterate inclination to punning and alliteration, as does a brief excerpt from "Guido the Gimlet of Ghent: A Romance of Chivalry":

Isolde the Slender stood upon an embattled turret of the castle. Her arms were outstretched to the empty air, and her face, upturned as if in colloquy with heaven, was distraught with yearning.

Anon she murmured, "Guido"—and bewhiles a deep sigh rent her breast. . . .

Willowy and slender in form, she was as graceful as a meridian of longitude. . . .

She was begirt with a flowing kirtle of deep blue, bebound with a belt bebuckled with a silvern clasp, while about her waist a stomacher of point lace ended in the ruffled farthingale at her throat. On her head she bore a sugarloaf hat shaped like an extinguisher and pointing backward at an angle of 45 degrees. . . .

The love of Guido and Isolde was of that pure and almost divine type, found only in the middle ages.

They had never seen one another. Guido had never seen Isolde, Isolde

had never seen Guido. They had never heard one another speak. They had
never been together. They did not know one another.

Yet they loved . . .

Years before, Guido had seen the name of Isolde the Slender painted on
a fence.

He had turned pale, fallen into a swoon and started at once for Jerusa-
lem.[22]

There is short distance indeed from Leacock's knights of the castle of
Buggenburg—including Hubert the Husky, Edward the Earwig, Agatha the
Angular, and Carlo the Corkscrew—to the slangy pseudomedievalism of
Lorenz Hart (derived from Mark Twain) in A Connecticut Yankee, in which
the verse lyric for "Thou Swell" begins

> Babe, we are well met,
> As in a spell met—
> I lift my helmet,
> Sandy,
> You're just dandy
> For just this here lad.

After this, could Damon Runyonland, with Harry the Horse, Angie the
Ox, and Nicely-Nicely Johnson, be far behind? A residue of Leacock and
Hart also survives in fragments of an operetta libretto that a twenty-two-year-
old Frank Loesser began but never finished with his equally inexperienced—
but later famous—friend William Schuman. The show was intended to be
a comic take on the life of Leonardo da Vinci. Kimball and Nelson, in The
Complete Lyrics of Frank Loesser, note the following titles, presumably for
songs, assigned to six successive scenes. (None of the full lyrics that follow
this outline match these titles, however, so their significance remains un-
clear.)

> Act 1, scene 1 "You're a Bounder, You're a Blighter"
>   "I've Lived for This Moment"
> Act 1, scene 2 "Here Comes a Patron of the Arts"
> [This is perhaps the waltz that Schuman recalled he wrote with Frank's
> lyric: "Here comes that drunken / da Vinci again / all filled with highballs, /
> stewed to the eyeballs."]
> Act 1, scene 3 "Here's to It, Whatever It Is"
> Act 1, scene 4 "One Word from You"
> Act 1, scene 5 "Dirty Work at the Crossroads"

> "I'd Love to Push the Plow with You"
> "Love Is One of the Those Things"
> Act 2, scene 1 "Bravo"
> "Unaccustomed as I Am to Public Speaking"[23]

Loesser's First Lyrics

Only titles and lyrics survive for many of Loesser's first songs, written and registered for copyright a few years before the operetta: "Melancholy Me," "Alone in Your Class (Little Girl)," and "Let's Incorporate" (all in 1929), "Ticker Tape Talk" (1930), and "Satan" (1932). Carl Rice, about whom nothing is known, supplied the music.

"Let's Incorporate" prefigures the wit of *How to Succeed in Business Without Really Trying*, although perhaps it is better understood as an offbeat Dada fantasy consonant with contemporary Wall Street tumults. After "two well-known stocks were spied / Lovemaking side by side" (in the verse), the conversational refrain goes:

> Look me over if you please,
> I've no liabilities,
> We're two separate companies,
> So let's incorporate. . . .
>
> See my proposition through,
> For I'm bound to rise with you.
> We will cause a panic too
> If we incorporate.

After these short efforts with Rice, Loesser teamed with Schuman to write, besides the partial operetta, some "nightclub material" and about forty other songs, according to early Schuman biographers.[24] The team saw one song published by Feist, "In Love with a Memory of You" (1931), which disappeared without a trace of success. The lyric is filled with romantic clichés ("moonlight," "honeysuckle," "whispers," "daydreams," "Lover's Lane"). They also managed to record two songs, with Schuman singing and Loesser at the piano, on a Speak-O-Phone machine in a Broadway shop: "Doing the Dishes" and "Where the Grass Grows Green."[25] Schuman told Vivian Perlis, "They are cute songs, of no consequence, but fresh. He [Frank] always had fresh ideas, and my tunes I would describe as serviceable—nothing more than that."[26] They also collaborated on at least one "Russian number" for the use of Violet Carlson (1900–1997), a young vaudevillian and operetta singer.[27]

Loesser's byword seems always to have been "collaboration," although the phrase "love-hate relationship" also comes to mind. He worked with at least ten different tunesmiths between 1929 and 1936 (see the biographical introduction). He frequently shared lyric-writing duties as well. It would seem that he was invigorated rather than cramped by a group of cocreators, apparently preferring to work this way for many years. Probably he had no choice. Loesser gave most of his attention to wordplay and poetic structure, although it also seems likely he was picking up musical techniques along the way. He was always a notorious stickler for detail in whatever aspects of a song intrigued him. Ultimately his feeling for the links between poetic and musical rhythm began to increase. Gradually his understanding of the varied dimensions of songwriting bore fruit in his own work.

For Loesser, embracing the milieu of New York popular music also meant embracing the world of working-class, Yiddish-speaking Lower East Side Jews, who figured prominently in the entertainment business. Many of these men and women were lovers of popular music and club life. They were swing dancers, fans of Tin Pan Alley and burlesque who had little use for high art, cultivated sensibilities, or the classical legacy valued by Loesser's family. According to reports in the unpublished papers of his biographer Vincent Persichetti, young Bill Schuman deliberately avoided this crowd; Loesser, on the other hand, was attracted to both the people and their milieu.[28] Far from the assimilated high-culture German Jews of his childhood, Loesser's tough-talking, working man's persona was acquired and reaffirmed in a party atmosphere. As if to cement his introduction into this new ethnic urban community, in 1934 he collaborated with Joseph Meyer on three songs: "Junk Man," "I Wish I Were Twins," and "The Old Oak Tree."

The first title sounds like a jazz tune, and indeed it was played by Benny Goodman's band as well as Isham Jones. It bears traces of old-fashioned ragtime hits (whose popularity had peaked around 1910). If it had been written much earlier, sheet music sellers would surely have classified it as a "coon song." The verse begins benignly enough:

Junk Man, Junk Man,
Moochin' roun' Harlem town when all the lights are dim . . .

The refrain, however, tells the tale with streetwise language ("moochin'," "you done me wrong") about lost love, threatened abuse, and finally violent revenge—shades of "Frankie and Johnny."[29]

> I'm gonna give that Junk Man my broken heart,
> The broken heart I got from you.
> I'm gonna give that Junk Man my broken heart
> For a loaded "thirty-two."
>
> Now I ain't braggin', no! no!
> But you can't throw me down.
> I'm gonna fix your wagon, yeah! man,
> So you can't go to town!
>
> I'm gonna do you right,
> 'Cause you done me wrong,
> I'm gonna do you black and blue.
> And then I'm gonna tell that Junk Man to come along
> And pick up what's left of you.

Urban mayhem, when it happened in Harlem, was still considered chic in 1930s popular culture, but the dialect genre was beginning to fade in popularity at the time.

Loesser's second lyric with Meyer, which he cowrote with Eddie de Lange, called "I Wish I Were Twins," was recorded originally by jazz keyboard virtuoso Fats Waller; it made the biggest hit up to that time among Loesser's lyrics.[30] Falling into what might be termed the "cute love" style, it would probably be unbearably cloying were it not for the wonderfully over-the-top wordplay around twinning that, when combined with a repetitive syncopated melody, makes a nicely unified effect. The opening musical phrase rocks back and forth between two notes a scale step apart, but all sections of the tune keep to a restricted range and allow us to hear the emphasis placed on the last words of each bit of text, with the open "u" vowel sound dominating. The underlined phrases below contain multiple partial rhymes, and the entire lyric repeatedly stresses "you" and "I," the essential romantic word combination:

> [*phrases 1 and 4*]
> I wish that I were twins,
> You great big babykins
> <u>So I could love you *twice* as much as I do.</u>

[*phrase 2*]
I'd have four loving arms to embrace you,
Four *eyes* to *idolize* you each time I face you.

[*phrase 3*]
With two hearts twice as true
What couldn't four lips do?
When four *ears hear* you saying, "I'm yours!"

Meyer's third song with Loesser suggests a parody on the ubiquitous sentimental songs of the 1890s or the perennial favorite, "The Old Oaken Bucket." Other titles produced around this time, like "Now I Lay Me Down to Sin" and "Oh! What a Beautiful Baby You Turned Out to Be" (with music by J. Fred Coots) confirm Loesser's enthusiasm for a broad range of satirical, outrageous, or risqué turns, the kind of sensibility that Broadway would later welcome in his full shows and had already begun to observe in the *Follies* of Florenz Ziegfeld.[31]

Loesser in Hollywood

Loesser joined the songwriting business in Hollywood at a moment when it was just beginning to appreciate the value of originally composed songs. The roots of Hollywood musicals were embedded in their immediate ancestor—live staged musical theater. The musical repertory that these works presented was far broader in style than what would later become the popular songwriters' norm. "Stage" music could and did include everything from modern French overtures to patriotic songs to spirituals to parlor music favorites of Stephen Foster's generation (such as "Jeannie with the Light Brown Hair").

From 1865 to 1915, homegrown operettas, burlesques, and farce comedies dominated the American musical stage. Thanks to competing chains of theaters spread across the country, all but the most isolated Americans enjoyed relatively easy access to European comic operas (especially in English, but also in German and French) and vaudeville (variety shows with as many as a dozen different live acts, many of them musical).[32] "Musical comedies," in their earliest days (the 1880s), amounted to little more than comic or melodramatic skits strung together with music interspersed. Their characters, whether conventional or exotic, sang songs using familiar themes (love, sadness, homely sentiment, patriotism, and nostalgia) and melody forms with words chosen for their steady rhythms and evenly paced rhymes.

Motion pictures took up where live theater left off, yielding an abundance of stories that concentrated on boy-girl romances, exotic adventures, melodramatic confrontations, and comic antics. As Clive Hirschhorn has noted, the film musical was "initially dependent on its parents—operetta and musical comedy."[33] Contrary to popular belief, there were few truly "silent" films, though original scores for silent films were rare before 1911.[34] The idea of supplying new music for movies gained momentum when prominent composers such as Victor Herbert and Henry Hadley were commissioned to write scores in the following decades.[35] Theaters built or adapted to house the growing audiences for moving pictures grew accustomed to providing continuous musical accompaniment either onstage or in an orchestra pit. The largest venues paid for pit bands with as many as a dozen players. If live musicians were not available, background music was compiled by linking together previously composed and recorded sounds appropriate for the film, with the selections ranging "from Bach to the latest pop song."[36]

By the late 1920s, the major studios had created music departments and contracted music "directors," often brought in from New York, whose principal job was to assemble an acceptable list of available musical segments, but not necessarily to compose at all. The first Academy Award for music was made in 1934, and for four years the prize was given not to an individual but a studio music department, tacit recognition that creation of the film "score" was an elaborate piece of committee work. Sometimes aspiring legitimate composers wrote new works to fill up a studio's in-house library, as William Grant Still did for Columbia. Clifford McCarty points out that "screen credit for composers did not become customary until the 1940s."[37] By the late 1920s, full scores with sets of individual instrumental parts (and detailed instructions) were regularly distributed to movie houses across the country, which employed at least a single keyboard player but often other musicians as well.[38]

The first major film with extensive music, though it lacked recorded spoken dialogue, appeared in 1926 (*Don Juan*, starring John Barrymore). The addition of coordinated musical sound throughout an entire film and technologically linked to the film itself was accomplished in 1929. MGM also released the first in a string of popular screen musicals, *Broadway Melody*, in that year. As a result of talkies, many theater musicians who had provided

live sound were thrown out of work, but the role of the song composer gradually increased as directors became more adventurous and the musicians'
union demanded the creation of new music and new recordings for each
new film.

The role of the songwriter was only one of many in the full process of
creating a sound-rich motion picture. By the time Loesser entered the business, Hollywood's production line was operating at an extraordinary pace
and level of efficiency. With the establishment of the "studio system," most
creative talent was signed up with specific requirements aimed at the rough
goal of finishing one film per week per studio.[39] A fast-working striver could
expect to be kept busy. Even in the financially strapped period of the early
1930s, Paramount employed a musical staff of thirty-six.[40] The majority of
the films for which Loesser provided lyrics were destined to become industrial artifacts, the inevitable results of formulaic procedures. Moviemakers,
even those with large staffs and adequate budgets, like most Tin Pan Alley
tunesmiths before them, made no pretense of doing anything else than producing a consistent product. Given the right combination of factors, however, well-executed formulas could turn into hits. Normally, films were only
as good as the necessarily speedy process allowed. McCarty has estimated
the average preparation time for film scores at about three to four weeks.[41]

Because moviemaking was taking place in a period when each new structural innovation or acting sensation had the potential to produce a huge
profit, songwriting also contained an element of adventure, an exploration
into unknown waters, for each new singer on film. Since the technology for
making a successful film was always changing, the business invited some risk
takers as well as imitative hacks. Individual creative talents, men and women
with an eye for novel scenarios or inventive costumes, virtuosic cameramen
and sound engineers, lighting specialists, as well as bankable star performers,
were in high demand.

Deciding what musical models to emulate depended largely on the
tastes of the producer and music director. In general, filmmakers agreed that
the most logical way of introducing a song into a spoken play was to have
the play itself concern the making of a show. The show-within-a-show fram-
ing device, already hallowed by its frequent use in live musical theater, was
easily adapted by cinema producers. (Furthermore, it did not require a full-
fledged continuous score of music, thus keeping down costs.) This format
soon became the dominant plot mode for film musicals. A favorite subcat-
egory of such shows, known as the backstage musical, involves the produc-

tion of a "big show," interwoven with the personal stories of the participants offstage. (A preeminent later example would be Cole Porter's *Kiss Me, Kate* [1948], which embeds sections of Shakespeare's *The Taming of the Shrew* within the personal trials of its principal players; the Judy Garland/Mickey Rooney juvenile collaborations of the 1930s, most famously *Babes in Arms* [1939], also depend on the concept.) Revues, similar to vaudeville shows but in which long lines of dancing showgirls were mixed with contrasting solo or duo specialty acts, were favorite types of shows for embedding, since virtually any individual actor or group could be incorporated. The quick-paced variety that was possible in the film medium overshadowed any lack of dramatic sense as the segments succeeded each other. Indeed, all was not lost even in the complete absence of a story, since a type of revue, sometimes described as "the scrapbook format," could be employed: typically, a narrator or host would introduce scenes from a musical or dramatic biography; the rest is flashback. Among the earliest and most fascinating of such efforts is *The King of Jazz*, on the subject of Paul Whiteman in 1930.[42]

A large number of flimsy pretexts emerged as acceptable means on which to hang a movie plot, and almost any show could include a song or two to create contrast along an otherwise commonplace story line. Even murder mysteries and adventures sometimes featured singing protagonists. College campuses were popular locales for comedic romps, presumably because those darn kids would try anything and had all the time in the world for high jinks. Out-of-the-way, exotic locales permitted the exposure of "native" skin, adding a dose of titillation to any plot however inane or improbable, while usually avoiding the wrath of censors. As the clouds of war loomed on the horizon and then arrived over America during the 1940s, military or patriotic plots came into fashion. Frequently shows were built around stars known to the public in predefined roles, thus absolving the filmmaker or film songwriter from having to develop a character. Jack Benny, for instance, frequently played the masterfully inept comic lover. Dorothy Lamour almost invariably appeared wearing her figure-flattering sarong. Betty Hutton was both plucky and attractive as a heroine, and she could sing to boot. All types of films might include a love interest, either serious or comic, and therefore love songs were ordered up to match any situation.[43]

With his quick wit, educated ear, and musical intuition, Frank Loesser fit right in with the company of Hollywood dream spinners, and he contributed to over one hundred musical films between 1937 and 1952 in all the types mentioned above: backstage shows or outright revues (*Jam Session, A*

Night at Earl Carroll's, Dancing on a Dime), campus capers (*College Swing, Sweater Girl, Freshman Year*), star vehicles (*Thank Your Lucky Stars, Neptune's Daughter*), patriotic heart stirrers or light comedies with a military setting (*Christmas Holiday, True to the Army, See Here Private Hargrove*), comic adventure/travel yarns (*The Hurricane, Happy Go Lucky*). He also wrote for cartoons and for short subjects.[44]

The shows in the late 1930s almost always demanded dances with their songs, and all of the manifestations of swing jazz, at the height of its popularity with young audiences of the period, can be found in the films. Among other steps, the Cuban rumba was much in vogue, popularized by bands such as Xavier Cugat's. Loesser wrote his first Academy-nominated song lyric, "Dolores," in *Las Vegas Nights*, another dance-oriented product of 1941. Although Clive Hirschhorn has described the film as having a "paltry excuse for existing," it was redeemed somewhat by managing to include Tommy Dorsey and His Orchestra as well as the twenty-six-year-old Frank Sinatra in his screen singing debut with this fine Louis Alter tune.[45]

In the 1930s and '40s, Loesser benefited from working with a string of excellent composers, not just the tunesmiths of his own generation, such as the prodigious Burton Lane, but the older, avuncular Hoagy Carmichael (1899–1981) and full-fledged symphonic specialists, including Alfred Newman (1900–1970), Frederick (or Friedrich) Hollander (1896–1976), and Victor Schertzinger (1880–1941). He met and befriended many experienced hands and never lacked for good examples of modern lyric writing. Verses from the pens of Lorenz Hart, Ira Gershwin, and Cole Porter were probably committed to memory on repeated hearings, and it is well known that Loesser most admired the phenomenally successful and prolific Irving Berlin. Indeed, Berlin's work would remain a lifelong touchstone. Both men wrote words as well as music; both were adept at comic as well as serious lyrics; and, of course, both made lots of money at the business.[46]

Loesser also knew that his star would rise when his songs were sung by attractive actor-singers in successful films. *The Hurricane* (1937), a spectacularly produced blockbuster mounted by Samuel Goldwyn, represented an early opportunity to see his name in lights, albeit small ones, since his lyrics were never sung in the film itself. The story of Pacific Island romance and adventure was directed by John Ford and featured the voluptuous young Dorothy Lamour, as well as a host of highly respected supporting actors: Mary Astor, Thomas Mitchell, Raymond Massey, and John Carradine. Loesser provided a lyric for this show to Alfred Newman's "The Moon of

Paramount Pictures publicity photo of Frank Loesser, 1940. Frank Loesser
Enterprises.

Manakoora," a predictably exotic love song for the leads, which Lamour later recorded.[47] The full score was considered worthy enough for an Academy Award nomination.

Loesser acquired a particularly helpful mentor in 1938, when he was assigned to work with Hoagy Carmichael at Paramount. Carmichael would later recall of this time, "Frank Loesser interested me. Frank was gifted and most energetic. It was a good thing that he worked with me for awhile; I had a sobering Indiana affect on him. He had a tendency to want to write things 'way out.' This may be because he was so packed full of ideas then that he was overlooked."[48] Later on, Carmichael told Loesser's friend Cynthia Lindsay more details about their collaboration: "At first the kid shook me up—his exuberance and his zany talk were too much for me. Frank didn't seem serious enough about the matter of writing songs. It wasn't the first time I was wrong. After we'd worked together a little while, I realized he'd only been joking with me to keep me happy and alive. Then one day, sitting at the piano, he said, 'How's this?' I said, 'Follow it with this—.' We reeled off a few stanzas, and I realized this was the lyricist I'd hoped he'd be. All the time we worked together, Frank never violated the rules of construction or what it takes to make a hit song. It didn't take any time for me to know he'd justified the confidence I'd had when I first saw him strutting across the lot at Paramount. We had a lot of hits—a lot of laughs."[49]

Carmichael's stories radiate the glow of happy bygone days, and he papers over his mixed first impressions of the cocky young Loesser with a dose of modest self-correction. Still, his recollections reveal that Loesser's emerging talent was becoming visible to his older and more seasoned professional colleagues. Loesser wrote the lyrics for Carmichael's tunes "Heart and Soul," "Small Fry," and "Two Sleepy People" in 1938. Probably most tyro pianists who joyfully bang through "Heart and Soul" are unfamiliar with the languid Loesser text or its use in a Paramount short subject called "A Song Is Born":

> Heart and soul / I fell in love with you.
> Heart and soul / the way a fool would do,
> Madly / because you held me tight
> And stole a kiss in the night.

The text of "Two Sleepy People," made to order for the light, crooning voice of Bob Hope in *Thanks for the Memory*, was inspired, according to Susan Loesser, by a comment ("Look at us: four sleepy people") from her mother, Lynn Garland Loesser, after a dinner party with the Loessers and

the Carmichaels.[50] Using the popular AABA thirty-two-measure form, the
strength of the song lies in the diversity of syllable counts in a series of mostly
short phrases, a clear Berlinism, in its first eight measures:

> Here we are,
> Out of cigarettes,
> Holding hands and yawning,
> Look how late it gets.
>
> Two sleepy people,
> By dawn's early light,
> And too much in love to say "Good-
> night."

The first notes leaping up to "we" and then down to "are" instantly convey a
sweet air of meandering drowsiness. The third line ending, the word "yawn-
ing," receives a push from the musical rhythm, as if one were actually yawn-
ing to sing it. The completion of the next four lines continues in relaxed
melodic movement, a series of descending scales, but crowding the most syllables into the penultimate (seventh) measure to generate some sense of forward motion. It makes an extremely satisfying phrase ending on m. 8, where
just one note and one syllable are held for four languorous counts. Loesser
works in a neat Cole Porter–like rhyme in the second eight measures ("cozy
chair" and "Frigidaire") and explains in the release that the romantic couple
singing this song is—surprise!—already married, but—surprise again!—they
are still in love.[51]

> Do you remember the night we used to linger in the hall?
> Father didn't like you at all.
> Do you remember the reason we married in the fall?
> To rent this little nest, and get a bit of rest.

"Small Fry" was written as a joke, claimed Carmichael, and found use
in a Bing Crosby film, *Sing, You Sinners*.[52] Crosby appeared as a crooner
who loves to play the horses, a hint of things to come with *Guys and Dolls*.
Loesser matched Carmichael's gently swinging tune ("slowly and lazily," says
the sheet music) with several typical Crosby exclamations ("My! My!" and
"Oh! yes, Oh! yes, Oh! yes") and a fun-making, conversational lyric, with
Crosby giving bits of preachy advice to a twelve-year-old Donald O'Connor
("Small fry, struttin' by the pool room / Small fry, should be in the school
room / . . . Now you put down that cigarette").

Scoring on *Your Hit Parade* and Writing Original Melodies

The hard times of the Depression made radio the perfect entertainment medium for the vast majority of Americans, who had neither the price of admission nor the wardrobe to attend highbrow theatricals or concerts, as broad as their tastes may have been. Thus, the surest way to certify the success of a songwriter during the 1930s was by identifying his or her songs on the radio. Filmmakers, of course, were aware of the benefits of wide exposure on the air as well. The standards by which popularity could be determined were created by the National Broadcasting Company in its weekly broadcast, *Your Hit Parade*, which, beginning in 1935, served as a sort of mediator as well as informal statistician, announcing and performing in lush, danceable orchestral arrangements the most popular songs sold in a given week. The hour-long broadcast consisted in playing the fifteen most highly rated songs of the previous seven days.[53]

In 1937 and 1938 no fewer than eight songs with Loesser lyrics scored on *Your Hit Parade:* "How'dja Like to Love Me?" "I Fall in Love with You Every Day," "Small Fry," Heart and Soul," "Two Sleepy People," "The Lady's in Love with You," "Strange Enchantment," and "Says My Heart" (the first to reach the top position).

The years 1939 and 1940 were Loesser's busiest, if one counts by the number of shows he worked on.[54] He contributed music for no fewer than sixteen musical films in each year and added another fifteen in 1941, averaging about two finished song lyrics per film. Although capable of extremely quick work at times, his regular habits for producing consistently good lines were well established by this time, and his name known in the studios. He picked up the first of five individual "solo song" Academy Award nominations in this year as well, for his lyrics to Louis Alter's "Dolores." (The others would come in 1943, 1947, 1949, and 1952; the only winner, "Baby, It's Cold Outside," was featured in *Neptune's Daughter* in 1949.)

The combined profits from radio play and movie work worked hugely to Loesser's benefit. His prosperity illustrated a new and powerful economic phenomenon in America: "In 1939 alone," reports Richard Crawford, "[Hollywood] studios released 376 films and collected $673 million at the box office; in every week of that year, 52–55 million people watched at least one movie. With movie theaters outnumbering banks and department stores, movies had come to be one of the nation's largest industries."[55]

By 1941, Loesser also was putting words and music together by himself.

Although most of his early lyrics shine with humor and clever wordplay re-gardless of who wrote the tune, his own first best combinations of melody and text tend toward the more serious side. His first published solo effort was "Seventeen," written for a movie of the same name in 1939 (although the film was not released until 1940). The title and plot of *Seventeen* were derived from the youthful and nostalgic best-selling novel by Booth Tarking-ton, a widely read author of the time.

The song serves satisfactorily as a character number for an ingenue role, offering a pleasant, well-balanced melody in thirty-two-measure binary (ABAB′) form. Without syncopations or vocal tricks, it wafts sweetly on its way, mirroring the teenage naiveté of its lyric, whose title word is repeated just as and where the old-timers of Tin Pan Alley said it should be — in the first and last lines.[56] The text also pushes the rhyming game a bit by eliding the seventh and eighth text lines together with rising melodic and harmonic (bass chord) notes (at "mem'ry of / When"):

> When you're seventeen and you're in love
> With some seventeen-year-old angel from above
> How she cuddles oh-so-close as you sail away,
> In your good old nineteen twenty-nine Model A.
>
> When you're seventeen, you're in a trance
> And the cut of your first tuxedo spells romance.
> There'll be nothing half as sweet in your life as the mem'ry of
> When you're seventeen and you're in love.

Undoubtedly "love" and "above" have been rhymed uncountable times, and precedents for the "romance/trance" combination exist in more than one Tin Pan Alley ditty, but taking these humdrum standbys and adding "-ry of" (to rhyme with "in love"), a "good old nineteen twenty-nine Model A," and "the cut of your first tuxedo" shows Loesser's word skills to good advantage. The melody jogs along in perfect company with its lyric and with the picture of its wistful singer. The image is sharp and musically straightforward. "Sev-enteen" is a charming song, apt for its setting.

More impressive is Deanna Durbin's number in the wartime film *Christ-mas Holiday* (1944), "Spring Will Be a Little Late This Year," a ballad that even the critical Alec Wilder calls "exceptional" among the songs for which Loesser wrote both text and tune.[57] The typically repetitive verse is not a throwaway (it begins "January and February were never so empty and gray"), and it unexpectedly foreshadows the pathos of the chorus to follow. As early

Example 1.1. "Spring Will Be a Little Late This Year" (chorus, mm. 1–5)

as the fifth measure of the verse, the melody plummets to a vocally low B-flat on the word "tragically," then leaps with drama to a flat sixth (G-flat) above, resolving to the note just below it (F) on "crying." This classical formula, used to depict painful and sobbing words on notes only one half step apart— dating back to at least the madrigals of sixteenth-century Italy—is then repeated in musical sequence on the even more poignant word "dying." This is strong stuff for a pop song, but here it is used to ingenious effect, and Loesser has not even gotten to the chorus yet.

Loesser turns a corner in the next lines, keeping sentimentality at bay: "But let's rather put it this way, 'Spring will be a little late this year.'" Such an understated phrase comprises a wonderful displacement of intense feeling. It forms a kind of poetic envelope and thereby allows the listener to freely imagine the depth of the emotion involved without unseemly wallowing. Hearing the song out of its cinematic setting (a depressing, down-market nightclub), we know not whether the singing character's separation from her beloved is temporary or permanent, long or short, but the song serves all causes.[58] It is a platform from which the character speaks from the soul. She will carry on, head held high despite adversity and loneliness. This verbal deflection of feeling—from person to season, so to speak—is more apt to draw tears than the overt self-pity in the "crying/dying" verse (which, in any case, was not sung in the film). Loesser's good sense in making this simple, quiet line his focus reveals a deepening creative power: the ability to link whole states of mind, as well as individual words, to melodies.

In the first gesture of the refrain, marked *molto espressivo*, the octave leap up on "dying" (from the verse) is mirrored in an octave descent on the first words "Spring will. . . ." Then, after short notes on "be a little," another leap occurs, this time up a ninth, and arrives on C with the word "late." Thus, the most powerfully connoted word of m. 3 and m. 5, "late," receives an accent of length, being held for three full beats. It is further reinforced by its placement at the beginning of each of those measures (ex. 1.1).

The third phrase of four measures then begins with the highest note of the entire melody, a high D-natural on the word "you." This pitch stands out

Example 1.2. "Spring Will Be a Little Late This Year" (chorus, mm. 9–16)

dramatically. It lies a tangy major seventh away from the key note of E-flat, which occurs just before it, and makes a clash with the A-flat/E-flat open fifth of the chord below it in m. 9. Hence, it is prepared by both its accompanying harmony and its preceding note to give the maximum affective kick. Any one of these small tonal inflections—the pitch itself within the key, its neighboring notes in the melody, or its harmony—by itself would not move us nearly so much as the combination of all three does. The total impact is extraordinary (ex. 1.2).

In addition to the poignant shapeliness of this melody as a whole, its exact temporal midpoint pitch, a low C-flat in m. 16, confirms the singer's wintry pessimism by its surprise arrival. This note, the deceptive flat sixth degree in the key of E-flat major, is approached by a large downward leap, so its strangeness is enhanced all the more. *All* comparatively long notes in this slow melody carry important words ("spring," "late," "year," "you," "old," "cold," "slow," "time," "fear"), which commence on accented beats at periodic intervals—the first and fourth measures in every phrase—and thus constitute sure evidence of a conscious effort to coordinate harmonic, melodic, and emotional effects.

"Wacky for Khaki"

Little has been written about Loesser's experience while composing both the lyrics and the tunes for a string of wartime morale boosters: *Skirts, P.F.C. Mary Brown, About Face! Hi, Yank!* and *Okay, U.S.A.!* Because they were aimed at overseas troops and not for stateside consumption, few of these scores are housed in the United States. These shows repay study and shed light on the full range of his pre-Broadway activity. They are more than mere variety shows. In the army's own words, these "GI Musical Revues [were] 'tried-out' at typical Army Installations under Army conditions and then

Pvt. Frank Loesser at work with pen and pipe, 1945. Frank Loesser Enterprises.

'blueprinted'—compiled into a book containing the entire script, lyrics, stage, complete orchestrations, dance routines, scenic and costume designs (including instruction on how to make them from waste and salvage materials) and general production notes."[59]

"Complete orchestrations" meant ready-to-play parts for piano, two alto and two tenor saxophones, three trumpets, two trombones, guitar, bass, and drums, plus a short score for the conductor and a vocal lead part—in other words, the "swing style" big band ensemble of the day. "The music [was] assembled so that each instrument [had] a complete routine of the show in proper sequence. . . . The orchestrations are voiced so that they sound well with a minimum of one trumpet, three saxophones, piano, and drums." Doublings and additions up to a full band were encouraged. "The pianist's and conductor's parts have been thoroughly cued. If necessary the entire show can be played by the piano alone."[60]

The second of these Blueprint Specials, as they were officially designated, was entitled *Hi, Yank!* It had no overriding plot, its contents amounting to

Frank Loesser presents the original copy of "Rodger Young" to President Harry
Truman, 1945. Frank Loesser Enterprises.

a series of skits and vignettes about military life, interwoven with songs (see
table 1.1). Pvt. Frank Loesser was given top billing in the sample program
provided for would-be producers, which lists four individual contributors for
"music and lyrics" (a single creative category).[61] His professional experience
apparently earned him the privilege of seeing his name first in a list of his

Table 1.1. The Skits and Songs of *Hi, Yank!*

Act 1

1. The Soldier's Friend
     Song: "Yank, Yank, Yank!"
2. Sad Sack
     Song: "The Saga of the Sack"
3. Message Center
4. Sports Section
5. Girl of the Week
     Song: "My Gal and I"
6. WAC Department
7. Camp News
     Song: "General Orders"

Act 2

8. Puzzle Page
     Song: "Classification Blues"
9. Strictly GI
10. Mail Call
     Song: "Little Red Rooftops"
11. What's Your Problem?
12. Report from the Caribbean
     Song and Dance
13. Post-War Department
14. Round-Up [Finale]
     Song: "The Most Important Job"
     Reprise: "Little Red Rooftops"

---

military superiors: Lt. Alex North, Lt. Jack Hill, and Sgt. Jesse Berkman. Seventeen names in all constitute the list of contributors. Alex North, who rose to the rank of captain, would later succeed as a film composer. José Limón choreographed the dances. There is no way to be absolutely certain which parts were provided by Loesser, but he certainly did not do the orchestrations, which were supplied by five of the other sixteen collaborators assigned to this task: Herbert Bourne, Bernard Landes, George Leeman, Lee Montgomery, and Robert C. Williams.

Several of the lyrics suggest Loesser-like wordplay. The tunes often reflect the studied simplicity of later Loesser melodies and the sometimes jazzy style of Loesser or Alex North, who later gained fame with the early (some say first) jazz-based film score for *A Streetcar Named Desire* in 1951.[62] Since Loesser was consciously cultivating his music-writing skills at this time, it is not unreasonable to guess that he had a hand in the tunes as well.

The first music in *Hi, Yank!* is a fanfare-and-medley overture, followed directly by an opening choral number ("Yank, Yank, Yank!"), a solo song with chorus, a comic ballet, a mildly wistful ballad ("My Gal and I"), three more ensemble numbers, another production number with dance on a Caribbean theme, and a patriotic finale. The first solo song, "The Saga of the Sack," depicts a familiar World War II cartoon character and contains a clever eleven-measure patter section, with a verbal turnaround saved for the seventh measure in each of the three sections:

I had so much romance in me, / I thought that I would burst.
I hurried off to see my gal; / my line was all rehearsed.
I rang the bell—she said, "So sorry, the Marines have landed first
—With full equipment!"
Anything can happen to a Sad Sack,
The Army's unluckiest guy.

The suggestive and rhythmically surprising extension, "With full equipment," doubles up skillfully on the joke about a Marine "landing."

Another number, "General Orders," is only one step removed from setting a telephone directory to music. The sung text appears to be a list of army regulations presented verbatim. The music consists of a through-composed, single-line melody and unrhymed text (of course), for mostly unison choral groups in alternation. It is held together by a repeated descending bass line, a steady rhythm, and a generally martial style, a tribute to the dullness of military routine without music. Harmony among the vocal parts and rhyming words are allowed only in the final ten measures, forming a sort of barbershop quartet coda:

These are Gen'ral Orders
Ev'ry soldier must obey
In the Army,
In the Army of the U.S.A.

The opening of the text is even less promising, and one can imagine Loesser viewing it as a challenge to his skills. It begins: "To take charge of this post and all Government property in view. To walk my post in a military manner, keeping always on the alert and observing ev'rything that takes place within sight or hearing. To report all violations of orders I am instructed to enforce. To repeat all calls from posts more distant from the guardhouse than my own. . . ." And so forth.

The song satirizes the familiar tensions of the time between professional,

"regular" army officers and so-called "citizen soldiers," the typical GI enlisted men. Allegedly the latter cared less about spit and polish than their
bosses, while the former were obsessed by discipline and the letter of the
military law. Like most of the songs in the revue, this one was aimed to appeal to the rank and file, not to the career servicemen and women in higher
ranks.[63]

"The Classification Blues" takes a comic swipe at bureaucratic inepti-
tude in the military, a theme that long predates Loesser's World War II experience, of course. Its lyric was matched with a sixteen-measure tune that, owing to its jazz flavor, might well have been the work of the more jazz-oriented
Alex North or Loesser and North together. Four individual singers complain
in turn about their army jobs, all joining in on the chorus (both verse and
chorus fill eight measures apiece):

> [Verse]
> I used to play the horses in Jamaica; (2)
> I made a million bucks before I quit; (2)
> So naturally the Cavalry is / Exactly where they put me, (2)
> Where they put me (1)
> Shovelin' it. (1)
>
> [Chorus]
> I got the Classification Blues, the Classification Blues (2)
> If they ever classified me right, that would be news (2)
> The somebody else's occupation [sic] / Living a life of aggravation (2)
> Oh, what a lousy Classification (1)
> Blues. (1)

By lacing the melody with dotted eighths and sixteenths and triplet divisions of many beats, the writers accommodated varying numbers of syllables
in a line while still keeping to a regular musical phrase length of four measures apiece. The mixture of beat divisions to achieve a larger rhythmic purpose is also characteristic of much of Loesser's later narrative song style.

The grand finale of Hi, Yank! —intended as a patriotic and tear-jerking
salute—is a nicely calibrated medley of two tunes, "The Most Important
Job" and "Little Red Rooftops" as a reprise. The basic form for the new tune
is straightforward—a thirty-two-measure chorus composed of four phrases
filled out in a typical Tin Pan Alley fashion (ABA'C) but glued together with
consistent rhythmic and melodic elements (ex. 1.3).

The melody uses a minor key applied in a martial manner, a swagger-

2. This is the biggest, the hardest, the battle 'em yard-by-yardest,
The most important job I ever did.
I used to keep the books in the Nat'nal Bank;
Now that's done by a fourteen-year-old kid.
Now I could sleep more, and shave more, and get me the dames I crave more,
But what's the diff'rence when you're fighting mad?
This is the biggest, the toughest, the ruggedest and the roughest,
The most important job I ever had.

3. This is the biggest, the strongest, the rottenest, and the wrongest,
The most important enemy I've met.
I once was in the ring fighting heavyweights,
But that was just a sissy minuet.
I could be cleaner, and neater, and temperament'ly sweeter,
But what's the diff'rence when you're fighting mad?
This is the biggest, the toughest, the ruggedest and the roughest,
The most important job I ever had.

Example 1.3. "The Most Important Job" (voice part)

Table 1.2. Mode and Phrase Chart for "The Most Important Job"

A mode: minor	This is the biggest, the toughest, the rugged- est and the roughest, The most important job I ever had.
	(8 measures)
B mode: minor	I used to hold a job in a groc'ry store, But now I've turned it over to my dad.
	(8 measures)
A′ mode: MAJOR	Now I could gripe more, and brood more, and holler about the food more, But what's the diff'rence when you're fighting mad?
	(8 measures)
C mode: minor	This is the *biggest*, the toughest, the rugged- est and the roughest, The most important job I ever had.
	(8 measures)

ing style that recalls the famous Civil War melody by bandmaster Patrick S. Gilmore (under the pseudonym Louis Lambert), "When Johnny Comes Marching Home."[64] The use of minor mode is rare in American popular song between 1840 and 1960, but its appearance in this tempo and style stokes up a sort of he-man assertiveness, tempered by a stoic mood, in contrast to its more usual association with sadness or exoticism (see table 1.2).

The A′ section, with the lightest couplet of the text in each verse ("Now I could sleep more, and shave more, and get me the dames I crave more, / But what's the diff'rence when you're fighting mad?"), is presented in F major, which in turn sets off and underlines the leap up from F to D-flat in the final eight measures. Such a modal slide—from minor to major to minor again, needing only one or two pitch adjustments—delivers a strong emotional punch without confusing singers or listeners. The final pair of lines returns to the baseline minor mode at a higher melodic pitch level, though not at an extreme, making an appropriately serious gesture that resists mawkishness. Each section of text below (for the concluding C phrase) receives two strong beats:

> This is the biggest, the toughest,
> The ruggedest and the roughest,
> The most important job I ever had.

That Loesser did not receive top billing for *P.F.C. Mary Brown: A WAC Musical Revue* may be attributed to gallantry or politics as much as to rank.

This show, fourth of the five military stage shows with which Loesser was involved, included women collaborators: Capt. Ruby Jane Douglass for music and lyrics and Mary Schenk, unranked, for costume designs. On the whole, it is musically less interesting than *Hi, Yank!* but by interweaving Greek gods and goddesses among its military characters it succeeds in creating the semblance of a plot. Pallas Athene (the goddess figure had been adopted by the military for its Women's Army Corps insignia) is talking with Jupiter on Mount Olympus, observing the activities below. She resolves to join up with the Americans—in disguise, of course—with a nom de guerre, "Mary Brown." Jupiter at first mocks, then objects when she dates regular soldiers. Coming down to earth to confront her, he is arrested by a burly MP, who assumes that only a crazy man would claim to be a Greek god, but finally "Jumpin' Jupiter" follows Mary's lead and enlists as a paratrooper for the duration. With the help of her new friends, Mary survives the rigors of basic training and proudly assumes her rank of private first class.

Like *Hi, Yank! P.F.C. Mary Brown* includes the requisite skits about military bureaucratic bumbles, but it concentrates on patriotic devotion, solidarity with the cause, and comradely good feeling expressed from a woman's point of view. It comprises twelve scenes and nine songs, with the title number reprised as part of the finale, the "WAC Hymn."

Both the lyrics and music of several numbers seem to bear Loesser's fingerprints. A female guard sings a minor-key lament, "Poor Lonely MP," with sinuous and rhyme-saturated lines, such as

> I walk my beat
> And my heart's keeping beat
> To the beat of my feet on the street.
>
> When folks see me coming,
> They start in a-running,
> So how can I sing
> About love in the spring?

The repeated three-note descending phrase, E-flat–D–C, with its obvious minor-key flavor, matches well with the self-pitying text ("Poor lonely MP / Nobody loves me.").[65] Its AABA form is installed at two levels, in the fashion of Russian dolls that contain successively smaller dolls within (see table 1.3). Three of the four stanzas consist of essentially the same music, just as do three of each set of four phrases (the first, second, and fourth) within each chorus. The syllables of this lyric at the release (the section labeled c c' in

Table 1.3. Formal Structure of "Poor Lonely MP"

4/4 meter	Chorus I	Chorus II	Break	Chorus III
(measures per section)	16	16	8	16
(4-measure phrases per section)	a a′ b a	a a′ b a	c c′	a a′ b a

Example 1.4. "Lost in a Cloud of Blue" (mm. 1–8)

table 1.3) are deployed so as to create momentum in the third of every four phrases, as well as in the break, a feature detectable in many other Loesser songs.

One of the patriotic insertions is a scene and dance number calling for Gay Nineties costumes, "New Style Bonnet," which segues into a fashion show, with representatives of all of the female units of the U.S. military—WAC, WAVE, SPAR, WASP, USMCWR, and the Army Nurse Corps—parading across the stage in their modern uniforms. If it is by Loesser, this would appear to be the first of several "fashion show" numbers, which in later years would include "On a Slow Boat to China" (used as an instrumental backup for Esther Williams on display in the film *Neptune's Daughter*, 1948) and the satirical treatment of such displays in *How to Succeed in Business Without Really Trying*, "Paris Original."

The show's most challenging scenic and musical moment occurs in the romantic ballad, "Lost in a Cloud of Blue," sung by Jupiter while dressed as a god, suffused in blue light, "sitting on cloud, [playing a] lyre," and accompanying an "Olympian ballet" troupe of twenty-four dancers. His melody (example 1.4) contains several vocally large leaps—an octave skip up at the fourth note and then a quick descent of a sixth two notes later—as well as a handful of chromatic inflections, which add poignancy and impart much the same feeling as other similarly moody popular ballads: Loesser's "Spring Will Be a Little Late This Year," but also Kern and Harbach's "Smoke Gets in Your Eyes" (1933), Cole Porter's "Ev'ry Time We Say Goodbye" (1944), and Erroll Garner's "Misty" (1954), with Johnny Burke's lyrics. It would be easy to successfully revive this tune as an independent number.

CHAPTER 2

The First Broadway Hit:
Where's Charley?

Where they hum and they strum
And they drum till the feeling is frantic,
And they call it romantic,
And so do I.
—"PERNAMBUCO," FROM *WHERE'S CHARLEY?*

F OLLOWING THE WAR, LOESSER RETURNED TO WORK AT PARAMOUNT and soon found his work, another strong ballad, again nominated for an Academy Award. "I Wish I Didn't Love You So" had been written as one of four songs for the Betty Hutton vehicle, *The Perils of Pauline,* a pseudodocumentary about the early days of filmmaking and the career of Pearl White, the original "Pauline." Like "Spring Will Be a Little Late This Year," "I Wish I Didn't Love You So" is enriched with note-to-note craftsmanship, but overall it is especially impressive for its harmonic sweep. Several minor chords (C minor, G minor, F minor) invoked in the A phrase—the form is AABA and the key is E-flat major—tilt toward a somber mood throughout. The story told in the lyrics is unoriginal, yet somehow the realization seems fresh: the singer tries to clear her mind and heart of a former love, but all in vain. Moody distraction sets in. A brief verse sets the stage for the first and title line of the refrain (ex. 2.1):

Example 2.1. "I Wish I Didn't Love You So" (opening mm. 1–8)

> After all this time without you, After all this time I find
> That it's still no use to say to myself: "Out of sight, out of mind."
> [*Refrain*]
> I wish I didn't love you so . . .

That the highest note of the refrain melody is also the very first one instantly conveys an impression of emotional strain. The singer, without warning, leaps to a self-pitying precipice. The pangs of lost love, starting with the personal pronoun on a whole note, persist for all thirty-two measures in a series of descending melodic phrases that suggest both fatigue and the futility of trying to expunge a memory that will not go away. ("My love for you *should* have faded long ago," the lyric insists.) The release, with a superficial swagger of confidence and a not so easily singable rhythm ("I might be smiling now with some new tender friend"), attempts to override the basic emotion, but of course it cannot sustain itself with the return of the title line in the final eight measures (ex. 2.2). Loesser drives home the heartrending effect by figuratively choking up the haunted singer, inserting an interruptive rest before she sings the last line: "Something in that heart says . . . you're still there, [*rest*] I wish I didn't love you so." The tune's basic shapeliness recommended it for use as the main title theme at the beginning of the film, and it later appears at a turning point in the action, when Pearl uses it to audition for agents who offer her a movie debut. Almost any straightforward ballad could have served the dramatic purpose in the film, but it works especially well in this context.

Hutton's most well-received songs of this set for *The Perils of Pauline* were a novelty piano number, "Rumble, Rumble, Rumble" and "Poppa, Don't Preach to Me," a rousing tune with an inventive lyric that points to later stage songs such as "Sit Down, You're Rockin' the Boat." The object of production numbers like "Poppa" was to create camaraderie in an audience and admira-

Example 2.2. "I Wish I Didn't Love You So" (chorus mm. 25–32)

tion for the featured performer, a communal cheer from the gathered throng of admirers both on- and offstage. Although the singer of this song is purportedly reading a letter from America, urging that she not go off the skids in the alluring city of Paris, listeners are pulling for her to throw off the shackles of hometown propriety. Hutton courts a similar sympathy with her comic novelty number "Sewing Machine" in the film's first scene, at a stifling garment factory job. It is probably the most cheerful song ever composed about sweatshop labor.[1]

While writing more complete songs on his own, Loesser had continued to collaborate as lyricist with others during the 1940s. Bette Davis sang his "They're Either Too Young or Too Old" to Arthur Schwartz's tune in the film *Thank Your Lucky Stars* (1943), a celebrity-filled extravaganza with a thin plot but at least a half-dozen sturdy songs besides this one. Loesser's list lyric, chronicling women's sexual frustration when the men are off to war, is his most sophisticated text of the mid-forties, and it netted him his second "solo song" nomination from the Academy.

> They're either too young or too old;
> They're either too gray or too grassy green.
> The pickin's are poor and the crop is lean . . .

> They're either too warm or too cold;
> They're either too fast or too fast asleep.
> So darling, believe me, I'm yours to keep . . .

> They're either too bald or too bold.
> I'm down to the wheelchair and bassinet;
> My heart just refuses to get upset . . .

The multiple similes, interwoven with sounds that echo within and across lines verse after verse (gray/grassy green/crop is lean; bald/bold/bassinet/get upset), show Loesser at an inventive peak. The two-syllable extension of the second and third lines of each stanza allows the word "fast" in the second to serve contradictory meanings (too fast/too fast asleep). Davis's demure performance, partly sung, mostly spoken, added strongly to the overall effect.

Table 2.1. distills data compiled by Thomas Hischak and Nigel Harrison: a partial list of Loesser's successes in the 1940s and 1950s. It provides only the names of individual songs, not albums or full show recordings or re-releases on compact disc (many of which achieved substantial sales). The list of recording artists is far from complete, but it includes the performers most popular in their day. (Both "The Moon of Manakoora" and "Spring Will Be a Little Late This Year" have been recorded over a dozen times; "On a Slow Boat to China" has enjoyed no fewer than twenty-two releases to the present.) As the table indicates, the number of recordings can be as strong an indicator of overall popularity as high placement on the hit parade lists.[2]

Where's Charley?

Loesser gained facility and dramatic character-painting skill from his Hollywood assignments and increased versatility and collaborative experience in connection with the army shows. During his military stint, he also had acquired a musically talented secretary, Milton DeLugg. Thus prepared, Loesser was ready to tackle more ambitious projects back in New York, even as he maintained his Hollywood ties. Friends Cy Feuer and Ernest Martin tapped him to write lyrics for the songs in a musical update of the 1892 British cross-dressing farce *Charley's Aunt*. Because Harold Arlen was unavailable to write the music, Loesser took that on as well. George Abbott, the show's guru and producer, had heard little of Loesser's music up to this point, but after a friendly audition he gave it his blessing, as did the star Ray Bolger. Loesser leapt at the opportunity by writing nine songs for the first act and four new songs (plus three reprises) in the second (see table 2.2).

Charley's Aunt was a classic farce, the only substantial hit by the British writer Brandon Thomas and a staple of the comic stage during the previous half century.[3] Its premise was simple but potentially hilarious (as a 1940 Broadway revival featuring José Ferrer and a 1941 film with Jack Benny had demonstrated).[4] Two Oxford undergraduates of the 1890s, Charley and Jack, wish to have lunch and make marriage proposals to their lady loves, Amy and Kitty, before the girls leave town the next day. But propriety does not allow them to meet without chaperones. The imminent arrival of a long ignored but fabulously wealthy aunt from Brazil, Donna Lucia D'Alvadorez, prom-

Table 2.1. Frank Loesser's Top Hits: A Partial List

Title	Performer(s)	Year of Issue	Highest Chart Position
"Anywhere I Wander"	Mel Tormé	1952	30
	Julius La Rosa	1953	4
"Baby, It's Cold Outside"	Ella Fitzgerald and Louis Jordan	1949	9
	Homer and Jethro	1949	22
	Sammy Kaye	1949	12
	Johnny Mercer and Margaret Whiting	1949	3
	Dinah Shore and Buddy Clark	1949	4
"Bloop, Bleep!"	Danny Kaye	1947	21
	Alvino Ray	1947	13
"A Bushel and a Peck"	Andrews Sisters	1950	22
	Perry Como and Betty Hutton	1950	3
	Doris Day	1950	16
	Johnny Desmond	1950	29
	Margaret Whiting and Jimmy Wakely	1950	6
#"Dolores"	Bing Crosby	1941	2
[Louis Alter]	Tommy Dorsey and Frank Sinatra	1941	1
#"The Fuddy Duddy Watchmaker" [Jimmy McHugh]	Kay Kyser	1941	11
"Have I Stayed Away Too Long?"	Perry Como	1944	19
	Tex Ritter	1944	28
#"Hoop-Dee-Doo"	Perry Como	1950	1
[Milton DeLugg]	Doris Day	1950	17
	Russ Morgan	1950	15
	Kay Starr	1950	2
#"I Don't Want to Walk without You"	Bing Crosby	1942	9
[Jule Styne]	Harry James	1942	1
	Dinah Shore	1942	12
	Baja Marimba Band	1969	121
	Barry Manilow	1980	36
"I Wish I Didn't Love You So"	Dick Farney	1947	13
	Dick Haymes	1947	9
	Betty Hutton	1947	5

Table 2.1. (*Continued*)

Title	Performer(s)	Year of Issue	Highest Chart Position
	Vaughan Moore	1947	2
	Dinah Shore	1947	2
#"I Wish I Were Twins"	Henry Allen	1934	20
[Joseph Meyer]	Emil Coleman	1934	8
	Fats Waller	1934	8
"If I Were a Bell"	Frankie Laine	1950	30
#"In My Arms"	Dick Haymes	1943	3
[Ted Grouya]			
#"Jingle, Jangle, Jingle"	Gene Autry	1942	14
[Joseph Lilley]	*Kay Kyser	1942	1
	Freddy Martin	1942	15
	Merry Macs	1944	4
#"Just Another Polka"	Eddie Fisher	1953	24
[Milton DeLugg]	Jo Stafford	1953	22
"Leave Us Face It"	Hildegarde	1944	29
[with Abe Burrows]			
#"The Moon of Manakoora"	Bing Crosby	1938	10
[Alfred Newman]	Ray Noble	1938	15
#"Moon over Burma"	Shep Fields	1940	26
[Frederick Hollander]	Gene Krupa	1949	23
"My Darling, My Darling"	Doris Day and Buddy Clark	1948	7
	Peter Lind Hayes	1949	20
	Jack Lathrop and Eve Young	1949	26
	Jo Stafford and Gordon MacRae	1949	1
"No Two People"	Doris Day and Donald O'Connor	1952	25
"Now That I Need You"	Doris Day	1949	20
	Frankie Laine	1949	20
"On a Slow Boat to China"	Larry Clinton	1948	25
	Eddy Howard	1948	6
	*Kay Kyser	1948	2
	Snooky Lanson	1948	24
	Art Lund	1948	12
	Freddy Martin	1948	6
	Benny Goodman	1949	7
	Emile Ford and the Checkmates	1960	3
"Once in Love with Amy"	Ray Bolger	1949	16

Table 2.1. (*Continued*)

Title	Performer(s)	Year of Issue	Highest Chart Position
"Praise the Lord"	Merry Macs	1942	8
	Royal Harmony Quartet (R & B chart)	1942	10 .
	Southern Sons (R & B chart)	1942	7
	*Kay Kyser	1942	1
"Spring Will Be a Little Late This Year"	Morton Downey	1944	25
"Standing on the Corner"	Four Lads	1956	3
	Mills Brothers	1956	
	Dean Martin	1956	22
	King Brothers (in the U.K.)	1960	4
# "Strange Enchantment"	Dorothy Lamour	1939	5
[Frederick Hollander]	Ozzie Nelson	1939	8
"Tallahassee"	Bing Crosby and Andrews Sisters	1947	10
	Dinah Shore and Woody Herman	1947	15
"Thumbelina"	Danny Kaye	1952	28
"The Ugly Duckling"	Mike Reid (in the U.K.)	1975	10
# "Wave to Me, My Lady" [William Stein]	Elton Britt	1946	19
"A Woman in Love"	Four Aces	1955	14
	Four Aces (in the U.K.)	1955	19
	Ronnie Hilton (in the U.K.)	1956	30
	Frankie Laine	1955	19
	Frankie Laine (in the U.K.)	1955	1
"Wonderful Copenhagen"	Danny Kaye (in the U.K.)	1953	5

= Loesser wrote lyrics only; [composer or coauthor]
* = Gold Record designate (500,000 units sold)

ises to solve the problem. But when Donna Lucia changes her travel plans, Charley convinces another friend, the flamboyant Lord Fancourt Babberley, to masquerade as his aunt in order to preserve appearances before Chesney (Jack's father) and Spettigue (Kitty's guardian). The unexpected arrival of the real Donna Lucia leads to predictable confusion, with much romping

Table 2.2. Musical Numbers in *Where's Charley?*

Act 1

	Overture
1. "The Years before Us"	Male chorus, Dance
2. "Better Get Out of Here"	Quartet of principals
3. "New Ashmolean . . ."	Quartet and chorus
4. "My Darling, My Darling"	Duet (Jack and Kitty)
5. "Make a Miracle"	Duet (Amy and Charley)
6. "Serenade with Asides"	Solo (Spettigue)
7. "Lovelier Than Ever"	Duet (Sir Francis and Donna Lucia)
8. "The Woman in His Room"	Solo (Amy)
9. "Pernambuco"	Chorus and principals, Dance
	Entr'acte

Act 2

10. "Where's Charley?"	Jack and chorus
11. "Once in Love with Amy"	Charley, Dance
12. "The Gossips"	Girls
13. Reprise: "The Years before Us"	Male chorus
14. Reprise: "Lovelier Than Ever"	Chorus
15. "At the Red Rose Cotillion"	Duet (Jack and Kitty) and chorus, Dance
16. Finale: "My Darling, My Darling"	Full ensemble

about and the final happy ending. Despite its convoluted plot, this comedy of manners seemed susceptible to musical adaptation. Musicals with college settings—such as *Leave It to Jane* (1917), *Good News* (1927), and *Too Many Girls* (1939)—had been staples of Broadway for a long time.

Feuer and Abbott's text revision of Thomas's play combined the original cross-dressing substitute aunt with Charley himself and cut much dialogue, while giving the show a crisper pace and more jokes.[5] The lines for the women characters are especially mordant and modern—putting their words somewhat at odds with the Oxfordian language of 1892. For example, when Charley waxes nostalgic with Amy by saying, "The few moments in the garden by ourselves were the happiest of all my life," she tartly replies, "I wonder how many people have said that?" When an elderly suitor offers Charley (disguised as his aunt) a flower, he responds, "Thank you. I'll have it stuffed," depositing it in his bodice; later he fires off a put-down line straight out of vaudeville: "I love your voice—just like a moose in mating season." Having deleted certain plot twists, the production team left plenty of time for the music and dance. On paper it looks to be an adequate adaptation, although some choices blurred the original Victorian flavor of Thomas's play.

Where's Charley? bears a resemblance to the campus caper films for which Loesser wrote in the 1930s. The play's situations were delineated with musical insertions, and other situations were added in logical sequence. Loesser begins everything with a song at the curtain. After the overture, an a cappella male chorus sets the scene squarely on campus:

> In all the years before us,
> Though fortune part our ways,
> How fond the recollections of
> These merry salad days.

All of the musical's numbers occur as plausible interruptions in the story (college students sing offstage, a band is heard outside, the lovers dance at a party, and so on), and they often provide underscoring for dialogue asides, scene changes, and climaxes in the action. The writers gave Loesser a broad field for displaying many musical styles. Naturally, the focus on dancing for the star, Ray Bolger, required pieces that could be choreographed, and for that the renowned George Balanchine was hired.

Balanchine and Bolger had worked together previously in the Rodgers and Hart show *On Your Toes* (1936), where Bolger was teamed with George Church and Tamara Geva for the ballet "Slaughter on Tenth Avenue." George Abbott, the unofficial but de facto director of the show, recalled the dance as "one of the best numbers I've ever seen in the theater, both musically and choreographically."[6] Before *On Your Toes*, dance numbers had generally been diversions from the plot. But that changed with the Russian-schooled Balanchine, who brought the skills to create storytelling dances for a book musical. In *On Your Toes*, Bolger was cast as a vaudeville performer turned college music teacher who becomes involved with a Russian ballerina and her jealous lover. "Slaughter on Tenth Avenue" did not attract imitators in other Broadway shows at the time, but it attested to Balanchine's originality and versatility.[7]

After appearing as the Scarecrow in the film *The Wizard of Oz* (1939), Bolger was tapped for a starring role in Rodgers and Hart's final Broadway collaboration, *By Jupiter* (1942). Robert Alton choreographed the show, and Bolger's rising popularity was confirmed. His fame enabled him to move directly from Broadway to the Far East when he entertained American troops in 1943.[8] Thus, both Bolger and Balanchine, dancer and choreographer, came to *Where's Charley?* prepared to shape it in fundamental ways.

And Bolger could also sing. The first vocal quartet for the principals, Amy

(Allyn McLerie), Kitty (Doretta Morrow), Charley (Bolger), and Jack (Byron Palmer), "Better Get Out of Here," while making modest vocal demands, includes a clever interlude, "Gavotte—à la Mozart," wherein Loesser decorously sets the antiquated scene while introducing the audience to the main characters. The arrival of Charley's aunt from Brazil suggested to the writers the need for a long Caribbean dance number, "Pernambuco," with segments devoted to both a samba and a tango, which grows—according to the indications in the score—successively "sexy," "rhythmic," "wild," and "wilder" at the end of act 1. No less than three other attractive duets rounded out the first act: "Make a Miracle," "My Darling, My Darling," and "Lovelier Than Ever." "Make a Miracle" has Amy exclaiming about the coming wonders of the twentieth century (in a book she is reading), while Charley attempts to divert her attention and make a marriage proposal. (This witty conversational duo is discussed later in this chapter.) "My Darling, My Darling" made it to the top of the hit parade in the latter part of the year, but the song with the most staying power over the long run did not appear until the second act. "Once in Love with Amy" was a soft-shoe feature for Bolger. An early concerted number (for Jack, Kitty, Amy, chorus, band, and dancers), "The New Ashmolean Marching Society and Students' Conservatory Band," provided another audience favorite in rousing march style.[9] A romantic waltz song, "At the Red Rose Cotillion," concludes the show.

"My Darling, My Darling" is an unremarkable but supple melody, composed of a series of gently descending phrases. Its pleasingly tripping lyric contains at least one rare Loesser rhyme word:

My darling, my darling,
I fluttered and fled like a starling.

The generic romantic (or perhaps characteristically Victorian) sentiment expressed by this tune attracted many singers, and it was profitably recorded by Jo Stafford, Gordon MacRae, Doris Day, Peter Lind Hayes, and Sarah Vaughan, among others.[10]

"Once in Love with Amy," with the first title lines coming directly from Thomas's script, is much celebrated. Its skipping rhythm in "soft-shoe tempo" carries a singable melody that makes the most of notes clustered about a secure key note in balanced phrases, a rough AABA form. Loesser avoids line-end rhymes in favor of midverse assonances (by her/afire, etc.) until the final couplet finishes strongly (will be/with me).

Once in love with Amy,
Always in love with Amy,
Ever and ever fascinated <u>by her</u>
Sets your heart <u>afire</u> to stay.

Once <u>you're kissed</u> by Amy,
Tear up <u>your list</u> — it's Amy, . . .

Ever and ever sweetly you'll <u>romance her,</u>
Trouble is, <u>the answer</u> will be
That Amy'd rather stay in love with me!

Bolger, allegedly plagued with a memory slip and then cued by a child in the audience (Cy Feuer's son Bobby), was able to convert this solo number into an audience sing-along. The ploy worked, and the song performed in this manner — and always encored — carried the show for many months.[11]

Following "Once in Love with Amy" comes another good example of Loesserian dramatic musical conversation. This concerted number (with act 1 reprises inserted), entitled "The Gossips," shows Kitty and Amy's girlfriends engaged in teasing banter with one another. ("But of course you've all heard? / No, tell us, tell us, tell us. / No, I promised I'd never breathe a word. / Oh!") Gayle Seaton observes a possible classical inspiration for this lighthearted number, which, given Loesser's interest in all things theatrical, should not be dismissed out of hand.[12] The alleged parallel scene comes from the second act of Romani and Donizetti's *L'elisir d'amore* [*The Elixir of Love*] (scene 4, "Saria possibile?" ["Is it possible?"]); both scenes set conversational chatter for at least a half-dozen high voices in quick four-beat meters with short, repetitive, overlapping phrases. Loesser's natterers actually demonstrate more varied expressions through tempo and texture changes than do Donizetti's. The lyrics of both are equally slight about the same subject — amorous secrets — and the music equally zesty.

With an abundance of good music and luminaries among the cast and creative team, the producers Feuer and Martin worked hard to make their show a hit. They had based it on an established play, convinced the best "show fixer" in the business to adapt it for Broadway, added a young composer-lyricist with a brief but good track record, and hired one of the preeminent actor/dancers of the period. Advance ticket sales amounted to a substantial $250,000.[13] The critics refused to rave, however. The virtually unanimous reaction to the show lauded Ray Bolger's lithe movements and the supportive character acting and singing of Allyn McLerie, but found the rest to be

Ray Bolger in drag as "Charley's aunt" among the gossips in the ladies' dressing room, *Where's Charley?* (1948). Theatre Collection, The Museum of the City of New York.

merely amusing, a kind of warmed-over Gilbert and Sullivan based on a plot that didn't quite catch the audience's attention. Some reviewers seemed a bit put off by the female impersonation required of Bolger, though others found him well suited to the task. Others felt that the nondancing segments moved too slowly; at least one questioned the advisability of the first act's dance finale. All deemed Bolger's presence essential to the show and celebrated his "shimmering anatomy and educated feet."[14]

Most critics noted George Abbott's fidelity to Thomas's original text and implied that further pruning would have benefited the whole affair even more. His direction was thought dutiful but unexciting. Robert Garland of the *New York Journal American* declared, "George Abbott—out of respect, perhaps, for the age of 'Charley's Aunt'—has directed 'Where's Charley?' with a not unwelcome let-down in his customary hoopla."[15]

Comments on the music varied also, although writers whose opinion Loesser valued registered unqualified enthusiasm and even financial support. Kudos poured in from the likes of Rodgers and Hammerstein and Cole Porter.[16] To the general public, Loesser was known at the time as the composer of a string of recent hits ("Praise the Lord and Pass the Ammunition," "Rodger Young," and "Spring Will Be a Little Late This Year"), and consequently high expectations were brought to bear. In light of this collective anticipation, and given Loesser's inclination to expand his horizons rather than repeat formulas, the critics' responses to Loesser's music, including the addition of a Caribbean dance as the act 1 finale, ranged from mild surprise to disappointment. With terms like "clever though not exactly what we expected from him" (Coleman in the New York Daily Mirror), "pleasant . . . but commonplace and unexhilarating" (Watts, New York Post), and "a routine score with only a bright spot here and there" (Morehouse, New York Sun), most shied away from either rave or outright pan.[17]

In retrospect, William Hawkins of the New York World-Telegram seems to have nailed Loesser's intention best by terming the "score . . . brisk and fresh without being deliberately tricky."[18] One suspects that Loesser would have liked that perception of apparently artless artistry—because the score is indeed well-tooled on several counts, its textures and tunes meshing well with the dialogue. In this regard, Brooks Atkinson noted in the New York Times that "Mr. Loesser combines song-writing with composing, which is a most acceptable notion."[19] What Atkinson seems to have meant with this compliment was that Loesser wrote music for full scenes, achieving a unified and seamless effect (as did Rodgers and Hammerstein), rather than placing isolated songs arbitrarily into the middle of dramatic scenes. Loesser's approach to the duet for Sir Francis Chesney, suddenly reunited with his long-lost love, Donna Lucia D'Alvadorez (the true aunt of Charley Wykeham), illustrates Loesser's technique.

The number is called "Lovelier Than Ever." The circumstances of the couple's previous romance and parting in the springtime are established and explained in act 1, scene 3, through half a dozen short dialogue lines and are then followed by thirty-eight four-beat measures. In most songs, these bars would form the verse, a lead-in to the main tune—often nearly monotonic in a popular song. In this instance, the verse measures comprise a series of short paired musical phrases, carefully supported by a variety of chords with added pauses for the singers to "remember," intertwined spoken lines, appropriate gestures of hand and eye, and orchestral comments meant to paint a spring scene. Sir Francis's first sung lyrics are:

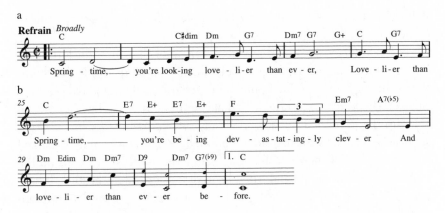

Example 2.3. "Lovelier Than Ever" (chorus), (a) mm. 1–5 and (b) mm. 25–31

> 'Twas a bright blue sky,
> And a lark sang high
> On a bough that was blossom laden.

The stage direction "He looks at Donna" covers the following two measures (eight moderately fast counts of time) and is accompanied by a short bird-call from the woodwinds. Loesser adds melodic or harmonic color for every moment of the next twenty-eight measures. And all this occurs before the song's main chorus melody begins ("Springtime, you're looking lovelier than ever"). This chorus tune is itself capable of standing on its own as a straightforward ballad. Formed as an ABAC melody—an appropriately old-fashioned form for this nostalgic moment—it directs us to another place and time by extending the second phrase (B) by two measures to accommodate the words "when I was seventeen" in a slower tempo.[20] The final phrase (C) contains the song's most ingenious lyric and word rhythm, "Springtime, you're being devastatingly clever," and so places it on the highest notes of the melody for added emphasis (ex. 2.3).

If all of this were not enough to grab a listener's attention, the succession of singing participants as the refrain is repeated intensifies the full scene operatically. After taking one full refrain by herself, Donna Lucia is spelled by Sir Francis, who begins the same melody in a lower, less vocally demanding key but supported by four-part chorus as backup. Sixteen measures into it, Donna Lucia returns to complete the repeat of the refrain. This device of layering voices was often used in romantically charged duets, such as "Make

Believe" in the justly famous first scene of *Show Boat* and in a long string of operettas.[21]

But Loesser pushes the dramatic envelope of this duet still further by having the two old lovers complete it by themselves alone (while the chorus leaves the stage). In this final phrase, taken at the higher, original key, they sing yet again the (C) phrase quoted above (mm. 25–31). The last note, an E-flat in the published full score, is sung for eight counts (or longer if desired, as indicated by the fermata), supported by an accompaniment marked *ff* (very loud). Raising the volume for solo voices in this way turns up the emotional heat in a tried and true means of musical intensification. It happens effectively and predictably, and audiences can be counted on to applaud. The number is a well-made piece, yet, in the context of the plot, it might represent dramatic overkill.

Ethan Mordden has described *Where's Charley?* as "conventional," which indeed it is.[22] But the problem it gave critics had less to do with its conventionality than with how its conventions interfered with each another. An emotional bath like "Lovelier Than Ever" makes a wonderful number for a nostalgia-soaked operetta. But how does it fit with the rest of this show? Was *Where's Charley?* intended as a romance or a farce or a blend of the two? After all, what is the dramatic significance of two minor characters' ancient love affair in relation to Charley's wedding prospects? Was it really wise to place three romantic duets—though admittedly highly contrasting ones—in succession in the middle of the first act? With more music yet to come, is it any wonder that this charming piece was more or less missed by the critics?

Although the reunion of Sir Francis and Donna Lucia as a constructed scene and "Lovelier Than Ever" as a romantic duet cannot be faulted for musical craftsmanship, the number might be too strong for its position in the show as a whole. The same can be said for the first-act finale, "Pernambuco," the work's only overt piece of South Americana. The farcical shenanigans of Brandon Thomas lose momentum from the clever but complicated choreography of "Pernambuco" even more severely than they do from the emotional intensity of "Lovelier Than Ever." From a traditional musical comedy perspective, an exotic chorus and dance are exactly what the recipe calls for at this time of the evening. The most drastic addition to the original play script, it seems to have been added for an obvious reason: the need for an up-tempo group number before intermission. Nevertheless, this dance has little to do with the plot, characters, or principal mood of the whole despite its "Brazilian" flavor and the opportunities it presented for Bolger. It lacks dramatic motivation.

Given the wildly divergent genre elements and because Loesser "scribbled off a lively score in a number of entertaining styles," a mixed critical response was probably inevitable.[23] Almost everyone found something to like and to quibble with in the show. Most felt that it failed to hang together well. Loesser would later be criticized on similar grounds for *The Most Happy Fella*. The seriousness of such charges should always be weighed against each song's and scene's function in the show.

Later critics proved considerably more positive about the music after a 1966 New York revival, with Vincent Canby nailing this reconsidered estimate with precision: "If memory does not deceive, Mr. Loesser's contributions to the show were originally taken rather lightly. However, in the context of this City Center season, it's possible to listen to the . . . score with new appreciation. . . . In 'Where's Charley?' Mr. Loesser was working within the prescribed limits of formula musical comedy. But even within such limits he was exhibiting the wit, perception and lyricism that later were to be so highly praised."[24]

That *Where's Charley?* appealed as much as it did to its first audiences—nearly 800 performances in its initial New York run—is testimony to the high quality of its many individual sections, not to any overarching concept or break with tradition. It looks even better when one realizes that it survived, even flourished, until Bolger left the show, all the while facing stiff competition from a string of high-powered contemporary hits: *Annie Get Your Gun, High Button Shoes, Kiss Me, Kate,* and *South Pacific.*

Although *Where's Charley?* has yet to become a staple of the musical comedy repertory, its power to delight audiences has persisted over the years. Music Theatre International reported seven licensed productions of the work in the United States during 2005 (versus eight for *The Most Happy Fella,* 158 for *How to Succeed in Business Without Really Trying,* and 515 for *Guys and Dolls*).[25] Its many musical virtues urge that it be better known. As Gerald Bordman summarized it, *Where's Charley?* belongs to a group of works that "defy easy classification," but which put old devices together in new ways.[26] Evidently Loesser had sensed the same wind blowing as Kurt Weill had in 1940, when the latter, recalling his first impression of *Porgy and Bess,* declared, "We [American composers for the stage] can and will develop a musical-dramatic form in this country, but I don't think it will be called 'opera.' . . . It will develop from and remain a part of the American theater — 'Broadway' theater, if you like. More than anything else, I want to have a part in that development."[27] Weill went on to help fulfill his dream with the highly innovative *Lady in the Dark* (1941), the Broadway opera *Street Scene* (1947), and the vaudeville-inspired *Love Life* (1948). Although Loesser probably never met Weill (who died in 1950), and later professed to dislike his music, both men shared a common cause and found an increasingly receptive milieu for their experimental musical ideas.[28]

Loesser and Counterpoint

By the late 1940s, Loesser was well appreciated for the brilliance of his lyrics, the beauty of his melodies, the aptness of his harmonies, and the breadth of his expressive range. He also prided himself on the esoteric formal effects he was able to achieve within a single number, most especially with devices that are known collectively in music theory as polyphony or counterpoint. Counterpoint enables a composer to combine and harmonize different melodies, or versions of the same melody, so that each may be heard independently. A single melody composed to be sung by singers starting at different times is also termed contrapuntal, specifically denoted as a round or canon. Schoolchildren are familiar with examples such as "Row, Row, Row Your Boat" and "Frère Jacques." But canons of more than a few notes can be difficult to compose. Loesser loved working out the challenges involved in such pieces. He would later refer to his taste for writing songs with "concurrent speech," which suggests contrapuntal musical devices.[29]

For most of recorded Western music history, an understanding of counterpoint has represented high technical achievement. Because counterpoint has not been necessary for American popular song composition, few songwriters have worked to master it. Indeed, its academic odor is powerful. (It tends to be associated with the classical music of centuries past, the bewigged Johann Sebastian Bach [1685–1750] often taken as the figure representing the peak in its development.[30])

This brief aside is intended to give a bit of context for Frank Loesser the intellectual, who was anything but put off by the puzzle-making character of contrapuntal writing. In his lyrics, he thrived on searching out unusual sound combinations and unlikely juxtapositions of poetic syllables and musical lines. At the same time, he resisted anything that smacked of an elite pedigree, which counterpoint sometimes does. Although Loesser spent relatively little time explaining his compositional techniques, he was delighted when his ingenuity was detected and appreciated. Susan Loesser reports that an anonymous correspondent (later discovered to have been a midwestern kindergarten teacher and musician's daughter), having been impressed by the clever double tune and supple rhythm of "The Inch Worm" from *Hans Christian Andersen* (see chapter 4), handwrote the following:

> Dear Loesser your song Inchworm makes me very happy; not only from an inchwormitarian point of view (I know you must realize people will not be so repelled by us after this) but from the aspect of downright beauty. It is conceivable that if Robert Burns and the god Pan, and Antoine de St. Exupery, and Euclid had gotten together for three days and three nights, they might have been able to write almost equally good words, but as I see it no group of musicians nor any other one musician could have written the beautiful music. It is simple, yet it is so intricate, the harmony is perfect and the counterpoint—well it just gives me a headache when I think of what it would be like to try to write it tho I suppose for you it was easy.[31]

The letter was signed "Respectfully, a Kansas inchworm." Loesser was so taken by this knowing but anonymous tribute that he placed a quarter-page advertisement as a thank-you note, complete with squiggly inchwormitarian lines, in the largest daily paper in Lawrence, Kansas, which finally moved the writer to reveal herself.[32]

Because it naturally suggests multiple singers, a contrapuntal song is also an ideal type to include in musical comedies. Contrasting styles and sounds are always welcome in an evening-long show. As operatic composers demonstrated in the eighteenth and nineteenth centuries, groups of two or more characters singing together can produce a climactic effect of shattering dramatic power. Far more appealing than the confusion of a multipart spoken conversation, sung ensembles are indispensable in well-rounded musical dramas. Historically—right up until the time of Rodgers and Hammerstein, in fact—the job of creating dramatic intensity in a musical had most often been fulfilled by a large chorus. Such is the animating power of counterpoint, however, that even a small group of, say, three or four strong individual singers can create a compelling effect, not unlike the visual excitement in a good game of mixed doubles tennis. Even a duo written in this fashion provides a pleasant dramatic enhancement.

Loesser clearly recognized the technical options possible with multiple singers and sung lines, and he enjoyed exploiting them even before he began to write full shows. There are very few nonchoral ensembles of this kind in any American musical theater before Loesser. When he collaborated with Joe Lilley on "Jingle, Jangle, Jingle" (in 1942), he might have observed that Lilley's tune, like many that make good canons, uses only a handful of basic chordal notes located on the strong beats. At any rate, when Loesser wrote both the words and the music for the duet "Tallahassee" five years later, he chose to apply a different kind of counterpoint while still inventing a catchy number. "Tallahassee" is not a strict canon, but it employs another contrapuntal device familiar to classical musicians, in which each part of the duet is given a highly distinctive rhythmic shape. (It is sometimes called a "double song.") He also had before him the models of Irving Berlin, who had been up to such tricks at least as early as 1910 with "That Opera Rag," the deceptively titled song "Play a Simple Melody" (1914), and "Pack Up Your Sins and Go to the Devil" (1922).[33]

When two singers sing the same word at different times, it is relatively easy for listeners to shift their attention from one to the other and fail to notice any passing clashes between the notes or accompanying chords. "Tallahassee" (written for the Paramount movie *Variety Girl*) charms in two separate ways: the large number of words in both parts are perfectly understandable and in fact work to reinforce a single central message ("Tallahassee [is] the Southland at its best"); yet the two musical lines contrast completely in character, with one part a smooth long-note ballad and the accompanying part a boogie-woogie bursting with dotted eighth- and sixteenth-note pairs and triplets.

Part 1: When you see land   kinda green and grass-   y,
Part 2:   Out of the window of a train   How in the
                                                                                           world can

Part 1:   Beneath a moon   bright beyond
                                                                                   compare,
Part 2: you complain?   You ought to see the way it shines,

Each of these parts keeps to its own time span. Even better than the clarity of the musical conversation, though, is that each part *rhymes* poetically within itself in a different scheme and makes sense, more or less, by itself:

Part 1:
When you see land kinda green and grassy,
Beneath a moon bright beyond compare,
When you hear blue jays chirping high and sassy,

And catch one sniff of southern cooking
Hanging in the evening air.

Part 2:
Out of the window of a train
How in the world can you complain?
You ought to see the way it shines,
The way it shines upon the pines.

The "moderate boogie" beat the score calls for here is a coded cue intended to suggest the "good, old" (antebellum) South. Using a romantic ballad to celebrate the Southland is a familiar Tin Pan Alley device, but Loesser pulled off a novel turn with this example. He and Abe Burrows performed it together over the radio on *The Abe Burrows Show* in 1947.[34]

"Make a Miracle," the second of the three romantic duets in the first act of *Where's Charley?* demonstrates how Loesser by 1948 had mastered the skill of isolating a basic series of notes and then using them to make both a melody and a repeating series of accompanying chords. Long before, back in Hollywood, he had found many ways to apply catchy rhythms and novel concatenations of rhyming words to other men's tunes. But "Make a Miracle" is probably the first example among Loesser's Broadway songs of what might be termed an interruptive duet. ("Sue Me" in *Guys and Dolls* is a later one.) One singer begins the chorus, only to be cut in on by the second singer trying to steer the discussion in another direction. The conversation goes back and forth on two different tracks, but it all rhymes and comes out together in the end:

AMY: I've just read a book on what's to be expected. . . .
    They'll have . . . Horseless carriages on the road,
    Breakfast cereals that explode—
CHARLEY: [*Spoken*] Yes, I know, I know, I know, I know, [*sung*] I know.
    [*Refrain*] Someday / they'll have horseless carriages that fly.
AMY: Horseless carriages that fly.
CHARLEY: Horseless carriages and
    Someday / they'll be roaring all about the sky.
AMY: Spelling out slogans: / "Buy a beer at Hogan's."
CHARLEY: But who knows when that age of miracles / will come to be?
    So meanwhile, darling, make a miracle / and marry me.

This all works musically, because clashes among the basic melody notes in both parts are carefully avoided. In "Make a Miracle" there are five basic

Example 2.4. "Make a Miracle" (a) melodic pitch vocabulary, (b) beginning of the refrain, and (c) chords accompanying the refrain

notes in the refrain: F (the key note), A, C, D, and B-flat. Arranged in order from low to high they appear in example 2.4a. Most pairings of two adjacent notes in this set will form the consonant interval of a third. Any three adjacent notes will form a triad, as such stacked third pairs are called.

In Loesser's melody (ex. 2.4b), the second note, the repeated F, is syncopated to match the determinedly pointed short-long utterance of "Someday." The chords underlying this melody (ex. 2.4c) are all variants of the notes in example 2.4a.

One does not need to understand much about harmony or counterpoint to observe the efficiency of this ploy. Limiting the number of different pitches (counting pitches in different octaves as the same) also limits dissonance. Backup singers and accompanists in many idioms employ a similar technique. Once a basic melody with its chords is stated, the composer needs only to shift the tune between the voices so as to keep the conversational lyric going. This is more call and response than counterpoint (if the term is strictly interpreted), but it reveals, nonetheless, a careful disposition of complementary sung parts.

In a 1952 *Life* magazine feature article on hit songwriters, Ernest Havemann cited "Make a Miracle" as revealing Loesser's consummate knack for "micro-engraving on the head of a pin," his ability to illustrate character, context, and action simultaneously and all within an extremely brief musical span:

> In what must be the most economical use of language since Genesis, Loesser accomplishes [scene setting] with 40 well-chosen words. He then goes on to run through a gay capsule history of recent scientific miracles: the radio, automobile, fountain pen, airplane and electric light, not to mention such less scientific developments as the breakfast cereal with sound effects and the short skirt and plunging neckline. While breezing merrily through this recital, he manages to inject a few bits of trenchant social observation and criticism. . . . In an aside of just six words, he gently chides the British for the nasal stuffiness produced by their damp climate. In another aside of just four words, he complains about the high cost of psychoanalysis.
>
> To most lyric writers, even the best, all this would seem more than enough for a three-minute song. To Loesser it is only the beginning. Packed into his lyrics is a good deal of character study. Loesser makes it clear that the young man singing his song is a conservative steak-and-kidney-pie Englishman who wears his rubbers when it rains but also has a rakish streak which makes him consider the short skirt and bare front the most desirable of all conceivable 20th century developments. Loesser also conveys very vividly the young man's growing impatience as the girls [*sic*] continues to interrupt him. Then, at the very end, to the listener's complete surprise, everything is wrapped up by the girl's suddenly agreeing to the marriage.[35]

Loesser's other triumphant duet of the late 1940s is his only Oscar-winning song, "Baby, It's Cold Outside."[36] After years of tryouts at parties, with Loesser himself and wife Lynn singing the parts, he was finally convinced to use it in a film, *Neptune's Daughter* (1948). Its tempo, "Loesser-ando" (which apparently equates with "relaxed," "nonchalant," or "casual") and its designation of parts for "The Mouse" and "The Wolf" mark its unique place in Frank Loesser's career. It is a not too distant cousin of Mozart's celebrated seduction duet "Là ci darem la mano" ("Put your hand in mine") in *Don Giovanni* (1787). It is a model of monomotivic development, which is to say he gets quite a long song by repeating a single short tune fragment for most of the dialogue (ex. 2.5).

Example 2.5. Basic motive of "Baby, It's Cold Outside"

With one rhythmic idea, "Baby, It's Cold Outside" uses the standard ABAC format of thirty-two measures and adds an unremarkable chord progression for foundation, yet its cumulative effect is so impressive that Loesser can be said to have built his little tune into a miniature dramatic scene, a *scena* in the operatic sense, in which two characters and the nature of their relationship are fully sketched with efficiency and emotional clarity. The call-and-response conversation of the characters is fraught with humor, danger, and suggestiveness. Yet it makes no judgments and allows the listeners to imagine what comes next and draw their own conclusions.

For years Loesser continued to profess that while he enjoyed writing comic or novelty songs, often rich in lyrical and contrapuntal invention, they were easier for him to make than more plaintive numbers such as "Spring Will Be a Little Late This Year" or "I Wish I Didn't Love You So." He consistently aspired to evoke the full range of emotional responses from his audiences by whatever musical means he could develop.[37] He also loved to subvert formulas and expectations through comic parody; he came up with new lyrics for other composers' Broadway hits and gave college students in the film *Those Were the Days* (1940) a fight song matched to the tune of "When Johnny Comes Marching Home." With Nashville music legend June Carter (1929–2003), he wrote some literally breathtaking lyrics for a country song send-up, "No Swallerin' Place" (1953).[38]

Ultimately, he was able to devote an entire musical to serious and pastoral songs rather than boffo stage numbers or comic tunes. (For a variety of reasons, that show, *Greenwillow*, when it finally reached the stage in 1960, lacked theatrical staying power.) But by the end of the 1940s, Loesser had already achieved a great deal: a string of hit songs, including an Academy Award winner; stage production savvy acquired through his writing of military shows; considerable professional prestige; and a single, highly success-ful Broadway hit, encompassing a variety of standard song styles and dance types. To continue exploring Broadway's possibilities must have seemed the natural thing to do. In the following decade, he was to find his greatest suc-cesses as well as his greatest artistic challenges in constructing more full-length musical comedies.

 CHAPTER 3

The Broadway Composer Arrives:
Guys and Dolls

My time of day is the dark time:
A couple of deals before dawn, . . .

Music I can wish you,
Merry music when you're young,
And wisdom when your hair has turned to gray.
—FROM *GUYS AND DOLLS*, 1950

The Genesis of *Guys and Dolls*

GUYS AND DOLLS OPENED AT THE FORTY-SIXTH STREET THEATRE on November 24, 1950, and on December 3, 1950, *New York Times* critic Brooks Atkinson declared,

Although "Guys and Dolls" is composed of the many bizarre elements essential to every musical show, it seems simple and effortless on the stage. Everything falls into place easily as though the play had been created in one piece, and every song and actor were inevitable. As a matter of fact, musical shows are put together out of sweat and tears by a couple of platoons of anxious workmen. But every now and then a perfectly-composed and swiftly-paced work of art comes out of the bedlam of Broadway producing and seems as if it had always been in existence in somebody's imagination. You have an irrational feeling that it had to be done sooner or later, exactly as it has been done by the people who have now composed it.[1]

Rave reviews by such critical arbiters as Atkinson had appeared before in the theatrical press, but seldom if ever can one find the terms "perfectly-composed" or "work of art" or the phrase "as though . . . every song and actor were inevitable" attached to a single musical comedy. In his second major outing on Broadway, Frank Loesser and his cocreators struck the rarest kind of Broadway gold: an example of both highly artistic and unapologetically popular creativity.

Guys and Dolls appealed to everyone, or so it seems. The other critics all agreed with Atkinson. The show's depiction of characters in Prohibition era New York was lighthearted and believable. Yet it was also so well constructed, thematically unhobbled by any too-specific historical facts, and so efficiently turned out that it has remained fresh in many later revivals. Its gestation and birth were difficult, but it has stood the test of time. It continues to be produced in theaters across America every year in numbers far exceeding Loesser's other hit shows.[2]

Guys and Dolls appeared roughly fifty years after the first Salvation Army girl of American musicals, Violet Gray in *The Belle of New York* (1897) wowed crowds in both New York and London with her song "The Purity Brigade."[3] Shortly after this transatlantic triumph, the patriotic and energetic romps of George M. Cohan—shows like *Little Johnny Jones* (1904) and *Forty-five Minutes from Broadway* (1906)—which essentially defined the genre of musical comedy for the first third of the century, came to town. To be successful, musical comedies in the days before Kern and Hammerstein's *Show Boat* (1927) had to be brash, fast-moving, plain-speaking star vehicles that showcased individual talents playing sympathetic characters involved in mildly coherent stories.[4]

But even before the blockbuster hit *Oklahoma!* the importance of the spoken script and fresh settings had begun to assume greater significance. Public and critics alike warmly greeted the Princess Theatre shows (1915–18) of Guy Bolton, P. G. Wodehouse, and Jerome Kern and Rodgers and Hart's hits in the 1920s, filled with innovative scenarios, witty lyrics, sensible scripts, and vernacular tunes. *Guys and Dolls* represents a peak comparable to those earlier landmarks, but for Atkinson to have used the phrase "perfectly-composed"—with the likes of *Pal Joey* (1940), the 1942 revival of *Porgy and Bess*, *Oklahoma!* (1943), *Carousel* (1945), *Annie Get Your Gun* (1946), *Street Scene* (1947), and *South Pacific* (1949) in the recent past—suggests just how highly Loesser's work was valued.

Vivian Blaine, the first Miss Adelaide in *Guys and Dolls*, costumed as a
"farmerette" on the cover of Mrs. Frank Loesser's own copy of *Life* magazine.
Vivian Blaine image by Milton H. Greene, © 2007 Joshua Greene,
www.archiveimages.com.

The World of Damon Runyon

After *Where's Charley?* Cy Feuer and Ernest Martin decided to move away from British farces toward American local color, and they warmed to the idea of transforming an unlikely love story about a fast-talking hustler and a Salvation Army evangelist into a Broadway musical. Apparently inspired by the incongruous pairing of Emile de Becque and Nellie Forbush in *South Pacific*, they found similar possibilities in "The Idyll of Miss Sarah Brown," published in 1932, by Damon Runyon (1884–1946).[5] They also knew Frank Loesser from his work on *Where's Charley* and liked him. (They also may have recollected Loesser's old ties to Paramount Studios, which held the rights to Runyon's tales, although that notion never enters into Cy Feuer's version of the story's development.[6]) Their hopes for Loesser's interest in a Runyon show were well-founded, however, and he quickly worked up "Luck Be a Lady Tonight," "Sit Down, You're Rockin' the Boat," and a handful of other numbers to convince potential financial backers. ("A Bushel and a Peck" and "More I Cannot Wish You" were already in his trunk.[7])

Once access to the stories was accomplished and many more songs were written, a problem arose in finding a librettist who understood and could adapt Runyon's picturesque and individual style. According to Abe Burrows, Feuer and Martin's original concept for *Guy and Dolls* had been closely aligned with Rodgers and Hammerstein's earnest, joke-free approach in *Carousel* and *South Pacific*, and only after much reconsideration were they persuaded to fully embrace Runyon's comic attitude.[8] Academy award–winning author Jo Swerling had produced a first-act script that realized the serious "music drama" conception originally called for; but when Feuer and Martin changed their minds, they knew this draft would not mesh with Loesser's songs.[9] In the search for the right book, at least a half-dozen writers were approached. Finally Abe Burrows, whose radio characters were close cousins to the residents of Runyonland, was hired to write a newer, funnier book for *Guys and Dolls*. He had almost no experience with writing for Broadway or legitimate theater, although he had turned out nearly 200 scripts for a popular weekly radio program, *Duffy's Tavern* (1941–45). Owing to Burrows's inexperience, one prominent backer of the show, Billy Rose, withdrew his support ($10,000), and he lived to regret it.[10]

A native of Manhattan, Kansas, raised in Pueblo, Colorado, Damon Runyon had been a third-generation newspaper man. Both his father and grandfather were proud products of the rough-and-tumble, "six-gun" West.

His mother succumbed to tuberculosis when he was still a boy, and the experience appears, not unsurprisingly, to have affected him deeply. He suppressed his grief, spoke little, and learned to listen to the stories of the people around him. Barely out of adolescence, he rode the rails as a hobo, fought in the Philippines during the Spanish-American War, and turned to sports and court reporting back home in Denver and San Francisco. At the age of thirty he headed for New York, where he became a vivid presence in the Manhattan of Loesser's youth. Like Loesser, Runyon seems to have possessed a cynical attitude toward politics, religion, corporate business, and the trappings of high culture. Both men, though of different generations, were hardheaded pragmatists who worked hard, played hard, and liked making money.[11]

One of his biographers, William Kennedy, declared, "When I was eleven years old [in 1939], I thought Runyon was the funniest man alive. He was a great newspaperman . . . our literary equivalent of his contemporaries, the Marx Brothers, . . . enduringly comic, thoroughly original."[12] Along with friend and fellow reporter Walter Winchell, Runyon depicted the free and easy atmosphere of a New York untroubled by efforts to enforce the Eighteenth Amendment to the U.S. Constitution, which took effect in 1920 and prohibited the "manufacture, sale, or transportation of intoxicating liquors within . . . the United States."

Runyon's sharp ear allowed him to catch and preserve in written form the authentic tone of his gangster and sporting-life acquaintances.[13] Part of Runyon's gift for recording language lay in his ability to take a verbose stream of slangy chatter among his pals and turn it into a witty, rhythmic poetry of the street. In other words, he was something close to a lyricist himself. Heywood Broun once declared, "To me the most impressive thing in [the book and lyrics of] *Guys and Dolls* is the sensitivity of the ear of Damon Runyon."[14] Jimmy Breslin claimed, "Damon Runyon invented the Broadway of *Guys and Dolls* and the Roaring Twenties, neither of which existed, but whose names and phrases became part of theater history and the American language. . . . He stressed fine, upstanding, dishonest people who fell in love, often to the sound of gunfire that sounded harmless."[15]

A sample from one of his short stories about a character named Feet Samuels makes the point well: "He is a big heavy guy with several chins and very funny feet, which is why he is called Feet. These feet are extra large feet, even for a big guy, and Dave the Dude says Feet wears violin cases for shoes. Of course this is not true, because Feet cannot get either of his feet in a violin case, unless it is a case for a very large violin, such as a cello."[16] With seven repetitions of the word "feet" in three loose sentences, this passage reads more like an irregularly accented poem than a descriptive paragraph. It is also perfectly suited to musicalization, although Loesser probably never set this particular text.[17] It is straightforward and clear in its imagery. It also makes no judgments. It may turn out that Feet is a killer, or at least a felonious kind of guy, but in this description he is just very much alive, someone Runyon has convinced us we *must* meet and see — especially his feet.

Loesser admired Runyon's literary grit and his method of storytelling, which in its reiterative style (and relentless adherence to the present tense) suggests a musical approach. Since most melodies use a limited vocabulary of pitches, motives, and phrases over and over again, it must have struck Loesser how well matched Runyon's material would be to a New York songwriter of similar sympathies — himself. At any rate, Burrows's script was interwoven with Loesser's already composed songs. (Burrows had once met Runyon in the company of his friend Walter Winchell, a reporter and radio broadcaster long associated with New York sports and nightlife. With his edgy, staccato delivery and catch phrases like "Flash!" and "Good evening, Mr. and Mrs. America," Winchell was an influential purveyor of Broadway's distinctive jargon, including such terms as "hit," "flop," "turkey," "wow" [as a verb], and "The Big Apple."[18])

Runyon's plots and characters appealed almost as much as his verbal style. The multifaceted quality of his underground world of gangsters, gamblers, and their molls struck both Loesser and Burrows strongly. Raymond Knapp has observed that "*Guys and Dolls* . . . brings a version of America's mythologized West to the heart of the American city . . . at the same time that it brings America's West-based literary tradition to the Broadway stage. The central figure of that literary tradition is unquestionably Mark Twain (1835–1910)."[19] The characters' high-toned and rapid-fire speech embodies a distinctive poetic quality, and their pseudophilosophical disquisitions bespeak both humor and pathos, while also recalling the strain of rebelliousness in the English-language comic opera tradition, epitomized by *The Beggar's Opera* (1728) by John Gay. Indeed, Kenneth Tynan referred to *Guys and Dolls* as "the *Beggar's Opera* of Broadway."[20]

Burrows himself called attention to the 1928 German updating of *The Beggar's Opera—Die Dreigroschenoper (The Threepenny Opera)*—and its connection with *Guys and Dolls*, when he was interviewed in 1974 by Martin Mann.[21] Written by Bertolt Brecht and Kurt Weill, this show was suppressed by the Nazis in 1933. It had appeared that year in its first English-language production on Broadway (though only for a week), but it did not return to New York until 1954, where after a jump restart in September 1955 it ran continuously off Broadway (at the Theatre de Lys, now the Lucille Lortel Theater, Greenwich Village) for over 2,600 performances.[22] It seems unlikely that Burrows would have known of the show before its New York revival. But his memory in 1974, however anachronistic, saw a significant link between it and *Guys and Dolls*:

> There's a word called integration they use, but that means where a number advances the plot and stuff like that. . . . I believe . . . Brecht's thing—*Threepenny Opera* was a good example. Those numbers were not integrated as being about the plot, but they curiously enough advance the character—gave you an insight each time. You see Brecht knew about that. *Threepenny* was on my mind. . . . *Guys and Dolls* was [like it] in spirit, even though God knows, it wasn't as courageous or as raffish; but it [had] bums, raffish people acting like ladies and gentlemen.
>
> The essence of *Guys and Dolls*, if anybody asks me [what] the secret of it was, [is] that these bums act like they are written by Noel Coward. That's what *Dreigroschenoper* was.[23]

Other Precursors?

Brecht, Weill, and Elisabeth Hauptmann's immediate successor show to *The Threepenny Opera*, *Happy End* (1929, Berlin), resembles *Guys and Dolls* even more closely, featuring a gangster enamored of a Salvation Army woman, though no one has ever suggested for the record that either Loesser or Burrows was aware of that show.[24]

Guys and Dolls also seems to bear a kinship with George Bernard Shaw's play *Major Barbara* (1905), a work in which the principal actions surround religious and moral questions, proper class behavior, and the character of a wealthy girl (Barbara Undershaft) who devotes her life to the Salvation Army. The second act (of three), set at the Salvation Army mission, even includes a wager concerned with the "saving of souls." While *Major Barbara*, like Shaw's other dramas, has much discussion of ideas taking place in a real-world London setting, it is also filled with action and energy, witty lines, and sympathetic characters on both sides of the moral issues in question. Major Barbara's fiancé, Adolphus Cusins, delivers a ringing retort to Barbara's cynical father, who questions Cusins's religious views and his attitude toward the Salvation Army: "I am a sincere Salvationist. You do not understand the Sal-

vation Army. It is the army of joy, of love, of courage: it has banished the fear
and remorse and despair of the old hell-ridden evangelical sects: it marches
to fight the devil with trumpet and drum, with music and dancing, with banner and palm, as becomes a sally from heaven by its happy garrison."[25] At
least the musical attitude of this passage accords with the optimism of Sister
Sarah's Americanized expression of religious fervor. Cusins's élan is also a
good match for Loesser's general enthusiasm.

There is no evidence that Loesser read *Major Barbara* or ever saw a production of the play, although a critically acclaimed movie version did appear in 1941, a period when Loesser was deeply involved in the motion picture industry.[26] Yet the two plays reveal a thematic resonance that both share
with many Euro-American dramas after Ibsen. *Guys and Dolls*, like *Major
Barbara*, succeeded at least partially because it raised ethical, moral, and religious questions not by preaching, but by cajoling, joking, and singing the
audience—yes, there is even live music in Shaw's play—into sympathy with
its characters and its dilemmas.

Guys and Dolls avoids the bitter, satirical edginess of *The Threepenny
Opera*, the overt political tone of *Happy End*, and the learned dialogue that
pervades long stretches of *Major Barbara*. It aims rather toward a kind of
amiability typical of many 1950s musical shows, yet seldom so well expressed.
The underground worlds of *The Threepenny Opera* and *Guys and Dolls* are
related in spirit. Each has its own rules, not necessarily mirroring the norms
of polite society. Yet in their self-consistency and their concessions to sentiment, both are reassuring, at times even comforting, and reveal that beneath
the surface human beings—saints and sinners alike—are pretty much the
same.

The special quality of the *Guys and Dolls* world—embodying both sincerity and smartness—was well timed and well suited for Americans in 1950.
But its circle of appeal only seems to have grown over time. By including
both hip modernity and a bit of old-fashioned romance, Burrows and Loesser
discovered a recipe that has touched and pleased a wide range of tastes.

Putting It All Together

Cy Feuer and Abe Burrows incorporated characters from another Runyon story, "Pick the Winner," to supplement those of "The Idyll of Sarah
Brown."[27] Burrows is credited especially with strengthening the humorous
side of the show, conceiving the Nathan/Adelaide romance as a parallel to

the Sarah/Sky pairing. Burrows's success as a radio writer and talk show personality—he had also written for Hollywood films in the 1930s and '40s—had tuned his ear. After he had begun to write the script, Feuer and Martin cajoled a reluctant George S. Kaufman to direct the show.[28] According to Burrows, Kaufman was won over by his trusted friend and producer, Max Gordon, who loved Loesser's new songs and cabled Kaufman, urging him strongly to take the job. Once committed, Kaufman encouraged Burrows to punch up the funny dialogue, an order contrary to what the writer had expected but which played to his strengths.[29]

Kaufman had become a high-profile figure on Broadway when Burrows was still a young man. They had worked together as panelists on an early television quiz show, *This Is Show Business*. As Burrows tells it, "On Sunday nights when we did *This Is Show Business*, we were colleagues. Equals. But when George became the director of *Guys and Dolls*, our relationship changed. He became my teacher."[30]

Burrows felt that the Runyon characters bore a strong resemblance to characters he had created for his radio program, *Duffy's Tavern*: salty, colorful, and funny, but who spoke a language free of profanity and double entendre.[31] Having learned his lessons well, Burrows enjoyed several Broadway successes after *Guys and Dolls* as both writer and director, including several shows with other collaborators besides Frank Loesser.[32]

The Book

The first hint of the show's deviation from a classic double-pair love story appears immediately after the instrumental overture, with an opening sequence of movement that is neither strictly dance nor chorus. Dubbed "Runyonland," this prancing display instantly presents the bustling, colorful, and shady character of the musical's setting, the petty criminal underground of New York, circa 1925 (though also with many recognizable 1950s features). Two dozen bits of choreographed stage business, filled with minor-league crooks and showgirls and an assortment of other urban types, are cued in score (usually with short phrases such as "two ready guys," "couple of tourists," "the cop and the pitchman," "the baby buggy," and so on).

These turns taken together resemble the kaleidoscopic cinematic street scenes of earlier decades, such as those Busby Berkeley created in *42nd Street* (1933), although no direct homage is apparent.[33] The concept of a nonchoral opening was borrowed from the commencement of Rodgers and Hammerstein's recent *Carousel*, which employed a similar pantomime dance to paint the background. (Unlike *Carousel*, however, *Guys and Dolls* begins with a traditional medley overture and its pantomime is less balletic.) After setting the tone of the play, this varied swath of music and choreography leads seamlessly into a conversation among three "tinhorns" (gamblers with more bluster than ready cash), checking the morning papers for tips on the daily horse races. This opening then segues to the heart of the story, the confrontation between the gamblers and the Salvation Army.

The dramatic arc of *Guys and Dolls* is one of the secrets of its success. Scene 1 moves with crisp efficiency. Directly after the initial call to sinners by Sister Sarah Brown and the Salvation Army band ("Follow the Fold"), we meet Nathan Detroit and hear about his problems—the need for ready cash to secure a safe location for his illegal crap game, the pursuit by police officer Lieutenant Brannigan, and Nathan's fourteen-year engagement to Miss Adelaide. In a dialogue of less than fifteen minutes' length, we also meet Sky Masterson, learn about his penchant for unusual betting, and see him tricked into wooing the proper but highly attractive Sister Sarah. Nathan, Nicely-Nicely Johnson, and the other guys sing about "The Oldest Established Permanent Floating Crap Game in New York."

Scene 2 zooms in on Sarah and Sky, establishing their characters and attitudes. Sky comes to the mission, where she correctly suspects his motives, but he is persuasive and promises to produce "a dozen genuine sinners" ready to confess if she will only consent to a dinner date with him. The scene concludes with an appropriate character-revealing song, "I'll Know [When My Love Comes Along]." Scene 3 returns to Nathan and Adelaide, explains their relationship, and contains her comic soliloquy, termed a "lament," as well as a comic dance number for all the Hot Box dolls, "A Bushel and a Peck." The title song follows immediately, a large choral number for the men led by Nicely-Nicely and Benny Southstreet.

At this point the dramatic tension is ratcheted up by a rapid succession of events: the arrival of General Matilda B. Cartwright, threatening to close the mission; Sky's repeated promise to deliver sinners to attend a midnight prayer meeting; Sarah and Sky's date in Havana (which reveals Sky's respectful gallantry and Sarah's looser, lighter side, as well as their growing attraction to each other); and the police raid on the crap game at the mission. Sarah's anger and shock at the deception suspend the action at a high emotional pitch before the act 1 curtain.

Weak second acts commonly plague Broadway musicals, but *Guys and*

Dolls avoids this problem. At the start of act 2, the pendulum swings back to Nathan and Adelaide, who sings "Take Back Your Mink" at the Hot Box club and reprises her solo lament. In dialogue, we learn that Nathan's crap game will continue driven on by the Chicago thug, Big Jule. In a brief scene at the mission, Arvide Abernathy sings a comforting song to Sarah, "More I Cannot Wish You." Scene 3 presents the crap game in the New York city sewer, with "Luck Be a Lady," the climactic dance number in which Sky wins the "souls" of his fellow crapshooters and compels them to attend a prayer meeting.

The appearance of the guys at the prayer meeting impresses General Cartwright, thus saving the mission and leading eventually to the two couples' reconciliation. This scene also contains the exuberant eleven o'clock number, "Sit Down, You're Rockin' the Boat," Nicely's hellish nightmare. The next-to-last scene offers a duo for Adelaide and Sarah ("Marry the Man Today"), a conversational interlude that completes the possible pairings among the four principals (Adelaide and Sky have had a dialogue at the beginning of act 2). The brief finale, set appropriately on the streets of New York, where the show began, celebrates Nathan and Adelaide's wedding about to take place at the mission. Sky and Sarah, having said their vows offstage, enter together, both dressed in uniform and performing as members of the Salvation Army band.

The show is sewn together not only with snappy and funny dialogue (and a running joke about Adelaide's psychosomatic head cold), but with orchestral interludes and introductions that signal the scenes or characters about to appear. Using such incidental music is standard operating procedure for *Guys and Dolls*; even these short segments of music are carefully applied. A bit of "Follow the Fold," for example, occurs no fewer than seven times after its first appearance. In its most complete reprise, it is sung by all the guys in the mission after "Sit Down, You're Rockin' the Boat," and it is always in the same key. In the final scene, "Follow the Fold" signals the arrival of Sarah and the onstage Salvation Army band (as it has previously), but in this instance it also provides a musical answer to Nicely's last quip. Nathan has finally agreed to marry Adelaide, but where can they have the ceremony? Nicely replies, "How about the Biltmore garage?" (the original subject of the betting in act 1, the garage is a sore point with Nathan). Instantly the band enters playing: of course—we understand even before Arvide can make the offer—the mission will host the wedding. Thus a double victory for the forces of tradition, order, and religion is achieved when both of the lead guys get hitched.

The Songs in the Show

Loesser eventually completed twenty-two songs for the stage version of *Guys and Dolls*, six of which were eventually dropped ("Traveling Light" "It Feels Like Forever," "Getting Dressed," "Action," "Shango," and "I Come A-Running"). Three more songs were added ("Pet Me, Poppa," "Adelaide," and "A Woman in Love") and five dropped ("A Bushel and a Peck," "I've Never Been in Love Before," "More I Cannot Wish You," "My Time of Day," and "Marry the Man Today") when the conversion to a motion picture took place.[34]

It was an instance of quintessential Loesser/Runyon humor to call the opening three-part round a "fugue," a nose-thumbing gesture for those who might want to point out that it fell short of being a true Baroque fugue. (Loesser first titled this piece "Three-Cornered Tune.")[35] Though it may lack full-fledged, Bach-like fugal form, this number demonstrates structural and lyrical cleverness surpassing nursery rounds. It has a canonic melody at the unison—that is to say, everyone starts on the same note—with each of the three tinhorns (Nicely-Nicely Johnson, Benny Southstreet, and Rusty Charlie) pleading the virtues of a favorite horse (Paul Revere, Valentine, Epitaph) in full-blown racetrack slang set to a catchy tune:

> I got the horse right here, / The name is Paul Revere,
> And here's a guy that says if the weather's clear,
> Can do, can do. / This guy says the horse can do.
> If he says the horse can do, / Can do, can do.
>
> I'm pickin' Valentine, / 'Cause on the morning line
> The guy has got him figured at five to nine.
> Has chance, has chance . . .
>
> But look at Epitaph, / He wins it by a half,
> According to this here in the *Telegraph*.
> Big threat, big threat . . .

In the second set of verses, three more vernacular expressions of probability like "can do" complete the picture: "likes mud," "needs race," and "shows class."

According to Jule Styne, Loesser picked up his jockey talk at a California racetrack years before. As Styne tells the story, "[Frank] was always working too hard, never had any fun. One day I took him to the races—he was crazy about the racing form and the phrase 'can do' after a horse's name. Twelve years later he called me and said that's where he got the idea for 'Fugue for Tinhorns.'"[36]

Wherever it came from, Loesser put this early tip to good use. The basic musical subject itself comprises twelve measures, three phrases of four bars each, with each singer repeating his part roughly three times. Part one is lengthened and parts two and three are foreshortened so that all singers can end together. (In ex. 3.1, the canon begins in the middle-voice part of the first system, the measure labeled 1. The final four measures [9–12] can be found in the uppermost part, in the second system, labeled 9.) The three parts are held together by a fourth one—a repeating two-measure accompaniment pattern based on the pitches B-flat, F, C, and F (bracketed in the bass line), which support the chords I–V^7–ii^7–V^7. Finally, a complementary eight-measure tag at the end (not included in ex. 3.1) reverses the order of entrances presented in the introductory "first call" to the starting gate. The descending fanfare of triplets at the start becomes a blended rising chord, including all three horses' names at the close. This busy and assertive conversation captures the flavor that racetrack touts often experience, with each man shouting for his favorite "hot pick" but "oblivious to the opposing and equally fervent views of the other two."[37]

Another of its vernacular gestures, the dotted, then syncopated, notes F–E–F–B–C–C ("I'm pick-ing Val-en-tine"), and a few chromatic inflections later on hint at the opening arch of Harold Arlen and Johnny Mercer's award-winning melody of 1941, "Blues in the Night" (which begins with the line, "My momma done told me"). Loesser undoubtedly knew this earlier song, since he kept close tabs on hit parade song picks and because he knew and admired Mercer's work in particular, but "Fugue for Tinhorns" is certainly no blues. After the slight melodic resemblance at the start, the tunes diverge.[38]

The tinhorns scatter when a Salvation Army band, led by the wholesome Miss Sarah Brown (first portrayed by Isabel Bigley), appears. Her goal is to save sinners in the heart of a sinning city, but she is not having much luck, and the band's stolid music is as different from the tinhorns' optimistic chatter as could be. The contrast registers instantly. Whereas "Fugue for Tinhorns" bubbles with quick, syncopated, polyphonic motion, "Follow the Fold" is slow, evenly paced, and nonchromatic, a melody accompanied in basic block chords (ex. 3.2).[39]

This number's rhythmic consistency closely parallels Lowell Mason's

Example 3.1. "Fugue for Tinhorns" (excerpt with all three singers in canon)

Example 3.2. (a) "Follow the Fold" beginning; (b) "Work for the Night Is Coming" (1864) by Lowell Mason and Anna Cogswell

strict time in "Work for the Night Is Coming" (1864) and skirts the edge of parody by means of rhyming word choices that speak directly to worldly issues. The urban white gospel song tradition of Peter Paul Bliss (1838–1876) and Ira Sankey (1840–1908) often used metaphors from everyday life ("A Shelter in the Time of Storm," "God Is an Anchor"),[40] but Loesser's message is more literal:

> Follow the fold and stray no more, . . .
> Put down the bottle and we'll say no more; . . .
> Tear up your poker deck and play no more; . . .
> If you're a sinner and you pray no more,
> Follow, follow the fold.

A small onstage band gives the number visual impact. Loesser knew that songs happened quickly, and that the audience had to understand the situations at first sight and first hearing. Like other theatrical composers, he constantly sought ways to make and fix a dramatic impression on his listeners' minds, whether that impression was labeled danger, romance, excitement, confusion, or, as in this case, simple—and slightly tattered—piety. As noted above, a fragment of this song is also repeated several times throughout the show.

The climactic final number of the first scene, "The Oldest Established [Permanent Floating Crap Game in New York]," takes a bit of tourist ballyhoo as its key text line, exuding what musicologist Stephen Banfield has termed the "celebratory unself-consciousness" characteristic of many crowd numbers in 1950s musicals.[41] (The number was actually a relatively late substitution to replace a song and dance for the two male leads called "Action."[42])

The problem of where to hold a high-stakes crap game without being discovered by the ever-vigilant Lieutenant Brannigan becomes the subject of a grand choral scene. It may be an unusual premise for a song, but the farcical setup is redeemed by the energy and the ever-growing crowd that greets chief fixer Nathan Detroit (first performed by Sam Levene), as more and more crapshooters enter and add their voices to the chorus:

> Why, it's good old reliable Nathan.
> Nathan, Nathan, Nathan Detroit.
> If you're looking for action, he'll furnish the spot.
> Even when the heat is on, it's never too hot.

The chorus breaks into glowing a cappella harmonies ("slower and forcefully"). Eventually the Handelian conclusion (the last five measures, repeating the title words and including a plagal cadence, are marked *Maestoso, quasi religioso*) underlines a reverence for tradition evinced even by pickpockets, rumrunners, and petty gamblers in a way somewhat reminiscent of the pirate and sailor madrigals in Gilbert and Sullivan operettas. Such a clash of musical form and dramatic characterization is itself a comic touch.[43]

With four musical sections clearly marked off, the structure of the first scene reveals a complete, miniature world in itself. The situations flow easily one to the next; all work together to make a vivid impression. The hustle and bustle of the opening music creates the visual space of "Runyonland," and the tinhorn trio introduces three of its inhabitants. Earnest Salvationists who sing bone-simple music reveal another side of urban life. In Geoffrey Block's observation, "'Follow the Fold' . . . illustrates a rare 'appropriate' use of a hymnlike style in Loesser's work. The concluding a cappella harmonies of the next song, 'The Oldest Established,' is far more typical of Loesser's predilection to translate the religious fervor of secular emotions with mock musical religiosity: gambling as a religious experience. . . . In all stages of his career Loesser would revisit the secular religiosity of his first hit, 'Praise the Lord and Pass the Ammunition.'"[44]

Finally Nathan and the gang complete the picture with their paean to gambling. The perky duple-meter tune (ex. 3.3)—rhythmically lively, with constantly shifting accents—follows a chantlike opening dialogue ("What's

Example 3.3. "The Oldest Established" at Bright tempo section (opening of chorus)

playing at the Roxy? I'll tell you what's playing at the Roxy: A picture about a Minnesota man / so in love with a Mississippi girl / that he sacrifices everything / and moves all the way to Biloxi. That's what's playing at the Roxy") that revolves around a small cluster of midrange notes to minimize the vocal challenges for this energetic lot. The quick tempo of the refrain seems to focus on the shifty and furtive attitude of life on the streets. Adding to Block's point above, Raymond Knapp suggests that the "sometimes religious tone of the song serves in part to parody religion, but more importantly to demonstrate the gamblers' innate affinities for the religious feelings they so overtly shun."[45] Salvationists and gamblers are brothers and sisters under the skin.

Because the spoken dialogue was written after the songs—not the normal procedure—it says all that is needed and no more. ("Loesser's songs were the guideposts for the libretto," Burrows reported.[46]) Burrows knew, because he worked so closely with Loesser and veteran director Kaufman, exactly what the songs had already taken care of and what did not need to be restated. It was advertised as "a musical fable of Broadway," with the fabulous element taken directly from Runyon.

That *Guys and Dolls* was not to be a vehicle for a single star actor was easy to assume—all the principals (Robert Alda, Isabel Bigley, Vivian Blaine, and Sam Levene) were only low-voltage celebrities at the time, known, at best, for their minor film roles. The show depends on ensemble work and reflects the attention its creators bestowed on this aspect. It also appeals because the plot comes as close to the heart of Broadway as any could. It was made by New Yorkers and set in a favorite New York neighborhood. Yet its concerns were not restricted to New York issues or themes. This double move—both toward and away from the particularities of time and place—helped to broaden its appeal. For example, a 1950s New Yorker hearing about

Table 3.1. Musical Numbers in *Guys and Dolls*

Act 1

    Overture
    "Runyonland" (opening dance)
1. "Fugue for Tinhorns"
2. "Follow the Fold"
3. "The Oldest Established"
4. "I'll Know"
5. "A Bushel and a Peck"
6. "Adelaide's Lament"
7. "Guys and Dolls"
8. "Havana"
9. "If I Were a Bell"
10. "My Time of Day"
11. "I've Never Been in Love Before"
    "The Raid"
    Entr'acte

Act 2

    "Hot Box [Night Club] Fanfare"
12. "Take Back Your Mink"
13. Reprise: "Adelaide's Lament"
14. "More I Cannot Wish You"
    "Crapshooters' Dance"
15. "Luck Be a Lady"
16. "Sue Me"
17. "Sit Down, You're Rockin' the Boat"
18. Reprise: "Follow the Fold"
19. "Marry the Man Today"
20. "The Happy Ending: Guys and Dolls"

"Mindy's cheesecake" in the opening dialogue would instantly recognize the reference to Lindy's restaurant, known to Damon Runyon. But failure to appreciate this bit of insider trivia would hardly detract from the effect.

The second scene, in the Save-a-Soul Mission, provides insight into Sister Sarah's predicaments and attitudes. Sky comes to the mission, where she correctly suspects his motives. To put off his teasing, she defends her feminine intuition about romance. Her song (echoed by Sky), "I'll Know," emerges from fourteen measures of sung verse interspersed with spoken dialogue. This opening forms a subtle parenthesis that fixes the starting pitches for the singers and makes for an intense exchange. Their words are carefully calculated to contrast with the release of tension that will flow from the song proper.

After Sarah says of her ideal, "I've imagined every bit of him, from his strong moral fiber to the wisdom in his head," Sky retorts, "You have wished yourself a Scarsdale Galahad, the breakfast-eating Brooks Brothers type!" The refrain arrives perfectly poised, exhibiting a characteristic melodic sweep and emotional focus, but it is no ordinary thirty-two-measure ballad. Encompassing a single ten-measure period (two related four-measure segments with a two-measure extension) and a repeat of the same, it also contains a final five-measure phrase to sum up the tune, adds a high note (E), and then clinches the emotional message with a final descent to the tonic F.[47]

The first two notes, D falling to C on the words "I'll know," form the simple but effective envelope to hold our attention. This sighing motive embodies a well of feelings: longing, confidence, hope, fortitude—even doubt. All seven recurrences of the word "know" fall on long notes (all Cs, all dotted half notes) at the beginnings of measures. These would have been heard as an exceptionally tedious string of phrases had they been placed in the normal pattern of four phrases of eight measures each, or had they not been interrupted by several vocally grateful leaps. But here they are transformed into anchors in an uncertain temporal sea. The two-measure extensions, rather than raising a legato line to a climax—as such extensions typically do—include rests that mitigate the absolute certainty of Sarah and Sky's "knowing," at least for a moment.

The long-note phrases are followed by brief pitches to which they sing, "[rest] But I'll stop / [rest] and I'll stare / [rest] at that face / [rest] in the throng." It is a subtle touch, a nod in the direction of vulnerability that Loesser often incorporates within romantic songs. The simple rhythmic motive pervading the ballad (a weak upbeat descending to a long note, followed by a string of shorter notes) is given the proper—somewhat darkened—emotional color with the help of richly modal harmonies (Dm^7, Gm^7, and Am^7) to supplement the other chords of F major.

"I'll Know" also demonstrates another favorite Loesser ploy, though it is by no means his personal property: creating a key or "hook" phrase at the very beginning of a song's refrain and repeating the phrase often enough that it is virtually burned into memory. Many of his songs, and others that have remained familiar for over half a century, it could be argued, have succeeded because of consistent recourse to this technique. Songs as different in mood, tempo, setting, and singing style as "The Inch Worm" (from *Hans Christian Andersen*) and "The New Ashmolean Marching Society and Students' Conservatory Band" (from *Where's Charley?*) both come to mind, but almost all of Loesser's commercial hits follow this pattern. He was not an accidental composer, but rather a perfectionist who knew what worked and consistently sought to exceed himself in applying basic principles.

Scene 4 (of ten in this act) is quintessentially Loesserian, a brilliantly constructed comic piece. Adelaide, alone in her dressing room, is reading a book about ailments induced by romantic frustration, a send-up of "expert" advice and psychological cures. This scene is established as comic before a word is said or sung because, having met Adelaide already in dialogue with Nathan, we know she is trusting, naive, emotional, and pointedly unintellectual. She has failed for fourteen years to see through Nathan's excuses. But she is loyal to a fault, and that makes her endearing.

Stumbling over big words and consulting the footnotes, Adelaide reads a text, enacts it, and reacts to it all at the same time. The punch line, "A person [pronounced poysson] can develop a cold," comes out perfectly in performance. Listeners are compelled to both sympathize with and laugh at her anxiety. The full effect is masterful, helped by Adelaide's showgirl drawl—a kind of Brooklynese (the score of the later cabaret numbers calls it a "doll voice"), a whining tone not normally associated with reciting medical terms like "chronic, organic syndromes, toxic or hypertense."[48] The verse, so carefully marked with stage directions and pauses that it takes on the character of an operatic recitative, has Adelaide quoting:

> The av'rage unmarried female, basically insecure,
> Due to some long frustration may react
> With psychosomatic symptoms, difficult to endure,
> Affecting the upper respiratory tract.

Her subsequent reaction to her own reading (the section equivalent to an aria if we continue the analogy to opera) is both a translation of the reading into nonmedical language and an extension of the humorous verbiage by a multiplication of examples.

> In other words, just from waiting around
> For that plain little band of gold,
> A person can develop a cold.

> You can spray her wherever you figure the streptococci lurk,
> You can give her a shot for whatever she's got,
> But it just won't work,
> If she's tired of getting the fish eye from the hotel clerk,
> A person can develop a cold.

Example 3.4. "Adelaide's Lament" (beginning at "In other words")

The number is filled with verbal dexterity, alliterative and assonantal rhymes at every possible point, and unexpected polysyllabic insertions ("psychosomatic" and "streptococci"). The full effect is secured by the musical details. The verse is delivered parlando (semispoken) style in short, repetitive bursts that lack a sustained, songlike character, allowing the singer to take an elastic approach—a feature of many verses, serving to heighten our expectations—followed (at "In other words") by a slightly quicker, more regular series of triplets in a distinct four-beat meter (see ex. 3.4).

The melody (on the notes A, G-sharp, F, F-sharp, G, and so on) in this more flowing section at first extends the slithery feel of the verse, but it also contains several critical skips that underline Adelaide's angry frustration by landing firmly on the tonic chord notes (F, A, C in ex. 3.4, later G) from six notes away, like leaps off a trampoline. The rhythmic pattern described above, when delivered with conviction, confirms Adelaide's intensity, sincerity, and self-assertion in a way that resembles a blues plaint's emotional honesty. Audiences don't just laugh at Adelaide. They cheer her tenacity and her passion, which somehow has survived a fourteen-year engagement complicated by maladies of the eyes, ears, nose, and throat.

Veteran composer and conductor Lehman Engel has explained how such a number as "Adelaide's Lament" makes its effect onstage: "Not only does the music make [the comedy] possible, but it gives the lyrics a framework, which . . . makes the *place* of the joke or 'pay-off' predictable, and if it is a workable 'pay-off,' the audience will wait for it expectantly, hopefully, and then will respond to it in the spot where the music allows 'space' for such a reaction."[49] Loesser and Burrows's attention to the overall architecture of their play is revealed when this running joke about colds and marital frustration is turned upside down in the final page of the script: as Adelaide describes the homebound joys of wedlock finally about to be hers, it is Nathan who lets out an "enormous sneeze."

With the scene set by "Runyonland," ensembles for tinhorn gamblers and the Hot Box girls delivered, and solos sung by three of the four principal characters (plus a song of greeting for Sam Levene's character Nathan Detroit—where the vocally challenged Levene would not actually have to sing), the title song, a sort of summary general statement of the show (like the song "Oklahoma" in *Oklahoma!*) follows naturally in scene 5. Set up by a "conversational" recitative by Nicely and Benny, "Guys and Dolls" had to be well crafted but straightforward, in order to be fitted securely for choral rather than solo presentation. It is not a simple song, however, and it proved sturdy enough to serve in reprise as the second-act finale as well. By capturing the humor and manic frenzy of guy–doll relationships, the song exemplifies in its verve something about the perennial appeal of sexual comedy. Once again, Loesser's instinct for rhyming to the saturation point is fully demonstrated:

> When you spot a John waiting out in the rain
> Chances are he's insane as only a John can be for a Jane.

> When you find a doll with her diamond in hock,
> Rest assured that the rock has gone to restock
> Some gentleman jock.

The musical frame, in line with the song's broadly positive but generic emotional character, is thoroughly traditional—a thirty-two-measure chorus in ABAC form with a tuneful arc and rhythmic pulse common to hundreds of Tin Pan Alley melodies—yet also distinctively original. Example 3.5 aligns (from top to bottom) small repeated sets of two or three notes in the first sixteen measures (the AB half of the tune) in order to illustrate the asymmetrical contrasts from phrase to phrase. It may look complicated, yet it flows with ease, sounding utterly casual and catchy. The text shown in the example, from the B phrase only, fits neatly with the quarter-note triplets that occur in this spot, the only place in the song to introduce this special bit of rhythmic variety. It provides a rapid succession of twenty-seven notes for twenty-seven syllables forming the run-on rhymes (seven more than occur in the rhymeless A phrases) and therefore reveals just how well Loesser understood the re-

Example 3.5. "Guys and Dolls" (chorus melody, mm. 1–16)

lationship between syllable count, musical meter, and comic timing—a skill that he shared with the wordsmith masters of his youth, Lorenz Hart and Ira Gershwin.

The trip to Havana and the Cafe Cubana contains a variety of dance tunes presented as a rumba, a tango, and a samba under the dialogue. Sarah gets pleasingly sloshed on milk and rum (the drink known as *dulce de leche*) and, in a manner described in the score as "very [free] and slightly tipsy," she sings her famous "bell song":

> Ask me how do I feel,
> Ask me now that we're cozy and clinging.
> Well, sir, all I can say is,
> If I were a bell I'd be ringing.
> From the moment we kissed tonight,
> That's the way I've just got to behave.
> Boy, if I were a lamp I'd light,
> And if I were a banner I'd wave.
>
> Ask me how do I feel,
> Little me with my quiet upbringing.
> Well, sir, all I can say is,
> If I were a gate I'd be swinging.
> And if I were a watch I'd start popping my spring
> Or if I were a bell I'd go
> Ding, dong, ding, dong, ding.
>
> Ask me how do I feel
> From this chemistry lesson I'm learning.
> Well, sir, all I can say is,
> If I were a bridge I'd be burning.
> Yes, I knew my morale would crack
> From the wonderful way that you looked.
> Boy, if I were a duck I'd quack
> Or if I were a goose I'd be cooked.
>
> Ask me how do I feel,
> Ask me now that we're fondly caressing.
> Pal, if I were a salad
> I know I'd be splashing my dressing.
> Ask me how to describe
> This whole beautiful thing.
> Well, if I were a bell I'd go
> Ding, dong, ding, dong, ding.

By having Sarah sing this tune under the influence, Loesser manages to make a believable dramatic event out of a lovely if potentially irrelevant list song. Avoiding clichés, he issues an extended series of metaphors about the condition of erotic enchantment (or delusion), while never mentioning the words "love" or "magic." From the outset, one suspects that this lyric is going to become a tour de force:

> Ask me <u>how</u> do I **feel,**
> Ask me <u>now</u> that **we're** *cozy and clinging.*

Both the how/now rhyme and the feel/we're half rhyme, nice enough, are topped and wittily extended with the double-syllabic pair, "cozy and cling-ing."

The "slightly tipsy" indication permits the singer to break the apparently regular rhythmic phrases into unsquare patterns and to inflect slightly off-beat three-note groupings (the high-low-low pitch sets match long-short-short rhythmic ones), a clever effect that is undetectable in the music notation but executed to perfection by Isabel Bigley on the original cast recording. There can be no doubt that Loesser's coaching as well as his written notes deter-mined the character of Bigley's superb rendition.[50]

Another standout technical accomplishment of "If I Were a Bell" lies in Loesser's employment of English gerunds and participles (those -ing words) with weak endings, and making them the highlight of the song, titillating and surprising us with each successive stanza—"clinging," "ringing," "up-bringing," "swinging," "popping"—only to land squarely on our feet with "popping my *spring*—ding, dong, ding, dong, *ding*." Furthermore, only three times in these thirty-two chatty lines, at the words "clinging," "kissed," and "caressing," does the lyricist even get close to describing physical contact between lovers. This condition has become almost a fantasy in the mind of the singing lover, yet Loesser wisely concentrates on describing the present moment, always savoring and anticipating but never quite finding a point of rest.

The concatenating syllables continue to appear, even as the second verse winds down and we hear *less*on echoed in ca*ress*ing and *dress*ing:

> Ask me **how** do I feel,
> Ask me **now** that we're *fondly caressing.*
> <u>Pal,</u> if I were a <u>sal</u>ad
> I know I'd be <u>*splash*</u>ing *my dressing.*

The effect can leave listeners, not to mention singers, breathless.

"If I Were a Bell" reveals unsuspected spunk in the normally restrained character of Sarah, and it underlines that she now fully comprehends the idea of sexual "chemistry," which she had pointedly scoffed at in Sky's part of "I'll Know." In her second verse, she sings, "Ask me how do I feel / From this chemistry lesson I'm learning," and Sky interjects, "Chemistry?" while Sarah

Example 3.6. "My Time of Day" (opening measures)

insists, "Yeah, chemistry!" lest the audience miss the parallel with the earlier song.

Sky's turn for self-revelation follows almost immediately. "My Time of Day" is a short, sweet, and introspective moment—only seventeen measures—for the normally extroverted gambler. Reportedly a favorite song of Loesser's, who shared Sky Masterson's predawn work habits, it is a full-blown operatic *recitativo*. "My Time of Day" is entirely devoted to the expression of intensified awareness and mood, with a few well-chosen but inconspicuous rhymed words and an absence of a marked or easily countable beat. A striking eight-note opening phrase (A–E–F–C-sharp–D–F–D–A-flat) feels uncomfortably rudderless, almost atonally suspended outside of a clear key area (ex. 3.6). Forced to listen to the words intoned sans obvious tunefulness, and accompanied by downright modern chords, we feel the gravity of Sky's declaration settling into our ears. The phrase "My time of day" is not here a springboard for comic display or a juicy emotional refrain, as in so many Loesser verses, but as introduction and conclusion. "My time of day is the dark time: a couple of deals before dawn," he begins. A snapshot of the city at sunrise is painted and then quietly concluded by a simple repetition: "That's my time of day, and you're the only doll I ever wanted to share it with me."

This last comes as a powerful revelation, almost entirely because of its compelling musical setting. It would feel right at home in the center of a Kurt
Weill opera.

Momentarily away from the hustle and bustle of the Runyonland crowd
and surprised by the intensity of their love, Sky and Sarah, like classic musical comedy couples must do, sing a pure and simple love song. The song's
structure is conventional, the emotion is familiar, and the poetry is restrained, with only one striking visual metaphor ("But this is wine / That's
all too strange and strong. / I'm full of foolish song / And out my song must
pour"). "I've Never Been in Love Before" signals a swing of the emotional
pendulum away from both the delight of "If I Were a Bell" and the introspec-
tion of "My Time of Day." As previously heard in the contrasting opening
sections ("Fugue for Tinhorns" and "Follow the Fold"), the alternation of
contrasting moods and melodies with "I've Never Been in Love Before," "If
I Were a Bell," and "My Time of Day" maintain the audience's interest by
providing both balance and variety.

"I've Never Been in Love Before" reflects an uncynical tone (somewhat
uncharacteristic of Runyonland), yet it fits as the final big tune of the first
act. We know, without having to be told again, how peculiar this sweet pre-
matrimonial pair is in a gangsters' underworld. Yet the duet also suggests that
Sky and Sarah—indeed, all the guys and dolls—share an intensity and optimism about life and love. The song also fulfills what Lehman Engel names
as essential to keeping the drama on track at this point: retaining audience
interest over the intermission.[51] The plot leaves several questions unresolved,
but the song supplies an important emotional layer; it urges the audience to
be both curious and sympathetic about the fate of Sarah and Sky.

Of course, this being a musical comedy, after all, we suspect that things
will end happily—but we cannot be sure yet. The first challenge of any work
of dramatic art is to create a world unto itself that an audience is willing to
accept emotionally, whose premises may just possibly differ from what we
expect, but where the results will finally satisfy our need or wish for closure.
The calibration of just the right means to achieve this psychological effect is
no small artistic feat. Here Loesser, Burrows, and Kaufman combined their
experience and melded the skills of the cast with hardly a misstep.

Balancing the central love story and the comic doings of secondary characters is the primary task of most musical comedy librettos. In the opening to
the second act of *Guys and Dolls*, we revisit Adelaide's place of employment,
the Hot Box nightclub, a location never mentioned in Runyon's "The Idyll

of Miss Sarah Brown" but imported by Burrows from other Runyon tales. The Hot Box may also have owed something to Loesser's early experience with Irving Actman at the Back Drop club on West Fifty-second Street.[52]

Loesser, for his part, creates outright parodies of burlesque numbers to show off the showgirls of the Hot Box, with "A Bushel and a Peck" and "Take Back Your Mink." The first, an instant hit in 1951, uses countrified metaphors ("bushel," "peck," "barrel"), slang phrases ("purty neck," "it beats me all to heck," "cows and chickens goin' to the dickens"), and farm sounds ("doodle, oodle, oodle") to make its simple point suitable for an audience of rubes, presumed to be the bulk of the tourist clientele present in the Hot Box.[53] The mildly risqué tone of a "A Bushel and a Peck" was either muted or enhanced, depending on one's perspective, by the "farmerette" costumes created by Alvin Colt, which featured gingham dresses, straw hats, and large daisy-petal brassiere cups with pluckable petals, so the girls could toss them away and scream, "He loves me, he loves me not," as the spirit moved them.[54]

In "Take Back Your Mink," the farm girls show their versatility by becoming "debutantes," scorning the gifts of lustful suitors in another kind of striptease. Adelaide ironically demonstrates her virtue by casting away mink, pearls, hat, gown, and other accessories in waltz and then foxtrot steps. The deliberate character of the melody allows ample room for dramatic embellishment. Although this number aptly shows off the talents of the Hot Box performers, it was a late addition to the show after Loesser realized he needed another musical number to prolong the suspense before the climactic crap game, which doesn't take place until the third scene. It turned into a showstopper.

The harmony in both the Hot Box songs is bare-bones, appropriately simple for the setting. The skipping melodies evoke an early twentieth-century style of winsome boy/girl duet singing. Strings of alternating long and short notes (in the line "a bushel and a peck and a hug around the neck," for example) bring to mind familiar favorites like Jerome Kern's 1905 hit "How'd You Like to Spoon with Me?" (see ex. 3.7).[55] The resemblance is entirely intentional on Loesser's part. An exaggerated effect that underlines this song's status as rural parody occurs with the strong accent indicated for the offbeat syllable "a" in "a-bout you." It evokes a saucy turning of the head, at once awkward, unnecessary, and rib-tickling. Similarly, many verbal indications in the score of "Take Back Your Mink" aim to clarify the singers' moods, gestures, poses, and attitudes.

"More I Cannot Wish You," a swaying modal number sung to Sarah by

Example 3.7. "A Bushel and a Peck" (beginning of chorus) and "How'd You Like to Spoon with Me?" (beginning of chorus, by Jerome Kern, 1905)

the avuncular character identified by Runyon as Sarah's grandfather, Arvide Abernathy, is singled out by Alec Wilder as "a very special song, shining with tenderness, as natural as if it simply happened. . . . [with a lyric] most distinguished and truly poetic."[56] Wolcott Gibbs, writing in the *New Yorker*, declared that "'More I Cannot Wish You' is possibly the most charming moment of the show."[57] The song's gentle touch and smooth line are enhanced by chords that oscillate between C major and D minor. The tune is entirely diatonic (without sharps or flats), which lends it a folklike character, and it is formed in regular phrases with almost no rests to separate them. It is a quiet song (mostly *pp*, only once rising to *mf*), whose continuous lullaby lilt provides a sweet interlude before the excitement to come—the long-awaited crap game and the appearance of arch-gambler Big Jule. The placement of this song amid so many other more comic and colorful scenes, not to mention its rendition by the seventy-year-old Pat Rooney Sr., was a masterstroke. But even the creators did not appreciate its powerful contrastive effect until after the critical response proved so positive.

The two big second-act group numbers, "Luck Be a Lady" (for Sky and the gamblers) and "Sit Down, You're Rockin' the Boat" (with Nicely-Nicely Johnson and the chorus at the Save-a-Soul Mission), are the ultimate proofs in this show that Loesser was master of the collaborative situation song. "Luck Be a Lady" and its "Crapshooters' Dance," like the pantomimed opening

Example 3.8. "Luck Be a Lady" (first chorus, mm. 27–33)

of "Runyonland," were choreographed by Michael Kidd, and even dance-skeptical director George S. Kaufman was impressed with the results. Kidd's program of movements is supported by Loesser's broad-stroke tune in AABA form (an easy and infinitely repeatable one for the dancers), which scarcely deviates from its narrow range and two-chord accompaniment. The "bright" tempo is an invitation to dance directors everywhere to show their stuff, and Kidd delivered. Yet the tune also contains its own harmonic power.

Loesser sets up a steady pulsation in the bass, an alternation between the tonic note (D-flat) and it upper neighbor (D-natural) on downbeats, changing back and forth on each measure (see ex. 3.8). The upward modulation by half steps in each of the first three phrases (sixteen measures each, plus two measures more for modulation—from D-flat major to D major to E-flat major) in the refrain and the somewhat surprising fall back to D-flat in the last phrase (mm. 78–104) are neatly matched to the lyrics elaborating the luck/lady metaphor. These techniques preserve both a dissonant edginess—the gamblers are tensely awaiting the outcome of the crap game—and the sense of stability that the moderately paced ostinato, the long-short-short rhythmic motive, and the harmonic return in the fourth phrase convey.[58] After the second (dancing) chorus, in the final twenty-five measures of "Luck Be a Lady" we hear Sky and the gamblers in a group crescendo that anticipates the final toss of the dice and the triumphant exclamation "Ha!" (marked *fff*, extremely loud). The full integration of choreographic and musical elements clinches the beauty and memorability of this theatrical stroke. Sky wins his game, and the souls of the gamblers are remanded to the mission precisely as the song ends.

"Sit Down, You're Rockin' the Boat" invites comparison with other pseudoreligious comic songs from the Broadway canon, most notably the Gershwins' "It Ain't Necessarily So" (and also Loesser's own "Brotherhood of Man" in *How to Succeed in Business Without Really Trying*, see chapter 4, and "Make a Miracle" from *Where's Charley?*).[59] The musical form for Loesser's song is short, while George Gershwin's is more discursive, but in both the text is clever and mildly irreverent rather than strictly biblical. Both songs are audience favorites sung by secondary characters. Three full verses and three differently worded choruses in "Sit Down" create a narrative to go with the relentlessly syncopated refrain. Yet the fun of the song comes from its repeated title phrase, delivered in gospel revival style:

> For the people all said, "Sit down, sit down, you're rockin' the boat."
> People all said, "Sit down, sit down, you're rockin' the boat."
> And the devil will drag you under
> By the sharp lapel of your checkered coat.
> "Sit down, sit down, sit down, sit down.
> Sit down, you're rockin' the boat."

Only three times among thirty-two repetitions (in three verses) of the phrase "sit down" does it begin on a strong beat of the measure, so a listener's sense of instability in a "rockin' boat," of being carried away by the devil perhaps, is teasingly imposed throughout the triumphant conclusion of Nicely-Nicely's dream of near damnation.

"Sue Me" was Loesser's solution to the problem of a major performer with limited singing ability. (Sam Levene as Nathan Detroit was originally slated to lead "Sit Down" and two other songs.) Nathan's rhythm in "Sue Me" closely follows the natural spoken word stresses of the lyric. His plaintive melody sticks closely to the comfortable home note of G and is built on a series of falling thirds, nearby intervals that seldom present problems to adult amateurs. Despite its modest tonal dimensions, "Sue Me" is an ingratiating song. Adding quick and contrasting patter (to convey her nearly exhausted patience) against Nathan's slow and loosely timed interjections, Adelaide sings most of the notes of the piece. Yet Nathan's part is more than sufficient for the scene, amounting to a sulky plea from a misbehaving child:

ADELAIDE: You promise me this, / You promise me that,
      You promise me anything under the sun,
      Then you give me a kiss / And you're grabbin' your hat
      And you're off to the races again . . .
      I could honestly die.

NATHAN: Call a lawyer and / Sue me, Sue me,
      What can you do me? / I love you.

Two snippets of the "Sue Me" tune also serve as memorable linking phrases between longer sections of the medley overture, a small but telling testimony to the strength of a carefully placed musical gesture.

As the conclusion of the play approaches, the two principal "dolls" meet and sing the final new song of the second act, "Marry the Man Today" ("and change his ways tomorrow"). The song summarizes an element of ambiguity in the characters' personalities and also some unsuspected parallels between them. "[Both] Sarah and Adelaide seem in the end reconciled to their future spouses' inadequacies and even willing to become, like them, gamblers," Knapp observes.[60] Sarah has now shed her earlier repressed persona as "mission doll"—while still remaining true to her calling—and Adelaide has finally secured what looks like a firm commitment. She even seems prepared to leave Nathan for good if he refuses to comply after all. The women are in command and secure in their feminine roles. Their shared agenda could not be clearer, and the domestic metaphors of the verse tell the story:

ADELAIDE: At Wanamaker's and Saks and Klein's
      A lesson I've been taught:
      You can't get alterations on a dress you haven't bought.

SARAH: At any veg'table market from Borneo to Nome,
      You mustn't squeeze a melon till you get the melon home.

The loping chorus rhythm, with rumbling oompah chords in a modified compound meter (changing from 6/8 to 4/4 but still keeping the triplets), supports a tune in the key of A minor (ex. 3.9). The composer's direction that it be sung "craftily" fits the song's calculating slyness to a T.

In a way, with its eccentric minor-mode humor and depiction of Sarah as a schemer, "Marry the Man Today" stands apart from the full roster of tunes

Example 3.9. "Marry the Man Today" (beginning of chorus)

in *Guys and Dolls*. Yet its function can be justified. It brings together the two principal females in their common cause at a key moment in the plot. It provides a thematically unified duet near the show's end that can be seen to balance the opening male trio, "Fugue for Tinhorns." It also enables Sarah to reveal her practical side, just as Sky had revealed his surprising biblical literacy in their first conversation (he had read Gideon Bibles placed in hotels during his wandering days). Finally, it juxtaposes a brief comic number before the impending finale, giving the male chorus time to recover from "Sit Down, You're Rockin' the Boat," which it has just finished.

All that remains to complete the action is the final appearance of the mission band with Sky in tow and Nathan with Adelaide to signal the happy ending. A reprise of the title song brings the full company onstage, celebrating the theater's oldest comic denouement, the mythical solution to all civil and personal ills: love and marriage.

The Quality of *Guys and Dolls*

Guys and Dolls is a tightly constructed, thoroughly organic show that does not call attention to its craft. All the contributors understood that the various components of a musical, not unlike early nineteenth-century European operas, needed to be "treated as a collection of individual units that could be rearranged, substituted or omitted depending on local conditions of performance, local taste or . . . whim."[61] Because they recognized so many possibilities for failure, the show underwent six weeks of tryout performances in Philadelphia before the New York opening, to allow enough time to refine and strengthen every element.[62] The fundamentals for creating a satisfying entertainment were thoroughly accounted for. The *Guys and Dolls* criminals are basically tenderhearted and never (except once in the person of Big Jule) resort to cruelty. The jokes, while mildly suggestive, shun profanity. All the principal roles are carefully fleshed out, and the religious characters are depicted as well-rounded human beings, not as caricatures, zealots, or saints. For these reasons, despite its shady situations, racetrack dialect, and occasional Broadway tricks, the whole is remarkably coherent and smooth.

Guys and Dolls contains no padding or filler, since even the extractable Hot Box songs function to heighten our appreciation of the talents of the long-suffering Adelaide. Its conventions, such as the double love story, the prop songs at the club, the choral dances, the innocent heroine, the use of soliloquy ("Adelaide's Lament") and reprise ("Adelaide's Lament" and "Guys and Dolls"), an early evening almost-love song ("I've Never Been in Love Before") and a rousing eleven o'clock number ("Sit Down, You're Rockin' the Boat"), all tightly adhere to the plot and give direction to the whole.

With this unbeatable combination of devices, *Guys and Dolls* managed to capture the traditional audience for lightweight 1920s Broadway shows as well as those who admired the more musically dense approach of Rodgers and Hammerstein. In the words of Broadway chronicler Abe Laufe, *Guys and Dolls* "recapitulated the history of the American musical theater, for it not only embodied all the assets of the earlier hits [such as *Irene* (1919), *Sally* (1920), and *Sunny* (1925)], but also included the innovations in plot and music integration characteristic of the better productions of the 1930s and 1940s."[63]

Some additions were made to the music when Frank Sinatra was cast in Nathan's mostly nonsinging role for the 1955 film version. But the basic solidity of the material in the live show itself was not influenced by this move. *Variety*'s movie reviewer (Abel Green) paid Loesser a backhanded but perceptive compliment with his observation that "the Frank Loesser songs constitute one of those durable scores which were not singularly boffo even in the original, despite the long runs, but have the plus value of being pleasantly lilting without being overly familiar."[64] Indeed, at least in the minds of some critics, the changes made for the movie proved unfortunate and confirmed the wisdom of the original Broadway sequence of events.[65] For the film Loesser wrote a new song for Sinatra, "Adelaide." "Pet Me, Poppa" was substituted for the Hot Box choral number, "A Bushel and a Peck." "A Woman in Love" took the place of "I've Never Been in Love Before." "My Time of Day" was retained only as underscoring.

Loesser was known in the business as a demanding perfectionist. He prided himself on polishing lyrics to a high gloss. When he added music of his own, he extended his standards to cover that art as well. After years of paying his dues and working successfully on teams of musicians, writers, directors, and dancers, he could now call the critical shots. Accordingly, he set the bar as high as he and his fellow artists could reach. It was very high indeed. While he was able to benefit from the dramatic wisdom of George S. Kaufman, he himself was the senior musical mind on the team. Cy Feuer, also an accomplished musician, understood just how reliable Loesser's intuition was on almost all issues that related to song.[66]

The Critics Agree

The 1950 New York premiere of *Guys and Dolls* was met by a unanimous critical reaction: unbridled and enthusiastic. John Chapman opened his critique by observing "only one defect, . . . The big trouble with *Guys and Dolls* is that a performance of it lasts only one evening, when it ought to last about a week." Williams Hawkins, in the *New York World-Telegram* and *The Sun*, came straight to the point with a sharp summary outline:

> Type — Fabulous Musical.
> Topic — Broadway — see title.
> Mood — Satirical, tender and jazzy.
> Cast — A new Milky Way.
> I find — I love it.[67]

Virtually all writers noted the teamwork that contributed to the finished product (including kudos for the book, sets, costumes, and direction), the presence of outstanding young actors, nearly all newcomers to Broadway, and a depth of talent covering even the smaller roles. Hawkins predicted a bright future for Isabel Bigley, recognizing that a great song such as "If I Were a Bell" was just the vehicle to launch a great talent. Loesser must have been cheered by the comparison to Gershwin and Cole Porter hits when Hawkins added, "It reminded me of 'I Got Rhythm' and 'My Heart Belongs to Daddy,' and what they did for a couple of other girls [Ethel Merman in *Girl Crazy* (1930) and Mary Martin in *Leave It to Me* (1938)]."[68]

Howard Barnes in the *New York Herald Tribune* and John McClain in the *New York Journal American* both saw *Guys and Dolls* as a natural successor to Rodgers and Hart's *Pal Joey* (1940); both shows featured lovable ne'er-do-wells in a racy, urban setting, with coherent scenes, adult humor, several good songs, and few slow moments. Michael Kidd's choreography was singled out for its energy and inventiveness ("Kidd has gone to the heart of Broadway high-jinks," wrote Barnes). Richard Watts in the *New York Post* went so far as to apologize for what he deemed an earlier misjudgment: "Mr. Loesser has long been recognized as a bright and resourceful song writer, and with the scores for 'Where's Charley?,' which I didn't at first properly appreciate, and now 'Guys and Dolls,' there is no doubt that he is a valuable addition to American musical comedy."[69]

Most reviews began and ended with a bow to Damon Runyon, while recognizing that the borrowing from Runyon's tales had required considerable artistry by the *Guys and Dolls* collaborators. Hawkins summarily declared, "The show springs from Damon Runyon stories. It recaptures what he knew about Broadway, that its wickedness is tinhorn, but its gallantry is as pure and young as Little Eva."[70] Even *New York Times* critic Brooks Atkinson, in a similar vein, noted "as its highest achievement the fact that [*Guys and Dolls*] has preserved the friendly spirit of the Runyon literature without patronizing and without any show-shop hokum."[71]

Atkinson's first review of the show, already cited partially at the beginning of this chapter, aptly captured the combination of artistry and ebullience that *Guys and Dolls* seems to have conveyed to New Yorkers in particular, which may well explain a significant part of its perennial appeal, especially in the Big Apple. "From the technical point of view we might as well as admit that 'Guys and Dolls' is a work of art. It is spontaneous and has form, style and spirit. In view of the source material, that is not astonishing. For Damon Runyon captured the spirit of an idle corner of the town with sympathetic understanding and reproduced it slightly caricatured in the sketches and story he wrote. 'Guys and Dolls' is gusty [*sic*] and uproarious, and it is not too grand to take a friendly, personal interest in the desperate affairs of Broadway's backroom society."[72]

Revivals on Stage and Screen

After its opening run of nearly three years and 1,200 performances at the Forty-sixth Street Theatre, *Guys and Dolls* hit the road and gradually began to fix itself in the national consciousness. Its tours and song sales on vinyl succeeded exceptionally well and brought recognition even beyond the boundaries of the United States.[73] It has enjoyed thousands of revivals during the half century after its American opening. It ran for 555 nights in London, the initial production there in 1953, which included several members of the original cast: Vivian Blaine, Sam Levene, Stubby Kaye, and Johnny Silver. The show returned to London with Bob Hoskins (Nathan Detroit) in 1982 and appeared again at the Royal National Theatre in 1996, this time with elaborate new production features and direction by Richard Eyre.[74]

New York's City Center mounted a modest effort of thirty-one performances, with Walther Matthau (Nathan) and Helen Gallagher (Adelaide) in May and June 1955, directed by Philip Mathias.[75] The film came out in November of that year with some significant retentions (Stubby Kaye, Vivian Blaine, and Michael Kidd's choreography), but also with substantial changes of personnel: Marlon Brando (rather than Robert Alda, the first Sky Masterson) in a rare singing role for him, and Frank Sinatra (Nathan Detroit), who sang much more music than in the original, but who also fought with Loesser and permanently alienated the composer. Sinatra resisted Loesser's vocal coaching, and Loesser disowned his artistic stake in the production (and later claimed never to have seen the movie). He also never spoke to Sinatra again.[76]

Critical judgment on the film has been mixed over the years. Abel Green, writing in *Variety*, praised it, calling the movie "a bangup filmusical, made-to-order for the young guys and dolls out front, and for the general family trade as well." He only found fault with some "drab Times Square street scenes" at the beginning and its excessive (over two and a half hours) length.[77] In his monumental work devoted to the Hollywood musical, Clive Hirschhorn admits that "the show, while totally failing to capture the convivial intimacy of the stage presentation was, nonetheless, full of good things — the best being Michael Kidd's spirited high-octane choreography." He judged Brando to be "better than expected" in the Sky Masterson role (for which Gene Kelly had been sought),[78] a conclusion that encyclopedist Thomas Hischak and others seem to share.[79] Gerald Mast's more dismissive assessment (in 1987) deemed the entire project misconceived. In noting the producers' combination of "the always quirky Marlon Brando as gambler Sky Masterson, the always casual Frank Sinatra as the Jewish Nathan Detroit, the dubbed English movie star Jean Simmons [who had played Ophelia opposite Laurence Olivier's Hamlet] as Sarah Brown . . . directed by Joseph L. Mankiewicz (who never directed a musical before or since)," he asks, "How could experienced showmen spend so much time and money putting together a package that was so obviously wrong?"[80]

Part of the answer, of course, lay in the hope for profit. Brando, Sinatra, and Simmons guaranteed a strong box office. But there was more: Samuel Goldwyn's film concept was far more grand and cinematic than the Broadway original, somewhat at odds with Burrows and Loesser's "musical fable." This grander idea worked for Green and many others; critical reaction to the film was not all or even mostly negative. English critic Robert Matthew-Walker recently described the cinematic *Guys and Dolls* as "an excellent version of a musical."[81]

In 1981 Ethan Mordden knocked the film on many counts, including its "labored pace," its "half real and half stagey" sets, and Vivian Blaine's "[overworked] lines and gestures."[82] But Mordden was mostly echoing one of the film's original critics, an unknown young musician and cinéaste in 1955, who made several subtle and balanced observations. Stephen Sondheim wrote for *Films in Review*, "The two major flaws of *Guys and Dolls* are Oliver Smith's sets and Frank Sinatra's performance. Samuel Goldwyn, Joseph Mankiewicz, and Mr. Smith apparently couldn't make up their minds whether the scenery should be realistic or stylized. As a result, they have the disadvantages of both, and these disadvantages work against the very special nature of Runyonesque story-telling. . . . *Guys and Dolls* has much more success as a screen transference of a stage musical than *Oklahoma!*, *Brigadoon* and *Kiss Me, Kate*, but is not so successful as *Cover Girl*, *Seven Brides for Seven Brothers*, and *Singin' in the Rain*, all of which were written for the screen."[83]

The larger audience, far more numerous than critics, loved the film, although one offended viewer took the trouble to complain in writing to the Production Code Administration (Hollywood censor's) office, headed at the time by Eric Johnston. For all its ranting tone, the letter touches on a few points raised by other critics on nonreligious grounds.

June 12, 1956
Dear Mr. Johnston:
    On April 2, the day after Easter, it was my misfortune to see Guys and Dolls, one of the rottenest movies I have ever had to sit through. I was so angry at the end of it, that I caught emotionally induced "flu" and was sick for a week.

Identifying himself as a man of good and modern taste and no prude, the letter writer, a Nevada clergyman, cites a "bill of particulars," focused on what he saw as the film's dishonesty, disrespect for religion, and lack of artistry. On the last point he employed outline form:

    3. It is inartistic.
    a. There is not a tuneful melody in the show.
    b. Sinatra never sang so poorly. Of course, he had nothing decent to sing.
    c. Brando should not even try to sing. If his "singing" was dubbed by a ghost, please get a new ghost.
    d. The choreography is hideous. I realize what lengths one must go to be different, but for goodness sake don't make the world uglier than it is. I like to dance, and appreciate good dancing. Guys and Dolls dances are horrible. Whoever planned them should be permanently retired in some institution for the insane.

After asking that copies of his letter be passed on to the "author of the libretto and the composer of the lyrics as well as the producer and the director," the writer closes, "Yours, in complete disgust, Felix A. Manley, Pastor."[84] Probably Frank Loesser never saw the letter. Given his penchant for pranksterism, however, perhaps that was just as well for the Reverend Manley, for Loesser rarely shrank from needling his critics. Manley's view, for all his indignant barbs, was clearly a minority one at the time, since the film took in more money than any other in 1955.[85]

    Guys and Dolls was brought back by the New York City Center Light Opera Company for a couple dozen evenings in April and May 1965 and in June 1966 (the latter run once again featuring Vivian Blaine as the psychosomatic Adelaide). But for over two decades *Guys and Dolls* played mostly away from Broadway, though individual songs were frequently included in periodic revues and medley shows.[86]

    In 1976, under Billy Williams's direction and with Abe Burrows's supervision, New York saw a version with an all-black cast starring Robert Guillaume (Nathan). The young, energetic players working with Guillaume and Williams produced an interesting cast album and drew curious crowds to

James Randolph (Sky) and Ernestine Jackson (Sarah) in the 1976 Broadway revival of *Guys and Dolls*. Billy Rose Theatre Division, The New York Public Library for the Performing Arts, Astor, Lenox and Tilden Foundations.

Robert Guillaume (Nathan) and Norma Donaldson (Adelaide) in the
1976 Broadway revival of *Guys and Dolls*. Billy Rose Theatre Division, The
New York Public Library for the Performing Arts, Astor, Lenox and Tilden
Foundations.

the Broadway Theatre for 239 nights. This intriguing production, reportedly first suggested by Loesser himself, was mostly true to the original, but
it made a few timely adjustments (such as relocating the Cuban escapade,
act 1, scene 8, to Puerto Rico) and allowed the actors to put their special in-
terpretive seal on the familiar melodies.[87] The songs alone—without their
libretto—were reused and joined with other Loesser tunes in a 1980 revue,
headed up by Jo Sullivan Loesser, called *Perfectly Frank*. Not surprisingly almost the entire score—fourteen songs—of *Guys and Dolls* was worked into
this series of skits in one place or another.

The most celebrated Broadway return of *Guys and Dolls* took place in
1992. Directed by Jerry Zaks, it featured Nathan Lane (Nathan), Peter Gallagher (Sky), Josie de Guzman (Sarah), and Faith Prince (Adelaide) in a stel-
lar production. It proved to be the big hit of the season and chalked up an
impressive 1,143 performances.[88] Theater historian Keith Garebian observes
that the production "redefined Broadway dazzle," yet preserved the Runyonesque attitude and language. While "nothing in the revival imprisoned the
show in the past," due homage, he felt, was paid to the colorful sets, costumes,
and stylizations of the original while adding an "extravagant iridescence."
The principal performers realized in exciting ways the letter of the script and
score, rather than merely imitating the past. Thus, the whole was made compelling for a contemporary audience, the way a classic should be.[89]

Several recorded versions of the full show can still be found on the market. Decca issued the original cast album, now available on compact disc.
The 1976 Billy Williams makeover was brought out by Motown Records, the
London revival was recorded on the Chrysalis label, and the 1992 version
was produced by RCA Victor. Jean Simmons and Marlon Brando recorded
the film songs, also released by Decca. Frank Sinatra, Dean Martin, Bing
Crosby, Jo Stafford, Dinah Shore, and Sammy Davis Jr. and other stars of
the early 1960s recorded most of the songs for Reprise Records in 1964. The
Miles Davis Quintet, consisting of Red Garland (piano), Paul Chambers
(bass), John Coltrane (tenor sax), Philly Joe Jones (drums), and Davis (trumpet), included "If I Were a Bell" on their 1956 Prestige release, *Relaxin'*.
Loesser's own demo recordings of eight *Guys and Dolls* songs were included
on *An Evening with Frank Loesser*, a CD produced by the Frank Music Corporation in 1992. In 1996 the full list of stage music plus the film songs and
"Traveling Light" (originally cut) were released on a compact disc set, with
Emily Loesser singing the role of Sister Sarah.[90]

Postscript

Guys and Dolls is now a classic among classics, a "uniquely unique" show in Mordden's words, presenting four equally balanced characters and the perfect intersection of two networks of humanity engaged with "life on the street and life in the Lord."[91] The jokes, songs, characters, and situations continue to draw new audiences because of their special oddity and charm, and because they seem to have achieved a sort of ahistorical universality. Only future productions will reveal how much life is yet left in the old vehicle, but it continues to receive hundreds of independent licensed stagings every year, far more than any other Loesser musical. Indeed, it may well be the most popular American musical comedy in the world (allowing for the difficulties in making an accurate global tabulation).[92] One suspects it will remain the single show with the widest appeal in Frank Loesser's legacy, so long as there are enough Broadway fans left to tell about their first experience of hearing and seeing this transcendent fable.

In his memoir, *Honest Abe,* Abe Burrows recalled his favorite review of *Guys and Dolls* as one "that never appeared in any newspaper," since the reviewer, Walter Kerr, had not yet become a drama critic.[93] "His notice wasn't a written notice," claims Burrows, "it was something he said to his wife. One day some years later he told me that when he and Jean first saw *Guys and Dolls,* he turned to her in the middle of the first act and said, "Am I wrong or isn't this the greatest musical we've ever seen?"

CHAPTER 4

Just Don't Call It Opera:
The Most Happy Fella

What other wish can I wish?
What other plan can I plan?
What other dream can I dream?
And what for? Whatever for?
—"MY HEART IS SO FULL OF YOU," FROM *THE MOST HAPPY FELLA*, 1956

IN THE "PERSONAL PREFACE" TO HIS 1924 PULITZER PRIZE–WINNING play *They Knew What They Wanted*, Sidney Howard linked his story with the mythic theme of Richard Wagner's music drama *Tristan und Isolde* (1859). Howard declared, "The story of this play, in its noblest form, served Richard Wagner as the libretto of the greatest of all romantic operas. It is shamelessly, consciously, and even proudly derived from the legend of Tristram and Yseult."[1] Howard's plot does not exactly mirror the story of either the medieval legend or the opera, but his mental association with it suggests something of the passionate intensity of the scenario he created.

It should come as no surprise that a tale of longing made in the mold of Wagnerian transcendent love, yet filled with unpretentious working-class characters, should have found a fan in Frank Loesser—a man who, despite all attempts to hide it, had absorbed idealistic German philosophy and Romantic nineteenth-century music with his mother's milk and never stopped looking for ways "to make you cry."[2] Ever since he had first started putting notes to words, he had favored expressions of pathos over humor. The opportunity to set a grand, emotion-filled tale akin to Howard's seems to have fit Loesser's creative mood in the wake of *Guys and Dolls*. He reportedly began to study technical music theory at this time, so as to further increase his ability to completely record the sounds in his creative ear.[3]

As he scouted about for a book to follow on the heels of the Runyon-inspired comedy, Loesser's encounter with Howard's play was serendipitous. At first he resisted its lure, or so he reported in the early Imperial Theatre playbill. But soon he was referring to his work-in-progress as "Project Three," giving it the ring of a clandestine government affair.[4] However, the launch of Project Three—*The Most Happy Fella*, as it was eventually named—took place about six weeks too late to have had the optimal anticipated effect. With a premiere on May 3, 1956, it was temporarily submerged in the wake of an even bigger blockbuster, *My Fair Lady*. (With 2,717 performances, Lerner and Loewe's clever and tuneful adaptation of Shaw's *Pygmalion* would become the most successful show of the decade, outlasting all the Rodgers and Hammerstein hits and Loesser's own *Guys and Dolls*.[5])

Nevertheless, *The Most Happy Fella* made a significant impact, with an initial run of 676 performances and a strong showing in revival despite a varied critical reception history. Even with the distraction of *My Fair Lady*, the critics and the fans of 1956 understood what an excellent show *Most Happy Fella* delivered. *Life* magazine declared it a "landmark musical."[6]

Loesser's most ambitious work to date was powerful stuff, and for a love story crafted in music from start to finish—and carrying much more emotion than talk to fill an evening—it registered more immediately with audiences than most other serious music dramas or quasi operas of the first half of the twentieth century. That said, Loesser found many compelling models for treating a serious story in music closer to home than Wagner or nineteenth-century European opera. Gershwin's *Porgy and Bess* (1935; revived on Broadway, 1942 and 1953) was filled with operatic music and a multifaceted American story. Rodgers and Hammerstein's *Carousel* (1945) contained a number of tragic elements, including the death of a leading character onstage. Likewise, Kurt Weill's *Street Scene* (1947) told the tale of struggling tenement dwellers during a sweltering New York summer. Another Weill show, *The Threepenny Opera* (revived and restaged in a slightly softened translation by Marc Blitzstein early in 1954) would provide Loesser with his first Rosabella and later his second wife in the person of Jo Sullivan, who appeared as Polly Peachum.[7] Leonard Bernstein had made yet another kind of hybrid with *Trouble in Tahiti* (1952), which Carol Oja describes as "a fusion of opera, musical theater, and television sitcom."[8] His music drama masterpiece *West Side Story* would come the year after *The Most Happy Fella*. All these works bear traits of musical comedy as well as opera. All contained a variety of music. Loesser, it seems, was seeking to write a show along the same lines, incorporating a number of Italian (especially Puccinian) operatic conventions such as recitative, but also pitching his "serious musical" at a regular Broadway audience.[9]

Always on the alert for something new that would also meet his own highest aspirations for novelty and quality, Loesser sensed the potential for Sidney Howard's play after it was given to him by Samuel Taylor, a writer and Hollywood colleague, with whom he had hoped to collaborate. But he also harbored doubts about how to bring it off. Taylor described the situation in an interview with Susan Loesser:

> Our idea was that I was going to write the book and he was going to write the score. But after working for a week, I realized that this wasn't going to be feasible, because I just couldn't live his kind of life. We were very good friends, but we were quite different. I couldn't stand those parties that went way on into the night, with all those characters, all trying to be "on" all the time. And Frank's work hours were a little bit strange.
>
> So after a week, I said to him, "I'm not going to do this." He was quite stricken. He said, "What will I do? Who will I get?" And I said, "Don't get anybody. Do it yourself."[10]

Taylor encouraged Loesser to produce effective dialogue by reassuring him, "Any time you have doubts about what you're doing, write a song."[11] Forty or so songs later, Loesser had constructed a Wagner-sized edifice, though it was hardly Wagnerian in style. Many cuts would be made before the show reached Broadway. But the core of a grand work was established.

The opportunity to raise two ordinary characters—a waitress and a grape farmer—and others of questionable poetic distinction to the emotional heights of opera proved an absorbing assignment for the composer. Like Wagner, he would write all the words and all the music. Like many opera composers, including Wagner, Puccini, Mozart, and the American Marc Blitzstein, he would make harmonic and melodic linkages with characters, symbols, and states of mind to assure continuity and clarity throughout a long work. But like Rodgers and Hammerstein, Loesser would insist that what he was doing was *not* opera first and foremost, but just a "musical with a lot of music." He resisted the idea that because a Broadway show explored tragic dimensions or used sung dialogue, it therefore needed to take a cultivated

Jo Sullivan (Rosabella) and Robert Weede (Tony) perform "Happy to Make Your Acquaintance." Billy Rose Theatre Division, The New York Public Library for the Performing Arts, Astor, Lenox and Tilden Foundations.

name. In this he strove to achieve something similar to but not precisely like Rodgers and Hammerstein: to paint complex and fluid dramatic situations with sustained music appropriate for the varied and often intense emotional content. There is no guarantee of a happy ending to *The Most Happy Fella* that can be distilled from the music alone until it actually occurs—a fact that some musical comedy aficionados perhaps found disconcerting. There is no sugar coating of the principal characters' feelings or reactions. As Loesser himself told *New York Times* writer Gilbert Millstein soon after the opening, "The purpose of this show is to portray emotional expression, as the play calls for, through songs. I tried to emotionalize everything so you know which way people are going. It's easy to recognize who a guy is and what he does. . . . But you don't really care. That's only a starter. What's he doing, what's he want? That's where the music comes in for me."[12]

But Loesser did not just use Howard's play as he found it. His transformation is summarized in table 4.1. The basic plot of both shows hinges on the well-worn dramatic convention of mistaken identity and its consequences. A successful, middle-aged vintner on his farm in the Napa Valley of California, Tony is seeking a wife and writes a letter to a down-and-out young waitress who had caught his eye while serving him in a San Francisco diner. Since she does not remember his face, he promises to send a picture. But fearing rejection, he substitutes a photograph of his strikingly handsome assistant, Joe, described by Howard as "dark, sloppy, beautiful, and young."[13] A restless, rootless political activist, Joe is inclined to wander from job to job, but he is devoted to Tony, a considerate boss, loyal friend, and good man. In the course of their correspondence, Amy agrees to marry Tony, but arrives at Napa only to discover the deception. Rushing to meet her at the station, Tony has an automobile accident and suffers serious injuries that make him an invalid for months. Feeling humiliated, trapped, and defiant amid the crowds of well-wishers and friends of Tony, Amy agrees to go through with the wedding and nurse him back to health as her first wifely duty. She also succumbs to the comforts of Joe for a night, and by him she becomes pregnant. Eventually Joe agrees to leave the farm, and Tony forgives Amy for her unfaithfulness as she has forgiven him for his deception with the picture.

Three motion pictures based on *They Knew What They Wanted* appeared after the play's Broadway run in 1925: one each in 1928, 1930, and 1940; it is possible that Loesser was familiar with any or all of them. (Howard was reportedly paid $50,000 for the screen rights before the third was made.) Using the working title *The Other Man*, this 1940 remake, directed by Garson

Table 4.1. Principal Dramatic Turns in *The Most Happy Fella* and *They Knew What They Wanted*

Loesser	*Howard*
Act 1	
Scene 1. A restaurant in San Francisco, January 1927	**Act 1.** The scene is a farmhouse interior. Morning, in early summer
We meet Cleo, a friend and coworker of Amy, through her song "Ooh! My Feet!" Just as the restaurant is closing, Amy finds a piece of jewelry left as a tip, along with a note in broken English: "My dear Rosabella. I call you Rosabella because I don no your name, and I am too scared to ast you. . . . I don no noting about you, where you ever go, wat you ever done. . . . Wat I see is kind of young lady I want to get marry."	Ah Gee, the Chinese cook, is decorating the room. Joe is singing a labor movement song and speaks first to greet . . .
	Father McKee, who disapproves of the upcoming marriage.
Amy (hereafter, Rosabella) is touched by the sweetness of the letter and the amethyst pin attached to it. She sings "Somebody, Somewhere."	The bridegroom-to-be enters grandly. Tony declares, "Looka me! I'm da most stylish fella in da world."
	Father and Tony talk. Father objects to the marriage on several grounds: their age difference; Amy is not from the neighborhood; she is not a Catholic.
Scene 2. The main street of Napa, California, April 1927	
The Postman arrives. He calls out deliveries to the strains of a tarantella and finally meets Tony, to whom he hands an envelope with a picture. Tony sings "Omma the most happy fella in the whole Napa Valley."	
Tony has his photograph taken by Max the photographer. We meet Marie, Tony's sister, who disapproves of his advances	

Table 4.1. (Continued)

to "that pretty little chippy in Frisco." [She presents the same arguments as Father McKee in *They Knew What They Wanted*.]	Tony is not swayed by these arguments but has a secret that is bothering him and that he will not confess to Father.
Comic relief arrives in the form of a male quartet. Herman, Jake, Clem, and Al sing "Standing on the Corner."	
Joe enters. [*He is big and young and strong—and in an animal sort of way, he is handsome. Although his disposition seems friendly and even generous, there is something cold and possibly brutal behind the smile in his eyes.*] He has a new travel bag and wants to leave town because he is "gettin' restless." He sings "Joey, Joey, Joey."	
Tony asks for Joe's picture, his "pitch," as a keepsake of "da best damn foreman ever come to work for me."	
Tony sings "Rosabella," pondering her beautiful picture and his ploy to bring her to Napa.	
Scene 3. In Tony's barn at twilight, a few weeks later (May or June 1927)	
Ciccio and Giuseppe, Tony's servants, are preparing for the wedding feast, led by Pasquale, the cook and paymaster. They sing "Abbondanza" ("Abundance")—the text is entirely in Italian—as they assemble the food, drink, flowers, and decorations for the banquet.	Tony leaves to pick up Amy. Joe and Father discuss the circumstances that have led to the impending wedding, including Amy's employment in a "spaghetti joint" called Il Trovatore in

Table 4.1. (Continued)

A Country Girl shows a City Boy around the barn and explains that Rosabella is due to arrive soon for this, her *sposalizio*, her wedding banquet. Tony comes in and greets the children.	San Francisco, the exchange of pictures, and the marriage proposal by mail.
Scene 4. In the yard in front of Tony's house, the next moment Townspeople enter and sing "Sposalizio." The arrival of Rosabella, indignant at not having been met at the station, interrupts the preparations. The Postman sings, "I put her in my buggy and I took her for a ride, / Special delivery, one bride!" The three servants sing a welcoming trio, "Benvenuta." Rosabella and Joe have a musical conversation. She sings, "Such friendly faces, . . . I'm sorry I got mad."	The "R.F.D." (Postman) arrives with what he calls a "piece of registered mail" outside needing Tony's signature; it is Amy, whom he has found stranded at the train station. Joe goes out to greet Amy and brings her in. Joe and Amy converse alone, with Amy assuming he is Tony. She relaxes as she meets the cook and two farmhands, Giorgio and Angelo, who speak only Italian and at the same time. When Father McKee and the Postman prepare to leave, Amy replies, "I'm pleased to have made your acquaintance." Unaware of the identity confusion, Joe and Amy continue to talk about their personal histories.
The revelation of the picture switch takes place in a few lines of spoken dialogue, which quickly leads to . . .	

Table 4.1. (Continued)

The arrival of the injured Tony. Rosabella sings "No Home, No Job."	Just as Amy says, "I guess we'll get used to each other in time. Don't you think we will, Tony?" Joe is only able to respond, "Tony? Say, I ain't . . . !" when a commotion is heard outside. It is the Doctor, who has arrived with the Postman and Father McKee. He announces Tony's automobile accident.
	All eyes are on Tony as he is carried in. Joe is solicitous. Amy is in shock, not quite understanding what has taken place.
Seeing Rosabella, Tony insists on going through with the wedding ceremony, which they do inside the house, offstage, but with the Priest's Latin words audible.	With Tony taken off to the hospital, Joe and Amy talk, and the deception of the photo—Joe's was sent in place of Tony's—becomes clear to Amy. Joe was not complicit, but she indignantly doubts him.
The crowd disperses and Rosabella comes out of the house sobbing. "I went through with it, didn't I? I said I'd marry him—Well, I married him." Joe takes pity on her and sings "Don't Cry."	Amy wants to leave but feels trapped. She finally resolves to stay in Napa as the only practical solution to her problems. "If he wants to marry me, I'm game. I'm game to see it through. It's nice up here. . . ." [*Joe stares in mute admiration as the curtain falls.*]
Rosabella at first resists his sympathy, then comes around. Mimed gestures—an embrace and a separation—take place, accompanied by emotional music. Finally, [*Joe with significant stealth comes toward her, and she, in turn, takes an expectant amorous step toward him.*]	*Howard* **Act 2** The scene is the same as the first act. Late evening the same day.
	Tony lies groaning, attended by the Doctor, while the feast

Table 4.1. (*Continued*)

can be heard going on outdoors. There is also a fireworks display.

We learn from their conversation that Tony has been allowed to return home from the hospital to get married, and that the marriage has taken place that afternoon. He will be laid up for six months.

Joe and Tony talk. Tony is concerned that Amy is angry and wants to make it up to her. Joe says, "Just be good to her and take care of her. That's what Amy needs." They have an extended conversation about women in general, but Tony still feels guilty: "I'm the most unhappy fella in the world. W'y? Because I been verra bad sinner an' God is goin' to get me for sure!"

With Joe in the room, Tony tries to win Amy over with a present of earrings. She reacts with wonder and gratitude (a parallel to the opening scene in *The Most Happy Fella*). Overcome with joy, she exclaims, "I don't know what to say! I don't know what to do!"

Amy is still angry with Joe, who doesn't yet know about the picture swap. To Tony's horror, she picks up the picture and hands it dramatically to Joe.

Joe now knows the score and resolves to leave town the next day. Tony protests that he needs someone to run the vineyard

Table 4.1. (*Continued*)

Loesser	
Act 2	while he recovers. Amy feels vindicated and glad to be rid of Joe.
Scene 1. A clearing near the edge of Tony's vineyard. Morning, a week later. [*The entire scene is one of continuous industrious activity*] for both vineyard workers and farm women.	Their conversation is interrupted by the Doctor and Father McKee, arguing over the evils of drink. The party guests come in and bid farewell to the newlyweds.
The workers sing "Fresno Beauties."	
Rosabella and Joe soliloquize in song together (facing opposite directions): "Cold and Dead."	
The Doctor enters and talks with Tony, urging him to take the "Love and Kindness" offered by his nurse, Rosabella, to heal faster.	
Tony apologizes to Rosabella for the picture trick, and they sing "Happy to Make Your Acquaintance."	Amy speaks warmly to the guests and to Tony, agrees to nurse him back to health, and wins over Father McKee.
Cleo enters—she has been brought up from San Francisco to surprise Rosabella—and reprises "Happy to Make Your Acquaintance" with Tony.	
	Tony is sedated, and Joe and Amy are again left alone. They argue, then make up. Amy asks, "You really . . . didn't know nothing about his sending me that photo of you instead of his own, did you?"

Table 4.1. (Continued)

Marie enters and speaks with Cleo, who distrusts her.
Herman enters and spies Cleo. They strike up a conversation, leading to "Big D" —they both hail from Dallas. The chorus joins for the scene finale.

 Amy puts up a brave front, then says, "I bet all those people are laughing at me. . . . I wish I was dead!"

 Joe and Amy embrace and kiss as Tony calls out. Amy rushes from the house, with Joe in hot pursuit.

Scene 2. The barn, a little later in May. Rosabella enters, pushing Tony in a wheelchair. [*Apparently they are continuing an Italian lesson.*]

 Song, "How Beautiful the Days." They sing the Italian words for the days of the week.

 Marie enters and then Joe as well, making a quartet to finish the song.

Scene 3. The vineyards, a month later

 Tony and Doc and later Rosabella and Marie watch the "young people" who "gotta dance." Rosabella joins them. Tony [*despondently watches the gay, youthful scene . . . with feeble resignation.*]

Table 4.1. (*Continued*)

Scene 4. Inside the barn
Cleo and Herman are working and are joined by Pasquale, who demands a cigarette from Herman, who gladly complies. Herman is unruffled by Pasquale's commanding attitude and to Cleo sings, by way of explanation, "I Like Ev'rybody."

Scene 5. The vineyards in July
Cleo and Rosabella, then Tony and Rosabella, sing: "I Love Him" / "I Know How It Is" and "Like a Woman Loves a Man."
Tony and Rosabella confess their love, now grown deep, in "My Heart Is So Full of You." They announce the long-delayed *sposalizio.*
All dance; Rosabella faints and is taken inside to rest.
Tony sings "Mamma, Mamma, how ya like-a my sweetheart?"

Loesser
Act 3
Prelude. Pasquale, "dressed in his cook's hat and apron," urges the audience members to take their seats. He begins "Abbondanza" with Ciccio and Giuseppe.

Scene 1. The curtain rises on the abundantly filled barn, with wine vats, cheese, etc.

Howard
Act 3
The scene is unchanged [*but the woman's presence has made itself felt*]. Three months later, midafternoon.

Tony, Joe, and Father McKee are having a political discussion.

Table 4.1. (*Continued*)

Cleo enters with luggage, apparently prepared to leave the vineyard. Herman is unfazed.	
The Doctor urges people to give Tony and Rosabella time alone together after the *sposalizio*. He and the chorus sing "Song of a Summer Night."	Amy enters and brightens up the room.
	The Doctor enters and declares Tony much improved, since he is already on crutches and enjoying Amy's expert nursing.
	The Doctor reveals to Joe that Amy is pregnant and suggests that they leave town together. Joe tells Amy about the conversation. They agonize over what to do.
Rosabella confesses all to Tony and returns the amethyst pin. He attempts to strike her but cannot, as she takes her suitcase and begins to leave. She sings, "Please let me tell you that I love you."	Amy works herself up to confess all to Tony and finally comes out with it.
Rosabella leaves, and Tony swears to find and kill Joe, whom he suspects of departing with her.	Tony is enraged, vows to kill Joe, and attempts to throttle him as he enters the room, but falls helpless to the ground.
Scene 2. The Napa depot, a little later	
Joe, who has finally decided to leave by train and without Rosabella, bids farewell to his friends.	Joe and Amy prepare to leave, but Tony comes around and begs Amy to stay. Everyone will get what they want: Joe a chance to move on, Amy a roof over her head, and Tony a wife and baby to call his own.
Rosabella awaits nearby for the Napa–San Francisco bus.	
Tony is gloomy and desolate, but he realizes that Rosabella	

Table 4.1. (*Continued*)

is utterly alone and that allowing her to leave will not help either her or the baby.	
Marie enters and tries to prevent him from helping, but he finally insists, with Cleo's help, that Rosabella will come home with him and they will raise the baby as his own. Marie sings [*with venom*], "You ain't young no more! And you ain't good-looking! And you ain't smart!" To which he replies, "No! In da head omma no smart, ma, in da heart, Marie. In da heart!"	Tony tells Amy, "What you done was mistake in da head, not in da heart. . . . Mistake in da head is no matter."
Cleo and Marie fight and are finally broken up by the suddenly stalwart Herman. He and Cleo sing "I Made a Fist."	
Tony gently approaches Rosabella, and they agree that the baby's "gonna be Tony's bambino." A rapid section of final music includes bits of "I Don't Know Not'ing about You," "My Heart Is So Full of You," and "The Most Happy Fella."	Joe leaves. Tony and Amy embrace.

Kanin, starred Carole Lombard and Charles Laughton as Amy and Tony. Loesser probably found the idea of beginning the story at Amy's workplace rather than Tony's Napa ranch in this film, but he seems not to have been influenced by other liberties taken with the plot by scriptwriter Robert Ardrey. In Ardrey's version, Joe is finally roughed up and driven from the vineyards in disgrace, while the fate of the lovers remains uncertain at the end. Father McKee, having heard the whole story from Joe, intercedes to counsel a distraught, guilt-ridden, and still unmarried Amy, as a forgiving Tony looks on. Whatever cues he may have taken from the movies, Loesser undoubtedly studied the original play closely and modeled the central action of The Most Happy Fella on it, retaining its most provocative plot element, Amy's adultery, which all the film versions handle in slightly different ways.[14]

The interlinked fate of the three lovers, Amy (called Rosabella in the musical), Tony, and Joe, forms the central action of Howard's play and Loesser's musical. But the approaches taken by playwright and author are markedly different. First of all, Howard begins in medias res, filling the audience in on how Tony has come to marry a woman he has never met. Loesser begins with Rosabella (Amy) at her diner job, which both clarifies her motives and delivers the plot in chronological order. Whereas They Knew What They Wanted is a play of discussion and confrontation on issues ranging from religion and Prohibition to labor politics and women's rights, most of which takes place exclusively inside a farmhouse, The Most Happy Fella eliminates all issues of politics and religion in favor of a grand tour of northern California.[15] Loesser is intent on keeping the story focused on the Tony-Rosabella relationship and creating musical motives that will reinforce it, but also on providing some comic counterpoint with a secondary couple (Cleo and Herman). In the play, Howard chooses to paint Tony's home, his friends, and his misgivings first, so that the viewer is drawn into his plans before meeting the object of his desire. He is a likable but shady character who probably operates an unlawful business (since the Eighteenth Amendment made the manufacture of wine illegal in the United States between 1920 and 1933); any such suggestion is entirely absent from the musical. The early dialogue of the play also clarifies the potential problems with Tony's impending marriage: Amy's youth, her non-Catholic religion, her city background, in short, her status as a total outsider in Tony's world. The priest, Father McKee (an important character in the play), is nearly written out of the musical, but his silence is compensated for by Loesser's addition of Marie, Tony's sister (in the musical but not in the play), who utters her own concerns about Rosabella's marginal position and sings of devotion and sacrifice for her "dumb, funny-lookin' big brother, Tony." Indeed Loesser wrote two songs for Marie that deepen her character considerably. Though not included in the original production or the published score, these numbers were first sung onstage at the New York City Opera in 2006.

The musical begins with Rosabella's desperation and moves at a brisk pace. From Cleo and Rosabella's bustling restaurant in San Francisco ("Ooh! My Feet" and "I Know How It Is") to the Main Street of Napa ("The Most Happy Fella," "Standing on the Corner"), to Tony's barn and vineyards for the celebratory crowd scenes ("Abbondanza," "Sposalizio," "Fresno Beauties," "Big D," "Young People Gotta Dance," and "Hoedown"), and finally to the train station for Joe's departure ("Tell Tony and Rosabella Goodbye for Me"), Loesser removed most plot elements that lacked clear suggestions for musical portrayal and added some incidental business to heighten continuity and modernize the plot. While often taking verbal cues from words in the play to drive the music (e.g., "Looka me! I'm da most stylish fella in da world" became "'At's-a me! Hey! Omma the most happy fella in the whole Napa Valley"), Loesser turned a somewhat introverted series of domestic discussions into an outdoor extravaganza while retaining the essential interior scenes and soliloquies, provided with different but equally compelling music.

Loesser also developed a technique by which to strengthen the drama through sung dialogue, which he described for Murray Schumach in a *New York Times* interview when *The Most Happy Fella* was approaching its premiere: "I've always had a flair for concurrent speech in my songs—take 'Sue Me' and 'Baby, It's Cold Outside.' So I worked on these self-descriptive songs, using concurrent speech whenever necessary."[16]

The first scene reveals Loesser's uncompromising approach to musicalizing the entire story. Cleo complains about her sore feet at the end of a hard day waiting tables:

This little piggy
Feels the weight of the plate,
Though the freight's
Just an order of Melba toast.

And this little piggy
Is the littlest little piggy,
But the big son of a bitch
Hurts the most!

Instantly we are told a lot about her. Cleo is honest, earthy, funny, and sympathetic. Her drawl in the subsequent dialogue marks her as a Texas native, a fish as much out of water in San Francisco as city girl Amy/Rosabella will be in Napa. Cleo's song was only one of two numbers that Loesser wrote prior to conceiving *The Most Happy Fella* (it was originally intended for a *Guys and Dolls* policeman), but it fits perfectly here.[17] Because of Cleo's up-close candor, we know something about Amy's problems before we meet her. As the waitresses close down the restaurant for the night, Amy's romantic dreams are stoked by finding a tip in the form of a piece of jewelry. An amethyst tie pin has been enclosed in a note addressing her as "Rosabella," because the customer did not know her name. Howard wrote a parallel scene in *They Knew What They Wanted*, act 2, where Tony presents Amy with a pair of earrings, not as a tentative expression of love but as an apology for the picture ruse. The introduction of this love token so early in the musical telescopes the action and helps to explain why Rosabella acts so decisively to move away from San Francisco and marry a man she does not know.

By presenting the action in chronological order, Loesser gains our sympathy with Rosabella by giving her the first scene with Cleo. In scene 2, the introduction of Tony, Marie, Herman, and Joe, and the picture-taking business (which later enables Tony to mail Joe's snapshot to Rosabella) all follow in quick succession. The lengthy opening dialogue of the play is gone, as is Ah Gee, Tony's Chinese cook. Rosabella's friend Cleo, and Herman, a comic male partner for Cleo, were added for the musical. (Loesser found the name Cleo in Howard's play, when Amy delights Tony by calling him by *his* name for the first time. She retorts, "Expect me to call my husband mister? That'd sound swell, wouldn't it? Tony. Short for Antonio. Antonio and Cleopatra, huh? Can you beat it? You'll have to call me Cleo."[18])

The presence of extra women characters in *The Most Happy Fella* is easy to justify on musical grounds. The play has no females except Amy, which effectively draws attention to her solitariness in Napa: an important goal for the spoken drama. The musical, however, needs a variety of voice types and singers to sound the range of emotional states during several hours of music. A lone female singer among a large male cast would pose a problem from a composer's perspective. In this light, Cleo and Marie are welcome additions to the ensemble.

The use of paired couples, one funny (Cleo and Herman) and one serious (Rosabella and Tony), was a convention hard for Loesser to resist, for he understood that only in the rarest of circumstances could a musical suc-

Frank Loesser, Jo Sullivan, Joseph Anthony (the director), and Mona Paulee (Marie) read through *The Most Happy Fella*. Billy Rose Theatre Division, The New York Public Library for the Performing Arts, Astor, Lenox and Tilden Foundations.

ceed without an attractive love interest. Most musicals relied on a double set of lovers to provide enough plot for an evening. But the individual characters here are not merely formulaic, and their differences are fully in keeping with the exuberant variety of the play's action. The additional figures of Joe and Marie place this set of characters well beyond the conventional requirements of a standard comedy.

How or whether the comic musical numbers, "Standing on the Corner," "Benvenuta," and "Big D," fit in with the serious musical sections is a different question and will be discussed later in this chapter. Although *They Knew What They Wanted* contains no separate comic scenes, it bristles with comic elements: the happy ending, the joking postman, the stereotypical Chinese cook, farmhands who only speak Italian, and so forth. Loesser chose to add comedy to his musical, fully aware of the useful counterweight it would give to the serious aspects of the show.

The Comedy and the Chorus

The Most Happy Fella's chorus, which Loesser playfully designates in the score as "all the neighbors and all the neighbors' neighbors," is engaging and diverting, and used in a variety of ways typically found in both operas and musicals. In act 1, scene 2, the presence of a chorus confirms the extrovert outdoor scenario by lending energy and visible momentum for the actions of the principals, especially Tony ("The Most Happy Fella"), and sums up the developments in his "mail-order love affair." Herman's ogling quartet ("Standing on the Corner") flows easily out of the larger group scene and proceeds just as naturally to Tony and Joe's dialogue, and finally to Joe's expansive solo about his need to move on ("Joey, Joey, Joey"), which gives Tony the idea to send a substitute picture for his own. "Sposalizio," the next chorus in scene 4, serves as prelude to Rosabella's much-awaited arrival; it can also stand alone as a spirited party song. The absence of a choral number from both the first and last scenes of act 1 is *The Most Happy Fella*'s most striking deviation from standard musical theater practice; to round off the drama convincingly—the hubbub created by Tony's accident, the anger welling up in Rosabella, and the comforting seduction of Joe—Loesser dispensed with choral singing entirely.

The second-act opening chorus, "Fresno Beauties," begins conventionally enough, accompanying a scene of "continuous industrious activity" in and around the vineyards, according to the score. Then, quite unconventionally, Loesser suddenly interrupts everything by freezing the group action midphrase at the moment when the now alienated Joe and Rosabella meet by accident. The effect is stunning when, for twenty-four slow measures (marked *Lento e lugubre*, ex. 4.1), the pair sing twin soliloquies culminating in the words, "It didn't matter then; it doesn't matter now. It's cold and dead, buried and gone, . . . And now ev'ry day the best we can do is nod good morning." At this point the uptempo chorus resumes precisely where it had so abruptly stopped.

"Big D" employs the chorus in characteristic Broadway style. After Cleo and Herman get acquainted and sing about their shared native city, everyone else in the vicinity jumps aboard to join in reprising the song about Dallas. "Big D" has showstopper stamped all over it, and this function is affirmed by the dance variation that follows. The penultimate choral song, "Song of a Summer Night," surprises in a different way. This chorus, led by the Doctor, shows off Loesser's tender, pastoral mode with lyrics of striking freshness:

Example 4.1. "Fresno Beauties" (*Lento e lugubre* section, at m. 104)

Song of the cricket call,
Song of the lazy breeze,
Song of a blossom falling
Down from the 'cacia trees! . . .
Song of a thousand voices
Full of a rare delight.

The quiet, palpitating quality of the close-harmony homorhythmic (block-chord) style in an easy gait is reminiscent of Stephen Foster's "Come, Where My Love Lies Dreaming" or any number of genteel nineteenth-century parlor song choruses by George F. Root and Henry Clay Work. It serves, not unlike the Humming Chorus of Puccini's *Madama Butterfly*, to depict the calm before the storm: Rosabella's impassioned confession to Tony and his initial murderous reaction.

In short, Loesser's use of the chorus substantially redirects the basic story by placing it within a larger community that regularly interacts with the main characters. In Howard's play, the Italian partiers and wedding guests form an *offstage* crowd, and so they do not distract our attention from the dialogue of Tony, Amy, and Joe. In the musical, Loesser always keeps the chorus and the dancers nearby to accomplish transitions, clarify scene changes, heighten dramatic turns of the plot, frame solo numbers, and finally reinforce a general sense of exuberance or mounting tension—in other words, to serve classic operatic functions.

Ensembles

Small ensembles (duets, trios, and quartets of singers) also play a major part in the musical action. By combining and interweaving spoken lines and sung ones at every turn, Loesser enhances the emotional and melodic flexibility that enables a deeper portrayal of individual characters, while simultaneously mixing up the musical textures. Freestanding solo songs built with multiple verses and refrains are far rarer here than in conventional musical comedies, but ensembles, usually restricted to finales, happen rather more often.

"Standing on the Corner," a male quartet, harks back to the barbershop song interpolations found in musicals from George M. Cohan's era (circa 1900). The next ensemble, in act 1, scene 3, introduces Tony's comic servants Ciccio, Giuseppe, and Pasquale, who are preparing for the wedding feast. They sing their song, "Abbondanza," as they work. This scene is the musical version of Howard's scene in act 1, with Ah Gee (the Chinese cook) and two Italian farmhands (Giorgio and Angelo) who speak only Italian and at the same time. It provides a lively comic interlude. Loesser was proud of this catchy number, seeing it as inseparable from the show; wary of overexposing his comic hits, he refused to license it for performance outside the musical.[19] "Benvenuta," performed by the same trio, includes an inventive bit of stage business as Rosabella is properly welcomed with flowers, food, flashing lights, and a painted banner. It also parodies operatic expression, as each member of the trio presents his gift and sings his personal, fulsome cadenza on increasingly higher notes (see ex. 4.2).

Example 4.2. "Benvenuta" (cadenzas, mm. 40–45)

The first ensemble in the second act depicts the growing trust between Rosabella and Tony. "Happy to Make Your Acquaintance" is a clever blend of lyrical and humorous work, another example of what Loesser termed "concurrent speech" songs.[20] In their first scene alone together—their marriage has occurred offstage—Tony apologizes:

TONY: You mad at me? [*Rosabella does not answer.*] Omma send you wrong fella's pitch. If I was-a send you *my* pitch you no come here. No? [*He waits through a thoughtful silence.*] Omma sorry about da pitch.
ROSABELLA: [*correcting him*] Pic-ture.

Their scene, ostensibly about etiquette and proper pronunciation, leads smoothly to the surprise arrival of Cleo and a reprise of "Happy to Make Your Acquaintance," this time as a duet for Cleo and Tony. The reprise demonstrates how a set of character relationships can be transformed in a moment through music. After Cleo's exit, Tony speaks his motives to Rosabella: "I was-a t'ink maybe you lonesome. . . . So omma send for you friend you was a-tell me about." Rosabella admits that she is not so lonely after all and that Tony is "a nice, kind man," a significant concession. They repeat the second half of the song (from "How do you do / Pleased to know you") in unison, leading to a firm cadence. The whole scene is tightly managed, musically efficient, and dramatically satisfying.

Another ensemble of a completely different character follows directly. Cleo meets Marie and each expresses her individual mood; Marie sees a potential ally against the marriage ("You understand / When the girl's too young for the man"), and Cleo is instantly suspicious of Marie's motives ("I don't like this dame"). Another kind of double soliloquy ensues. As Marie's voice "diminish[es] to a whisper" and her rhythm predicting "a million kinds of trouble, trouble, trouble" is picked up by a staccato saxophone solo (ex. 4.3), Cleo decides to hold her tongue, noting that "since I'm company right now, into her eye I can't exactly [spit]."

Their superficially amicable first meeting, with clearly differentiated musical motives, nicely foreshadows the open hostility to come in the final act. Loesser underlined the cool disparity between the women in this number by consciously invoking "an ultra-classical form, a sort of two-part invention, . . . derivative of the time of Bach," to explain his duet's unusual feel, although he denied any covert historical allusions. "I use the form because I like the sound of it and I don't think [it] belongs in any special niche."[21]

The stylistic differences between the meeting songs of the second act, "Happy to Make Your Acquaintance" and "Big D" (after Herman first notices Cleo), merit further comment. Rosabella and Tony get to know each other through an etiquette lesson in the form of a call-and-response duet. (The whole consists of two sixteen-measure sections, the words in one part repeated immediately in the other. Later on, "How Beautiful the Days" will reverse the roles, with Tony singing the days of the week in Italian and Rosabella repeating after him.) The mood here is "free and lyrical." "Big D," in contrast, wastes no time becoming a full-fledged production number, with everyone praising Dallas in one voice. In form (AABA'), its syncopated first

Example 4.3. "I Don't Like This Dame" (mm. 144–55)

phrase (A) contrasts with the strong downbeats of the release (B) ("And that spells Dallas"). "Big D" is celebratory and extrovert. Its general exuberance fits it for performance outside the musical. "Happy to Make Your Acquaintance" and "How Beautiful the Days," while tuneful and lighthearted, appear to have no subject apart from the specific "instructional" one in the show. They suggest the beginnings of intimacy between the lovers by their deftly understated business. "How Beautiful the Days" becomes a quartet with the addition of Marie's and Joe's contrasting sentiments, but it retains an easy, intimate quality and never aims at choral grandeur. The ensembles, like the choruses and the solos, are never present merely to fulfill typical expectations, but instead to provide musically appropriate illustrations of the emotional situations at hand.

The Conclusion

The dramatic climax and denouement of the story follow slightly different arcs in the two shows, and Loesser contrives carefully to complete the drama with all major characters accounted for, including the new ones he has invented. Both versions have three acts: standard form for a play but completely atypical, if not unique, for a musical.[22] Loesser takes a full second act to develop the serious love story and bring it to a musical climax in "My Heart Is So Full of You." Then Tony, in musical soliloquy, reflects on his good fortune ("Mamma, Mamma"), which ends the act. How to present Rosabella's fate once Tony discovers her pregnancy by Joe is the center of the dramatic problem in both Howard's and Loesser's third acts. In the play the Doctor reveals Amy's condition to Joe, who in turn informs Amy (as if she did not know herself). This dramatically improbable plot twist was removed by Loesser, who lets Rosabella figure things out with Cleo after she faints in the middle of her dancing party. In the musical, unlike the play or the film versions, Joe is never aware of Rosabella's pregnancy; his leave-taking is unrelated to qualms about Tony and Rosabella's future happiness and impending parenthood. Both of these modernizing adjustments to the original 1924 script sharpen the focus and bring us more closely into sympathy with the principal characters.

Some intermediate business with Cleo and Herman prolongs the action in the musical and therefore heightens the suspense before Rosabella's final confession to Tony. Marie's presence allows Tony to vent his anger and to reason out for himself how things stand. He realizes and accepts that he is as much at fault as Rosabella.

In the play, Tony finally forgives Amy, thus showing a degree of growth in his character, which was Howard's object.[23] But the dialogue's moralistic tone also seems to finger Amy as the chief offending party. In the musical, Marie becomes the heavy. She speaks the most judgmental lines, but she is roundly put down for doing so. Between Tony and Rosabella, the blame, if blame there is, seems to be more equally shared. The forces of reconciliation are more balanced. Loesser's brief section of dialogue and music leading to the finale has no exact parallel in the play. But it is a crucial scene, absolutely necessary before the happy ending can take place. It depends on musical repetition for its effectiveness. Tony reassures Rosabella by confessing his fear when he first saw her, beginning in straight dialogue:

> TONY: Nunja be scared, Carissima. It's-a bad to be scared. . . . I should-a know what I want an' say what I want. Now, tonight, we start all over. I sit in da ristorante. You wait on me. Omma no scared. Omma say, "Young lady—what's-a you name?"
>
> ROSABELLA: Amy.
>
> TONY: Amy. Dat's-a nice name.
>
> TONY: [*singing now*] I canno' leave you money on da table. You look too nice. An' so I give you my genuine amotist tie pin.
>
> ROSABELLA: [*speaking*] How can you be so good to me? How can you be so kind? So kind, after what I . . .
>
> TONY: [*singing what Rosabella had sung from his letter in act 1, scene 1*] I don' know not'ing about you, where you ever go. . . . What I see is kind of young lady I wanna get marry!

Rosabella's spoken interjections and Tony's melody are intertwined until Rosabella is convinced of Tony's sincerity. This segues easily to the finale, a reprise of "My Heart Is So Full of You" and "The Most Happy Fella." But the musical and emotional crux is the reprise of "I don' know not'ing about you." This Puccinian gesture of recollection virtually guarantees any listener's sympathy, because the audience knows these are precisely the words (and notes) that Rosabella sang in the opening scene, the words that introduced her to Tony in the first place. (Tony has sung them once again to Marie.) But in this final reiteration they are much more weighted and poignant. Indeed, he now knows *all* about her but still wants to get married and still accepts their mutual failings. The circle of their relationship is finally completed with his honesty and mature depth of feeling.

Choosing the Cast

The Most Happy Fella requires an unusual combination of singer/actors for a Broadway show. The role of Tony needs a mature operatic voice in the body of a superior character actor, while the female lead must simultaneously be able to project naïveté and to deliver sustained, demanding vocal lines. A Broadway belter would be inadequate for either role. Cleo is a more familiar Broadway type—a brassy confidante in the mold of Ado Annie in *Oklahoma!*—but she also has important lyrical moments. Joe must convey swaggering self-assurance yet also project sensitivity and humor in dialogue and put over a few soaring high notes in his solo number. The role of Marie originally called for more songs of operatic dimensions, so again a normal Broadway casting call probably would not have netted the right individual.

Loesser found his first Tony in baritone Robert Weede, who had enjoyed a long career singing major Italian roles at the Metropolitan Opera, the City Center Opera Company (later the New York City Opera), and the San Francisco Opera, among other venues.[24] Weede had made his Metropolitan debut as Tonio in *Pagliacci* (1937) and created the role of the emperor of Haiti, Jean-Jacques Dessalines, in William Grant Still's *Troubled Island* (1949) at the City Center Opera Company. After *The Most Happy Fella*, he ended his Broadway career with appearances in *Milk and Honey* (1961) and *Cry for Us All* (1970).

Rosabella fell to Jo Sullivan, who had been spotted by Lynn Loesser singing the role of Polly Peacham in the critically acclaimed revival of Brecht and Weill's *Threepenny Opera* (1954). Lynn urged Frank to invite Sullivan for an audition.[25] Sullivan had grown up taking voice lessons in her home state of Missouri, won a singing contest sponsored by the St. Louis Symphony during her high school years, and then found advanced instruction in New York, including music theory and composition classes at Columbia University, before gaining experience in a variety of shows. She nailed a spot in the chorus of *Oklahoma!* during the last year of its initial run, sang the roles of Julie in *Carousel* and Adele in Johann Strauss's operetta *Die Fledermaus*, both at City Center, and appeared as the star of a short-lived Broadway production (five performances) of Benjamin Britten's "entertainment for young people," *Let's Make an Opera/The Little Sweep* (1950), a show directed by Marc Blitzstein, who also helped to create the English version of *The Threepenny Opera*, for which she then auditioned.[26]

Lynn Loesser cast another Metropolitan Opera veteran, Canadian mezzo-soprano Mona Paulee, for the role of Marie, Tony's sister. A singer of enormous breadth who had begun her career as a cabaret chanteuse, Paulee recorded songs of Romberg, Cole Porter, Gershwin, Bizet, and Rimsky-Korsakov, among many others in her long career. The 2006 revival of the show, with two of Marie's cut arias restored, explained why a big opera voice was necessary for the part. (Originally thought too operatic for a Broadway audience, Maria's arias were omitted at the urging of the show's first director, Joseph Anthony, and producer Kermit Bloomgarden.) Fully realized, Marie is a rich and even sympathetic character, who expresses herself most completely in song.

Susan Johnson, who created the role of Cleo, combined a brash, comedic speaking style with a strong mezzo-soprano. Loesser especially admired her plucky determination when she auditioned for the part, singing through a massive head cold without complaint. Country-and-western singer Shorty Long, who had recorded "Rodger Young," was selected as the first Herman. Yet another opera singer, baritone Morley Meredith (who later sang at the Met from 1962 to 1992), was originally tapped for the part of Joe, but when he proved too polished and pallid to suit the sexy but rough-and-ready role of cowboy/lover, a swing-band singer named Art Lund was substituted to supply the required charisma.[27]

Once the roles were created, of course, casting for revivals was somewhat simplified, since directors now at least had a clear idea of the show's basic requirements. The renowned Metropolitan Opera bass Giorgio Tozzi and Sharon Daniels were well received in the lead roles in a 1979 Broadway revival, but critics were especially enthusiastic in praising a modest production (with an orchestra consisting of two pianos, guitar, concertina, and accordion) at the Goodspeed Opera House (East Haddam, Connecticut) in 1991, featuring Spiro Malas and Sophie Hayden and directed by Gerald Gutierrez. This version reopened at Manhattan's Booth Theatre on February 13, 1992, and ran for 229 performances. For audiences lately accustomed to song-and-dance shows with little or no dialogue (such as Evita in 1979 and Cats in 1982) and others demanding substantial operatic singing (Sweeney Todd in 1979, Les Misérables in 1987), the more intimate Most Happy Fella at last felt utterly right for Broadway. In March 2006 another critically praised revival, this time using full orchestral forces, was mounted at the New York City Opera. Its biggest draw and weakest musical link was Paul Sorvino as

Tony. A famed television actor with previously unsuspected musical talents, Sorvino delivered a convincing characterization but struggled with the vocal challenges.

The Music

How listeners react to *The Most Happy Fella* probably hinges most directly on their responses to the exceptional amount of continuous music. If you don't like recitative singing in place of (or interlaced with) dialogue, then it may appear to be overly stylized. All those incomplete melodies that are less than songs—the term "arioso" is sometimes used to describe such half songs—may seem superfluous or distracting, and there are nearly two dozen such places in the score. If, on the other hand, one is drawn into the web of emotions that arise from a complex of overlapping vocal and instrumental lines, then the high jinks that accompany the presence of Cleo and Herman, or the vivid action numbers of the Doctor, the Postman, the servants, and the farmhands, may seem like lapses of mood. But to put it this way is far too analytical. What Loesser has woven together, overlapping spoken words and musical responses, cannot easily be changed without doing fundamental damage. His "concurrent speech" songs are essential to the whole.

Among some forty sections of *The Most Happy Fella*'s spoken dialogue, barely half a dozen exceed twenty lines, taking up a total of no more than fifteen minutes on the clock. Most of the spoken sections are quite brief, and several work with music like the final scene between Tony and Rosabella. What's more, it is often hard to tell from the words on the page which ones are intended to be spoken and which sung. A consistent adherence to everyday language binds the show as tightly together as does the music.

Richard S. Hill, an astute early reviewer of *The Most Happy Fella* for the Music Library Association's journal *Notes*, observed in the show "a font of melody closely allied to American speech patterns, . . . a constant interchange of modes of presentation smoothly integrated."[28] Loesser's apparent plan of musical work, reflected in the sixteen sketchbooks that survive in the New York Public Library from the years of *Fella*'s genesis, and discussed at some length by Geoffrey Block in an article for the *Musical Quarterly*, confirm several fundamental facts: (1) Loesser preferred to have a fixed text before proceeding to write musical notes to his words; (2) he derived and notated basic musical rhythms in synchrony with the natural speech stresses of titles or key lines of the lyrics for all the major songs; (3) he tended to build

Table 4.2. Basic Song Rhythms in *The Most Happy Fella*, Act 1

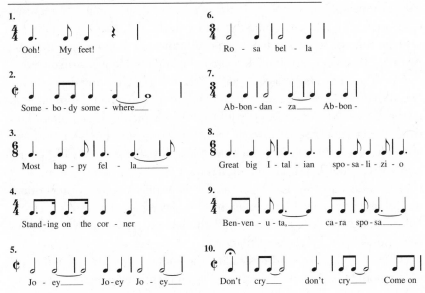

entire songs around a prominent opening rhythm; (4) he was far more apt to change pitches rather than the underlying rhythms during the course of revision; (5) he wrote virtually all the music for *The Most Happy Fella* specifically for the show; very little came from the proverbial Tin Pan Alley songwriter's trunk.[29]

For example, table 4.2 illustrates the constantly varied character of the basic rhythms of the first ten numbers (in act 1) of *The Most Happy Fella*. Except for no. 7, each song bears a meter signature different from its predecessor, and despite the technical identity of the 3/4 time signatures for no. 6 ("Rosabella") and no. 7 ("Abbondanza"), the contrast between the two in other respects (tempo, mood) is marked. Loesser's consistent attention to lively contrast marks the entire score.

The presence of such a large number of sketchbooks also reveals the painstaking process by which Loesser worked out the final forms of the melodies in his show over the course of weeks or even years of labor. He carefully matched musical techniques with the emotional temperature of the words. The sketchbooks demonstrate how completely Loesser accepted the idea that a song's essential character inheres in its most characteristic rhythmic figures.

Loesser took for granted the idea that any sustained piece of music (a work comparable to a spoken drama or concert dance program) required an element of continuity, some thread drawn through over the duration of a whole song or scene, such as a repeating melodic fragment, a dramatic rhythmic statement, or a motive treated sequentially. Hence, virtually every song in *The Most Happy Fella*—as well as much of the sung dialogue between the fully developed songs—takes no more than a half-dozen notes to establish a quickly recognizable pattern, which is then repeated often. This structural fact about songwriting helps us appreciate how quickly a tune can be made to attach itself in the memory as well as the difficulty of the task Loesser set himself. On one hand, frequent repetition of a strong musical element risks boredom for singers and listeners alike. A lack of repetition, on the other, may lead to incoherence. Achieving a balance of effects requires dedicated effort over time, and most composers only rarely reach this goal. Loesser did much more than write a dozen clever songs to bring off his Project Three. To avoid misleading the audience into thinking that his work amounted to an endless stream of undifferentiated operatic music and hardly any dialogue, Loesser made sure that the show's original printed program spelled the twenty-one principal songs with capital letters.

Entertainment professionals know they must hold an audience's attention at all costs. Loesser understood that continual motivic repetition had to be paired with variety in order to maintain listeners' interest. He achieved this end in *The Most Happy Fella* principally through changes of key, basic meter, tempo, and combination of singers (solo, duo, trio, and so on). Table 4.3 illustrates how he variously shifted these four traits in the musical's twenty-one principal numbers. Notice that the nonuniform succession of changes among the four columns guarantees a kind of kaleidoscopic effect, with differing forces creating either links or breaks from number to number. For example, where the number of singers ("solo") remains the same from no. 1 to no. 2, the key and tempo change. All elements shift from no. 2 to no. 3, but from no. 3 to no. 4 the key is retained, and so on. It is unnecessary to understand all the different meter signs or Italian tempo indications to detect this patterned, selective adjustment of the four elements.[30]

Of course, normally such variables would be absorbed more or less unconsciously by the audience. Few listeners will take conscious note of a specific set of key or meter changes in a work of music theater. That said, certain linking gestures are more noticeable on the surface than others, and these can

Table 4.3. Basic Meters, Keys, Tempos, and Ensembles in *The Most Happy Fella*

Title	Meter	Key	Tempo	Ensemble
Act 1				
"Ooh! My Feet!"	4/4	E-flat	*Pesante*	solo
"Somebody, Some-where"	¢	G	*Lamentando*	solo
"Most Happy Fella"	6/8	C	*Tempo di tarantella*	solo + chorus
"Standing on the Cor-ner"	4/4	C	*Allegro moderato*	quartet
"Joey, Joey"	4/4	D-flat	*Moderato*	solo
"Rosabella"	3/4	B-flat	*Moderato*	solo
"Abbondanza"	3/4	b/D	*Allegro con brio*	trio
"Sposalizio"	6/8	C	*Allegro con brio*	chorus + dancers
"Benvenuta"	4/4	C	*Moderato*	trio
"Don't Cry"	¢	A-flat	*Lento*	solo, then duet
Act 2				
"Fresno Beauties"	2/4	D	*Allegro*	chorus
"Happy to Make"	¢	C	*Allegro giusto*	duo
"Big D"	¢	A	*Allegro con spirito*	duo + chorus
"How Beautiful"	¢	E-flat	*Andante tranquillo*	duo
"Young People"	3/4	G	*Moderato con rubato*	solo
"Warm All Over"	¢	G	*Con molto espressivo*	solo
"I Like Ev'rybody"	¢	C	*Allegro ma non troppo*	duo
"My Heart Is So Full"	¢	D-flat	*Moderato appassionato*	duo
"Mamma, Mamma"	6/8	B-flat	*Lento*	solo
Act 3				
"Song of a Summer Night"	¢	D′	*Andante*	solo + chorus
"Please Let Me Tell You"	4/4	D	*Molto espressivo e lagrimoso*	solo

serve as cues to recurring moments of a particular emotional or affectional type. For instance, Rosabella's recitative on the words "No home, no job" and Joey's song of comfort, "Don't Cry," both feature short unstressed notes repeatedly moving to longer ones at a relatively slow pace. This amounts to a familiar kind of sighing motive, whose significance is instantly grasped as sorrow and sympathy. The two getting-to-know-you or first-meeting songs, "Happy to Make Your Acquaintance" and "Big D," are linked by multiple means: syncopes in their melodies; bouncy tempi; identical meters; and larger-than-solo ensembles. Both are cheerful and warmhearted in feeling, not just because of their words, but because of their musical elements.

The Solo Songs

No musical, even a well-knit operatic one, could achieve significant popular approval without a handful of infectious melodies. Several songs in *The Most Happy Fella* stand out for their individual attractiveness. "Joey, Joey, Joey" is perhaps the most difficult to classify because it seems neither truly operatic nor inclined toward Broadway brashness. Nevertheless, as Gayle Seaton has argued, the character of Joe, as Loesser has placed him in the plot, possesses an ambiguous quality that is clearly mirrored in this signature song.[31] He is dreamy but down to earth, loyal but wayward, seductive but honorable. He also anticipates a later, less successful Loesser character, Gideon Briggs in *Greenwillow*, who is similarly restless and tempest-tossed but fundamentally goodhearted.

Joey's verse (to be sung "mysteriously") evokes "a perfumed woman / smellin' of where she's been . . . Oregon cherries /or maybe Texas avocado . . . or Arizona sugar beet." The leitmotivic refrain begins at m. 23 in D-flat major (ex. 4.4), adopting a moderate but shifting tempo, and unfolds in an expansive AABA song form (four times sixteen measures) with a six-measure coda. Through the verse and the A phrases, two melodic pitches, C and A-natural, constitute understated dissonances against the accompanying drone (A-flat over D-flat in the bass). Augmented chords (stacked major thirds in the harmony) move with sliding parallel thirds in the accompaniment to enhance a feeling of instability that comes with the plaintive and mysterious call of the wind. The B section lyrics shift the diction back to earth for an eleven-measure interlude about the creature comforts taken for granted (the soft bunk, the good food, and "the ladies in the neighborhood") that must be sacrificed to wanderlust. The wide dynamic range (from *ppp* to *f*) and relatively lofty reach—to a high F—of the final A phrase and ending provide a head-tossing flourish to conclude (and court applause), but they do not upset the warm, pastoral aura established by what has come before.

None of the solo ballads in *The Most Happy Fella* are entirely ordinary in form and style. Rosabella's two solos, "Somebody, Somewhere" and "Warm All Over," show especially clearly how Loesser makes fresh harmonic turns serve emotional expression. The first asserts a dozen times over (in five suc-

Example 4.4. "Joey, Joey, Joey" (mm. 23–29)

cessive, similar eight-measure phrases) a single rhythmic and melodic motive:

By omitting a contrasting release (B) phrase from the form and shifting each melodic segment to a different pitch level, the composer builds the listener's sense of anticipation, producing an irresistible forward momentum, a gesture recalling a similar move in "Hello, Young Lovers" (Rodgers and Hammerstein, *The King and I*, 1951) and anticipating one in "Who Can I Turn To?" (Leslie Bricusse and Anthony Newley, *The Roar of the Greasepaint*, 1965).

"Warm All Over" (ex. 4.5) is one of Loesser's most adventurous melodic/harmonic excursions, in a class with "My Time of Day" from *Guys and Dolls* and "Spring Will Be a Little Late This Year." David Jenness and Don Velsey note that its opening note (the sixth scale degree, that is, E in the key of G major) is not a member of the tonic triad underneath (G–B–D), the blend

Example 4.5. "Warm All Over" (mm. 11–18)

creating "a Schumannesque effect."[32] The melody proceeds with several large leaps to chromatic notes outside the G scale, often accompanied by four-note (seventh) chords that obscure the song's direction. Yet, as if to explain the meandering notes and start-stop rhythm, "The words are wonderfully well-controlled. . . . The 'high' vowel of *smile* is followed by a series of long dark *o* sounds, connecting introduction to chorus (*glow* / *so* / *know* / *o-ver*), before *smile* is heard again. There are then no more bright vowels until one word, *feel*, in the release, and its affine, *feeling*, at the end. Added to this control is a miraculous attainment of an innocently sexual tone in the title phrase, as sung unconsciously by a naïve young woman. For the auditor, picking this up is like not hearing the key-tone (m. 8): you recognize it, but you don't stop to think about it."[33]

Arguably the jewel in the crown of this score is "My Heart Is So Full of You," the love duet shared by Tony and Rosabella toward the end of the second act. The dramatic deployment of this song is cunning, since the professions of love are coming late in the play, but not yet as a denouement or capstone moment, since the secret of Rosabella's pregnancy by Joe has yet to be divulged to Tony. This final revelation, still hovering in the air, adds poignancy for the audience members, who, like Rosabella, have reason to fear Tony's reaction and its consequences. The prominent word "heart" also foreshadows the concluding reconciliation embodied in lines from both the original play and the musical book. In forgiving Amy, Howard gives Tony the line, "What you done was mistake in da head, not in da heart." The parallel passage in Loesser's text is dialogue between Marie and Tony. She sings "(with venom)," "You ain't young no more! And you ain't good-looking! And you ain't smart!" To which he replies, "No! In da head omma no smart, ma, in da heart, Marie. In da heart!"

The unusual structure of "My Heart Is So Full of You" is based on a long-breathed forty-three-measure passage in the key of D-flat major, with two distinct melodic elements unfolding simultaneously: a true melody and a second, nonimitative part. The second tune, which does not begin until m. 12, rather than forming an independent statement, adds intensity. Loesser begins with what might be termed an expanded AA'BA" song form, expanded because only the B phrase contains the standard eight measures (the others being either three or five measures longer: A = 11, A' = 11, B = 8, A" = 13). Despite the oddity of the phrase lengths and a few sizable leaps for the singers, the main melody moves simply and easily to illustrate the full and mutual emotion that the characters are expressing (the tempo being *moderato appassionato*). The top note of Tony's first main melodic phrase, a chromatic F-flat, occurs in m. 10 on the word "more." The top note for Rosabella appears in the penultimate measure in the third (B) phrase. By consistently placing high and emotional notes (on the words "more," "for," and "heart") as late in each phrase as possible, Loesser ratchets up the cumulative effect of high volume, high range, and rich harmony. The relatively slow speed gives the tune plenty of time to sink into listeners' ears. Furthermore, everything flows together because the composer has neatly overlapped Tony's phrase endings with Rosabella's entrances and vice versa. Tony, who sings the first section (A) of the main melody by himself, sounds like he will be landing on the key note (D-flat) in m. 12, but in fact Rosabella begins her part on that pitch in m. 12, while Tony rests for a beat and begins the contrapuntal part immediately after (see ex. 4.6). Tony then bubbles over into dialogue *and* recitative in succession—a musical display of confused excitement—to announce the *sposalizio* (the wedding banquet). Finally the couple repeats together the A' phrase of the main melody, but this time in unison, making for a powerful and solid conclusion. The counterpoint in this song—highlighting emotional words, but also easing singers smoothly into dialogue—goes

Example 4.6. "My Heart Is So Full of You" (mm. 1–20)

a step beyond the call-and-response duets that appeared in earlier Loesser numbers such as "Make a Miracle" in *Where's Charley?*

The Ariosos

The show's musical variety is further enhanced by many transitional sections of sung dialogue. Block cites the absence of a full libretto among the sketchbooks to support his claim that Loesser planned from the beginning to keep spoken lines to a minimum.[34] Richard S. Hill declared that "Loesser's passages of accompanied dialogue generally pass into a type of writing that is difficult to describe but which may well be Loesser's most significant contribution. . . . [He] has gone a step further than what is generally understood by the term *arioso* [a half-way point between full-fledged song and pitched recitation], and once the melodic phrases are shaped, he builds from them a wide variety of freely organized song forms."[35] Such a claim bears careful scrutiny.

The opening scene contains several passages that fit Hill's description.

"Seven million crumbs and a gravy spot" begins fourteen measures for Cleo to elaborate on the kind of tips she gets (*not* the amethyst tiepin that Rosabella has received from Tony). The following passage (*maestoso*, majestically), in which Rosabella quotes Tony's letter, "I don't know notin' about you" is a mere twelve measures, yet it recurs memorably throughout the whole show. Originally Rosabella's first full-length song at this spot was entitled "Wanting to Be Wanted," but it was deemed too dark and was cut long before the premiere, only to be rediscovered by Jo Sullivan Loesser in the 1990s. A remnant of the original tune remains in the published score as a seven-measure introduction to "Somebody, Somewhere."[36]

In the third scene, Tony dreams about fathering "plenty bambini" with his new bride. Accordingly, he sings a version of this phrase five times in succession spread over twenty-nine measures, picking up the fast waltz tempo still left in our ears by the previous number, "Abbondanza." A full-blown song would overwhelm the simple sentiment, but this arioso moves the action along expeditiously. The repetition of another simple phrase, "Tell me, aren't you *glad* I'm here?" constitutes Rosabella's next arioso and anticipates her misidentification of Joe as Tony. Once Joe explains himself, the remainder of the scene is played out in spoken dialogue, followed by dramatically underscored speech and finally stark recitative as the injured Tony is brought in to join a stunned Rosabella. Only at Joe's comforting song, "Don't Cry," does a full thirty-two-measure AABA song emerge. The act concludes with Joe's seduction of Rosabella as underscored pantomime. Their affair takes place offstage.

In the second act, the line between arioso and recitative (dramatic statement without a strict beat) fades in importance. Rosabella and Cleo complain to each other about her man's lack of amorous attention, through twenty-five lightly accompanied measures. Rosabella, urged on by her confidante, then dramatically sings her complaint (a similar melody) directly to Tony. In retrospect, this extended conversational passage draws us powerfully to the climactic and fully formed duet "My Heart Is So Full of You," in the same manner that a good verse in a Tin Pan Alley song leads to its refrain. In another arioso passage, Tony takes a moment for himself to reflect on his good fortune: "Mamma, Mamma, up in heaven / how you like my girl?" On paper this reflective soliloquy appears to follow an AABA closed form, but, like "Joey, Joey, Joey," it contains enough changeups in the vocal line to avoid giving the impression of a rigidly made aria. The last dozen measures are studded with high Fs and Gs, following a staccato interlude (the B section) in mixed meters (three times switching between six and four counts per measure) meant to suggest an Italian folk song ("in Palermo, Mamma, when I was a young man"). These rhythmic shifts and the emotional tug of Tony's communing with his mother impart sufficient weight to close the act decisively in only fifty-nine brief measures. In an even shorter passage during the third act, Loesser shapes Rosabella's emotional farewell to Tony, "Please let me tell you that I love you," again by reiterating a single rhythmic motive accompanied by rich harmonic underpinning.

More about the Musical Mosaic

Weaving together the separate and discrete songs and dances of *The Most Happy Fella* by means of shorter melodic segments is not merely an interesting technique that Loesser adopted for his private amusement. To understand what he seemed to be striving for, we can liken his process to the construction of a mosaic. In this familiar Byzantine art form, the size, color, and placement of many small bits of tinted glass may vary but their collective presence in the right light guarantees the brilliance of a complete image when viewed from a distance. A few bits of missing tile or mortar will not significantly damage the artwork, but if more than a handful of pieces are absent, the gaps will begin to weaken the total impression. The optical illusion will not hold.

Even the music without words in *The Most Happy Fella* is implicated in the full texture of the drama. For example, in the delicate moment following Tony and Rosabella's wedding vows, before Joe attempts to offer comfort, a brief orchestral introduction to "Don't Cry" quietly echoes motives from "Joey, Joey, Joey" and "Somebody, Somewhere," subliminally placing Joe and Rosabella within the same emotional frame for the audience. The operatic expectation at this point is for a duet, but Rosabella has no lyrical line to sing here. As Gayle Seaton has observed, after Joe finishes his first phrase an orchestral *agitato* in effect substitutes for a complementary melody line on her part.[37] Following the already interrupted presentation of several phrases is a further angry exchange in accompanied recitative: "He's an *old man*, an *old man*. I don't want him leaning all over me." The power of this short phrase of repeated text from earlier in the scene is guaranteed when "old man" is matched with the identical musical interval (a descending fourth) and rhythm from the first occurrence (see ex. 4.7).

Tony is similarly tongue-tied at Rosabella's touching farewell mini-aria

Example 4.7. (a) "No Home, No Job" (mm. 158–60); (b) "Don't Cry" (mm. 51–56)

Example 4.8. Dramatic minor ninths in "Wanting To Be Wanted" and "I Love Him"

"Please let me tell you that I love you" in act 3, whose introduction seems to be a vestigial echo of the basic motive of an omitted aria of similar intensity in the first act, "Wanting to Be Wanted" (replaced by "Somebody, Somewhere"). Each contains an ear-catching minor ninth leap in a chromatically rich passage. A more precise reuse of the omitted aria's notes, however, occurs early in act 2 in Rosabella's frustrated recitative, "I love him, I love him, / But he treats me like a baby" (see ex. 4.8).

This connective tissue provided by underscoring and motivic repetition in the middle of a number, like the ariosos discussed above, are critically important to the full musical mosaic. Bits of music that are developed in the longer songs or that refer to common musical mottoes are often distinctive on their own and bind the whole work tightly together.

In the opening scene of act 1, Cleo commiserates with Rosabella's complaint about the obnoxious cashier. With the notes for "I know how it is" (ex. 4.9), Loesser creates a distant musical cousin of the famous fate motive from Bizet's *Carmen* (in the bass line below). Although it is an inexact quotation and much less significant as a portent of doom in the Loesser dramatic com-

Example 4.9. "I Know How It Is" and the fate motive (above) from Bizet's *Carmen*

edy than in the Bizet tragedy, the six-fold repetition of those five words and the descending rhythmic arch of the notes provide a musical cue on which to hang Cleo's frustration and fatigue, as well as her sympathy and common-sense advice.[38] When Tony later brings Cleo to Napa as a surprise for Rosabella, this motive recalls their sisterhood of shared hardship at the restaurant. Cleo repeats the identical words in another tête-à-tête with Rosabella about her love for Tony in the final scene of act 2 (just before the climactic duet for Tony and Rosabella). By interweaving Cleo's support with Rosabella's need to take action, Loesser suggests how Cleo's decisiveness can assist Rosabella at a point of uncertainty. Another version of the sentence is spoken rather than sung, when Cleo is completely unable to help her friend. Her being forced to speak this sentence adds a tone of despair entirely in keeping with her sympathy:

> ROSABELLA: What am I going to do? Cleo, what am I going to do [about the pregnancy]?
> CLEO: [*lost*] I don't know how it is. Don't ask me.

Rosabella's affair with Joe occurs offstage, and when the state of their relationship needs further explanation early in act 2—now they are avoiding each other out of shame—a different but still alienated attitude is conveyed by alternating fourths (the "old man" interval noted in ex. 4.7) once again. These bald two-note intervals (played in the orchestra by lower winds and strings) slowly seesaw back and forth for fourteen measures, leading to the words, "Cold and dead, dead and buried, buried and gone." The singers alternate with each other, sometimes harmonizing with the alternat-

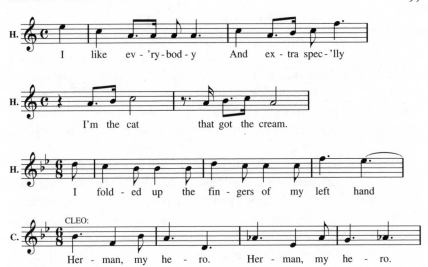

Example 4.10. Rhythmic motives for Cleo and Herman

ing fourths, sometimes not (see the bottom staff beginning in m. 104 of ex. 4.1).

The music for the comic couple, Cleo and Herman, displays shared features too. Both seem to like bouncing dotted notes and rolling long-short figures in compound meter (see the short extracts in ex. 4.10). The sprightliness of Herman's lines in "Standing on the Corner" and "I Like Ev'rybody" match up well with the duo's affirmation of his newly acquired backbone in "I Made a Fist" (act 2, scene 3)—not a literal note repetition but an attitudinal one.

Geoffrey Block has traced leitmotifs for Rosabella and Tony in his book *Enchanted Evenings*, noting Loesser's own feelings on the limits of motivic integration.[39] A detailed parsing of every song and arioso in *The Most Happy Fella* would extend the discussion here far out of proportion to the rest of this book, and it is unnecessary to do so to demonstrate Loesser's prowess. It should be clear by now that the show's strength comes not merely from its sheer quantity of musical material but also from the various internal, organic relationships among the parts and how they are used to further the story. *Where's Charley?* was filled with musical variety, as was *Guys and Dolls*, but no other Loesser show ever attempted quite such a knitting together of so many elements with such effective results.

The Critical Verdict

As almost all of the show's first critics noticed, musical variety can get out of hand, and Loesser was accused of carelessly juxtaposing operatic and Broadway conventions, of yielding to an uncontrolled impulse to add too many different musical parts to the detriment of the whole. What one set of ears hears as a string of refreshing novelties, another perceives as stylistic chaos.[40]

One of the elements that some listeners relish in a musical is, paradoxically, the *absence* of music at several key points—the fact that the music has stopped a while ago and is now about to begin again. In most traditionally structured shows, even those not deemed to be "integrated," the dialogue leading to a song is underscored by a musical introduction. At such a moment, listeners are being told, in effect, to relax and enjoy a break in the action of the plot. Rational thought is not required here. Emotional buttons are about to be pushed that will shift your attention to a different place, usually a reflective or comic one. In shows where the music is more continuous, as in all of grand opera, it is less easy to notice such shifts or to detect their meanings for the action. When so much of the dramatic business is musicalized, plain speech functions somewhat differently as a dramatic device. In *The Most Happy Fella*, *most* of the critical plot turns—Rosabella's first discovery of Tony's mash note, her confusion over Joe's identity, Tony's accident, Rosabella's pregnancy, and Tony's decision to shoot Joe—are all handled in dialogue alone. Yet the lion's share of the action is conveyed purely through music, which bears all the marks of the opera house. Perhaps Loesser was correct to eschew the word "opera" on technical grounds, but his operatic sounds belie him.

Despite issues of genre identification and pacing, Loesser was willing to run the risk of overloading the musical menu in order to fully realize his epic. Its sheer size was touted as a virtue, and Columbia proudly produced its longest original cast recording to date, on six LP sides.[41] Loesser seemed to have achieved a goal that Kurt Weill had articulated a decade before, although there is no evidence that he was aware of Weill's precise formulation: "The special brand of musical entertainment in which I [Weill] have been interested from the start is a sort of 'dramatic musical,' a simple story told in musical terms. . . . This form of theatre has its special attraction for the composer, because it allows him to use a great variety of musical idioms, to write music that is both serious and light, operatic and popular, emotional and sophisticated, orchestral and vocal. Each show of this type has to create its own musical style, its own texture, its own relationship between words and music, because—as a truly integral part of the play—it helps to deepen the emotions and clarify the structure."[42]

Yet the early critical judgment regarding *The Most Happy Fella* was mixed. Among the more negative reviewers, Walter Kerr of the *New York Herald Tribune* declared that "the evening at the Imperial is finally heavy with its own inventiveness, weighted down with the variety and fulsomeness of a genuinely creative appetite. It's as though Mr. Loesser had written two complete musicals—the operetta and the haymaker—on the same simple play and then crammed both into a single structure."[43]

Has this criticism stood the test of time? A closer look at the stylistic details might help us come to grips with the professed disorientation (or at least the dismay) of viewers such as Kerr at the premiere. Some of the confusion no doubt can be attributed to the associations the original audience made with the disparate array of musical sounds. Admittedly, this was far from typical Broadway stuff at the time. As Geoffrey Block has pointed out, however, "Even those who condemn Loesser for selling out cannot fault him for composing songs that are stylistically inappropriate."[44]

Many varieties of Italian music are sung and danced by the Italian characters in situations where ethnicity is expressed. Whether we prefer the tarantellas of the title song, "Abbondanza" and "Sposalizio," the nostalgically tinged barcarolle of "How Beautiful the Days," the quasi recitative of the "Benvenuta" trio, or the romantic, Puccinian heights of "My Heart Is So Full of You," each flows from an easily identifiable Italian source.[45]

The plaintive or wistful songs, such as "Joey, Joey, Joey" and "Don't Cry," match the waywardness of Joe's character. Cleo, who sings about her aching feet ("Ooh! My Feet!) and craves a sit-down job, contrasts neatly with her comic partner, Herman, who *stands* on the corner to watch "all the girls go by." Even the jaunty "Big D," often cited as the number most out of line with the idea of a fully "integrated" and homogeneously etched score, was placed clearly within a particular context. The stage direction for the dance portion of "Big D" reads, "This is a slightly countrified version of a whole gamut of inane specialties peculiar to the late 1920s [when the play is set]." Its fast tempo (half note = 132–138) is modified by the phrase "Dixieland style."[46] (Dixieland jazz burst out of New Orleans and Chicago onto the larger American scene in the 1920s.) If this city-style piece feels a bit askew next to the pastoral romance of Tony and Rosabella, then maybe that was how it was intended to be.

A longer historical perspective reminds us that a pastiche of different musical styles has often been deemed more a virtue than a vice in American musical theater, and works that illustrate the point can be found as far back as the late eighteenth century.[47] Blackface minstrel shows, which arose in the 1840s, knew both racial caricature and opera parody, and they prized novelty and diverse elements as their lifeblood. Variety shows, revues, and vaudeville always sought an ideal combination of contrasting routines, even as contemporary operettas and some musical dramas around 1900 began to work on integrating songs and dialogue.[48] The show-prolonging technique whereby leading singers could add lines and songs of their own choosing was known as "interpolation." This process, often ungoverned by the dictates of composer, director, or conductor, was the norm with most loosely plotted musical comedies as late as the mid-1920s.[49] But, of course, after the innovations of Rodgers and Hammerstein, and much ink spilled about the maturation of the American musical, some confusion was inevitable.

What most critics seem to have missed about *The Most Happy Fella* was its connections with Loesser's earlier musical work, which have already been cited in chapters 2 and 3. When Loesser told Gilbert Millstein of the *New York Times*, "If a song sounds like Verdi, Berlin or Scarlatti, it's entitled to. I don't invent languages. I make use of them," he was only identifying himself with an ancient tradition.[50]

As of 1991, it would seem that audience attitudes had finally caught up with Loesser. The rich variety and operatic slant were no longer troublesome. Kevin Kelly in the *Boston Globe* praised the Goodspeed Opera House revival (in East Haddam, Connecticut, directed by Gerald Gutierriez), writing "[*The Most Happy Fella*] makes you want to stand up and cheer." When this version reopened on Broadway in the following year, *New York Times* critic Frank Rich even bestowed canonical status, placing it "on the hit parade of Broadway classics" such as *Carousel* and *The Music Man*. Speaking in virtual unanimity, the critics found the lead performers Spiro Malas (Tony), Sophie Hayden (Rosabella), Liz Larsen (Cleo), and Scott Waara (Herman) to be touching, soulful, sexy, and funny as required.[51]

Loesser was a great admirer of Marc Blitzstein's opera *Regina* (1949, based on Lillian Hellman's play *The Little Foxes*), and in his program notes for the 1958 Columbia recording, Loesser characterized Blitzstein's accomplishment eloquently. In some measure this also seems a self-reflective state-ment, a judgment that suggests something of Loesser's own aspirations in *The Most Happy Fella*, which he had completed just two years earlier:

> Blitzstein knows that the very purpose of song is to provide extravagant but somehow clear expression for emotional outburst. Time and time again . . . the composer-adaptor has found these outbursts and made them resound unforgettably for me. Some are like bells, others like thunder, some piteous and some sprightly, some viciously angry and others full of heroic triumph. But altogether they form more than a chain or series of illuminations. They make a bright new cloth out of the whole strong fabric of the original play— always true to its meaning, but never giving slavish or pious adherence to the mechanics of it.
>
> . . . with his astounding craftsmanship, he has poured in all his sense of the emotional, his instinct for finding and coloring those exclamation points in human drama (tragic or comic) at which the speaking voice can no longer contain itself and emerges as music. . . . [In the end, the musical work] does not have to reach for the cleverness of "integration." The integrity is in the soul—or the guts or the heart or whatever you want to call it—of [the com-poser] himself.[52]

Intermission in Hollywood

Many of Loesser's loveliest songs never performed in a Broadway musi-cal of his own compilation were written for the 1952 film *Hans Christian An-dersen*. The list includes "The King's New Clothes," "The Inch Worm," "I'm Hans Christian Andersen," "Wonderful Copenhagen," "The Ugly Duck-ling," "Anywhere I Wander," "Thumbelina," and "No Two People."

As early as 1938, Samuel Goldwyn had begun to entertain the idea of making a musical film using stories by the famed Danish children's writer. At first he envisioned Gary Cooper and later Jimmy Stewart in the title role, floated the idea of obtaining music from Rodgers and Hammerstein (who de-clined), and apparently approached George Balanchine to choreograph the dancing. These ideas failed to catch fire, but Goldwyn went ahead and com-missioned treatments from several writers, none of which were found satis-factory until Moss Hart took the job and completed it during three months of work in 1952. Goldwyn's friend Sylvia Fine, a songwriter and the wife of rising star Danny Kaye, recommended her husband for the singing role— observing reasonably that Jimmy Stewart's musical gifts were limited—and hoped to be hired herself to provide the songs. Kaye was signed on but not

Fine, because Hart urged that Loesser be approached to provide the music—his success with *Guys and Dolls* having pushed his fame and name recognition (as well as his commission fees) to new heights.[53] Cost notwithstanding, Goldwyn wanted to produce a spectacular show with a surefire creative team; Loesser willingly interrupted work on *The Most Happy Fella* to return to Hollywood after being promised 10 percent of the net profits in exchange for eight songs.[54] He, Hart, and music director Walter Scharf worked closely to shape the musical segments and place them comfortably within the fictional plot.

Far wide of true biography, the film story includes an invented trade (shoe cobbling) for Andersen and an apprentice named Peter (played by Joey Walsh). Andersen is banished from his hometown in punishment for inducing truancy by schoolchildren distracted with his tall tales. He falls hopelessly in love with a ballerina (played by Renée [Zizi] Jeanmaire, wife of the film's choreographer, Roland Petit), who to his distress is already married to her stern dancing master (Farley Granger).[55] Finally Hans, although thwarted in love, succeeds in bringing his tales to the attention of enthusiastic patrons. He and his loyal assistant head home, where we know that soon shoemaking will be put aside permanently in favor of creative writing.

The syrupy plot, though drawing critical scorn, left juvenile audiences unfazed. The songs perfectly captured the show's innocent and sentimental mood, succeeding with youngsters and adults alike. Having been expertly marketed via television segments—featuring stars as different as Dinah Shore, George Burns and Gracie Allen, and Edward R. Murrow—in addition to recordings by Frank and Lynn Loesser of "The Ugly Duckling," "The Inch Worm," and "The King's New Clothes" (for MGM Records), the film was released in November 1952, in time to attract huge holiday crowds. A restive Danish press and foreign ministry at first protested such an entirely fanciful depiction of their national author, but they were placated by Goldwyn's publicity machine, which touted the film as not strictly biographical "but [rather] a fairy tale about this great spinner of fairy tales."[56]

The film grossed six million dollars in its initial run and netted six Academy Award nominations, including one for "Thumbelina" as best song of the year (which lost, however, to the title song from *High Noon*.)[57] It eventually ranked as Goldwyn's third-largest career moneymaker (trailing only *The Best Years of Our Lives* in 1946 and *Guys and Dolls* in 1955).

Most of the songs were multiply recorded. Frank and Lynn Loesser de-

lighted their own children with home performances and made private recordings of "Wonderful Copenhagen" and "No Two People."[58]

The prize for most deftly worked lyric among the songs belongs to "The
King's New Clothes." Hans begins his story in direct speech ("One day, two
swindlers came to see the king to sell him what they *said* was a magic suit
of clothes. . . .) which soon turns into a dramatic and rhythmic announce-
ment ("Isn't it grand! Isn't it fine!") and finally into a rollicking melody that
plays repeatedly on the word "altogether" through five varied refrains, set
off by more spoken verses, comprising more than 100 separate lines of text.
("The suit of clothes is altogether, / But altogether, it's altogether / The most
remarkable suit of clothes / A tailor ever made. . . . / The king is in the altogether . . . / He's altogether as naked as / The day that he was born. / And it's
altogether too chilly a morn!")

The two most musically ingenious songs, "The Inch Worm" and "No
Two People," are both duets. The first combines two contrasting metrical
patterns in a manner rarely found in popular songs: while the children at
school recite their sums ("Two and two are four, four and four are eight")
in a strict duple pulse (alternating strong and weak beats), Hans sings a
slow triple-time waltz (strong-weak-weak) pattern as he observes the insect-
bearing marigold just outside the schoolhouse window ("Inch worm, inch
worm, measuring the marigold"). The steady accompaniment and standard
harmony (which sticks close to the basic chords in the key of F major) allow
listeners to enjoy the rhythmic play simultaneously with a simple, ingratiating tune.

"No Two People" is an economically constructed double song blending
strings of skipping triplets (on the words "Never before and never again could
anything more romantic and beautiful . . .") with descending open fifths,
echoing back and forth between the parts (labeled "He" and "She" in the
published score) on the words "been so [in love]." Never at a loss for rhymes,
Loesser simultaneously summons and pokes fun at the oldest of romantic
clichés and finally tops them: "No two people have ever mooned such a
moon / Juned such a June / spooned such a spoon / . . . / been so in tune /
as my macaroon and I."

Not usually given to false modesty, Loesser dismissed "Thumbelina," despite its Academy Award nomination and audience-pleasing capacity, as an
embarrassment best forgotten, "not a real song." But it features some of the
same directness that made "Praise the Lord and Pass the Ammunition" a

runaway hit a decade before.[59] The exceptionally plain melody consists of a
four-note descending scale line treated sequentially in a series of brief, equal-
length phrases. With a bone-simple rhythm, it is easy to sing along with. The
limited range of notes repeated in short patterns reinforces the miniature
metaphor for a thumb-sized girl and her friends.

One of the most attractive features of the songs in *Hans Christian Andersen* is their psychological aptness. Loesser was assigned to write tunes that
could be performed by and for children, and he succeeded precisely in that
deceptively difficult task. All the stories chosen by Hart and Loesser for the
film are, in effect, therapeutic fables, aimed at assuaging common childish
fears: being freakishly different ("The Ugly Duckling"), too small for your
age ("Thumbelina"), publicly embarrassed ("The King's New Clothes"), or
just lonely and needy ("Anywhere I Wander"). Of course, adults are free to
appreciate them as well. But because the target audience is children, adults
perhaps can accept the sentiments with less defensiveness. In any case, we all
want to like the songs because they make us feel better. They are completely
unpretentious and yet still cleverly worked out. The composer's genial salute to Copenhagen rounds off the set with a toast in praise of comfortable
camaraderie. Clinking and drinking "neath [the city's] tavern light," we are
always among friends young and old. "Wonderful Copenhagen" serves up a
splendid nightcap.

Sooner or later it was bound to occur to someone that these winning
songs, performed so successfully by Danny Kaye on-screen, would be more
than adequate to supply a staged musical comedy shaped roughly along the
same plot lines as the film. On December 17, 1974, the London Palladium
hosted just such a show, prepared for the stage by actor Tommy Steele in
the title role, assisted by writer Beverley Cross and producer Harold Field-
ing. Called simply *Hans Andersen*, this posthumous Frank Loesser musical
never made it to America, although it registered well with English audiences
for more than three years. Marvin Laird wrote two new songs ("Happy Days"
and "Ecclesiasticus"). Loesser's "Truly Loved" from *Pleasures and Palaces*
(see chapter 6) was also added to the mix.[60]

CHAPTER 5

Another Way to Write a Broadway Hit:
How to Succeed in Business Without Really Trying

Now I hear it! I hear it! I hear it!
Suddenly there is music in the sound of your name . . .
What a crescendo!
—"ROSEMARY," FROM *HOW TO SUCCEED IN BUSINESS WITHOUT REALLY TRYING*, 1961

W HEN FEUER AND MARTIN FIRST PRESENTED LOESSER WITH THE
idea of deriving a musical from Shepherd Mead's guidebook for
the young man on the make, *How to Succeed in Business Without Really Trying: A Dastard's Guide to Fame and Fortune*, he found it ab-
surd as a theater vehicle.[1] But as with *Guys and Dolls*, Abe Burrows came to
the rescue. *How to Succeed* succeeded first with Burrows, who realized that
Loesser—as a skillful dealmaker himself—was ideally placed both to sympathize with and satirize big business onstage. Mead's book provides a long
list of ingredients—in the form of scenarios, roles, helpful hints, and sample dialogues—that only needed to be arranged properly to create a plausible story line. Several character names (J. Pierrepont Finch, J. B. Biggley,
Bratt, Gatch, Womper, Bud Frump); Biggley's alma mater, Old Ivy, and its
rival's mascot, the Chipmunk; the wickets business; on-the-job situations described in chapters entitled "How to Apply for a Job" and "How to Rise from
the Mail Room"; and the general tone of happy-go-lucky cynicism all come
straight out of Mead's book.[2]

Burrows also brought his additional experience gained as a Broadway in-

The "Coffee Break" number for the chorus of *How to Succeed in Business Without Really Trying*. Billy Rose Theatre Division, The New York Public Library for the Performing Arts, Astor, Lenox and Tilden Foundations.

sider during the decade since *Guys and Dolls*. He had worked with Robert Morse and understood the young, rubber-faced actor's star appeal. He could easily imagine Morse in the role of Pierrepont Finch. Morse had recently enjoyed good reviews for his supporting spots in *Say, Darling* (1958) and a musical version of Eugene O'Neill's play *Ah, Wilderness!* entitled *Take Me Along* (1959).

As Burrows tells it in his autobiography, what he and Loesser puzzled over most were the central *musical* issues: How was it even conceivable for clerks and stenographers to dance and sing during a typical office day? Where was the humor? Where was the hook for the audience? Loesser finally proposed a solution with the song "Coffee Break," not part of Mead's book. "We knew that during a coffee break everyone in the office relaxes. . . . Then Frank, who was a coffee addict, said, 'Hey, how about if somebody goofed and there's no coffee in the machine?' Then he came up with a sad

Example 5.1. Basic motives for the orchestra (a) and singers (b) in mm. 4–7 of "Coffee Break"

song written in appropriately Latin rhythm that said something like, 'If I can't take my coffee break, something inside me dies.' It was a helluva number and suddenly we saw daylight."[3]

Bob Fosse also saw the kinetic possibilities for original choreography in a set of jerky, angular moves that parodied buttoned-down, uptight office attitudes. The idea for a Latin number at the mention of coffee harks back to the Brazilian showstopper "Pernambuco" in *Where's Charley?* (when the conversation turned to the home country of Charley's mysterious aunt). But rather than serving as a plot-stopping, act-ending tour de force, Loesser and Fosse's "Coffee Break" turns robotic office slaves into live-wired bodies, their caffeine-deprived condition depicted wittily by the combination of two jumpy, accented rhythmic fragments, one for the singers, one for the orchestra, and both for the dancers (see ex. 5.1).

With this breakthrough achieved in one number, Loesser agreed to join Burrows, who had already contracted to write and direct the show. Of course, returning to work with his old friend was partly an act of homecoming for Loesser, since it conjured up the happy days of *Guys and Dolls*. As Burrows suspected, the script also pushed Loesser to draw on his personal knowledge of the business world. Having started Frank Music Corporation in 1950 and later Frank Productions in 1960, he had a well of experience to tap in the service of parody and humor. Yet without the catalytic presence of Burrows, the project would never have gotten off the ground. Burrows relished satire and possessed a gift for comic writing. Left to himself, Loesser seems generally to have preferred romantic plots with as many opportunities for emotional music as possible. For *How to Succeed*, the Loesser–Burrows chemistry was just right.[4]

As it eventually developed, *How to Succeed* skewered a host of inhabitants of early 1960s corporate culture. As reviewer Howard Taubman described it, "Not a bypath in the honored folkways of big business avoids a going over. The mailroom, plans and systems, president, chairman of the board, the executive conference, secretaries, stenographers, cleaning women, the coffee break and even the executive washroom are sources of anything but innocent merriment."[5] Greedy opportunists, philandering bosses, husband-hunting female secretaries, craven yes-men, and work-averse drones all come in for lampooning.

Faceless corporate drudges hardly seem apt objects for happy musical treatment. But since at least the time of Molière, social and occupational climbers have been the butts for farces in the *How to Succeed* vein. Burrows and Loesser, once convinced that their concept would work, proved inventive and intrepid. Their touch was light enough to hit the mark and suitable for a public familiar with daily office life. The story was perfect for the time and the audience. Mocking but not bitter, it was a send-up of patriarchal business mores that found fun with everything from nepotism ("The Company Way") to sexism ("A Secretary Is Not a Toy") to old school ties ("Grand Old Ivy"). Stuart Ostrow, who served as Loesser's assistant during the making of *How to Succeed*, credibly argues that "A Secretary Is Not a Toy," with its protofeminist message, is less a political statement than it is a Frank Loesser valentine to his loyal assistants, office staff, typists, copyists, and clerks. Perhaps it is enough to say that Loesser's basic decency shaped this song and its companions in a pointed but unspiteful way.[6]

In sync with this attitude, the book adduces just enough sympathy for the scheming protagonist, J. Pierrepont Finch, to make everybody feel good about the outcome. Rather than despising Finch for his shameless climb up the corporate ladder, the audience, much like his destined mate Rosemary, find his approach so endearing and whimsical that one can only laugh at the effrontery of it all. (Although Burrows lifted a lot from Mead's manual, much of the show's comic libretto was developed from a play script by Jack

Weinstock and Willie Gilbert that had come into the hands of Feuer and Martin.[7])

Besides the need to find humor in the business world, Burrows was also challenged by Loesser to create a love interest. For this the character of Rosemary, who does not exist either in Mead's book or in Weinstock and Gilbert's play, was created by Burrows. As it evolved, the show finally combined several overlapping elements: a solid comic plot, a young and appealing (though slightly odd) romantic couple, a well-turned satirical script, some barbed social commentary, clever and sharp-edged choreography, and swinging, up-to-date music.

The score accounted in no small way for the accolades that How to Succeed garnered, including the Pulitzer Prize. Loesser's curiosity once again had led him in a direction that no one could have predicted. But neither his musical talent nor his intuition for musical and dramatic continuity failed him once the basic scenario had been fixed.[8]

Satire with a Heart of Gold

How To Succeed was Loesser's first show since his military days to use a modern setting and the first to depend on satire. Its appeal lies partly in the critical distance that satire creates. The chance to work in parodic mode probably helped to capture Loesser's attention for the project, since it represented a new challenge. The satirical target—day-to-day life in the business world—was growing gradually larger as corporations prospered in the postwar era. Billy Wilder's popular film The Apartment (1960) began what would become a string of movies and shows mocking corporate ethics; it featured Jack Lemmon as a harried insurance clerk who gets ahead by lending his apartment as a "trysting-place for his philandering superiors."[9] Several Broadway productions followed How to Succeed in picking up on the business theme. But such shows as I Can Get It for You Wholesale (1962), What Makes Sammy Run? (1964), and Promises, Promises (1968), a musical based on The Apartment, failed to retain the light touch of How to Succeed.

Integrating Shepherd Mead's occupational advice within a musical comedy remained a challenge. Burrows recalled earlier contacts and conversations with businessmen as part of the process of plot construction; Loesser, for his part, hewed to his penchant for romantic and emotional scenes and insisted that the role of Rosemary be enhanced as much as possible.[10]

As it was finally developed, the story unfolds with Finch washing windows on a scaffold and reading the "How to Succeed in Business" manual. He is literally on the outside, looking into the World Wide Wickets corporate headquarters and dreaming big. He sings the title song and then contrives to bump into the boss, J. B. Biggley, but remains unnoticed until secretary Rosemary Pilkington, who is instantly charmed by Finch, strikes up a conversation. Through a misunderstanding about his relationship to the boss, he is hired to work in the mailroom. Rosemary is impressed and dreams aloud about married life with a successful young executive. Burrows described "Happy to Keep His Dinner Warm" as "a pathetic, masochistic love song" despite its pleasant tune.[11]

> Oh, to be loved / By a man I respect
> To bask in the glow / Of his perfectly understandable neglect!

Once inside the door, Finch schemes to rise through the ranks on a fast track. The equally ambitious Bud Frump, the boss's nephew, suspects Finch's motives but is temporarily distracted by his seeming goodwill. Frump and the office workers sing and dance about their caffeine addiction when the coffee machine breaks down:

> If I can't make three daily trips
> Where shining shrine benignly drips,
> And taste cardboard between my lips,
> Something within me dies . . .

Finch pledges his loyalty to the company on the advice of his mailroom supervisor, Mr. Twimble; they both sing "The Company Way." In a distant echo of Sir Joseph Porter ("the ruler of the Queen's Navee" in Gilbert and Sullivan's *HMS Pinafore*), they agree that utter deference to the wishes of one's superiors is the best way to keep your job. Twimble begins:

> When I joined this firm
> As a brash young man,
> Well, I said to myself,
> "Now, brash young man,
> Don't get any ideas."
> Well, I stuck to that —
> And I haven't had one in years!

With his first big promotion — he becomes a vice-president's assistant — Finch and his colleagues receive more good advice from Mr. Bratt, the per-

sonnel director: "A Secretary Is Not a Toy," a line taken directly from Mead's
original guidebook.

> A secretary is not to be
> Used for play therapy.
> If that's what you're doing,
> You're quite misconstruing
> Her function while in your employ.
> No, a secretary is not,
> Definitely not, a toy.

After work, Rosemary and Finch, observed by her best friend, Smitty (a
woman), imagine romantic dinner dates in parallel soliloquies, "Been a
Long Day." Waiting for the elevator, they sing in a back-and-forth conversational style with short lines reminiscent of "Baby, It's Cold Outside," while
Smitty acts as interlocutor:

> SMITTY: Now she's thinking—
> ROSEMARY: I wish he were more of a flirt.
> SMITTY: And he's thinking—
> FINCH: I guess a little flirting won't hurt.
> SMITTY: Now she's thinking—
> ROSEMARY: For dinner we could meet.
> SMITTY: And he's thinking—
> FINCH: We both have got to eat.
> SMITTY: Then she says—
> ROSEMARY: [*spoken*] Achoo!
> SMITTY: [*sung*] And he says—
> FINCH: [*spoken*] Gesundheit!
> ROSEMARY: [*spoken*] Thank you.
> FINCH: [*sung*] Well, it's been a long day.
> ALL: [*sung*] Well, it's been a long, been a long . . . day.

Loesser prided himself on being able to invent winning and catchy music about a range of unpromising subjects: sore feet, dripping faucets, noisy
neighbors, caterpillars, and elevators (the "Elevator Dance" occurs later in
this show). In its homely, familiar subject, "Been a Long Day" is quintessential Loesser. Surely the gist of the conversational exchanges could have been
handled by dialogue alone or even by spoken soliloquies. Yet Loesser the
composer saw the opportunity to offer a novel, inventive solution to a classic dramatic challenge: how to reveal the inner feelings and motivations of

two key characters as they begin to fall in love at the same time and the same place.

The effectiveness of this number rests in the idea, intuitively understood by viewers, that all the *musical* lines sung are unheard by the others onstage, whereas the inserted *spoken* lines are audible to all. Loesser had used a similar technique in the "Cold and Dead" and "I Don't Like That Dame" duets in *The Most Happy Fella*, but this midpoint between spoken dialogue and a full-blown, through-sung duet has many other precedents. Lorenz Hart had explored a peculiar kind of rhyming dialogue in the Al Jolson film musical *Hallelujah, I'm a Bum* (1933), and Rodgers and Hammerstein's famous "Twin Soliloquies" for Emile and Nellie in *South Pacific* (1949) exemplified the idea of "unheard" simultaneous songs. The music of this trio is briefly reprised with new lyrics for boss Biggley, Hedy LaRue (a new hire at the company and Biggley's paramour), and Frump, who has just overheard their compromising conversation. Biggley instantly promotes Frump to buy his silence. All three conclude, "It's been a long, been a long, been a long day."

Early the next morning, Finch is discovered by Biggley asleep at his desk, apparently having spent the night in the office hard at work (since empty coffee cups and office papers are strewn about to create this impression). He further ingratiates himself by humming a college fight song, implying to Biggley that they share the same alma mater. Biggley approves of old school ties, of course, and they launch into "Grand Old Ivy," a waggish parody boosting the home-team Groundhogs against the rival Chipmunks.

Finch is soon promoted to vice-president of plans and systems, and Rosemary becomes secretary to another vice-president. To impress Finch and the others at a welcoming reception, she buys a designer gown as "love insurance," only to discover a string of other female partiers with the same, obviously mass-produced "Paris Original." Meanwhile, Frump once again schemes to put Finch out of favor with Biggley, but Rosemary rescues him, and Finch, finally love-struck, proposes marriage to her. In the final scene of act 1, all appears to be going well until Finch interrupts himself amid a passionate embrace with Rosemary. He needs to call a painter whose job it is to inscribe the gold letters for J. PIERREPONT FINCH on his new office door. Rosemary is dismayed at Finch's confirmed self-centeredness, and Frump once again vows to quash the upstart.

The first act contains the normal amount of musical material for postwar Broadway shows (twelve major songs), and it leaves the audience as most

Rudy Vallee (Biggley) and Robert Morse (Finch) celebrate the boss's alma mater, "Grand Old Ivy." Billy Rose Theatre Division, The New York Public Library for the Performing Arts, Astor, Lenox and Tilden Foundations.

comedies do: with a sense of sympathy with the main characters, feeling a degree of satisfaction about what has happened so far but also aware of unfinished business or clouds on the horizon.[12] But How to Succeed's formulaic elements were unobtrusive, allowing the novel features to stand out: the sharp, angular dance moves, the broad-brush acting gestures of the principals (especially Finch, Frump, and Biggley), and Robert Randolph's two-dimensional, line-drawn, flat-colored sets, their exaggerated, cartoon qualities according well with the show's satirical style.

As the second act begins, Rosemary has resigned her job and broken off her engagement with Finch. Smitty and their fellow office workers beg her to reconsider, noting, "it's not a matter of money. He's a vice-president. That makes him automatically a prince. . . . so you are automatically a Cinderella." They sing encouragingly,

> You're a real live fairy tale,
> A symbol divine.
> So, if not for your own sake, please,
> Darling, for mine,
> Don't, don't, don't, Cinderella, darling,
> Don't turn down the Prince. . . .

To keep his new job, Finch needs a "big idea" to boost the company's image and sales. Frump, pretending to be helpful, suggests that Finch pitch Biggley a giveaway scheme, involving a "treasure hunt" for hidden stock certificates, which Frump knows Biggley already hates. In the next scene, Hedy prepares to walk out on Biggley and World Wide Wickets if he cannot find her a job suited to her talents. Together they sing "Love from a Heart of Gold." Finch enlists Hedy to sell his treasure hunt idea to Biggley. Meanwhile, Frump and the other junior executives are bent on stopping Finch once and for all. Finch stiffens his resolve by singing a pep talk to himself, "I Believe in You." At the big meeting, Biggley agrees to Finch's plan, provided that Hedy is chosen as the "Treasure Hunt Girl" for a national television broadcast. The plan fails miserably, the company's offices are ransacked for the hidden stocks, and Finch is fingered as the scapegoat. But Wally Womper, World Wide Wickets' board chairman, comes to Finch's aid. As it happens, both are former window washers, common men at heart, who have worked their way up from the bottom. To get Biggley off the hook, Finch reveals to Womper that the treasure hunt idea had originated with Bud Frump, but he urges the CEO to show mercy:

[*sung verse*] One man may seem incompetent,
Another not make sense,
While others look like
Quite a waste of company expense.
They need a brother's leadership,
So please don't do them in.
Remember mediocrity
Is not a mortal sin.

[*chorus*] We're in the brotherhood of man . . .

All join in on the spirited refrain. But Womper has one more surprise. He has decided to retire as chairman of the board and take a round-the-world honeymoon trip with his new wife—Hedy LaRue. He appoints Finch as his successor, provided that Finch's *wife* approves of the plan. Rosemary is finally able to seize her opportunity.

ROSEMARY: Darling, I don't care if you work in the mailroom, or you're Chairman of the Board, or you're President of the United States. I love you!
FINCH: Say that again.
ROSEMARY: I love you.
FINCH: No, before that.

Still president of his company but clearly worried about his new boss, Biggley screams, "Take a wire to the White House. Watch out!" as the full cast reprises "The Company Way."

The Production

The discovery of an actor who could simultaneously embody both a shameless opportunist and a charming naïf helped the creators envision a winning protagonist. Robert Morse's personality did not come out of central casting, and virtually all the reviewers recognized the remarkable skills that fitted him for the part. His body language was simply over the top. Walter Kerr, in his first-night rave for the *New York Herald Tribune*, said it best:

Mr. Morse is also charming—in an alarming sort of way—when he isn't so sure of himself. His sudden look of deep seal-like shame when he realizes a girl has hooked him for lunch; his habit of using his hands as though he'd skip rope if he only had a rope; his practice of seeming to try to shake water out of his ear when a damsel has an undue effect on him—all of these are graphic studies in the nature of man, pre-coordinated man. Whether he is darting around high on a windy penthouse or taking off from the horizon as in a very spiritual movie, he is a magnificent (if cunning) shambles. Of course, Mr. Morse is spastic. But they'll probably never be able to cure it, and he'll go right on being as funny as he is at the 46th Street.[13]

The physical demands placed on Morse—or that he placed on himself—night after night impressed audiences and critics alike. Abe Burrows proudly recalled the backstage visit he and Morse received postperformance from the quarterback and wide receiver of the New York Giants, Y. A. Tittle and Del Shofner, who were also bowled over by Morse's feats of physical dexterity.[14]

While adept at providing music for both romantic scenes and comic set pieces (where a single actor performs a clever lyric), Loesser had never before tried to musicalize an almost entirely satirical script. He understood that all elements, including the dance numbers and acting gestures, had to fit the edgy style to consolidate the overall effect. This comedy required arched eyebrows and bent limbs in every scene from all the actors. His prodigious musical production for his three earlier hits strongly favored a familiar sort of choreography, despite some unusual moments (such as the gamblers' sewer scene in *Guys and Dolls*). But the question Loesser faced in *How to Succeed* was, How should music behave so as to enhance the satire without finally becoming spastic or just chaotic?

Films have traditionally made comedic music in a manner that film historians refer to as mickey-mousing, in which the physical gestures of actors or drawn animated figures (such as Mickey Mouse) are accompanied by obvious sound effects: a "bam" to go with a punch in the face, a "swoosh" to signal a slip on a banana peel, and so forth. Interestingly enough, several critics have referred to the "cartoonish" features of *How to Succeed*: a term useful to describe the actors' exaggerated gestures, the burlesque humor (notably with the appearance of the buxom Hedy as President Biggley's girlfriend), other stereotypical character types, and comic scenes related to vaudeville and circuslike antics. A cartoonish allusion could also be seen in Finch's entry-level job as a window washer in the World Wide Wickets company, which takes a page from the silent-film scenarios of Charlie Chaplin and Buster Keaton.[15]

Certainly part of Rudy Vallee's appeal in the Biggley role as passionate alumnus of "Grand Old Ivy" lay in the audience's knowledge of his own earlier collegiate song fame at Yale and the University of Maine and his subsequent status as the one of the first crooners during the 1920s and '30s. Music

to exaggerate what was already known to most of the audience would naturally stoke laughter in this cartoonlike setup.

Loesser's music goes far beyond action mimicry, but the need to coordinate and magnify the principal points of the plot and the physical gestures of
the actors required a variety of sounds: full-fledged dance patterns, music to
enhance comic poses or regular stage movement for the actors, and melodic
material or vamps that would provide appropriate background sound during
scenes of general bustle or random activity. Most of this musical filler was
absorbed unconsciously by the audience, but its effect was fully appreciated.
Once the other creative talent, but especially Loesser and Fosse, were convinced that Burrows's book had comic substance, love interest, and musical
possibilities, they jumped into the project with gusto. The casting of Morse,
Vallee, Virginia Martin, Bonnie Scott, and Charles Nelson Reilly confirmed
everyone's best hopes for what could be accomplished with a diversely talented and (except for Vallee) young cast.

The Music

The music of How to Succeed follows the familiar Broadway model of
the period, with more songs in the first act than the second and a liberal
number of reprises throughout to ensure continuity (see table 5.1). The published piano-vocal score includes twenty numbers in the first act with nine
principal songs, and seventeen numbers in the second act with four major
songs plus an extended dance number. Each of the fourteen major pieces
has its own personality, yet all contribute to the plot and action in a distinctive manner. The other musical numbers for the most part consist of music
for scene changes, background, or fanfares. How to Succeed, while not needing the reflective, emotion-laden recitatives or poignant melodic outcries
indispensable to musical dramas, nevertheless was crafted to fit the action in
microscopic detail. This was the essence of its novelty.

Loesser's return to a simpler, more traditional Broadway song sequence
should not be understood as a retreat to formula, but rather as an attempt to
maintain continuity while neither overwhelming the action nor slowing its
pace. Comedy relies more than drama on quick, efficient pacing. Extended
breaks in the action for reflection or expansive emotional statement would
have doomed the effort.

Each of the show's major songs falls into one of three musical catego-
ries, defined by what could be called "rhythmic attitude." The first of these

Table 5.1. Principal Songs in *How to Succeed in Business Without Really Trying* (as listed in 1961 program)

Song	Performer(s)
Act 1	
Overture	
1. "How to Succeed in Business . . ."	Finch
2. "Happy to Keep His Dinner Warm"	Rosemary
3. "Coffee Break"	Frump, Smitty, Dancers, Chorus
4. "The Company Way"	Twimble, Frump
5. "The Company Way" (reprise)	Dancers, Chorus
6. "A Secretary Is Not a Toy"	Bratt, Dancers, Chorus
7. "Been a Long Day"	Finch, Rosemary, Smitty
8. "Been a Long Day"	Biggley, Hedy, Frump
9. "Grand Old Ivy"	Biggley, Finch
10. "Grand Old Ivy" (reprise)	Biggley, Finch
11. "Paris Original"	Rosemary, Girls
12. "Rosemary"	Finch, Rosemary
Finaletto	Finch, Rosemary, Frump
Act 2	
13. "Cinderella, Darling"	Smitty, Girls
14. "Happy to Keep His Dinner Warm" (reprise)	Rosemary
15. "Love from a Heart of Gold"	Hedy, Biggley
16. "I Believe in You"	Men, Finch
17. "The Yo Ho Ho"	Dancers
18. "I Believe in You" (reprise)	Rosemary
19. "Brotherhood of Man"	Finch, Miss Jones, Men
Finale	All

attitudes consists of a steady beat and meter, a strict tempo, a continuous line of melody notes, and a straightforward optimism in the lyric. "Happy to Keep His Dinner Warm," "A Secretary Is Not a Toy," and "Grand Old Ivy" clearly fit into this category. One almost irresistibly wants to move to the beat of these songs. They are dance numbers in spirit, if not in fact. ("Happy to Keep His Dinner Warm," while not choreographed, is marked with a dance tempo.)

The second attitude reflects a more jazz-inspired edginess. They are also dance-oriented, but the beats and rhythm patterns here are casually synco-pated (that is, musical accents often land in unexpected places). More rests interrupt the flow in the melodic lines, and steady foundational bass-note patterns (ostinatos) impart a driving feeling. "Been a Long Day," "Coffee

Break," "The Company Way," and "Brotherhood of Man" belong in this category.

The third attitude can be characterized as broadly romantic, but also
tinged with overdone nostalgia. The melodies of this type employ a relaxed
tempo, have fewer and longer notes, and, because their rhythms are less busy,
they induce a release of tension. The type was an early Loesser specialty.
"Rosemary," "Paris Original," "Love from a Heart of Gold," and "Cinderella, Darling" share these qualities. Gayle Seaton suggests that "Love from
a Heart of Gold" "adopts the style of a 1940s movie-musical love song."[16]
"Rosemary," with its false authority owed to an obviously borrowed classical quotation, enhances the singers' and audience's imagination of ideal
love. Finch's lyric in the final section of the song, "Rosemary, just imagine
if we kissed / What a crescendo . . ." is followed by nine measures of Grieg's
A-Minor Piano Concerto before he completes the rhyming couplet with the
words, "not to be missed." Such a sudden and dramatic extension rings true
with the general thrust of the show, calling attention to Finch's comic ego-
centrism and grandiosity.

The centerpiece song, "I Believe in You," exhibits traits from all of these
attitudes, but its overall vocabulary is closely related to the other ballads. By
employing this family-resemblance method of songwriting, Loesser avoided
the need to invoke explicit melodic quotations, transformations, or leitmotifs
as we have seen in *The Most Happy Fella*. His approach was validated by observations from the opening-night reviewers, such as Richard Watts Jr., who
declared in the *New York Post* that "it is possible that Frank Loesser's score
lacks any outstanding hit song, but it is invariably gay, charming and tuneful,
and it has the enormous virtue of fitting in perfectly with the spirit and style
of the book's satire. In his lyrics, Mr. Loesser is characteristically bright and
ingenious, and in the right mood. It is this *fitting together* [emphasis added]
of all of the parts, from the brisk imaginative dance numbers to the excellent
settings, that is the distinguishing feature of 'How [to Succeed in Business],'
and gives it such a comforting feeling of all being well."[17]

As with the songs for *Guys and Dolls* and *The Most Happy Fella*, Loesser
built his melodies in *How to Succeed* on the normal speech accents of the
most important words. For example, "Happy to Keep His Dinner Warm,"
Rosemary's first solo in the show, a hymn to self-sacrifice at the altar of do-
mesticity, presents a commonplace line of English text with the musical
stresses matched precisely to the way in which the line might be spoken in
direct conversation (see ex. 5.2).

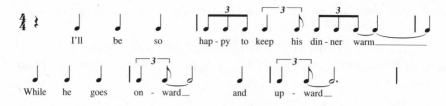

Example 5.2. The conversational rhythm of "Happy to Keep His Dinner Warm"

The biggest musical difference between *How to Succeed* and *The Most Happy Fella* is represented by the far jazzier idiom of the more recent show. Jazz elements had not loomed large in 1940s or early '50s Broadway musicals, but much had changed by 1961. Through the efforts of figures such as Dizzy Gillespie, Charlie Parker, and Dave Brubeck, jazz was being reconfigured in the mainstream American public consciousness as a progressive idiom, appealing to wider audiences than its earlier manifestations as a marginalized black cultural product (for instance, in the New Orleans–style improvisations of Louis Armstrong or Bessie Smith's searing blues) and as a dance phenomenon (expressed in the swing craze of the mid-1930s, spearheaded by Benny Goodman). The highly successful marketing of the long-playing 33 rpm vinyl disc also had increased audiophiles' opportunities to hear extended improvisational passages on home sound systems, since the new format allowed a single recording to last more than twenty minutes.

In other words, contemporary jazz in the late 1950s was becoming "hip," "cool," and widely accessible. A small but growing group of middle-class whites began to savor the technical complexities of black bebop and became at least superficially familiar with the racial argot of big-city black neighborhoods.[18] The musical codes of jazz signaled not just urbanity but sophistication, and they began to appear in record stores, at the movies, and on the radio. In an era when rock 'n' roll was a mere infant, jazz—or at least a jazz-flavored popular style—represented the height of fashion and could boast cultivated aficionados who welcomed its strains into their living rooms, private clubs, and even concert halls.[19]

Leonard Bernstein's *West Side Story* burst on the Broadway scene in 1957, followed by a popular movie version in 1961, many regional and international productions, and substantial sales of the original cast recording.[20] Bernstein's use of several syncopated and Latin elements expanded audiences' ideas of what the urban soundscape was like. The show confirmed both the danger and the vitality of the big city by providing an energetic and rhythmic sonic backdrop for Tony, Maria, Anita, and the other Sharks and Jets.

That elements of jazz expression should appear in a satire about American urban business life seems logical in retrospect, especially coming from a composer who had so smoothly worked to assimilate many earlier musical idioms into his shows. Even before the overture to *How to Succeed* is concluded—with its last fifty measures marked "Fast Swing in 4"—any alert listener will suspect that syncopated tunes and jagged offbeats are going to be actively shaping the musical textures to come. Moreover, it serves multiple purposes in the show. Jazz is both background for the bustle of city business life and also a sly counterpoint to the stodgy and rigid old regime doomed to give way before the ingenious younger generation epitomized by J. Pierrepont Finch.

The play's musical vocabulary also suggests several other musical markers, whether jazz-inflected or not, denoting the urban setting: a higher density of dissonant clashing chords, chords formed with stacks of fourths rather than thirds (stacks of fourths were also assuming more prominence in jazz chord voicings at the time[21]), more twists and turns in melodies to include notes not in the major scale, and the frequent presence of ostinatos. The beginning of the title song (see ex. 5.3) features such an ostinato of a sort often found in Latin dance numbers (with 3 + 3 + 2 eighth-note groups in the bass).

The importance of dance movement and rhythm is reflected elsewhere in the score for *How to Succeed*, with expressive terms borrowed directly from dance tempos: "Happy to Keep His Dinner Warm" is an "Easy Schottische," an old-fashioned round dance that bespeaks a traditional sentiment; "Coffee Break" is directed to be done in an "Ominous Cha-Cha Tempo"; and "A Secretary Is Not a Toy" was famously converted into a compound meter (12/8)—four moderately paced triplets per measure—for a "Soft Shoe Tempo," suggested by Bob Fosse to go with a production number for all the secretaries in the office. A "light swing" tempo backed by another ostinato and orchestrated with modern jazz instrumental colors is invoked for "Been a Long Day."

"The Company Way" also seems to be marked by a breezy rhythmic swagger. The basic pattern of the song emphasizes two moderately quick beats per measure, but with so much flexibility and syncopation on the shorter notes within the measures that it gives the impression of being made

Example 5.3. "How to Succeed in Business Without Really Trying" (opening mm. 1–7)

up on the spot. We might wonder whether it was based on a loose set of general directions, rather than being sung precisely "as written." A listener cannot tell at first by ear alone—and that casualness may be the root of its attractiveness and function. "The Company Way" fundamentally represents the subject of its lyric, the fawning flexibility of World Wide Wickets employees (Twimble, Frump, and chorus) and their conformity to shifting corporate demands. The music itself is also pliant, which is to say easily altered or modified. Indeed, as a musical metaphor it is the perfect parodic tune (ex. 5.4).

The final second-act number, "Brotherhood of Man," with a similarly flexible rhythmic line, meter, and speed, exhibits a parallel vein of aroused

Example 5.4. "The Company Way" (eight measures at rehearsal C)

good feeling. Less snide than "The Company Way" (in which a duo sings, "Your brain is a company brain. / The company washed it, and now I can't complain"), "Brotherhood of Man" invokes a religious phrase in its title to justify the good old boys' pecking order. The insincerity of its claim is not hard to ferret out. After all, the chorus sings, despite our different clubs (Elks, Shriners, and Diners), we are all members of "a benevolent brotherhood. . . . Your lifelong membership is free. . . . Oh, aren't you proud to be / in that fraternity?" Loesser knew the theatrical effect of this kind of delivery, having previously used such intensified quasi-religious metaphors with great success for "Make a Miracle" (*Where's Charley?*) and "Sit Down, You're Rockin' the Boat" (*Guys and Dolls*).

The hit song of the show, "I Believe in You," can be performed in as many different moods, attitudes, and settings as singers can muster, and, what is more, it makes perfect sense outside of the play. Apart from the immediate theatrical context of *How to Succeed*, "I Believe in You" is an attractive number, a solid example among the many happy songs of encouragement lodged in Broadway shows.

> x You have the cool, clear eyes
> Of a seeker of wisdom and truth;
> x Yet there's that upturned chin
> And the grin of impetuous youth.
> y Oh, I believe in you,
> I believe in you.
>
> x I hear the sound of good
> Solid judgment whenever you talk;
> x Yet there's the bold, brave spring
> Of the tiger that quickens your walk.
> y Oh, I believe in you,
> I believe in you.

Example 5.5. "I Believe in You" (two measures at rehearsal K)

    z And when my faith in my fellow man
        All but falls apart,
   z′ I've but to feel your hand grasping mine
        And I take heart, I take heart.

    x To see the cool, clear eyes
        Of a seeker of wisdom and truth,
    x Yet with the slam, bang, tang
        Reminiscent of gin and vermouth.
   y′ Oh, I believe in you,
        I believe in you.

The similarity of the song's first, second, and fourth sections would seem to suggest the use of a most familiar convention: the standard AABA phrase pattern of countless thirty-two-measure Tin Pan Alley favorites. But this song in both form and harmony is a rare item, if not a unique one. Each A section, with six lines of text, is actually composed of twenty-four measures, each divided into three equal-length, eight-measure subunits, with the first two being musically identical, as shown below. It is thus a much more extended repetitive pattern of basic materials than is usually found in this format:

A			A			B		A		
x	x	y	x	x	y	z	z′	x	x	y′
mm. 8	8	8	8	8	8	8	8	8	8	8

The melody's most prominent pitch, the note A, is the reiterated sixth scale step. With open parallel chords in the accompaniment to provide a dash of

Example 5.6. "I Believe in You" (two measures at rehearsal J)

modal flavor, a poignant plagal effect ("amen" cadence) occurs on the refrain notes for "Oh, I be- [lieve in you]," in which the singer's high E-natural
makes a sweetly dissonant seventh over the major chord (ex. 5.5). Lest we
miss the intensity of Finch's fervent "belief" and the musical pun that comes
from stressing the two chords built on the notes F and C, Loesser has marked
the measure *religioso e molto legato* (religiously and very smoothly).

The B section follows the dimensions of a classic pop song's bridge passage: sixteen measures of melody starting on the lowered sixth degree of
the scale (A-flat in the key of C) and then moving up through B-flat to the
tonic C again. The final measure of this section is marked with *three* verbal
directives (*tenuto*, meaning "sustain"), leaving no doubt in the singer's mind
that each note at the start of this single measure must be as slow and drawn
out as musical sense and dramatic timing will allow (ex. 5.6). The direction
was probably repeated because it directly contradicts one of Loesser most famous "rules" of singing: avoid holding notes out to their full notated length.
(In the majority of cases, such shortening gives them more "punch," but not
so here.) This kind of expressive cue appears nowhere else that I know of in
Loesser's music. His famously insistent demand for clear, loud, and enunci-
ated singing did not usually require such a modifier. Notes attacked clearly
and sung forcefully by singers (for the sake of audibility) *always* trumped
beautiful, sustained "tones" in Loesser's performance handbook.[22]

Judged as an isolated number, "I Believe in You" reveals a master crafts-
man at the top of his form. It is a charming song, complete with the jungle
cat and alcoholic metaphors. Indeed, Loesser wrote it as a straight love song.
Who could ask for anything more by way of rhyme, key word repetition, harmonic variety, expressive clarity, and confident attitude? Yet to have Finch
sing this song to *himself* in the executive washroom mirror—the scenario
proposed by Burrows—amounts to a coup de théâtre that raises its impact
further. Moreover, to provide a second melody calling in violins and a kazoo
band to imitate the sound of electric shavers in the hands of plotting male

Robert Morse (center) with fellow business climbers in the executive wash-
room. "I Believe in You" / "Gotta Stop That Man." Billy Rose Theatre Division,
The New York Public Library for the Performing Arts, Astor, Lenox and Tilden
Foundations.

choristers ("Gotta stop that man, / I gotta stop that man / Cold . . . / Or he'll
stop me") all in the same washroom at the same time, exceeds even Loesser's
usual resourcefulness in devising music for comic tableaux.[23]

The Pulitzer Prize in Drama . . . for a Musical Comedy

How to Succeed picked up the 1962 Tony Award for best musical, Morse
won the same award for best actor in a musical, and the show's team garnered six other Tonys. So much was easy to predict from the critics' raves.
But to win the Pulitzer Prize was something else again. First presenting the
award to a drama in 1918, the judges took another fourteen years before a
musical comedy script pleased them enough to win amid an assortment of
straight plays. After *Of Thee I Sing* (1931), for which the composer George

Frank Loesser and Abe Burrows at the time of their Pulitzer Prize award, 1962. Frank Loesser Enterprises.

Gershwin received no prize (since Pulitzers were not then being given to musicians), only *South Pacific* (1949) and *Fiorello* (1959) among musicals had succeeded in picking up this honor. Burrows and Loesser (despite Frank's joke name, the "Putziller") were deeply gratified, and the original run continued through May 1965, totaling 1,417 performances, more than *Guys and Dolls* had achieved in its initial run and more than any other show of the 1950s except *My Fair Lady* (1956) and *The Sound of Music* (1959).[24]

Subsequent critical recognition echoed the general praise at the premiere. Signaling their impatience with Broadway sentimentality, critics latched on to the book's charming effrontery. Walter Kerr happily declared the script "deadpan and deadly."[25] Morse was seen to be a brilliant compound of Horatio Alger and Machiavelli (Kerr). Rudy Vallee (whose frayed and aging ego tried the patience of the producers, especially Loesser) was "merely magnificent."[26] The newcomer Charles Nelson Reilly, in the role of the president's nephew Frump, "turned in a most hilarious and artful performance . . . like Mephistopheles on needles," "a major achievement in hilarious exaggeration" (Nadel). "No one could suffer as exquisitely as he does" (McClain).[27] The critics found few faults and excused the paucity of blockbuster songs, pointing to the brilliant lyrics and the skill with which music knit the whole show together. Loesser's love of in-jokes and classical allusion were not lost on the critics, who duly noted and lauded his "romantic" quotation of Grieg's piano concerto during "Rosemary," when Finch and his girlfriend come to the clinch.[28]

After a year in office, President Kennedy chose *How to Succeed* for his first theatrical outing to New York in January 1962. The *New York Daily News*'s front page captured the moment with a photo of the president's arrival underneath the neighboring Imperial Theatre's marquee. The caption: JFK LEARNS: HOW TO SUCCEED.[29] According to Abe Burrows, the president liked the show so much that he recommended it in a cabinet meeting.[30] Burrows even recalled that a contingent of the original American Mercury program astronauts, led by John Glenn and Alan Shepard, attended the show. Since then, *How to Succeed* has traveled around the world; it was successfully mounted in London, Melbourne, Sydney, Paris, and Vienna (adapted), even before the end of the original New York run in March 1965. The film version appeared in 1967, trimmed of five original songs ("Cinderella, Darling," "Heart of Gold," "Happy to Keep His Dinner Warm," and the Pirate ballet number, "Yo Ho Ho"; "Paris Original" was used only as underscoring). Directed by David Swift, the movie retained much of the original stage show, including the performances of Morse, Vallee, Ruth Kobart (as Biggley's prim secretary, Miss Jones), and the second Rosemary in the Broadway production, Michele Lee.[31]

Revivals since the premiere have been less frequent, but the 1995 production, featuring Matthew Broderick as Finch, achieved substantial plaudits. Some changes were made in the direction of political correctness (the original bimbo Hedy LaRue was now played as a wilier and more calculating character, for example), ticket sales were excellent, and the critics were divided. A reprise of "The Company Way" sung by aspiring women executives replaced "Cinderella, Darling," but most of the original songs were retained, albeit with new orchestrations (by Danny Troob) that at least one listener likened to an assault on the ears.³² The choreography and sets were updated, and the stage action made even more busy than the original had been, leading to charges of heavy-handedness on the director's part.³³ The *Wall Street Journal*'s Donald Lyons blamed director Des McAnuff for misjudging the show's underlying motivation. Lyons deplored the production's "mindless lack of irony," which celebrated what in his view Loesser and Burrows had intended to satirize: conformity, hypocrisy, and sexual mischief in the workplace. The flat office spaces of 1961, he observed, had been replaced by flashy movable sets. The intentionally insincere "Brotherhood of Man" was treated as a straight-up rock gospel number (and brought the house down). The originally crisp caricatures were gone from a show now encrusted with too much staginess and too much noise; to Lyons, this *How to Succeed* represented the loss of "charm, intimacy, and humanity," washed away in a torrent of technology.³⁴

Still, almost all the critics professed to like the show, with *Variety* declaring it "as good as it gets."³⁵ Apparently, office politics turned out to be a hardier perennial theme than Loesser and Burrows could have imagined in 1961, satire or not.

CHAPTER 6

The Unknown Loesser:
Greenwillow, Pleasures and Palaces, Señor Discretion Himself

What a blessing to know there's a devil
And that we're not exactly to blame
For all guile and all greed
And each rotten misdeed
Which might blacken sweet mankind's good name.
— "WHAT A BLESSING," FROM GREENWILLOW, 1960

Transition

THE ROAD FROM *THE MOST HAPPY FELLA* TO *HOW TO SUCCEED IN Business Without Really Trying* was neither straight nor smooth. By the late 1950s, Frank Loesser was enjoying the notoriety and freedom of action that came with a string of Broadway and Hollywood successes. His fame had reached an all-time high, and his regular frenetic pace of work showed no signs of slackening. *Where's Charley?* and *Guys and Dolls* had both been produced in film versions by this time. In 1958 English actor Norman Wisdom assumed Ray Bolger's role in a highly touted London production of *Where's Charley?*[1] The Samuel Goldwyn/RKO movie *Hans Christian Andersen* had netted huge profits for the producers, and *The Most Happy Fella* had proved a solid critical success, further validating Loesser's astonishing breadth. Accompanying all this were major changes in his per-

Table 6.1. Songs and Singing Ensembles for *Dream People*

Act 1	
"Dream People" (Opening)	Ensemble
"Imagining"	Duet (Doris and Eva)
"Dream People" (Part II)	Duet and ensemble
"At the Home Appliance Show"	Solo (Roy)
"Marshmallow Magic"	Duet (Doris and Ted)
"We Harmonize"	Duet (Doris and Ted)
"Won'tcha Settle for Me?"	Mixed sextet (characters unnamed)
Act 2	
"Amateur Psychiatrist"	Solo (Doris) and ensemble
"For the Fam'ly Album"	Solo (Butch) and ensemble

sonal life: his family's move from Beverly Hills to New York in May 1956, followed by his divorce from Lynn Garland and his deepening relationship with Jo Sullivan in 1957. Loesser's business interests also prospered. To assist in the mounting of *Greenwillow* (1960) and eventually other shows, Loesser formed Frank Productions to accompany his music publishing firm, Frank Music, which he had founded in 1950.

During the same period, Loesser had noted the potential of television to create income for musicians by incorporating their work into broadcast advertising. He and his staff would later provide tunes for a variety of companies. Understanding the legal intricacies of licensing and copyright was proving to be essential in the high-stakes ventures that Broadway theatergoers craved. Frank Music and Frank Productions together ensured the continued diversification of Loesser's interests, and both firms added considerably to his wealth.

Loesser's prodigious energy and his curiosity about new scripts and production concepts rarely abated. In 1956 he began discussions with Garson Kanin about Kanin's whimsical, romantic, and unproduced play *A Touch of the Moon*, pondering its potential as the book for a future musical. And he did more than just thinking between September 1956 and August 1957, managing to write a full script, at least nine sets of lyrics, and music to match them before postponing and finally abandoning the project in 1959.[2] As well as the songs listed in table 6.1, two other lyrics were apparently considered for the show, although not indicated in the script: "The Green-Eyed Monster" and "Take Me Now."[3]

Various names were suggested for the projected musical, but Loesser settled on *Dream People*. Its story centers on a pair of idealistic lovers who separately live humdrum lives but daydream about their perfect soul mates before actually meeting them. Robert Kimball and Steven Nelson describe the work as "an odd mix of ethereal stage effects and conventional musical comedy romance."[4] The main characters consist of Doris, her confidante Eva (their personalities as expressed in the lyrics suggest a kinship with Rosabella and Cleo), her everyday suitor Roy, and her ideal lover Ted. Doris and Ted's imagined "younger son" in a family portrait is named Butch.

The rhyming lines of "Marshmallow Magic" speak the comic-romantic Loesser language through and through, though they might give modern listeners sugar shock:

> DORIS: Ooh, you marshmallow magic,
>   You choc'late and strawberry flame.
> TED: Ooh, you car'mel pecan mystery,
>   You flavor I can't quite name, . . .
>
> TED: Dextrose, fructose, glucose,
>   I can take them or leave them
>   Till the day I die,
>   For you are my lifelong sugar supply.
>
> DORIS: Ooh, you marshmallow magic,
>   You pure maraschino supreme.
> TED: Ooh, you carbohydrate symphony,
>   You sweeter-than-sweet sweet dream.

The title song is sketched as a lush ballad, filled with large melodic leaps and finished off with some stratospheric close harmony for three high sopranos. In the second act, "Amateur Psychiatrist," with calypso rhythms and background ensemble chanting, echoes Leonard Bernstein's *Trouble in Tahiti* (written in 1952; produced in New York in 1955), another fable of comfortable but bored, "modern" men and women looking for talk therapy, romance, and escape.[5] The chorus repeats the words "free-floating anxiety" over and over as Doris pines: "Amateur psychiatrist, / All my friends cannot resist / Advising the couch instead / Of the nice warm double bed."

Greenwillow, the Novel

In the midst of his work on *Dream People*, Loesser was offered another story in short novel form with a similarly ethereal character but with more

dramatic incident. *Greenwillow*, by B. J. Chute (1913–1987), was recommended to Loesser by actor-manager Robert Willey. Although he had not
met the composer, Willey imagined Loesser to be the artist most capable of
imparting the proper "heart" and "human feeling" to Chute's book.[6]

The novelist hailed from Minnesota. She had attended college and
worked as her father's secretary before writing a series of juvenile sports stories and children's books as a young adult. While living in New York during
the 1950s, she turned her attention to mature readers and eventually produced a number of successful novels and dozens of short fiction pieces for
magazines such as *Redbook, McCall's, Saturday Evening Post, Harper's Ba-
zaar,* and *Cosmopolitan.* While *Greenwillow* (published in 1956) was allegedly aimed at adults, it showed every sign of being a coming-of-age story appropriate for adolescent readers as well. Its attractiveness lies in a plangency
and quaintness of language, combined with a gentle, amusing nostalgia that
pervades virtually every page. It sold out eleven printings in its first six years
on the market.[7]

The village of Greenwillow—somewhat like that Broadway fantasyland,
Brigadoon, with bits of Chute's native Minnesota thrown in—exists in a
vague past time, with a rural, middle-American flavor. Its residents say things
like, "We dusted our knees together, asking for salvation. That's why I'm a-
sitting here now," and "Don't take that passel of kin along with you [to the
barn]. Cows got a right to their peace." Wise women prescribe home rem-
edies such as "assafetty [asafetida], whiskey, and rock sugar," and old men
debate the existence and exact whereabouts of the devil on earth.[8]

Chute was flattered that her work intrigued Loesser and Willey, and she
cooperated enthusiastically when they brought the project to completion. In
her notes for the original cast album, the novelist explained that "the village
of Greenwillow is an invention, and its time and place are left to the reader's imagination. I have been told variously that it is located in such diverse
regions as Vermont, Corsica, Denmark and the Kentucky Mountains. One
deeply involved reader settled it comfortably into Jane Austen's England,
and then quarreled vigorously with a friend who claimed with equal spirit
that it was plainly her home town in Indiana."[9]

Not on any map, but lying next to the pacific Meander River, and far up-
stream from the grubbier towns of Cheever, Middlemas, and Croke, Greenwillow preserves the values, speech patterns, and charming habits of a bygone era. Its opening sentence locates it squarely in a mythic zone: "Long

PLAYBILL

a weekly magazine for theatregoers

GREENWILLOW

Playbill cover for *Greenwillow*. Anthony Perkins (center) as the troubled
Gideon Briggs stands next to cheerful Rev. Birdsong, played by Cecil Kellaway.
Billy Rose Theatre Division, The New York Public Library for the Performing
Arts, Astor, Lenox and Tilden Foundations.

ago, centuries perhaps, the village of Greenwillow had been stood in the corner and forgotten."[10] Its characters are ideal types, in some cases almost Jungian archetypes who might be thought to represent aspects of mind, desire, conscience, and experience—hence Chute's willingness to leave the precise location of Greenwillow to our "imagination."

Most of Greenwillow seems free of worldly cares (and modern appliances), and few of its inhabitants wish for change, even while they sense that change is inevitable. In this Arcadian scene we meet Dorrie and her two elderly guardians, Miss Maidy and Miss Emma. Our heroine is an orphan, but utterly content and at home in Greenwillow. She lives to cook, clean, care for her guardians, nurture small animals, and charm the neighborhood children by her innocent kindness. Sixteen years old, she finds herself attracted to the eligible but troubled Gideon Briggs, whose family is cursed by his father's and indeed all his first-born male ancestors' wandering ways. The source of this "call to wander" is never explained but is understood by all to be irresistible. It is the most singular, mysterious, and mythic feature of the plot.

The religious life of Greenwillow is superintended by two pious men. The tall, thin Reverend Lapp, whose dour view of life holds to the harsh principle that newborns who die unbaptized go straight to hell. He is concerned in general about human unresponsiveness to the need for salvation and to anyone insufficiently alert to the devil's presence in their midst. His opposite number is the rotund, joyful, and angelic Reverend Birdsong, who always looks on the bright side of life and lives up to his name by singing to his feathered friends.

Soon after the novel begins, Amos Briggs returns home and with his wife, Martha, conceives a new child (which will bring their total offspring to seven). Amos and Martha's oldest, Gideon, not wanting to fall victim to his father's irresponsible and neglectful ways—Amos invariably departs within days of his infrequent visits—resolves to build up their farm to prosperity, thus leaving all in good order when the call to wander comes to him, as he assumes it must. He also vows never to marry or to produce children of his own, so that his departure, while sad in itself, will at least see the ending of the family curse.

Other inhabitants of the village consist of Aggie Likewise, the landlady for Reverend Birdsong; town drunk Little Fox Jones; a greedy and disgruntled farmer, Thomas Clegg; the irascible Gramma Briggs (a former girlfriend of Clegg); the remaining Briggs children, all of whom have names from Hebrew scripture, such as Obadiah, Micah, and Shadrach; the boy Tattery, who works for Clegg; and assorted townsfolk.

The action of the novel and the musical revolves around the various customs, superstitions, and manners of Greenwillow's inhabitants. Themes include anticipation of the "call" and its effects, the impending birth of another Briggs child to Martha, and the desire of the Briggs family to possess a cow, owned by the stingy Clegg (though tended by Gideon), whose milk could feed the new baby. Even in this idyllic setting, of course, faultfinders and rumormongers dwell. Evil is thought to lurk in unsuspected places.

Why do bad things happen to good people? Does misfortune come about by divine agency or through human choice? And is the hand of the devil always to be found nearby as well? To what extent are our lives governed by fate and destiny? How do hard work, upright behavior, selfless dedication, love, and religious observance affect the picture? These are the questions that seem to occupy most of the novel's characters. The Briggs family are kindly but not churchgoing folk and do not seek religious comforts. Whence the call to wander? Are the Briggs males "cursed" by the devil for their impiety or merely compelled by some force to desert their homes when the spirit summons? Such questions, which amount to a fairly temperate critique of Calvinist predestination, form the novel's core and shape its action.

Mythic fable though it appears, the story is neither puritanical nor cautionary, nor is it squeamish or evasive about sex. When Amos Briggs comes home to "plant" his latest baby, the action and its probable result—another child nine months down the road—is spoken of frankly by the elders. As for the nature of the wandering impulse, little is clear. The temptations strong enough to draw fathers from their homes and the powerful source from which they flow, implied by the words "call" or "curse," are left undefined and the caller unnamed.

Conversion for the Stage

Owing perhaps to its distinctive blend of candor, charm, mystery, and well-drawn characters, Loesser and Willey apparently needed little convincing about the novel's potential for Broadway. But how to musicalize a quasireligious fable? How to place it appropriately in a Broadway setting that was unused to sectarian fervor, philosophical musings, and imitation folk song? *Greenwillow* appears to have had few obvious antecedents, but Loesser loved a challenge, and so he pushed ahead.[11]

Table 6.2. Musical Numbers in *Greenwillow*

Act 1

1. "A Day Borrowed from Heaven"
2. "Dorrie's Wish"
3. "The Music of Home"
4. "Gideon Briggs, I Love You"
5. "The Autumn Courting"
7. "The Call to Wander"
8. "Summertime Love"
9. "Walking Away Whistling"
10. "The Sermon"
11. "Could've Been a Ring"
12. Reprise: "Gideon Briggs, I Love You"
13. "Halloweve" [*sic*]
13. "Never Will I Marry"
14. "Greenwillow Christmas"

Act 2

15. Reprise: "The Music of Home"
16. "Faraway Boy"
17. "Clang Dang the Bell"
18. "What a Blessing"
18. "He Died Good"
19. "The Spring Courting"
20. Reprise: "Summertime Love"
21. Reprise: "What a Blessing"
22. "The Call"
23. Finale: "The Music of Home"

Nine other songs were composed but unused in the production. See Kimball and Nelson, *Complete Lyrics*, 211–13.

Loesser and his collaborator, Hollywood screenwriter Lesser Samuels, used a conventional dramatic framework for *Greenwillow*, making relatively few changes in the novel's succession of events. Act 1 contains ten scenes and act 2 five, with most of the action taking place at the Briggs farm and the town square. The ministers have one scene to themselves in church. Most of the major songs are introduced in act 1; the children's number, "Clang Dang the Bell," Birdsong's solo, "What a Blessing," and Dorrie's haunting "Faraway Boy" are saved for act 2. Two songs are reprised in act 2. "Never Will I Marry," the emotional and vocal highpoint for Gideon and the most challenging solo number of the show, is placed just before the first-act choral finale, "Greenwillow Christmas." There is nothing unusual or unexpected in this basic layout of material (see table 6.2).

Lyrics by Loesser

Loesser, following his usual modus operandi, extracted key words and dramatic moments in Chute's story to build the verbal framework on which he could later drape the music. For example, the clergymen Lapp and Birdsong reveal their contrasting perspectives on life through a contrapuntal duet, "The Sermon."

LAPP:
The coming of winter, the coming of winter,
The coming of wretched cold, cold winter is a warning,
A warning to repent.
Repent, repent, repent, repent, repent.

BIRDSONG [*in canon with Lapp*]:
The coming of winter, blessed old winter,
Nights of long deep featherbed sleep
And a hot plum porridge in the morning.
Rejoice, rejoice, rejoice, rejoice.

In the second act Loesser also gives Birdsong a solo number, a series of saucy limerick-like lyrics that clarify his carefree position on free will and human nature. There are about a dozen stanzas in all; the following two convey the general idea.

What a blessing to know there's a devil
And that I'm but a pawn in his game;
That my impulse to sin
Doesn't come from within,
And so I'm not exactly to blame.

What a blessing to know there's a devil
Ever leading me into some vice.
And though easily led,
I can hold up my head
Knowing I'm fundamentally nice.

Loesser makes the most of the other possibilities for comic breakouts in the elders' duet "Could've Been a Ring" and the gossipy ensemble about the "flint-hearted, evil-eyed, blaspheming, poison-tongued" Thomas Clegg, who against all odds "died good," in other words, allegedly right with God.

Because Chute's story can be interpreted as a morality tale aimed at youngsters still barely aware of the powerful "calls" (besides sex) that will be coming to them, Loesser created lyrics and music that reify a number of traditional, even universal, themes appealing to all regardless of family, clan, tribe, or native habitat. This agenda is clear from titles such as "The Music of Home," "Never Will I Marry," "Summertime Love," "Faraway Boy," and "Greenwillow Christmas (Carol)." All point to domestic scenes, simple, sensuous pleasures, seasonal celebrations, and rites of passage—incidents that enrich the texture and fit comfortably within lives, hearths, and homes everywhere. Characteristically, Loesser distills the essence of his songs in a few key lyric and melodic phrases. He consistently lands on concrete words, as shown in the excerpts below:

"The Music of Home"
Just hear the teakettle sing,
"Away, awee, away, awee,"
And Clegg's old cow
Moo in the meadow,
And hear the morning chimes . . .

"Never Will I Marry"
Never, never will I wed.
Born to wander solitary,
Wide my world, narrow my bed.
Never, never, never will I marry.
Born to wander 'til I'm dead.

"Clang Dang the Bell"
Clang dang the bell,
Gather by the well.
Sprinkle joy on baby boy
So's he'll not go to hell.

In one particular way these lyrics resemble Loesser's more famous comic and romantic texts within more successful shows: they sound much less silly once music is applied. The show's modest reception history should not be blamed on the lyrics, however, since they capture a number of appealing and compelling sentiments quite successfully.

Loesser, ever the conscientious lyricist, understood that the addition of music to text creates an odd chemical reaction. Just as fog, water, and ice are all forms of H_2O, yet strike our eyes and hands in contrasting ways, words heard in song are fundamentally changed from words read or words spoken.[12] The intoning of notes with text always makes connections invisible to the eye, softens some syllables and hardens others, and highlights elements of meaning that may not stand out apart from their melodic clothing. The resulting product enters the audience's collective ear as an emotion-bearing object, partly subliminal in its effect. This remains true even if we firmly *believe* we are hearing and understanding every word in a merely cognitive way. Loesser had no exclusive or secret access to this branch of lyric-writing art, but he consistently demonstrated a sure command of it.

The Musical Language of *Greenwillow*: Folk Scales and Tripping Rhythms

The "folkishness" of *Greenwillow*'s music was developed without actually borrowing preexisting folk tunes. In accordance with Chute's geographical vagueness, Loesser's general rural sound was created so that listeners would not automatically be reminded of the hills of Tennessee or the highlands of Scotland or other specific locales. Yet the menu of musical techniques he employed can be found in many traditions and represents a kind of collective folk heritage, a bank of sound segments that he selected and adapted in a variety of ways. These common musical building blocks are shared so widely around the world that their careful manipulation effectively precludes any too strong association with any particular country or region. Because Green-willow's location was left to the audience's imagination, Loesser's *Greenwillow* music uses a potpourri of flavors to good effect.

The single most important scale in Western music during the last four hundred years or so is the major scale, which most of us learn as children. Along with its cousin, the minor scale, it has become normative and the mainstay of classical, folk, pop, jazz, and most other types of Euro-American music.

Scales that use fewer than seven pitches per octave often have within them intervals greater than a whole step (the space between *do* and *re* or *re* and *mi*, for example). Because of these large intervals, tunes based on so-called gapped scales possess an audibly different character than those made from a full major or minor scale. A gapped scale is often used when a "folk" sound is needed. Among the familiar gapped scales is the pentatonic, with five notes within each octave. The most common pentatonic scale consists of the first, second, third, fifth, and sixth notes of a major scale. Many popular American hymns, including "Amazing Grace," use this vocabulary. Accord-

Example 6.1. "Amazing Grace" (first two phrases)

ingly, in the key of G, the fourth and seventh notes (C and F-sharp) are omitted (see ex. 6.1).

Another immediately perceptible characteristic of all music is the relationship between the sounds and the silences, with the rests being as important as the notes in setting up a rhythm. Both speed (tempo) and regular
accentuation or the lack of it (beat) instantly convey a rhythmic profile and
mood, even in the absence of a clear melody; likewise, certain rhythms often
have folkish connotations (think of a favorite march or waltz). Melody and
rhythm together, then, work on our ears to answer the basic questions about
style that an attentive listener brings to any heard music.

Several aspects of performance determine our sense of a scale's or a
rhythm's presence, including tempo, note repetition, the spacing of successive pitches in melodies, the instruments or voices that are sounding, and
so on. Knowing all this, composers can readily invent new combinations.
By carefully deploying eccentric scales and other elements—fresh rhythmic
patterns, chords, and timbres—that are less familiar, a distinctive and, more
to the point, instantly recognizable sound can serve the purpose of taking us
to a distant or unknown place. Loesser deployed several devices of this kind
to construct *Greenwillow*'s musical world.

The Songs

Greenwillow's songs make prominent use of drones, sustained bass notes
called "pedal" tones, and static ostinatos (especially short, emphatic rhythmic patterns heard in lower parts) suggesting a pastoral, otherworldly atmosphere, both sweet and dreamy. Loesser begins "Faraway Boy," for example,
with rolled harp chords (short arpeggios in the accompaniment), which suggest association with other strummed folk instruments (such as the banjo,

Example 6.2. "Faraway Boy" (first phrase)

guitar, zither, or mandolin). The alternative scale (in this instance the Phrygian mode) emphasizes the closeness of the notes F and G-flat. The key word "faraway" is painted in the main melody with a large skip from the first note on the home or tonic pitch of F to the high second, third, and fourth notes: E-flat, D-flat, E-flat. The first E-flat is distant or faraway in at least two senses. The singer's leap of a minor seventh from the F is a large one, and the pitch of E-flat is absent from the typical F-major scale, the key for which the verse has prepared us. In effect, Loesser introduces an aural surprise even before the Phrygian G-flat is heard two measures later (see ex. 6.2). Using this "folk" mode for a melody in a moderately slow and unemphatic rhythm imparts a whiff of the exotic or alien. For these several particular technical reasons, the melody, even before it gets started, seems to be leading us (and the singer, Dorrie) into obscure memories.

"Greenwillow Christmas" employs another modified scale (the Mixolydian mode) in a hymnlike setting, with voices sounding in parallel rhythm. Both this scale and its arrangement for four choral voice parts evoke a vaguely English pastoral scene, since both features mark the traditional English carol. Another "old English" trick is played with the close juxtaposition of different chromatic versions of a note (e.g., B-natural and B-flat in mm. 3 and 4 in ex. 6.3), a gesture sometimes called "cross relation" that carries a lengthy English pedigree.[13]

Certain major and minor chords not generally considered appropriate neighbors in standard chord progressions are added to this mixture to link the piece securely to a bygone era, before modern harmonies were in use. These transient pinprick dissonances and unexpected harmonic sequences figure prominently in ancient and some types of choral folk music, so they effectively support the image of the Greenwillow folk as a community "out of time." To reiterate: *all* the foregoing individual elements are built into the tune, and, while not always blatant, they depart enough from everyday pop

Example 6.3. "Greenwillow Christmas" (opening measures)

song practice to deserve our notice. Since all are inserted without fuss or
fanfare, however, they also serve the composer's purpose of creating a novel
sound world.

Dorrie and Gideon's love duet, "Gideon Briggs, I Love You," is captivat-
ing in its evocation of folkish sweetness. The melody, while concluding in
E-flat major, is nevertheless dominated by minor chords, the mode mixture
being a clear folk marker (as we have already noticed elsewhere, and which
Loesser used effectively in the *Guys and Dolls* gem, "More I Cannot Wish
You"). The tune alternates between two bare notes a fourth apart, B-flat and
E-flat, supported by C-minor seventh and G-minor seventh chords. Loesser's
secure control of harmony and his alertness to sustaining an already powerful emotional moment can be heard in his overlay of countermelody (just
three rising quarter-note segments: B-flat–C–D, D–E-flat–F, and D–E-flat–F
in the upper range of the accompaniment, mm. 10–12).

Example 6.4. "Gideon Briggs, I Love You" (opening)

These decorative links make an emotional mark because they sustain our interest and elevated feeling at moments when the music might normally relax, as the poetic meter of the lyric does in example 6.4. An effective portrayal of the shyness with which Gideon and Dorrie at first express their mutual love is achieved by a highly elastic tempo (not explicitly indicated in the score) performed on the original cast album. Hesitations, stops, and starts at the very beginning of the main melody on the words "Gideon Briggs, I . . ." and later "Dorrie, I truly . . ." give way to the higher, longer notes on the word "love" with a pleasant effect. This technique is simple to describe and to observe, but it is not always easy to execute, since its ultimate effectiveness hinges on the singers' intuitive reaction to a text.

"The Music of Home," into which snippets of "Gideon Briggs, I Love You" occasionally are inserted for dramatic continuity, begins with vintage Loesser word painting; teakettle squealing, cows mooing, and village chimes are mentioned in the verse. The main melody features a nearly pentatonic array (a C scale minus the leading tone of B and with only one A), used to

Example 6.5. "The Music of Home" (beginning of chorus melody)

construct a consistently plain and simple tune and an equally straightforward lyric. The many leaps in the melody (shown in ex. 6.5) are somewhat reminiscent of those in "Spring Will Be a Little Late This Year" and can be difficult to deliver effectively. The first six notes bear a strong family resemblance to the opening pitches of "Home for the Holidays" (a Perry Como Christmastime favorite recorded in 1959, five years after it was written by Al Stillman and Robert Allen), with the word "home" being stressed in both—though it is stretched one step higher in Loesser's more challenging vocal phrase.[14] The link between the two may have been unintentional, although such resemblances are common in the history of popular song. Being harder to sing and using a less visually evocative lyric, "The Music of Home" has faded into obscurity, while Stillman and Allen's song has remained a perennial.

The wistful exuberance of the refrain of "Summertime Love," Gideon's optimistic solo number, is prefaced by a verse in free rhythm (Loesser calls it "recitative," a half-sung, half-declaimed vocal style for delivering text that introduces a full-fledged song or aria), accompanied by drone (parallel, open) fifths in the bass. The song refrain itself is a melody filled with long, sustained notes for the singer but supported by a steady rhythmic engine, a mildly syncopated set of three unequal notes, and a bass line that changes pitch infrequently. This sort of quiet pulsation fit well with the mellow warmth of vocalists Rosemary Clooney, Eddie Fisher, and Harry Belafonte, all of whom recorded "Summertime Love" after its premiere by Anthony Perkins.[15]

"Never Will I Marry" (ex. 6.6) and "Walking Away Whistling" were both inspired directly by Chute's text. The first, despite its self-pitying lyrics, has been recorded by singers as different as Vic Damone, Barbra Streisand, Liza Minnelli, Sheena Easton, and Nancy Wilson.[16] The bleak verse ("Any flimsy-dimsy looking for true love / Better look her looking some other way"), sung in an elastic recitative style like "Summertime Love," is delivered quickly over a sustained five-note chord, a vaguely dissonant grouping spaced from low bass to treble over an octave and a half, a span echoed also in the solo voice part. These gaps between chord notes and among successive melody

Example 6.6. "Never Will I Marry" (mm. 1–4)

1. No burdens
2. To bear ____
3. No conscience
4. nor care ____
5. No mem'ries
6. to mourn ____
7. No turning
8. For I was

Example 6.7. Repeated three-note motive of "Never Will I Marry"

notes collectively suggest the distances that come from "wandering" (Amos Briggs has even sailed to China and India, according to the novel), as well as the sadness, solitude, and pain that separation brings. The song's emotion is intensified by the pressure of an ostinato—the three descending notes D, C, and B-flat on the second, third, and fourth beats—in no fewer than twenty-one of the twenty-four measures of the refrain's bass line (scored for extra emphasis in the trombone part) and then picked up in the singer's part at the release (B section) of the AABA melody (ex. 6.7). For depicting pain and isolation, Loesser never wrote a more poignant or graphic song.

"Walking Away Whistling," which also leans toward darker emotions, fills an entirely different place in *Greenwillow's* musical/emotional landscape. This truly original evocation features an unusual orchestration by Don Walker. A minor-mode melody and the echoing whistle in the piccolo are accompanied by ultrahigh strings (not indicated in ex. 6.8), lending a shimmering aura to each phrase. Furthermore, Loesser's preference for elastic

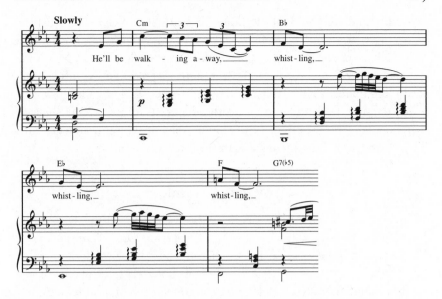

Example 6.8. "Walking Away Whistling" (opening)

rhythms and plain harmonies here saturate an already peculiar melody with an eerie sense of instability, as if the one walking away were proceeding into a thick fog.

Along with the powerful manifestations of nostalgia and melancholy in *Greenwillow*, Loesser included several bouncy numbers meant to bring comic relief to this subdued and serious plot. A racy duet in a quick duple meter is sung hoedown style by elders Thomas Clegg and Effie (Gramma) Briggs. "Could've Been a Ring" crackles with delight about an almost-but-not-quite-consummated affair recollected from their younger days:

> We came to the brink distinctly,
> Cozy close to mostly,
> Mighty near to nearly,
> But we never.
>
> Oh, yes there
> Could've been a ring,
> Could've been a ring-ding,
> Could've been a ring-ding-dee.[17]

The Briggs children are also assigned a musical number, "Clang Dang the Bell," to celebrate the birth of a calf. The tune is short and bright, the text only mildly clever, and the humor downright perverse. The kids love using big words like "Nebuchadnezzar," and they repeat adult expletives like "Hell" over and over. Had *Greenwillow* ever made it out of New York, perhaps its verve would have won over pious skeptics. On the other hand, Birdsong's upbeat waltz, "What a Blessing" (originally just called "Blessing Song"), sounds fresh and current nearly a half century after Cecil Kellaway first recorded it for the original cast album. Abba Bogin was nominated for a Tony Award for his conducting and music direction of this show.

"Anywhere I Wander"

If *The Most Happy Fella* was Frank Loesser's take on the *Tristan und Isolde* story, then *Greenwillow* was his *The Flying Dutchman*, an earlier Wagner opera about a cursed and wandering sailor. The "wandering" call of Chute's novel points to the restlessness of all adolescents, the need to take a journey to find themselves. But it contains none of the crime or faithlessness that lead to the tragic wanderings of Coleridge's Ancient Mariner or Wagner's Dutchman. Dorrie is young and innocent; her "calling," no less evident than Gideon's, is toward domestic stability. She cooks, cleans, and tends animals, joyfully and unselfishly, seldom complaining except when it comes to Gideon, whose skittishness about marriage she does not share.

Unlike Lerner and Loewe's Brigadoonians, the natives of Greenwillow may leave town, and newcomers may enter and depart at will. The arrival of the meek and cheerful Reverend Birdsong, who embodies the forgiving side of Christian love, lends a fairy-tale quality to Chute's story. Such mythic threads present many opportunities for moral lessons and appreciating nature. The dream quality of the setting is thoroughly charming, and both Willey and Loesser were excited about its possibilities for stage adaptation. Judged by its musical and lyrical parts, *Greenwillow* is a solidly built show. The book is evocative, the dialogue is reasonably clear, and the characters appealing and clearly drawn. The songs exhibit the craft and imagination we have come to expect in Loesser's Broadway vehicles. So why did the show disappoint?

In the end, the most attractive features of the book—its wistfulness, its homespun quality, its immersion in nature and agrarian life, and its spiritual aura—proved hard to translate to the stage. Bilberry cakes, stray pigs, pregnant cows, and family outings to the neighboring farm could not sustain audience interest for a full evening, and the array of musical moods available to Loesser was ultimately limited, despite many individually attractive numbers.

The arcadian world of B. J. Chute was musicalized at a consistently low decibel level, perhaps too low to register on Broadway's pizzazz meter. Something calm, sweet, and smooth emerges embodying Gideon and Dorrie's inner searching and turmoil, and of course the love story ends happily, but the obstacle posed for Gideon by the impending "call" never proved convincing enough for most audiences to credit. The resolution of his problem is all too simple when it happens. No melding of personal story and mythic quest is ever witnessed. Perhaps it comes down to the particular situation: an empty space or a sense of absence is a hard thing to give dramatic reality to. Unlike the world of *Guys and Dolls*, the fabulous village of Greenwillow has little independent resonance.

Loesser sought help from many quarters to write a sturdy libretto for *Greenwillow*, but he was turned away by those who most appreciated the difficulties. The distinguished movie scriptwriter Paul Osborn told him, "It's not one of those [plots] where it's obvious where to grab hold of it, or where you go after you have."[18] What Osborn needed to find and couldn't was the element of identity: Who were these people? What were they about? Where was their sense of tradition grounded? What dialect did they speak? Although thoroughly countrified, Greenwillow's residents were neither hicks nor yokels, so their story could not easily be turned to farce—and farce was not what Loesser was looking for, either. Abba Bogin believed that the show's lack of a strong ethnic flavor constituted a dramatic handicap.[19]

The story may have had an aura that pointed toward uplift, but it had little visual or concrete historical basis. History, whether actual or fictionalized, occasionally provides a solid basis for great musical theater, as in *South Pacific, Fiddler on the Roof*, or *Miss Saigon*. Yet a show that is adamantly ahistorical is asking for trouble if at the same time it wants to be as evocative of a material world as *Greenwillow* does, with all those "bilberry tarts," "fancy embroidery," and "Clegg's cows" that keep cropping up. Loesser thought he had solved his biggest challenge when Hollywood screenwriter Lesser Samuels agreed to cowrite the libretto with him. Although Samuels's work on the Billy Wilder classic *Ace in the Hole* (1951) and *The Silver Chalice* (Paul Newman's first movie in 1954) was well-regarded, his lack of Broadway experience may have limited his ability to convert a fundamentally undramatic novel to the musical stage.[20]

If *The Most Happy Fella* showed Loesser at his most exuberant, blending

operatic arias and Broadway showstoppers, *Greenwillow*, which premiered
in New York in March 1960, was the most restrained of his shows—the nar-
rowest in emotional range and the least invested in comedy. This low-voltage
tale of small events was not so much panned as dismissed with faint praise
and perhaps even a tinge of embarrassment for the brash urban composer of
Guys and Dolls.[21]

One Boston critic, Elliot Norton, who heard the tryout and loved it—
filling his review with words like "amiable," "good-humored," and "lighthearted"—still had to admit that *Greenwillow* after all was "no blockbuster,
no slambang smash hit."[22] Once *Greenwillow* reached New York, the *New
York Times* was pleased, but it stood alone among the city's newspapers in
its generally positive view of the work.[23] Kenneth Tynan, writing for the *New
Yorker*, declared, "On the whole it is barely credible that this simple-minded
extravaganza is the work of the man who created *Guys and Dolls*. In the
last ten years Mr. Loesser has traveled from urban ingenuity to grass-roots
ingenuousness; with *Greenwillow* he has reached the end of the line and we
must all wish him a rapid recovery, followed by a speedy return to the asphalt
jungle."[24] With such barbs in his ear, Loesser could hardly have done better than to riposte with *How to Succeed in Business Without Really Trying*,
a thoroughly modern and urban story as biting and prickly as *Greenwillow*
was mellow. *Greenwillow* hung on for ninety-seven performances. New York
revivals in 1970 and 1979 failed to yield improved reviews, although a 1991
mounting at the Goodspeed Opera House, directed by Gerald Gutierrez,
found an enthusiastic fan in the *Boston Globe*'s critic, Kevin Kelly, who declared it "as captivating as the first day it appeared," "a miracle of composition," and "one of the all-time great Broadway musicals."[25]

Intermission with Jean Anouilh: *Leocadia*

Amid the long-running subsequent success of *How to Succeed*, in the
spring of 1962 (news of the Pulitzer Prize came to him on May 7), Loesser
took up a project based on a Jean Anouilh play originally published under
the title *Leocadia* (1939) and renamed in its English version as *Time Remembered*.[26] It serves up a wistful story about a young French milliner tricked into
helping an eccentric duchess console her grief-stricken nephew, who also
happens to be a prince. Its witty repartee pits sensible middle-class attitudes
toward life and love against the foolishness of an idle aristocracy. Susan Stras-
berg, Helen Hayes, and Richard Burton acted the roles of milliner, duchess,

and prince in a 1957 Playwrights' Company production at the Morosco Theatre, and the critics raved.[27]

Loesser ceased work on the project when Anouilh refused to grant permission for a new staging, but not before having written four sets of lyrics and a handful of musical sketches between March and August 1962. Nothing from this stillborn musical comedy was published or recorded at the time. However, Kimball and Nelson have included the lyrics in their anthology: "Only the Rich," "I Am a Jolly Peasant," "Speak to Me," and "You Live in My Heart."[28]

The first lyric declares, "Only the rich may dine on orchids / Or sleep in a sequined toupee (don't try it), / For only the rich may be peculiar / Without being put away." Presumably intended for a scene between the milliner (Amanda) and the duchess, the song's references to lunatics and orchids come directly from Anouilh's (and translator Patricia Moyes's) dialogue. The other lyrics were probably meant for the prince's scenes. In particular, "You Live in My Heart" could have served a useful dramatic function in a reprise performed by Amanda or Prince Albert or both. When first sung, the text would have focused on the prince's obsession for his dead beloved, Leocadia; its repetition could then signal the prince's and the milliner's new love for each other. Such a double dramatic use of a single song is a common way to spice up a simple reprise. Loesser was fond of the device, which he had used for the title song in *Guys and Dolls*, for "I Believe in You" in *How to Succeed*, and especially for "The Music of Home" in *Greenwillow*.

> You live in my heart,
> Radiant and beautiful;
> Yes, you live in my heart,
> Close to me, still close to me,
> While I walk in a world
> Shimmering with memories.
> From my own exquisite world
> Why should I ever depart
> When forever
> And forever
> You live in my heart?

Loesser did not finish enough material for *Leocadia* to reconstruct a full show, but Anouilh's play exudes a tenderness that hints at what he might have done with it.

Pleasures and Palaces

During a minor thaw in the Cold War, when the Soviet Union momentarily appeared less threatening than it had in the 1950s, Alfred Uhry (later famous as the playwright for *Driving Miss Daisy,* but in this period writing theater song lyrics for Robert Waldman's music) proposed the idea of a Russian-themed musical to Frank Loesser and handed him a play by Sam Spewack entitled *Once There Was a Russian* (republished in 1961 as *The Prince and Mr. Jones*). The play had lasted for only one performance on Broadway (February 18, 1961) and did little for the careers of Walter Matthau in the role of Potemkin or Julie Newmar as the sultry Sura. It included a long list of colorful characters but garnered withering reviews. Howard Taubman in the *New York Times* declared, "Sam Spewack's new play looks and sounds like a farce, though it is described as a comedy. Regarded as a farce, it is ponderous and formula-ridden. Regarded as a comedy, it is a farce in the pejorative sense."[29] But Loesser was enthusiastic about the idea of blending the historical figures of Catherine the Great and the American naval hero John Paul Jones—who apparently did cross paths in 1788—into a musical love story that would make comic fun out of American-Russian "relations" from a safe distance.[30] A still young Bob Fosse, fresh from his directorial debut for *Redhead* (1959) and his work with Loesser on *How to Succeed,* was eager to direct and choreograph some dashing Russian dances.[31] Robert Randolph was engaged to produce monumental sets, and Freddy Wittop designed costumes appropriate for the luxurious eighteenth-century courtly scenes.

Starting in the fall of 1963, Loesser and Spewack set to work on the adaptation. A visit to New York by Moscow's Bolshoi Ballet seemed a good omen in 1964; Gwen Verdon, famed Broadway dancer and the wife of Fosse, later told Susan Loesser that Fosse and Loesser instantly grasped the possibilities for topical references to the occasion: "The Bolshoi had just appeared in New York for the first time. They did so many tricks that Frank and Bob decided that they should come up with something in response. So Bob made all kinds of jokes. One man did a great big jumping split—at which point, with sound effects, his pants would rip. Another man would do a cartwheel and his hairpiece would come undone. We didn't have enough [male dancers], so after various protests, they finally dressed the girls up like men and put mustaches on them. Kathryn Doby taught them to do *kazatskies* [squat kicks]."[32]

The show was at first dubbed *Holy Russia!* then changed to *Ex-Lovers,*

Principals in costume for *Pleasures and Palaces*, 1965. British actors Hy Hazell (Catherine the Great) and Alfred Marks (Dmitri Potemkin). Billy Rose Theatre Division, The New York Public Library for the Performing Arts, Astor, Lenox and Tilden Foundations.

and finally to *Pleasures and Palaces*, borrowing the opening lines of America's most popular nineteenth-century song, "Home, Sweet Home."

> Mid pleasures and palaces
> Though we may roam,
> Be it ever so humble,
> There's no place like home.

To remind listeners of the source of this borrowing, a snippet of melody from "Home, Sweet Home" makes repeated appearances throughout the title song.

Loesser and Spewack eventually completed a full script (and then some)[33] and fifty-five musical numbers, including underscoring and instrumental pieces, although no more than twenty-two were actually performed onstage, and only one, "In Your Eyes," was ever published.[34] The creative team worked at full tilt throughout 1964. Much hoopla was generated. Advance publicity made much of the casting process—"some two hundred persons were auditioned, questioned, and scouted" for the part of Potemkin, according to *Impresario Magazine,* for instance.[35] Rehearsals commenced in January 1965, and the tryout period began on March 11 with a month of performances at Detroit's Fisher Theatre.

Despite a menu of attractive elements—humor, clever songs, Russian-flavored dancing, handsome costumes, and a hardworking cast—the Detroit critics hated *Pleasures and Palaces,* their comments distressingly reminiscent of the straight play's premiere four years before.[36] Show doctors were brought in to no avail. After weeks of fretful rewritings and adjustments, Fosse still had hopes for recovery and wanted to go on to Boston. But Loesser deemed the project irreparable, and, since he was paying the bills, his view decided the matter. The show closed permanently after the Detroit tryouts, with Loesser taking a loss of nearly half a million dollars.[37] *Pleasures and Palaces* has never been heard of again, save through a handful of separate recordings of individual songs: "Thunder and Lightning," by Carol Ventura; "Truly Loved," by Tommy Steele, Joanne Brown, and Bernard Cribbins; "Barabanchik," by the Four Lads (who had had an earlier hit with "Standing on the Corner"); "Ah, To Be Home Again," by Jan Peerce; and "Pleasures and Palaces" by Pearl Bailey and Lena Horne.[38]

None of these recordings appear to have been big sellers, but a few gems amid the manuscripts and LPs show some potential for revival. "Thunder and Lightning," conceived as a duet for the voluptuaries Sura and Potemkin, uses a familiar metaphor to describe a tempestuous romance. Here Loesser employs several augmented second intervals in the main melody to mark "Russian" exoticism. "Neither the Time nor the Place" is a comic tango (Loesser called it a "Sex Fandango"), in which Potemkin tries unsuccessfully to maneuver Empress Catherine into bed.[39]

Perhaps the most historically prophetic song in the entire Loesser corpus is a mildly amusing character number assigned to a rather starchy John Paul Jones, "To Marry."

> I am glad to say as I travel abroad
> And I hear of a lawful marriage
> That my mind's relieved over alien folk
> Whom I normally would disparage.
> In a foreign land, when a wedding's planned

In an hon'rable forthright way,
I detect the fast-growing influence of the U.S.A.

It is somehow so American to marry,
So unflinchingly American when two hearts,
With benefit of clergy, unite.

As the lyrics would have it, Americans possess an unusual fondness for the institution of marriage. Jones tips his hat to the colonial dames Mrs. Martha Washington, Mrs. Betsy Ross, Mrs. Molly Pitcher, and Mrs. Dolly Madison. When this theme was conceived as pure farce in 1964, Loesser could have had no way of knowing how topical it would be forty years later, with serious pieces of legislation being promulgated to "defend" the vows of millions of heterosexuals against those seeking to validate same-sex marriage ceremonies.

Not counting songs that were replaced, cut, or unused, nineteen sets of lyrics are included in Kimball and Nelson (see table 6.3). All but two were registered for copyright as unpublished songs. "I Desire You" was never registered. "In Your Eyes" was published and appears in the anthology *The Frank Loesser Songbook*, compiled by Frank Music Corporation in 1994.

"In Your Eyes" deserves to be better known. A romantic ballad with familiar poetic tropes but an ungendered persona, it could be sung or recorded by almost any singer inclined to its mood and melody. With a clear meter yet a vocal line avoiding downbeats, Loesser imparts a gentle urgency to the lover's statement, which is to be sung "slowly and very expressively." Large intervals, long notes, and a languid tempo require a literally breathtaking performance, suggesting a breathless and light-dazzled lover:

> [*rest*] In your eyes
> [*rest*] I have seen the light . . .
> [*rest*] The light of goodness
> [*rest*] and truth divine . . .

Loesser preserves the smoothness of the melody, despite several large leaps, with appropriate harmonic support: a B-flat (the tonic) is sustained in the bass part through fully three-quarters of the melody, while at telling moments clashing major seventh intervals and minor thirds (forming diminished chords) lend modernistic spice to the accompaniment. The apex note of the melody, a high G rarely seen on popular song sheets, is sustained for six slow beats on the word "light," resolving by leaping dramatically down an unfilled major sixth to the final pitches: three B-flats for the syllables "in

Table 6.3. Songs Used in the Detroit Tryouts of *Pleasures and Palaces*

Title	Original Singer (Character Name)
1. "I Hear Bells"	Alfred Marks (Potemkin)
2. "My Lover Is a Scoundrel"	Hy Hazell (Catherine) and ensemble
3. "To Marry"	John McMartin (John Paul Jones)
4. "Hail, Majesty"	Ensemble
5. "Thunder and Lightning"	Phyllis Newman (Sura), Marks
6. "To Your Health"	Sammy Smith (Von Siegen), Eric Brotherson (Radbury)
7. "Neither the Time nor the Place"	Marks, Hazell
8. "I Desire You" [to replace 7]	Marks, Hazell
9. "In Your Eyes"	Newman, McMartin
10. "Truly Loved"	Hazell and ensemble
11. "Sins of Sura"	Newman
12. "Hoorah for Jones"	Ensemble
13. "Propaganda"	Mort Marshall (Kollenovitch), McMartin, and ensemble
14. "Barabanchik"	Marks, Marshall
15. "What Is Life?"	Marshall, Leon Janney (Bureyev)
16. "Ah, to Be Home Again"	McMartin plus Michael Davis, Howard Kahl, and Walter Hook (three prisoners)
17. "Pleasures and Palaces"	Newman
18. "Tears of Joy"	Marks, Hazell
19. "Far, Far, Far Away"	Marks, Hazell

your eyes." The gesture is analogous to a high dive into deep water by an expert athlete.

Pleasures and Palaces' long list of rejected material demonstrates once again that the art of creating a hit musical comedy is a highly complex, chancy process. The essentially collaborative nature of the enterprise admits of numerous pitfalls, which even seasoned professionals risk. It is possible that Fosse's intuition was right and that the show might succeed in revival. Loesser, in any case, moved on quickly; he may have been relieved simply to have avoided another *Greenwillow* letdown. There was always the financial situation to be considered. As the head of Frank Productions, Loesser heeded the omens about the show's shortcomings and made a prudent business decision, even though Fosse's youthful enthusiasm wanted to push on with it.

Loesser's personal life continued to flourish in the mid-1960s. He found a cherished family retreat, a waterside house in the small Long Island village of Remsenburg, which he purchased in September 1965. His older daughter, Susan, had married in the previous spring, and his youngest child, Emily, had been born on June 2. Loesser took up woodworking and sailing, among other pastimes, and continued to expand his business ventures.[40]

Señor Discretion Himself

Loesser used the word "mystique" to express what often attracted him to a play or story. The mystique of Budd Schulberg's short story "Señor Discretion Himself," first published in *Playboy* magazine in January 1966, began to operate on Loesser a few months before, when Schulberg offered it to him. He gave up on it only after two years of work.[41]

The story tells of the small Mexican town of Tepalcingo (for Loesser, Tepancingo) and a poor widowed baker, Alphonso (Pancito), whose only pride and joy, his daughter Lupita, seems about to be wooed away by a rival businessman, the smooth-talking Hilario. In a fit of rage, Pancito dictates a letter to be sent to Hilario demanding satisfaction for an imagined insult to Lupita, but fate intervenes in the person of the idealistic and diplomatic scribe and teacher Martinez (Martin), who secretly substitutes a complimentary letter of advice to Hilario. Hilario for his part is so surprised and impressed by the letter that he declares Pancito to be preternaturally discerning and wise, indeed "Señor Discretion himself." Martin pursues his own suit with Lupita successfully, and finally the plot is untangled when the truth of the substitute letter comes out. Hilario is induced to wed Carolina, Pancito's older, less attractive, but more practical daughter. The two bakers, having resolved their personal antipathy, go into business together.

Loesser decided that he needed to add other characters to fill out the plot, which over the course of two years grew to include a trio of comic priests (reminiscent of the trio of Italian servants in *The Most Happy Fella*), Manuel, Orlando, and Francisco, and other residents of Tepancingo, Julio and Negrin. But the process of working over the story continued to frustrate him, and he never expressed satisfaction with the book, believing that he had diffused its strength with too many strands of action. After sending manuscripts to his friend the author John Steinbeck, producer Cy Feuer, his erstwhile and reliable orchestrator Don Walker, and director Abba Bogin, and receiving mixed reactions, he gave up work on the show in March 1968.[42] To Schulberg he sent a letter of regret about his exasperation with the project. He may have also begun to sense the approach of his own death, which

Example 6.9. "You Understand Me"(opening vocal parts)

would be caused by lung cancer only fifteen months later.[43] Before the date
of abandonment, Loesser completed an outline of the music, the lyrics for
twenty-seven songs, and a full libretto, some three hundred pages of material. Most of the lyrics are included in Kimball and Nelson's collection.[44]

Two of the most beautifully wrought songs in the show are "You Understand Me," intended for Hilario and Pancito, and "I Cannot Let You Go,"
the love duet for Martin and Lupita. The former's Latin rhythm and close
harmony project a playful comic picture, taking place at the point in the
play when Pancito puzzles over Hilario's reaction to his supposedly insulting letter. The song's supple lines (see ex. 6.9) seem to invite mugging from
Pancito, while Hilario does his best to project utter sincerity. The full text, as
sung by Jo Sullivan Loesser and Emily Loesser in a 1992 recording, runs as
follows:

> You understand me. You understand me,
> Though you and I have points of view great oceans apart.
> You understand me as nature planned me;
> You see my faults with open mind and generous heart.
>
> I am at times a fool, a fool yet you comprehend.
> You are so calm, so cool, so cool you can afford me for a friend.
>
> How did I find you, sweet gentle kind you,
> In all the world of heedless hearts where sadly I dwell?
> Oh, please command me, poor badly planned me.
> You understand me so very well.[45]

"I Cannot Let You Go," like certain other unbridled declarations of romantic sentiment, seems to have stimulated Loesser to expressive heights.
By placing the words "I cannot" (and also "I am both" and "I can hear") at
eight successive rhythmic points, well before the strong or "down" beat of the
phrase, Loesser has imparted a plaintive urgency to the personal pronoun

Example 6.10. "I Cannot Let You Go" / "Goodbye Agitato" (excerpt from contrapuntal section)

and its verb in every phrase of this song. Poignant pleading by Lupita, with a series of short text phrases fairly tumbling over one another, is answered by a similarly intense melody by Martin (ex. 6.10).

While each sings:

> To think of losing you,
> Losing you even for a little while
> Chills my heart,
> And I cannot smile and be brave;
> I am both captor and slave.

the other repeats the first three lines, interweaving the following three as they proceed:

Arena Stage program illustration for *Señor Discretion Himself,* produced in 2004, Washington, D.C. Courtesy of Mike Benny.

I cannot let you go.
I cannot let you out of my arms,
Now that your lips are warm upon mine . . .

Thanks to their contrasting rhythms and ranges, all the words for both singers are instantly audible, and the unity of the shared emotional expression is
redoubled in power.

A Surprise Revival

The story of *Señor Discretion Himself* does not end with Loesser's abandonment of the project or even with his death. In 1985 a version of the music
was featured in a showcase at New York's Musical Theater Works.[46] More
significantly, some fifteen years later, Jo Sullivan Loesser traveled to Washington, D.C.'s Arena Stage to view a much-praised production of *Guys and
Dolls* during the 1999–2000 season. Impressed with the work of its director,
Charles Randolph-Wright, she invited him to New York for dinner and then
pitched this now forgotten show to the astonished Wright by mailing him virtually all of Loesser's manuscripts for it. Wright and Jo Loesser subsequently
engaged the talents of Ric Salinas, Herbert Siguenza, and Richard Montoya,
a Chicano-Latino performance cooperative calling itself Culture Clash, to
rework and update Loesser's original material, especially the book.

A further injection of Mexican authenticity went into the preparations
when Doriana Sanchez assumed duties as choreographer, Joey Arreguin was
hired to prepare the dance arrangements, and Emilio Sosa was brought in to
create the costumes. A *curandera* (traditional ceremonial healer) character
was invented to frame the action and provide additional context for the "miracle" of reconciliation supposedly achieved by Pancito. A predominantly La-
tino cast was selected, and Arena Stage mounted the show's first production,
with Budd Schulberg and Jo Sullivan Loesser in the audience, in April and
May 2004. Jo Loesser, as this book goes to press, still sees *Señor Discretion
Himself* as a work in progress and is encouraging further productions on the
West Coast.[47]

 CHAPTER 7

The Legacy of Frank Loesser

I want to go push a lot of buttons
And sign a lot of deals
And swing my horn-rimmed glasses
With my fellow business wheels.
—"STATUS," UNUSED SONG FOR HOW TO SUCCEED
IN BUSINESS WITHOUT REALLY TRYING, 1961

You understand me.
You understand me,
Though you and I have points of view
Great oceans apart.
—FROM SEÑOR DISCRETION HIMSELF, UNPUBLISHED,
REGISTERED FOR COPYRIGHT 1985

B ROADWAY WAS ALIVE WITH ACTIVITY IN THE LATE 1940S. AFTER THE difficult Depression era and war years, financial support for new musicals seemed to be there for the asking. Between 1945 and 1947, ambitious shows by established writers like Rodgers and Hammerstein (*Carousel*) and Irving Berlin (*Annie Get Your Gun*) were joined by the work of songwriters of Loesser's generation, such as Harold Rome's *Call Me Mister* and Burton Lane and E. Y. Harburg's *Finian's Rainbow*. All attracted large audiences. Some highbrow musicians got into the act even before the war ended.

Leonard Bernstein wrote *On the Town* in 1944, and the classically trained Morton Gould turned out *Billion Dollar Baby* in 1945. The work of Kurt Weill has already been mentioned. The eminent Aaron Copland, composer of *Appalachian Spring* (1943) and a string of other serious compositions, was tempted (by a $2,000 advance) to compose a "dramatico-musical" in 1945, although the show, based on Erskine Caldwell's novel *Tragic Ground*, remained unfinished and unproduced.[1] Following up on such prewar experiments as *Pal Joey* and *Lady in the Dark*, Broadway was broadening its horizons.

Hence Frank Loesser's first mature Broadway show, *Where's Charley?* appeared before an audience willing to consider modern musical plays as well as the familiar turns of Ray Bolger. By supplementing Bolger's dancing and cross-dressing with several well-made lyrical songs and a nostalgic subplot, Loesser seemed to bridge the gap between old-fashioned, lighthearted musicals and the newer, self-consciously serious ones of Rodgers and Hammerstein. *Guys and Dolls* struck a similar balance by combining comic scenes and lively characters with kinetic musical numbers.

Loesser's next major completed Broadway show, *The Most Happy Fella*, placed him within a select group of 1950s theatrical writers who could devise both song lyrics and book dialogue of a sufficiently high quality to power a hit show. This small club of lyrical-literary geniuses included among its members godfather Oscar Hammerstein II, Alan Jay Lerner (for *My Fair Lady* and *Camelot*), Sandy Wilson (*The Boy Friend*), E. Y. Harburg (*Jamaica*), Meredith Willson (*The Music Man*), Betty Comden and Adolph Green (*Bells Are Ringing*), Truman Capote (*House of Flowers*), Dorothy Fields (*Redhead*), and Rick Besoyan (*Little Mary Sunshine*). But few among even this talented crowd could boast of *musical* achievements comparable to Loesser's.

Jimmy McHugh (1894–1969), the composer of "I Can't Give You Anything but Love" and other hits, declared, "Any composer will tell you that a good lyricist is the rarest talent in the world—and any tunesmith lucky enough to have found one prizes him above gold."[2] Loesser not only combined the two skills, he frequently sought to fit his songs into interesting dramatic scenarios so as to tell a longer story. Continuity in itself attracted him; the making of long, coherent narratives was a goal that seems to have lain behind his notoriously fussy and critical coaching. Many have observed Loesser's special talent for writing lyrics for "characters who talked like people everybody knew,"[3] and then finding just the right music to match their dramatic character. Lehman Engel pointed out that Loesser's characters in *The Most Happy Fella* "*speak and sing* in the American vernacular" [emphasis added], citing the lyrics of Cleo, the exhausted server:[4]

> Ooh! My feet! My poor, poor feet!
> Betcha your life a waitress earns her pay.
> I've been on my feet, my poor, poor feet,
> All day long today!
> Doing my blue-plate-special ballet![5]

Although these lines are set to music, they could just as easily have been spoken, and no one would have objected. Loesser chose to have them sung to intensify the picture of Cleo's fatigue. The phrase "blue-plate-special ballet" sticks in the memory because it created a fresh metaphor: scurrying waitress as ballerina. Michael Stewart once recalled "Frank Loesser [saying] that when a scene reaches a pitch that is too strong to be spoken, *whatever the emotion* [emphasis added], then it must be sung."[6] Stewart's remark suggests the need for music at climactic moments, of course; but Cleo's scene comes at the very beginning of the show, before any plot has even been developed. (There is also some fine music at the start of *Guys and Dolls* and *How to Succeed.*) It would seem that Loesser not only understood where music *must* appear, but also was more than willing to use it wherever he could—to attract our sympathy for any character at any time.

When a composer, writer, or choreographer consistently puts a recognizable personal stamp on a work, and especially when he or she can do this repeatedly, audiences often notice the artist's distinctive perspective. Cy Feuer once said of his friend and colleague Frank Loesser, "He always excited me. His turn of mind would always have a sort of curve. And the way he used to sit and pick at the piano, and these inventive things that would come out *musically*, that fascinated me too."[7] Besides the raw talent, Feuer noticed a special turn of mind. Mark N. Grant adapts French critical (auteur) theory to explain his view of a unifying creative agency in musicals. The shoe seems to fit Loesser snugly and may help to explain the staying power of his shows:

> The great writers of the Broadway canon were indeed artists with a consistent point of view sustained through a body of work. Such Broadway auteurs started back in the nineteenth century with Ned Harrigan. . . . George M. Cohan's worldview was a red, white and blue merger of Rudyard Kipling and Horatio Alger. Cole Porter apotheosized the swank and soigné that could be

admired by average Joes. Lorenz Hart was the verbal virtuoso of unrequited love. . . .

Hammerstein wrote "Make Believe" for *Show Boat* and then rewrote it as "If I Loved You" for *Carousel*; the very self-plagiarism bespeaks an obsession with both songs' themes. Harburg wrote "Over the Rainbow" for the movie *The Wizard of Oz* and then rewrote it as "Look to the Rainbow" for *Finian's Rainbow* for the same reason: he was reworking the same creative issue the way great painters repaint the same scene.[8]

Whether they express a full-fledged "auteurial point of view" or merely consistent idiosyncratic details, Loesser's musicals contain a number of striking elements that seem to reflect his individual personality: dark or distant romantic situations (Donna Lucia and Sir Francis in *Where's Charley?* Sky's song "My Time of Day" in *Guys and Dolls*, almost all of *The Most Happy Fella*); social misfits as leading characters (Finch, and also Frump, in *How to Succeed*, Gideon in *Greenwillow*); irreverent humor and headstrong, cocky attitudes (everywhere). Jerry Herman once told Sheldon Harnick, "[Growing up] I loved Frank Loesser for the bite and strength [of his lyrics]."[9]

This mischievous tone pervades Loesser's best work, but his sharpest lyrics are almost always softened by playfulness as well. Even the most serious shows, *The Most Happy Fella* and *Greenwillow*, contain comic scenes and happy children. When Sky takes Sarah to Cuba and Nathan lies repeatedly to Adelaide, it is clear that the men are up to no good, but mean-spiritedness is absent. From the deceptive Charley Wykeham to the picture-swapping Tony Esposito to the rude and raucous Dmitri Potemkin (in *Pleasures and Palaces*), Loesser could never resist a rogue. But his scamps are likable and successful even while they behave badly—and they don't behave *all* that badly. Indeed, this description sounds much like Loesser in real life: a scalawag and a joker who excelled at multitasking. Jo Sullivan Loesser is on record more than once in noting that, as difficult and demanding as Frank Loesser could be, he was always fun to have around.[10] He cherished his one minor movie-acting role, the part of a piano-playing gangster named Hair-do Lempke, as a fitting alter ego.[11]

Many early accounts of Loesser in Hollywood describe a brooding or constantly pacing spitfire of a man, a smart-mouthed cock of the walk, sparing no one and fueled by a steady supply of coffee and cigarettes. For the young Frank Loesser, it appears that all newcomers were guilty until proven innocent. At best, he was irritating and unpredictable to work with; at worst, he was abusive. At a point of frustration in rehearsing the *Guys and Dolls* song "If I Were a Bell," he slapped Isabel Bigley across the face—to the shock of all present—although he also moved quickly to apologize and patch up the quarrel.[12] He famously rowed with Frank Sinatra and Rudy Vallee. Yet, years later, in fondly told accounts, Loesser seems to have become the best boss in the world. In this mature phase, he is often described as playful, irascible but considerate, inspirational, and as ready to compliment as to criticize, devoting hours of free time to counsel and advise others. Which picture of Loesser is the more true to life? Richard Rodgers remembered him as "a man [who] is a book in himself. He was happy; he was strong; he had enormous peaks and frightening depths. This is only to say that he was intensely human."[13]

Perhaps the best way to appreciate the many sides of Loesser's personality can be found in the variety of his interests and activities. The legendary lyric skills were hard won but lightly worn. Even as a teenager, he could generate witty words for all occasions, and when presented with a catchy melody he instantly became absorbed in the challenge of combining the elements to make a whole. As if possessed with finding the solution to an intractable crossword puzzle, he would concentrate, go into a mental shell, pace the floor, smoke one cigarette after another, and arrive at his answer, to the delight of previously skeptical coworkers. They put up with his behavior because he got good results. Such a mode of operation lends itself to myth making.

When it came to inventing both words and music himself, the pacing and the smoking (and probably the shouting) continued, but now the process was more often more inwardly directed, a dialogue between Loesser and his piano rather than with other humans. Whatever he did, he did it with enthusiasm. Abe Burrows reported that "[Frank] had some fascinating things, . . . the stuff was pouring out of him. It was always there. He read a lot, he asked questions a lot, he knew a lot. He was fascinated with words, . . . he lived with dictionaries. Not rhyming dictionaries. A terribly literate guy. Loved words—and loved to toy with them. And he used to work very hard. Always."[14]

Besides his intense work sessions, indeed essential to them, were his recuperative catnaps sprinkled through the day (since he slept few hours at night). Susan Loesser describes the childhood shock of inadvertently waking her father during a morning siesta only to hear a shower of abusive language that said, in no uncertain terms, "Daddy must not be disturbed."[15] His work time and his rest breaks were equally important to him.

When Loesser moved on to running his own businesses and hiring other writers, he must have appreciated how the roles were reversed; the intense working habits of other songsmiths needed their own special kind of nurturing. It was not so much that Loesser's creative habits had changed, but that the scope of activities had expanded to reveal all sides of a highly complex individual. A man who could quote great literature as he rhymed and swore, and who required only four hours of sleep a night, was also the prankster who once answered a complaint letter as if he were King John confronted with the Magna Carta—a combination of bluster and hilarious punning (and with a postscript directing that copies be sent to the pope).[16] Lynn Loesser reported that when Frank came across the key line of the *Guys and Dolls* best-selling song, "I love you a bushel and a peck and a hug around the neck" in *Other Voices, Other Rooms*, Truman Capote's celebrated debut novel she had passed on to him, he was so excited that he immediately rushed to the piano to write the tune down before going to bed.[17] Virtually everything inspired him, although nothing caught his attention as quickly as a fresh rhyme.

Loesser the Collaborator

All writers of musicals, no matter how strong their personal style, are collaborators. Despite the skills he brought to the making of a show, Loesser never hesitated to seek help in solving problems as he encountered them. Collaboration and the ability to bring together strong artistic temperaments were Frank Loesser specialties. From his adolescence, he worked with others out of necessity—usually musicians whose contribution to a fully developed song he needed. Yet even as he recognized the desirability of working with partners, he could be demanding, loud, and rude in the process. Burton Lane was one of the early songwriters to experience the sting of "collaborating" with Frank in the white heat of inspiration:

> He was a difficult guy even then. Very secretive. He'd sit across the room from me, and I'd say, "Well, what are you thinking about?" He wouldn't tell me. He'd keep it to himself. And then I'd see him smile. I'd say, "All right, Frank, what is it? Don't keep it to yourself; let me know the goodies too!" And suddenly he'd jump up, and he had it all written down, a complete lyric. I'd put it on the piano, and he'd want me to sing it right away. Hell, I

hadn't even seen the lyric yet! And if I'd stumble, he'd yell, "God damn it, can't you read?" Here I was, trying to think of what I'm doing, and reading his handwriting, which was terrible, and I've never seen the lyric before, and he's yelling at me![18]

Lane recalled this exchange from the salad days of both men, the prewar Hollywood environment of 1938, but even in Frank's later years his feistiness seldom waned. He invariably strove for a working environment that would stimulate the best from everyone involved. Stress and creativity seemed to go together for him. With enough coffee and cigarettes, the free association of ideas and sounds, jokes and jibes and quibbles added to the mix, and a song or scenic concept eventually emerged.

Despite the intensity of his personal creative process—the brooding silences, the angry outbursts, and the feverish bouts of trying to get everything down on paper—Loesser knew a lot about human nature and could draw on a well of common sense when it came to imagining situations and character relationships. He was a realist who harbored no illusions about the goodness of humankind, yet he always seemed to preserve a sense of optimism about life in general. His ability to translate psychology into song and gesture aided his ability to find the moments in the stage life of even the most unlikely character for a song to break forth. The severely melody-deprived Nathan Detroit, for example, in *Guys and Dolls* found just the right tone for his character with the musically modest plea, "Sue Me."

Loesser's "joyous" versatility in this regard impressed many of his most famous fans, including Richard Rodgers, who in his preface for *The Frank Loesser Song Book* declared:

> The well-tempered songwriter creates his own sort of "scherzo"—not necessarily fast, but surely joyous. It is difficult to listen to "Standing on the Corner" without wanting to giggle, not just at the words but at the music. This gifted man could wander off the conventional thirty-two-bar reservation without getting lost. Thus, "I Believe in You" is a full-fledged aria with a beat. It is also a statement of self-faith. Was Frank singing to himself? He was entitled to do it.
>
> Perhaps you would like a change of pace. There is a sweet affectionate waltz for you in "Wonderful Copenhagen." Are you in the mood for muscle? You have "Praise the Lord and Pass the Ammunition" or "What Do You Do in the Infantry?" Is your feeling of personal affection a little shy and a bit delicate? Sing "Once in Love with Amy." For the full gamut, sing everything in *Guys and Dolls*.[19]

Loesser also had a manager's talent for watching over all the elements of a production in progress, and he knew whom to call on to fix loose ends. Knowing his own talents and limits, he freely consulted others whose judgment he trusted: his close friend, the novelist John Steinbeck, music director Abba Bogin, his orchestrator Don Walker, script doctor Abe Burrows, and anyone else whose expertise he felt would benefit a current project. All these individuals were men of creative substance and strong opinions. He especially respected those "unseen and hidden collaborators" whose work is key to making a Broadway show happen: the arrangers, music directors, conductors, sound technicians, instrumentalists, copyists, and lighting designers.[20]

Professionally trained collaborators shape a musical in fundamental ways. As Burton Lane explained it, "When I do a show, I sit with an arranger. Then I select the conductor, and he and the arranger and I will decide on the best instrumentation for the score and how many musicians we need in the pit. I don't select them. The conductor works with a contractor from the musicians' union."[21] Loesser worked in a similar way. He normally presented melodies with a few chords or accompanying parts to a secretary or conductor who would supply a piano arrangement. Loesser, hearing the arrangement played back, would verbally edit until he was satisfied. Then the orchestrator would take over and try out different instrumental combinations.[22]

One of Loesser's most important collaborators, Abba Bogin, served with the composer "in capacities ranging from musical secretary to musical director" starting with *The Most Happy Fella* and lasting through Loesser's last shows. Bogin confirms Loesser's focused attention to every musical detail, as well as his phenomenal memory and complete comprehension of the harmonies he sought to create.[23]

Sometimes it is not clear what part of a show that an audience finds attractive is owed to the composer and what part to performers or other collaborators. But the reviews of a 1974 *Where's Charley?* revival illuminate the case of Frank Loesser well. Writing for the *New York Times*, Walter Kerr began with a rare admission: "Revivals are never a waste of time. You always learn something, even when the entertainment being trotted out for a second go at the track is something as inconsequential as a musical version of 'Charley's Aunt.' Certainly I didn't realize, when I first saw [it], precisely how delicate—how deliberately delicate—Mr. Loesser's gentlemanly score was." Kerr noted with approval a six-piece chamber ensemble used in this Circle-in-the-Square Theatre production, rather than the original full orchestra. The critic of course understood that Loesser had arranged neither the original nor the revival, but he felt better able to appreciate the composer's melodic and harmonic ideas in the more softly rendered 1974 version: "Mr. Loesser knew what he was doing in the first place [in] creating a chamber musical for a mezzotint world, paying a constant compliment to springtime. . . . We just didn't quite hear it the first time for the simple reason that in those days—about 26 years ago—we expected musicals to come down upon our heads with a cymbal-proud thump."[24]

Kerr lauded what he called a previously unnoticed "imperturbable intimacy" in this "duet-and-solo show," and continued:

> Perhaps that's why, when "Where's Charley?" was first done, it seemed only a fairish entertainment boosted to success by Ray Bolger. Now, listening with ears that don't demand thunderclaps by the dozen, we can hear Mr. Loesser's filigreed intentions more clearly. Oh, we always knew that "Make a Miracle" was a superb duo; it was imitated so widely in the following decade that I fully expected it to replace the National Anthem. . . . But what about "My Darling, My Darling," in which [the singers] slip so demurely into their expressions of mutual admiration that you're scarcely aware of the furtive crescendo they're building? It's a stunning surprise to discover that a song that seems no more than a conventional romantic ballad, and sung with Edwardian discretion at that, should be sneaking to such a finish.

Words like "gentlemanly," "imperturbable intimacy," and "discretion" are not generally associated with Loesser the extrovert. Kerr was on to something important. The key insight of his review lies in the suggestion that we can listen beyond the 1948 instrumental arrangements and recognize *Where's Charley?*'s musical essence as the product of Loesser's creativity rather than the arranger's. Other 1974 critics reacted to the revival with more mixed praise. Raul Julia, who re-created the Charley Wykeham role, was often the focus. (Clive Barnes's headline seemed to sum up the general feeling: "Dated Musical Retains Charming Aspects."[25]) While most liked the production more than the show itself, Martin Gottfried, in the *New York Post*, declared Julia "miscast" and the supporting players "mostly on the level of summer tent productions . . . mediocre."[26] But Gottfried too approved of the music:

> The show was Loesser's first [one] and it is remarkable how easily he switched from free-standing pop songs to songs to fit a story—songs to be part of a score. His combination of melody, lilt, theatricality, simplicity, and instinctive musical sophistication is still impressive. As a composer-lyricist he had

the advantage of unity—the same spirit in the words and in the music. This is no minor quality. Whether talking about the sophistication of Cole Porter or the simplicity of Irving Berlin, the same identity behind the words and the music can only be approximated by partners. Also, Loesser's lyrics seem as deceptively simple as his music. In fact they are crafty.[27]

Gottfried tells us that Loesser, despite a string of collaborative successes on individual songs, was finally his own best collaborator. Furthermore, his craft embraced a calculated balance of simplicity and sophistication, elements associated with two of his more famous contemporaries. Frank Loesser would not have denied the relationship.

Loesser the Businessman

Beyond his best shows and songs (including a total of nearly seven hundred separate lyrics), Loesser made other gifts that outlived him. Just as his early musical and verbal aptitude foreshadowed his songwriting talent, his eventual success in the business end of music could have been predicted from early on. Even as an adolescent, Loesser's salesmanlike intensity struck those who met him. A guy who partied and joked at the drop of a hat, he was never accused of shyness. But he also treated the mundane and private details of his craft conscientiously. As an adult, he kept to a strict work schedule, getting down every morning to the business of writing lyrics and melodies. And he transferred these habits of diligence to a business office where he called the shots.

The business of music should loom large in any history of American arts, since Old World sources of patronage—courtly aristocrats and donors from established churches—have never played a large role in North America. To become a musician in the United States, unless one was independently wealthy, has almost always meant getting involved in some aspect of music vending or production. By the late nineteenth century, American music comprised a variety of commercial ventures that included teaching, publishing, managing theaters, and conducting bands. American musical artifacts—sheet music, recordings, phonographs, and musical instruments—are therefore commodities as well as artistic products, and the economic success of American composers (regardless of whether they are supposed to be "classical," "folk," or "popular" in orientation) demands close attention if we hope to assess their influence.[28]

Loesser was both money-conscious and full of business savvy, and these traits fed his musical artistry. He saw no contradiction in doing good work that made a profit. He wanted to please the public as well as himself. As his daughter learned during her days as gofer at the Frank Music Corporation, "His rules were simple: Be clever. Be creative. Make money."[29]

A brush with poverty after the death of his father had alerted him at age sixteen to the dangers of failing to put bread on the table. Almost everyone faced privations during the Great Depression, of course, and Loesser was among them. Burton Lane reports visiting Frank and Lynn Loesser in their first year in Hollywood and realizing that the "dinner" he was offered would be canned beans and an apple, which was all the young couple could then afford. Loesser knew what it was to scrape by, but he never acted as if poverty were his ultimate fate.[30]

Unlike some survivors of early scarcity, however, Loesser also loved to be generous and never hoarded his wealth. He was famous as a grabber of checks. He sent candy to soldiers in Vietnam and flowers to his leading ladies. He ordered limousines to transport carless friends and coworkers and used his influence to arrange auditions, playing jobs, and interviews for young newcomers.

Loesser could be bullying one minute and shower his victim with gifts the next. When his apprentice Stuart Ostrow opted to leave his employ and strike out on his own, Ostrow remembered both Frank's "annoy[ance]" with him and some handsome farewell gifts, including a new grand piano and a check for $10,000.[31] His longtime secretary Betty Good declared, "[Frank] was twenty-eight different people. What a horse trader he was. It was beautiful—he'd do everything to best you, then give it back to you under the table."[32] He reveled in the give-and-take of haggling, and he loved the taking and the giving that his wealth and wily habits afforded him.

Loesser's beloved New York and Broadway provided him with all the models he would ever need for "how to succeed in business." He studied all facets of songwriting, including the economic and social ones. Uninterested in school as a youth, he always did his homework in life. He was a voracious reader and loved to learn even the arcane details of any subject that caught his interest, from sketching to carpentry to the law. Loesser knew the trail he was blazing, and he drew particular lessons from Irving Berlin's career. He understood that Berlin succeeded so handsomely in part because he was his own publisher. Hoagy Carmichael reported that, in the early days, "Frank always wanted to be Irving Berlin" and used Berlin's career as a model for his own.[33] Kimball and Nelson observe that Loesser was so intent on following

Berlin's business career that he even hired Berlin's lawyers to represent his interests: Irving Cohen in Los Angeles and Francis Gilbert in New York.[34]

Loesser's experience as an apprentice in the Hollywood studio system of the 1930s, where every transaction—with virtually every word and note under contract—was assigned a dollar-and-cents value, also conditioned him to follow the reports of his song sales closely. His pragmatic attention to details, indeed his obsession with them, served him well both as a creator of musicals and as a businessman.

At his death in 1969, the West Coast trade publication *Weekly Variety* described him as a "songsmith-librettist-music publisher-producer" with an estate valued at $4 million. The paper "ranked [him] with Irving Berlin and Cole Porter as a topmost ASCAP performing rights earner," and declared, "when Samuel Goldwyn paid $1,000,000 for the screen rights to 'Guys and Dolls' it set a new high mark at the time for a Broadway musical's film rights."[35] Considering that ASCAP's entire annual payout for the early 1960s came to about $33 million, it is clear that Loesser was a major player by any standard.[36]

Loesser and the Media

Billboard had been listing top-selling Tin Pan Alley songs since 1890, but the business of tracking hit songs on the broadcast media of Loesser's day (the radio and later television), with its evident commercial implications, began in a public way in 1928, when the National Broadcasting Company assembled a group of sixty-nine affiliated stations across the country.[37] In 1935 NBC introduced a prime-time show entitled "Your Hit Parade," which was broadcast on radio and then on television through the 1950s. Sponsored by Lucky Strike cigarettes, this show devised the now familiar countdown format for presenting what were claimed to be the fifteen "most popular" songs of the week past, based on statistics determined from sheet music and record sales, broadcast time on NBC stations, and requests submitted to popular bandleaders.[38]

"Your Hit Parade" offered instant feedback about community tastes, but the radio show was heavily influenced by the personal preferences of Lucky Strike's tobacco tycoon owner George Washington Hill, the show's sponsor. His wishes were made clear and his edicts firm: danceable songs with an accent on the familiar were the only acceptable fare. Hill decreed, "The show shall consist of the songs that made Broadway Broadway," with the emphasis placed on the past tense. He forbade "extravagant, bizarre or involved arrangements" and insisted that all songs be performed by a standard group of musicians: an orchestra of forty plus a small group of assorted vocalists. The show's preferred orchestral sound favored medium-tempo ballads and dances no more exuberant than a foxtrot. Such biases favored Loesser's career, since he could deliver lyrics for these kinds of songs with ease.[39]

"Your Hit Parade" continued to air on radio until 1959. While it represented only one type of index, it was an important gauge of national as well as regional appeal. Despite its debatable statistical methods—*Variety*, among others, observed that "Your Hit Parade" criteria were subject to manipulation, to say the least—the comprehensive quality of the index was a helpful marketing yardstick for the makers of records and sheet music.

In the late 1930s, the music publishing firms associated with the major motion picture producers (Paramount, where Loesser worked, owned Famous Music) dominated the selections for "Your Hit Parade."[40] For the fastidious Loesser, such a ranking for one of his songs provided useful supplemental information about what the public seemed to like. And, of course, good rankings tended to encourage more recordings, which in turn boosted sheet music sales still further. As has already been noted, by the end of World War II Loesser's songs had appeared on several top-seller lists. Given the sustained enthusiasm for "Praise the Lord and Pass the Ammunition," "On a Slow Boat to China," and "My Darling, My Darling"—all million-copy sellers reappearing for at least a dozen weeks apiece on the charts—Loesser's reputation in the music business was secured.[41]

"Let's Incorporate"

Loesser first began to secure his creative efforts legally and officially in 1948 by founding Susan Publications Inc., named after his infant daughter. He had help from his friend E. H. "Buddy" Morris, one of the early codirectors for Warner Brothers' music division (who also challenged Warner with an antitrust suit in 1950). Morris knew the legal ins and outs of the publishing business; in Susan Loesser's words, "he did the nitty-gritty work."[42] Loesser knew the producing end of it, of course, and he was becoming a well-known force in the industry.

Loesser must have been thinking ahead, even as he broke free of restrictive Hollywood lyric-writing contracts. Since the establishment of Susan

Publications occurred before October 1948, when *Where's Charley?* opened, his original object was to secure clear control and copyright of his own works and to pick up other unprotected songs along the way. In the early days of broadcasting, the details of music copyright law (established in 1909) consisted of information that publishers, record producers, and promoters kept close to their chests. But, ever following Berlin's example, Loesser retained the rights for as many of his songs as possible. He realized that ASCAP's practice of dividing its money equally between publishers and authors would benefit him if he were both author and publisher.[43]

Loesser also understood that films could include songs that would boost earnings for everyone. Movie musicals were especially popular between the opening of *The Broadway Melody* in 1929 and the granting of authority to the Production Code (censorship) committee in 1934.[44] In 1935 well over half of the fifty top-selling songs had been heard first in motion pictures.[45] For a variety of reasons, then, tunes that Tin Pan Alley or Hollywood failed to exploit interested Loesser, who had a keen eye and ear for such orphans. The sustained popularity of movie musicals also explains why two of his biggest commercial song hits of the 1950s, "Anywhere I Wander" and "Thumbelina," had no connection to his major Broadway shows; both came from his score for *Hans Christian Andersen*, which in the first week after its release had a bigger audience than any live Broadway run could ever attract.[46]

As these examples show, while musicians' profits were less than publicity sheets might contend, songwriters who managed to secure adequate control in negotiations with publishers, producers, studios, and performers, and who refused to sell their songs outright for a one-time fee, could make a good living.[47] Because the major corporate entities—recording companies, studios, and broadcasters—cut favorable deals among themselves, it behooved all participants in the process—from top executives down to lowly copyists—to define by contract their roles and terms of remuneration. Teams of lawyers were required. Formal incorporation was a commonsense move when one's interests were as broad and diverse as Loesser's.

The intensity of business dealings grew so great, in fact, that by the early 1950s charges of monopoly and payola—the bribing of radio disc jockeys to favor specific recordings in airplay—were beginning to be heard. Loesser's name was never associated with such scandals, but many former habitués of the Brill Building could later recall the "sharks" in the neighborhood, the "evil" often accompanying Top 40 strivers, and the "race to get on the [rating] sheet."[48] Success in the music business could mean big profits, and failure could bring big losses. But Loesser, who possessed a gambler's streak, rarely failed to spot a sure thing and invest in it.

Loesser the Mentor

Loesser's habit of giving helpful advice to colleagues dated at least as far back as his Hollywood years. Jule Styne concludes his anecdotes about his early contacts with Frank, and their collaboration on the 1941 hit song "I Don't Want to Walk without You, Baby," with a Loesser maxim for choosing lyricists: "Don't ever write with smart-ass rhymers. Write with people who have something to say with their words. Fellows who are thoughtful and literate, and have wit."[49]

As his own star continued to rise, Loesser always kept an eye open for young talent. Jo Sullivan Loesser would later recall one of Frank's favorite mottos as "Improve the breed."[50] This generous attitude made a big impression on Robert Wright and George (Chet) Forrest. Loesser had known about the successful adaptation of Edvard Grieg's music by the young team for *Song of Norway* (1944). But by the early 1950s, they had gone a long while without another hit.[51] Susan Loesser reports how her father astonished them at their first meeting. The two were astounded by his interest in and knowledge of what they considered some of their "most complicated and unsuccessful lyrics" from the musical that was to become *Kismet*. "Before that afternoon came to an end," both men told Susan, "Frank said, 'I'd like to publish your score.' I don't think we gave it a second thought. We had had a contract with Chappell, but they had shown a distinct lack of interest and had let it lapse. So we were free. Frank was very close to the show—brought everybody to hear it. And Lynn [Loesser] and Dick Gray plugged the score. Nothing was ever exploited like that score was. I think there were something like thirty-six different records made before the show ever left its California tryout for Broadway."[52]

The full-court press through print advertising and advance recordings by Loesser's company paid off. *Kismet*, based heavily on music by the nineteenth-century Russian Aleksandr Borodin—in a Romantic vein that Loesser recognized as golden—produced two huge hits: "Stranger in Paradise" and "Baubles, Bangles, and Beads," along with a half-dozen other attractive numbers. Chalking up 583 performances, *Kismet* ended its run as the second most attended Broadway musical of 1953 (following Cole Porter

Frank Loesser casting a critical eye. Frank Loesser Enterprises.

and Abe Burrows's *Can-Can* at 892). Wright and Forrest had less luck in shows based on their own tunes, such as *Kean* (in 1961, a biographical play about the famous English actor Edmund Kean), or in recycling the music of Rachmaninoff for *Anya* (1965), a Russian-themed show about the mysterious Grand Duchess Anastasia. Nevertheless, Loesser supported the team through thick and thin. His combination of direct business dealings and a willingness to take a chance on new material endeared him to these men and many others.[53]

Despite a fiery temper and a patron's air in dispensing favors, Loesser was nothing if not loyal to his writers, assistants, secretaries, and coworkers. Reminiscence after reminiscence confirms his entrepreneurial spirit and sense of commitment. He rewarded the individuals who helped him along the way by passing on the favor to others. He treated his colleagues as family. Business for Loesser was about the people who did the business as much as it was about money, although he never disdained the money.

Among others he took in hand, he marketed the songs of Richard Adler

and Jerry Ross, taking them, as Kimball and Nelson note, "literally and figuratively" from "Rags to Riches" (their hit song of 1953) to their two blockbuster shows, *The Pajama Game* (1954) and *Damn Yankees* (1955).[54] Among
other favors, Loesser introduced them to Broadway's legendary director, producer, and show doctor George Abbott, who eventually presented them with
Richard Bissell's novel *7 1/2 Cents*, the basis for *The Pajama Game*.[55]

Jerry Herman's account of meeting Loesser is characteristic of many
others:

> When I was about eighteen and had just started to go to Parsons School of
> Design, my mother made me bring a bunch of my songs to Frank Loesser. A
> friend of hers knew someone who knew him. I was very shy, scared to death.
> He said, "I want you to play everything you've ever written."
>   When I finished, he sat me down like a Dutch uncle. "I'm not trying to
> tell you this is an easy business. Some people make it and some people don't.
> But you can tell your parents I think you have what it takes." Then he drew a
> picture of a train with a caboose. "This is what makes a good song," he said.
> "The locomotive has to start it. The caboose has to finish it off. Those are the
> bookends. Then you fill in different colors for the cars in the middle." It was
> such a graphic, beautiful lesson about how to write a song. It stayed with me
> forever.[56]

Loesser, whose doodles and sketches reveal above-average drafting skill,
chose precisely the right medium to encourage a young man studying art at
Parsons.

Not all the lessons he taught were so immediately profitable, but Loesser's directives often revealed his uncompromising standards. He sometimes
held out for the unattainable and lost in the bargain. He once told Adler and
Ross he was doing his best to sell one of their songs but refused to let them
part with it for only $2,500, insisting it was worth much more. No buyer ever
paid the price and, according to Adler, the song remains unpublished and
unrecorded.[57]

Loesser's mentoring could be quite specific and immediately useful
for the performers who could take his directness. Donna McKechnie's first
Broadway role was as a chorister and understudy in *How to Succeed in Business Without Really Trying*. As she tells it,

> Frank Loesser was my first vocal coach. He could be the most romantic of
> men—he wrote those lush melodies—but he was also like one of those guys
> standing on the corner in *Guys and Dolls*. Once he came down the aisle of
> the stage: "Hey, honey, make the gesture first."

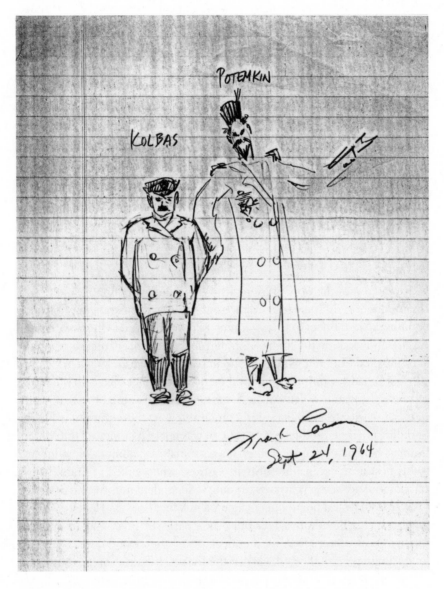

Frank Loesser's signed pencil drawing of two costumes for characters in *Pleasures and Palaces*, 1965. Loesser was a lifelong maker of sketches and doodles. Frank Loesser Enterprises.

"What?" I asked. I didn't understand.

He repeated. "Make the gesture first."

He was right, of course. The gesture comes first; it works that way. You mimic your organic response, do whatever your physical impulse is, then follow it with your voice. Like in A *Chorus Line*, you cross your arms and grab your chest before you sing, "God, I'm a dancer . . ." I began thinking about my physical life, what I do with my body.[58]

Loesser did not stint on praise even when he witnessed the triumph of a potential rival. When Stephen Sondheim, only thirty-two at the time, scored big with the music and lyrics for A *Funny Thing Happened on the Way to the Forum* (1962), the older man shot off a memorable congratulatory letter that Sondheim treasured. "Sometimes even a composer's working partners, to say nothing of the critics, fail to dig every level and facet of what he is doing. But *I* know, and I wanted you to know I know," wrote Loesser.[59]

The list of favors and advice dispensed goes on and on. Loesser took an active interest in the work of Meredith Willson and supported him through the production of *The Music Man* (1957).[60] Individuals ranging from pop composer Mark Bucci to prize-winning playwright Alfred Uhry to longtime lyricist and book writer Betty Comden and veteran chanteuse Margaret Whiting credit Loesser with giving them lessons to live and work by.[61]

As a Broadway intimate and loyal New Yorker concerned with the future of musical theater in general, Loesser realized the value of making common cause with his fellow musical comedy creators. This impulse led to the founding of Frank Productions in 1960. It was not that he viewed the competition as benign, of course. Rather, his passionate sociability was connected to his best business instincts. Stuart Ostrow, who worked at Frank Music Corporation for seven years before going independent in 1961, was a twenty-two-year-old would-be producer when he first met Loesser. He dates the beginning of his Broadway career from their earliest conversations: "He told me in no uncertain terms: 'A producer is someone who knows a writer—loud [singing] is good—and work in the theatre because you'll always have someplace to go after dinner.' Armed with these commandments, I began my Broadway journey. There were dozens of young producers trying their wings in the fifties, which is one reason why the theatre soared."[62]

The mottos are vintage Loesser, and Ostrow's count of "dozens of young producers" explains the significance of Loesser's role as adviser, go-between, and ear to the ground. Loesser was clever, clear, tough, and generous—and always focused on communicating the essentials. Ostrow's anecdote also affirms Loesser's deep understanding of the social component of the music business in shows, on radio, or on television. As a boss he was demanding but open-handed, and he seems to have noticed everything that went on around him. Having "someplace to go after dinner" is not only a choice one-liner, it speaks to an essential part of the process. Socializing with theater people was a key part of business strategy. His friend and lawyer, Harold Orenstein, once remarked, "Frank never took a chance, . . . he had every angle figured. He played the marvelous game of being the last one to fit the piece in the puzzle."[63] Loesser's loyal longtime secretary, Mona Lipp, told Susan Loesser, "You couldn't top him. Frank would always do you one better."[64]

Just as radio and early sound recordings had propelled popular tunes and performers of the Roaring Twenties across the country and the world, the production companies of Broadway set up tours and spread the newest Broadway melodies via traveling shows with professional actors. Frank Productions was in the thick of this action.

Abe Burrows subtitled his autobiography "Is There Really No Business Like Show Business?" adding a whimsical perspective to Irving Berlin's song title as well as to his own relationship with the theater. But his close friend Frank Loesser, for all his ebullient high spirits, took the business of show business very seriously and to a level of precision all its own. The Frank Music Corporation office files were impeccably organized. Loesser and his staff could account for every paid use of his music and similar deals with other hired writers long before computers made the task comparatively easy. All contracts were carefully preserved.[65] Loesser would have understood the meaning of the modern expression "24/7," for he loved to talk shop all the time.

There seem to be almost as many Frank Loesser anecdotes as there are musical comedy veterans who knew him, but many of the stories share a central theme. They illustrate basic points about song making and musical power. They get down to essential elements. They encapsulate operating instructions for professional or would-be professional musicians and lyricists. They reveal Loesser at his analytical best: an intellectual in tough-guy clothing who understood that artistry, energy, and effort must be interwoven in order to produce the illusions on which stagecraft depends.

Whether or not Loesser actually articulated all the ideas for which he is given credit, a larger point emerges: Loesser and his working methods were associated with integrity and attention to musical structure. He paid attention. He taught the way to build a show, and he had a sense of history. Composer Charles Strouse, for instance, in defining "authenticity" and "sophistication" in the making of musicals, once declared, "you've got to be aware of what Michael Bennett and Jerome Robbins and Elliott Carter and perhaps Frank Loesser have done" (probably the only instance in the literature of the musical in which Elliott Carter's and Frank Loesser's name appear in the same sentence).[66] Abba Bogin insisted that Loesser was ever the stickler for originality and guarded carefully against inadvertently copying anyone else's tunes.[67]

Many Loesser stories carry the aroma of urban legend, enlarged in the retelling to underline the genius, the open-handedness, and the eccentricities of a born wheeler-dealer. Yet as a quick-witted teacher and perceptive critic, he could efficiently deliver astute judgments about personal talent, assessing the quality of a song or even a whole show on the spot (although he seems to have lost some of this knack regarding his own work after *How to Succeed*). His diagnoses, when positive, fed the dreams of Broadway aspirants. Even his mistakes in judgment reflected integrity and a belief in doing your best work. His mentoring, whatever form it took, filled the needs of his most talented associates. Stuart Ostrow and others stress that Loesser always told the truth as he saw it—as hard as it might be to hear. He issued no gratuitous compliments and refused to call mediocrity anything else.[68] Still, as his friend the writer Cynthia Lindsay declared, "Knowing Frank Loesser was a rare and rewarding experience. . . . no matter who and what you were, he made you better. Whether it was your talent, your humor, your confidence in yourself, you came away from him more creative, funnier, more perceptive about yourself and lighter in spirit; a prettier woman, a stronger man—in fact, crazy about yourself, because he made you the best of what you were."[69]

Loesser himself had received less of this kind of guidance than would have been ideal. His mother and older brother never saw his work as more than meretricious. Receiving honest but supportive feedback from Hollywood professionals and watching the work habits of his compatriots at Paramount, he discovered a career. Ultimately, he found great satisfaction in passing on the tricks of the trade he had learned along the way.

As we have seen, Loesser lured many young comers to his office. He enjoyed the rough and tumble of deal making, and he especially enjoyed the discovery and promotion of new talent. As Kimball and Nelson have written,

"No one in the American musical theater since George Gershwin did more than Loesser to foster and encourage the work of his colleagues."[70]

"A Producer Is Someone Who Knows a Writer"

The transformation of Susan Publications into the Frank Music Corporation in 1950, a few months after the opening of *Guys and Dolls*, confirmed Loesser's sure sense of business timing. Road companies and an original cast recording for that show followed its Broadway success in short order. Later in the decade Loesser would go on to develop Music Theatre International (MTI), a show licensing company (still in operation), and then in 1960 Frank Productions, through which he would produce his own show of that year, *Greenwillow*.[71] In this second set of business enterprises, especially MTI, Loesser was again following the lead of other colleagues—in this case, Rodgers and Hammerstein, whose underwriting of other writers' productions was profiting them handsomely. Such secondary licensing, as it is called, for amateur and professional productions around the country was a logical outgrowth of Loesser's commitment to Broadway. He found a need and filled it. The list of Frank Productions, now owned by Freddie Gershon (who in the 1970s produced a large number of shows in London, including *Hair*, *Jesus Christ Superstar*, and *Sweeney Todd*), came to include *Gentlemen Prefer Blondes*, *Call Me Madam*, *High Button Shoes*, *Pajama Game*, *Damn Yankees*, *The Music Man*, *A Funny Thing Happened on the Way to the Forum*, *Candide*, *Fiddler on the Roof*, *The Fantasticks*, *Jesus Christ Superstar*, *Les Misérables*, and *Miss Saigon*.[72]

As Frank Music's catalog expanded in the 1950s, it acquired several notable tunes: Hy Zaret and Alex North's "Unchained Melody" from the film *Unchained* (1955) and Arthur Hamilton's "Cry Me a River" (1955), the latter made famous partly by the highly successful Barbra Streisand recording in 1963 on Columbia's *The Barbra Streisand Album*. The former received an Academy Award nomination, and the latter, as the eighth-best-selling album of the year, sold enough to win a gold record and several Grammy Awards. Loesser's coaching and marketing assistance led directly to individual song sales and establishing hit shows, as has been noted already (see table 2.1 in chapter 2). In 1976 Frank Music was bought by CBS and eventually became a part of MPL Communications, Paul McCartney's music publishing company, where it remains today.[73]

The Coming of Television

In 1951 Loesser associated himself with the newest entertainment medium of the day—television—when he composed the theme song of *The College Bowl* (not to be confused with the later 1960s quiz program), starring Chico Marx. Like many other things Loesser did, this led to a major commitment. Not surprisingly, he quickly came to realize television's potential for spreading his music, and after conversations with advertising executives he began to develop ways to be further involved in the medium, especially in the highly remunerative work of putting together commercial jingles. General Electric and its cartoon spokesman of the 1960s, Mr. Magoo, adapted "The New Ashmolean Marching Society and Students' Conservatory Band" to sell soft white lightbulbs.[74] When Gold Medal Flour, part of the General Mills Corporation, needed a television pitch in 1966, Loesser was ready to offer his "Fugue for Tinhorns" to entice homemakers across America to buy the product:

> Create a chocolate cake,
> Create a cherry pie.
> Create a stack of golden biscuits ten feet high.
> Can do, can do,
> With Gold Medal you can do,
> Can do, can do.
>
> It gives you confidence
> Down to your fingertips.
> Your white thumb tells you that you can't miss.
> Can do, can do,
> With Gold Medal you can do,
> Can do, can do.[75]

According to music business historian Russell Sanjek, "Broadcasters spent $3.5 million on jingles in 1962. Music publishers got up to $50,000 for the use of a hallowed standard by Cole Porter in a nationwide advertising campaign and anywhere from $750 [*sic*] for a current hit to be used on a regional- or local-market schedule."[76] Compensation on this level certainly caught Loesser's attention, and he evinced no artistic snobbery about it. He was too busy being clever, being creative, and making money. According to Susan Loesser, "Frank Music Corporation produced jingles for Sunkist Lemonade, Halo Shampoo, Newport Filter Cigarettes ('A hint of mint makes the difference'), Sanka Aroma Roast, and various (and very local) beers. My father just enjoyed it to tears."[77]

Censorship in the Fifties

Loesser's development of businesses encircling his shows suggests that he was committed to a grand idea—bringing Broadway, or a close facsimile of it, to everyone who would listen or watch. He knew well that theatrical productions and musical shows were larger-than-life fantasies—*Guys and Dolls* was billed as a "musical fable of Broadway"—that could be inhabited and embraced by viewers, expanding their imaginative lives if only for a few hours of an evening. Businesses spun off the basic product helped to perpetuate the total enterprise. Loesser was unembarrassed about connections between business and music, because he maintained that the music being sold adhered to the highest standards of quality. Commodification per se was not a problem for him, so long as the original artists were fairly compensated in the process.

Because Loesser valued his work so highly and respected the difficulties of the creative process, he resented attempts to cut or modify his songs on other than artistic or functional grounds. Not surprisingly, he found meddlers and censors annoying. Unfortunately, he had to cope with them throughout most of his professional career, starting in the 1930s, when the forces seeking to police Hollywood and the movies began girding for action. Scripts and song lyrics had to be submitted for all proposed films to the Production Code Administration's Joseph I. Breen and his review committee.[78] This censorship board routinely objected to specific lines of dialogue and lyrics, as well as film segments that were deemed to be overly suggestive of immoral behavior. By the late 1930s, censors in selected screening locations across the country regularly filled out and submitted check-off "analysis charts" in which questions about each film's content were posed: "Illicit sex?" "Any killings?" "Any racial angle?" "Any foreign angle?" Settings were noted ("bedrooms?" "church?" "beach?"), and the portrayal of particular types of characters (including lawyers, judges, doctors, "Negroes," children, and policemen) was asked to be rated as "good," "bad," or "indifferent." Immoral behaviors could be depicted as long as nudity and overtly sexual behavior were avoided on-screen and criminal perpetrators received proper punishment before the end of the film.[79]

Approval of a lyric or script was requested and usually awarded by form letter ("Please advise if the enclosed lyrics have your approval"; "I am happy to report that these lyrics meet the requirements of the Production Code"). In the relatively frequent instances where only a line or two was found wanting, a brief comment was issued: "The following lines seem suggestive and should be changed." Sometimes changes were refused and the original lines stayed in, at least in the early days.[80]

The Catholic Legion of Decency and the Production Code board were ever-present watchdogs over the conduct of actors, singers, and writers. But what had been an onerous though relatively automatic process in the 1930s intensified during the Cold War era. Anticommunism fed the rise of McCarthyism, and the combination of old-fashioned prudery with Atomic Age fears stoked social uneasiness during the 1950s. The Production Code committee's one-page "analysis chart" of 1937 had grown by 1951 into a booklet of seven pages, most of which sought remarks about issues of special interest to the censors: "the portrayal of professions," "races and nationals," "liquor," "crime," and "sociological factors" (a rubric covering everything from depictions of praying congregations to courtroom decorum to marriage ceremonies).[81]

Movie moguls Jack Warner and Samuel Goldwyn were called to testify before the U.S. House of Representatives Committee on Un-American Activities (HUAC) in 1947, and they admitted to Hollywood's having sheltered "Communists" in its midst.[82] Abe Burrows, among others, was caught up in the net of suspicion and blacklisted for several years. Given these pressures, which were felt in Hollywood during most of Loesser's time there, it is hardly surprising that he found more job satisfaction in the relatively free atmosphere of live theater in New York during the late 1940s.

The official guardians of American middle-class morality were targets Loesser found hard to resist. As a military veteran and composer of "Praise the Lord and Pass the Ammunition" and "The Ballad of Rodger Young," Loesser's patriotic credentials were impeccable, but he was always a lyrical libertine. He loved to push the limits, and, preserving an artisan's sense of proprietorship for theater pieces, he arrived at every potentially constraining situation prepared with a retort against those who would repress irreverent spirits, especially his own.

Loesser's personal attitude to Production Code dictates and religious and governmental censorship can only be inferred from the record and his lifelong habits of irreverence for sacred cows. To his credit, his friendship with Abe Burrows remained solid in the face of the charges made against

Burrows. Apparently Loesser was never called before Congress to testify or threatened with blacklisting. But he loudly objected to the censoring of his songs on moralistic grounds, when the criticism came from an individual producer, performer, or audience member.[83]

The Loesser Spirit

Playwright and screenwriter Paddy Chayefsky (1923–1981) once claimed that "Frank has the most original mind in musical theatre," and he echoed Bob Fosse in calling Loesser "the inventor of the anti-hero."[84] Duly noting Rodgers and Hart's *Pal Joey* as having introduced a bad-guy protagonist on Broadway well before Nathan Detroit or Sky Masterson, perhaps Chayefsky saw Loesser himself as the prototypical "anti-hero." Loesser certainly flaunted an irreverent attitude, while also exercising his highly original mind.

Loesser's position in the history of musical comedy is neatly summed up by Martin Gottfried: "[Jule] Styne and [Frank] Loesser are the last of America's great pop songwriters to have crossed show business's great divide— from Tin Pan Alley to Shubert Alley, from pop music to theater. The theater composers after them were all stage specialists. Styne and Loesser brought the unpretentiousness of the music business with them."[85] Composer Mark Bucci, a protégé of Loesser's at Frank Music from 1957 to 1960, told Susan Loesser, "I heard he was fond of developing writers, so I just called him up. I used to meet with him at his apartment. My music was always too science-fictiony, too fancy, I think, for Broadway. But I wanted to write a commercial musical. And Frank, having done *The Most Happy Fella*, wanted to write an 'important' opera. Every time I'd come up with something he'd say, 'Write more down to earth. Write another "California, Here I Come."' "[86]

Loesser's best instincts always led him to stick with the vernacular, but to maintain that impulse as Broadway was changing challenged some old habits. His songs of the 1930s and 1940s often automatically ended up in a dramatic setting—the movies. A song's commercial success was achieved partly from exposure in films. But as Gerald Mast has observed,

> Another subtle shift in postwar musicals, with artistic and commercial consequences, was the divorce of America's show music from its pop music—actually the divorce of its theater music from its dance music. While Broadway shows once came from Tin Pan Alley, Tin Pan Alley had moved from West 28th Street to Motown and Mersey and Nashville. Even in 1943, when Rodgers joined Hammerstein, the period of American popular music that

produced the standard jazz and popular repertory had ended, when songs
that were once sung or danced on theater stages and movie screens were the
songs to which Americans danced offstage and offscreen as well.

Hit songs, the name of the game for Berlin, Gershwin, even Kern, depended on dancing, [especially] paired social dancing. . . . Broadway musicals of the [1950s and 1960s] chose to have little to do with the [uncoupled
style of rock dancing], for the musical patterns and styles that defined character were based on the alternative dancing tradition of engaged pairs.

The divorce of American theater music from its dance music made it
more serious and more grand, even as it made it less American and less popular—particularly with the young.[87]

Mast has honed in on a point of interest in most of Loesser's musicals:
namely, how dance was used or integrated within the whole. In general the
composer seems to have found a happy medium. The dances in Loesser's
two most popular shows, *Guys and Dolls* and *How to Succeed*, were devised
by celebrated choreographers working at the top of their game. (The earlier
collaboration with Balanchine in *Where's Charley?* was less significant.) Both
received accolades for their efforts and were seen as essential to their shows.
Where's Charley? was built around a star dancer who did much of his own
choreography. *The Most Happy Fella* and *Greenwillow* incorporated strong
dance numbers, but they were sometimes viewed as disconnected from the
rest of the show. Even the failed *Pleasures and Palaces* was conceived from
the start with a large dance component. The 2003 mounting of *Señor Discretion Himself* revolved around its dance elements.

Had he lived, Frank Loesser would surely have taken careful note of the
innovations in the 1970s, including some of the dancing shows and so-called
concept musicals, and even tried his hand at them.[88] His taste for experiment
and grand gesture (wanting to write "important" shows) and his knowledge
of the history of Broadway dance songs and movie musicals would have made
such projects seem natural, especially given what took place in the work-
shops of John Kander, Fred Ebb, and Stephen Sondheim over the course of
time. Dancing could be innovative without being pretentious, a welcome
component for a vernacular entertainment.

The Sources of the Loesser Aesthetic

One of the small ironies of Frank Loesser's career, but also perhaps a
key to his long-term success, appeared with the unexpected sales of "Praise

the Lord and Pass the Ammunition" in 1942. That a patriotic quip attributed to a Navy chaplain should have been the inspiration for the fairly irreligious Loesser seems at least odd. How right the song was for the moment was summed up well by Frank's equally intellectual and secular older
brother, Arthur, in 1950: "The nature of the tune . . . reveals a great canniness. It refrains from modern, urban, musical slang; it avoids any suggestion
that anyone might consider disreputable, anything Negroid, jazzy, Jewish,
Broadwayish or night-clubby. Instead the melody has an affinity for that of
the *Battle Hymn of the Republic*; it tastes like school, church, grandma, and
biscuits: a master stroke of diplomacy, aptness, and good business."[89]

Arthur seems to have understood his half brother's talents, even though
his compliments often contained more than a whiff of condescension.
Clearly, both men shared much and brought similarly keen intellects to their
work. In 1954, Columbia University professor and historian Jacques Barzun
had this to say in his preface to the older brother's latest book: "Nothing
that is or was relevant is too slight for his notice; nothing that can entice the
imagination of the curious and the thoughtful is too impalpable for him to
convey. . . . he could never have made [his most recent work] in seven years
or seventeen, if he had not started with a large fund of general culture and
miscellaneous reading. . . . Mr. Loesser, it is clear, is a man of strong and vivid
opinions, and they color his work. No one but a pedant would want it colorless . . . his entire work is of a piece, free alike from witless gush and hollow
gravity."[90] So much sounds exactly like Frank, and despite their difference in
age the brothers apparently enjoyed each other's company and mutually reinforced their shared passion for artistic detail. Susan Loesser notes that her
father "never once spoke harshly of Arthur," despite the elder's superior attitude.[91] Yet the brothers were intellectually and emotionally dissimilar also,
and Arthur disrespected Frank's best music chiefly because it was popular. In
short, Arthur was a snob.

Between the publication of "Praise the Lord" and Arthur's article eight
years later, America would see and undergo fundamental political and cultural changes that permanently reconstructed the social matrix within which
Frank Loesser would find his greatest success. Things "Negroid, jazzy, [and]
Jewish" would continue to vex and provoke the body politic and affect developments in popular culture. But while Loesser's take on social issues can be
inferred from some of his work, on the whole he avoided politics and showed
little inclination to treat topics of the day as Oscar Hammerstein chose to do
in *South Pacific* (1949) or *Flower Drum Song* (1958), or as Bernstein did in

West Side Story (1957). He accepted American society for what it was and could be and worked with the forms he had inherited.

As we have observed already, Loesser liked to compare himself (and was compared by others) to Irving Berlin and Richard Rodgers.[92] He was a near contemporary and close friend of Jule Styne (1905–1994), but their careers followed slightly different trajectories, and of course Styne outlived Loesser by twenty-five active years. Gerald Mast draws an intriguing but incomplete parallel between the Broadway works of Leonard Bernstein—*On the Town* (1944), *Wonderful Town* (1953), *Candide* (1956), and *West Side Story* (1957)—with Loesser's four hits from 1948 to 1961: "Leonard Bernstein, Frank Loesser, and the team of Alan Jay Lerner and Frederick Loewe, the most distinguished postwar creators of musical plays, were both causes and effects of the musical's vitality in the decade after the war. Bernstein and Loesser took opposite roads only to arrive at a similar place."[93] Bernstein migrated from classical training and symphonic composition to Broadway musicals, culminating in the vernacular musical drama, *West Side Story*, Mast explains, whereas Loesser's early experience in the pop song and Hollywood music realm led to musicals and his most serious musical play, *The Most Happy Fella*. Both men set at least two of their hits in New York City and a third in "a world apart."[94] Both had catholic musical tastes, were superb speakers and teachers, and were somewhat divided in their own self-assessments, though always casting their lot on the side of accessible, democratic art.

Jerome Kern, who died in 1945, before any of Loesser's fully mature musicals appeared, suggests another kind of comparison. With his earliest interpolated songs, the justly famous Princess Theatre shows—which he put together with writers P.G. Wodehouse and Guy Bolton—and the incomparable landmark *Show Boat* (1927), Kern tracked a similar career path to Loesser's a full generation earlier. Kern was a youthful prodigy, took early lessons with his mother, and later studied at New York's College of Music.[95] Loesser's training was much more spotty. He probably picked up basic technique from observing his father as well as friends, adding self-disciplined practice and observation later, although he studied and prepared through reading conscientiously in the early 1950s. His early knowledge and instincts about harmony were acquired first by ear rather than through books or instruction.

Kern served his apprenticeship years shuttling between New York and London as a song plugger for T. B. Harms (the publisher who practically cornered the market on production music). Loesser famously split his time between New York and Hollywood, having first worked at the Back Drop nightclub and then heading west to work for Paramount as it emerged as one of the great film companies.

Both men had the good fortune of being mentored by masters of their craft and enjoying opportunities to work with peers who possessed complementary talents to their own. Kern was taken under the wing of Edward Rice, one of the great producers of the late nineteenth century, who placed his songs into the English import *Mr. Wix of Wickham* (1904).[96] Loesser's good relations with George Abbott in *Where's Charley?* helped his cause. Both Loesser and Kern made strong "practice" runs with shows leading up to their most famous works. For Kern, the successes of *Sally* (1920) and *Sunny* (1925), with remarkably high numbers of performances (at 570 and 517, respectively, the third and sixth largest runs of the decade), were crucial. *Sunny*, featuring the outstanding dancing turns of Marilyn Miller in a transatlantic love story and a production by the influential Charles Dillingham, probably encouraged him to press ahead with the grand conception that became *Show Boat*. It was also the first show in which he worked with Oscar Hammerstein II.[97]

Where's Charley?'s dancing star Ray Bolger and charming ingenue Allyn McLerie similarly fared well with the public, and the show achieved a spot among the top ten musicals for the 1940s.[98] Its impact also included the aftermath of fame and success for the songs "Once in Love with Amy" and especially "My Darling, My Darling," not to mention the impetus it provided for Loesser to write down a flock of tunes about Damon Runyon's short stories, in anticipation that a serviceable libretto would eventually be developed.

Both Kern and Loesser, thereafter, with the help of popular performers and excellent books written by well-tempered partners, created the singular musical of their careers. Both *Show Boat* and *Guys and Dolls* are based on the work of authors with reputations outside the theater, and as Mark N. Grant observes, both have affixed themselves in American cultural memory far more firmly than their literary progenitors.[99] Like Loesser, Kern was involved in the business end of music, having bought a part interest in Harms early in life. Both men took pride in their work and insisted that singers sing their songs the way they wrote them.

Kern was forty-two years old in 1927, and Loesser was forty in 1950. Both continued to produce other admirable work at the highest level of quality immediately following their hit shows, but neither superseded himself in the eyes of generations of fans: *Show Boat* and *Guys and Dolls* will remain into the foreseeable future the most important works for their respective composers. Both men died unexpectedly within twenty years of their pinnacle achievements.

Perhaps more significant than the parallel incidents of their careers and personal stories was the attitude both men shared upholding a particular principle of popular music writing: that a sober and artistically demanding attitude toward musical craftsmanship need not detract from a song or a show's accessibility to a wide audience. What Hammerstein had to say about his old partner Kern's perspective on "popular song" ten years after his death in 1945 could have been applied almost word for word to Loesser at the time the words appeared in print in 1955:

> Jerry had neither lofty illusions nor false modesty about his work. . . . He loved the tunes he wrote, and once his notes had found their right words, he would play his piano, close his eyes, and screech out the song ecstatically.
>
> He could not abide the phrase "serious music." Quite willing to admit that some music had more stature than popular songs in musical plays, he nevertheless would not grant that a musician who called himself "serious" was automatically a better artist than one who wrote light music. Bad serious music was certainly not better than good light music. . . .
>
> "What a wonderful life!" I can hear some readers musing—"a fun-loving man who, in between jokes, tossed off bright and lively and wonderful tunes." Well, musing reader, that isn't the way it happened. No good things are ever tossed off by anybody. The smooth and effortless melodies [of Kern's] are the result of unstinting and meticulous work. To begin with, it takes many industrious years to attain craftsmanship like Jerome Kern's. And then after you've got it, you have nothing more than the tools with which to do more and harder work. . . .
>
> Jerry was a worker who would never stop polishing until he was satisfied that a melody reached its destined shape. The high standards of his own exceptional taste were applied to every note he wrote.[100]

Of course, there were differences between the personalities and the songs of the two men. Although both knew the classical repertory, they grew up in different times and places and had different expectations of what a musical comedy should be. Kern started and finished his career as a musician, whereas Loesser, while highly valuing musical quality, was always a wordsmith first. Loesser once declared, "I'd like to have composed 'Begin the Beguine,' 'Younger Than Springtime,' and *Don Giovanni*." According to record producer Joseph Weiss, this meant "he wanted to write great works of sophistication, romanticism, and musical drama." Weiss goes on to observe: "He not only achieved these goals over the span of his career, he achieved them all in *The Most Happy Fella*."[101] Loesser's pipe dream and Weiss's comment merit further discussion.

The significance of Loesser's having singled out Cole Porter, Rodgers and Hammerstein, and Mozart and Lorenzo Da Ponte (the librettist for Mozart's three great Italian operas *Le nozze di Figaro*, *Don Giovanni*, and *Così fan tutte*) is suggestive. "Begin the Beguine" has been touted as the longest popular song ever written, ingeniously contrived to sustain a 108-measure refrain in a genre where the thirty-two-measure chorus is the norm. It never loses our attention with its undulating and ever-changing melody. In 1963 ASCAP ranked it among the top sixteen sellers of its hit parade for the previous half century.[102] In short, it was both innovative and highly successful.

Hammerstein's lyric in "Younger Than Springtime" from *South Pacific* uses simple yet fresh images ("younger than springtime," "softer than starlight," and so on), and although the noun "love" is absent, he works in "lovely" and "lover" as unhackneyed soundalikes. The straight-to-the-heart pathos is enhanced by a somewhat elevated text lacking rhyming word pairs. Hammerstein, like Loesser most of the time, understood how jangling and distracting too much rhyming could be. Rodgers's music fits like a glove.

As for *Don Giovanni*, the work was an updating of an old, popular, ribald, and socially provocative Spanish story, the legend of a rake named Don Juan (Sir John, in English). It is filled with ingratiating melodies, is rich in clever wordplay (the Don's servant Leporello famously recites a voluminous "catalog" of conquests made by his insatiable master), and blends comic and serious scenes. It is funny and bawdy, but casts a dark shadow with its talking statue returned from the dead. Furthermore, the drama is scaffolded upon a series of brilliant contrapuntal ensembles of the sort at which both Mozart and Loesser excelled. Like the guys of *Guys and Dolls*, Giovanni is a devilish, but devilishly clever—and loudly singing—scoundrel. He is eventually dragged off to hell, but not before enjoying a rousing good time. *Don Giovanni* goes far beyond farce to plumb deeper emotions. Indeed, Loesser's three models all have undertones of tragedy and loss, pointing perhaps to a broader and more personal sense of identification.

Like most prolific composers, Loesser found inspiration in a wide variety of sources, and he freely pilfered ideas large and small as it suited him, while being careful not to break the copyright laws.[103] On the lyric side is his evident admiration for and imitation of Stephen Leacock, Lorenz Hart, W. S.

Example 7.1. (a) Frank Loesser, introduction to "The Ugly Duckling," and
(b) J. S. Bach, "Fugue in C," mm. 9–10, *Little Clavier Book for Wilhelm
Friedemann Bach* (BWV 953)

Gilbert, and Ira Gershwin. On the musical side, we have noted shades of
Irving Berlin, Johnny Mercer, Jerome Kern, Richard Rodgers, Cole Porter,
and Mozart.

Loesser's debt to classical composers other than Mozart is less prominent, but it is clear that he grew up hearing a variety of classical works and
possessed a highly retentive memory.[104] It is unsurprising to find classical
fragments in his music from time to time. Such usage was simply part of his
tool kit. Quoting Grieg's piano concerto as a signifier of romantic awaken-
ing works nicely in *How to Succeed*, as does the Mozartean military flourish in a song with a military theme, "To Marry," in *Pleasures and Palaces*.
While such allusions or recollections may be viewed as isolated instances
of musical coloring, Loesser's ingenuity and memory also aided his use of
musical elements over longer stretches of a song. For example, the use of a
"waddling" accompaniment figure as an introduction and linking orchestral
theme in "The Ugly Duckling" (from the film *Hans Christian Andersen*) reveals once again how Loesser habitually sought to match musical mood and
technical gesture. Inspection of the Bach-like figure in example 7.1 suggests
little in the way of historical allusion, pun, or parody, but the similarity in
sound between the two excerpts is clear. His ear knew, if his eye did not, that
a sonic relationship exists here. It is possible that sometime during his formative years, Loesser actually heard this fugue from the *Little Clavier Book for
Wilhelm Friedemann Bach* (BWV 953) played by his father, his brother, or

one of their pupils. (Similar passages can also be found in Bach's works for unaccompanied violin and cello.) That some subtle reference was intended by Loesser for this fairly benign bit of passagework seems unlikely. It appears the natural result of a musician's unconscious mind coming into play.

This is not to say that Loesser denied his classical proclivities. He seems always to have stood ready to make use of the larger musical world that he had experienced. Unlike his half brother Arthur, he showed no snobbery when it came to musical genre. Marc Blitzstein, the composer of *The Cradle Will Rock* (written in 1936–37, on Broadway in 1938) and *Regina* (1949, rev. 1953) and the translator/adapter of Bertolt Brecht and Kurt Weill's *Die Dreigroschenoper* as *The Threepenny Opera*, was one of many living models that Loesser emulated. "When Blitzstein caught [Loesser] in the audience [of *Regina* for the] fourth time and asked him why, the songwriter replied, 'I'm studying,'" reports Blitzstein's biographer.[105] When the original cast recording was made (1958), Loesser discussed Blitzstein's work in incisive terms: "Beyond delivering neat musical capsules that conveniently paraphrase steps in the narrative, Blitzstein gives a special magic illumination to the whole thing, making the already enormous emotion of the story even more wonderfully memorable than before."[106]

Bringing the "magic illumination" of "enormous emotion" to enhance memorability seems also to have been a Loesser priority. Moreover, he insistently aimed at the widest possible audience. In his German grandparents' era, culturally ambitious Americans spilled much ink and expressed deep concern over the waves of immigrants landing on American shores and their effect on America's cultural life. The essence of "Americanness" was frequently debated in the press or defined by academics, pundits, and politicians in racial and ethnic terms.[107] But while many immigrant groups brought music from the home country to the United States, many of their children's generation embraced the new country's culture in preference to the old. One result was the music now often referred to as Tin Pan Alley: urban songs produced for wide distribution and aimed at middle- and working-class city dwellers. This commercial industry, which encompassed thousands of songs, had a lasting effect across classes and regions. As Charles Hamm has written, "Tin Pan Alley did not draw on traditional music — it created traditional music."[108] Other musical fruit that grew to maturity in the first two-thirds of the twentieth century included ragtime; jazz; gospel hymns; "ultramodern" symphonic, chamber, and choral works; neoclassical or neoromantic music for the screen and stage; and, of course, Broadway songs and shows. These all existed simultaneously and were recorded repeatedly; together they made for a vibrant public soundscape.

Loesser, like his most talented contemporaries, pushed ahead with his art using musical idioms and vernacular language rooted in American experience, tradition, and literature. His choices were eclectic but not eccentric. He was overt about his goals: to entertain, to make money, and to express or evoke an emotional response as directly as possible—and to do all these things with skill, care, and apparent ease. He wanted his music to be accessible but finely crafted. He went about his work with intensity, mischievous glee, and complete commitment to the job at hand.

In Kantor and Maslon's introduction to the companion book for the video series Broadway: The American Musical, the authors evoke a fairy tale: "Once upon a time, when New York theater was the most prestigious performance art form in the country, Broadway musicals were the boldest, bravest expression of the American character. Even though the theater lost its preeminence over the course of the last century, its journey to redefine itself and prove relevant again makes for a compelling story, indicative of many trends and tensions in our popular culture. The musical has always reflected different social and political forces—patriotism, skepticism, commercial consumption, escapism, revolt, globalization—and has put those onstage for everyone to see."[109] It would appear that Loesser's life and work touched on all these forces, with a few points of contact amounting to a passionate embrace. As a patriotic, commercially productive, mid-twentieth-century American man, Frank Loesser manufactured a type of popular entertainment that matured in his lifetime from mere escapism to become a "generative form of cultural imagery" (in Mark N. Grant's grand phrase), containing music with "a heart, a conviction, a soul, a rootedness" that sets it apart from the run-of-the-mill.[110] As representative works, Loesser's shows both conform to and rebel against social norms. They express skepticism about certain cultural values (most obviously in How to Succeed) and they affirm a few universal truths about human feelings, relationships, and communities. Because they succeed so well in their extrovert manners, sometimes audiences miss their subtler elements.

It must be admitted that Loesser wrote many fewer hit songs than his idol Irving Berlin. He has yet to make the impact of the glamorous and much shorter-lived George Gershwin. Rodgers and Hammerstein transformed the formal dimensions and dramatic expectations of the American musical comedy, while Loesser can only be said to have produced a handful of masterpieces in the genre. Nevertheless, Loesser stands out in at least one respect: from the first time he put notes together with lyrics until he stopped composing altogether, he took himself and his friends seriously as creative popular musicians. He avoided the rhetoric of the cultivated concert world, not because he disliked operas or classical music, but because he saw nothing wrong with popular music. On the occasion of the grand opening of the Lincoln Center for the Performing Arts in 1965, Loesser received a descriptive brochure from his lifelong friend, the center's director, William Schuman. Loesser could not resist responding with a needling, mirthful critique, part of a memorable, friendly letter that nevertheless contains some deeply serious observations about the fundamental definitions for words like "performing arts" and "center":

> Dear Billy, . . . It seems to me that your prospectus does not include a few of the performing arts, for instance: professional wrestling, bull fighting, auto races, burlesque comedy, radio and TV announcing, news & weather reporting, political debate, religious oratory, figure skating, strip tease, diving, auctioneering, stilt walking, juggling, restaurant greeting and seating, marching and drilling exhibition, etc., etc., etc. Please, Billy, don't suppose that I am pushing for a more vulgarian tendency in your program. I am pushing for nothing but simply pointing out that THE PERFORMING ARTS ARE NOT NECESSARILY THE NIFTY PERFORMING ARTS OR THE DIVINE PERFORMING ARTS OR THE ACCREDITED PERFORMING ARTS. Let me submit here that Hemingway—a high-class fellow, found something noble in bull fighting, and that Fred Allen, the much esteemed wit, started as a juggler, or that Victor Moore, who gave such a sensitive performance as Gramps in "Borrowed Time," learned his craft in burlesque; that Billy Graham is more effective as an actor than Sir Laurence Olivier; that the Indianapolis Speedway has · a bigger and more avid audience in any one day than do the combined performances of LA TOSCA in this country over a 10 year period—even though both audiences are there enjoying the smell of imminent death; that there is an abiding thrill for millions in the performance of those boys marching across the field at West Point; and that sky writing, parachute jumping, and fireworks (—all performing arts) make one look up in awe and wonder.

He goes on to admit that he himself prefers "ballet, drama, opera and musical comedy and not too many other kinds of performance." Furthermore, "[All of] New York *is* a center, a world's fair and a den of thieves, and a house of miracles. Sometimes I like my hotdogs at Nathan's, and sometimes the gentile kind at ball games. . . . I walk in Central Park and also on Madison Avenue, and sometimes around in circles in my study—and when I read,

sometimes it's the Herald Tribune, and sometimes the Talmud and sometimes your Lincoln Center brochure. In short, I have lots of places to go. It
isn't that one is better than the other, but simply that it is different from the
other."[111]

In light of this declaration and the variety of subjects to which he gave
creative attention, Loesser might justly be claimed as the ultimate democratic composer. His working life embraced as many "performing arts" as he
could squeeze into a day. His musicals, as full of wit and warmth as he could
make them, and free of ulterior motive, give pleasure to all sorts of audiences. All of his songs (well, most of them), whether rousing or relaxed, mellow or dramatic, invite listeners to take away what they like and then "walk
away whistling."

Disciples who worked with Loesser a half century ago still pass on his
words and stories as precious gems, because they were of a piece with the
personality of the man: a unique character who always lived life at full
throttle. His complete gift package—a combination of joyful works, a the-
saurus of sage professional advice, and a substantial business empire—was
bequeathed to family, friends, and colleagues with occasionally startling directness. Finally, the impact of his words and music, like the aftershocks of
an earthquake, will help to guarantee Frank Loesser's immortality—to the
extent that such is ever possible in the confected and ephemeral world of
American musical theater.

Stage Works by Frank Loesser

[*Leonardo da Vinci*]
ca. 1933
Incomplete operetta on the subject of Leonardo
Music: William Schuman
Lyrics: Frank Loesser
Libretto: Schuman and Loesser
No productions or recordings

Hollywood Be Thy Name
ca. 1933
Vaudeville act for Mary Nolan (1906–1948)
Music: Jean Herbert
Dialogue and lyrics: Frank Loesser and Jean Herbert
No production information available

The Illustrators' Show
New York opening: 48th Street Theatre, January 22, 1936
5 performances
Revue with sets based on designs by the Society of Illustrators
Music and lyrics: Charlotte Kent
Principal songwriting team: Irving Actman (m) and Frank Loesser (l)
Additional songwriting teams: Edgar Fairchild (m) and Milton Pascal (l), Frederick Loewe (m) and Earle Crooker (l), Michael Cleary (m) and Nat and Max Lief (l), Berenece Kazounoff (m) and Carl Randall (l)
Sketches: Donald Blackwell, Harry Evans, Fred Cooper and Frank Gabrielson, Max Liebman and Hi Alexander, Kenneth Webb, Will Glickman, David Lesan, Napier Moore, Otto Soglow
Stage and dance directors: Allen Delano and Carl Randall

Music director: Gene Salzer
Producer: Tom Weatherly

Skirts
London opening: Cambridge Theatre, January 25, 1944

"An all-American musical adventure in 15 scenes"
Music: Pfc. Frank Loesser, Pfc. Harold Rome, Leslie Stuart, Val Guest, and others
Sketches and lyrics: Lt. Arthur G. Brest, Pfc. Frank Loesser, Pfc. Leslie Weiner, Ben Begnal, Sam Locke, Pfc. Harold Rome, Leslie Stuart, G. Gabrielson, Cliff Gordon, Eric Spear, and others
Choreographer: Wendy Toye
Producer and director: Lt. Arthur G. Brest for Special Services, Eighth Air Force

About Face!
New York opening, Camp Shanks of the
New York Port of Embarkation, May 26, 1944

"GI Musical Revue, Blueprint Special"
Music and lyrics: Pvt. Frank Loesser, Pvt. Hy Zaret, T/Sgt. Peter Lind Hayes, Pvt. Jerry Livingston, Lou Singer
Sketches: Pvt. Arnold Auerbach, Mort Lewis, Howard Harris, Sid Zelenka, Dave Schwartz
Director: Robert H. Gordon
Production supervisor: Maj. Harry Salter

Hi, Yank!
Opening: War Department Theatre No. 5,
Fort Dix, New Jersey, August 7, 1944

"GI Musical Revue, Blueprint Special"
Music and lyrics: Pvt. Frank Loesser, Lt. Alex North, Lt. Jack Hill, Sgt. Jesse Berkman
Sketches: Lt. Ben Eastright, Lt. Jack Hill, T/4 Ed Milk, Pvt. Martin Weldon, Pvt. Arnold Auerbach
Director: Cpl. David E. Fitzgibbon
Choreographer: Pvt. José Limón
Producer: Capt. Hy Gardner

P.F.C. Mary Brown
ca. 1944

"WAC Musical Revue"
Music and lyrics: Capt. Ruby Jane Douglass, Pvt. Frank Loesser, Pvt. Hy Zaret, Arthur Altman
No production information available

Okay, U.S.A.
Opening: School for Personnel Services,
Lexington, Virginia, January 1945

"GI Musical Revue, Blueprint Special"

Music and lyrics: Frank Loesser
No production information available

It's the Goods
1945
Musical comedy
Music: Dave Mann, Frank Loesser
Lyrics: Frank Loesser, Dave Mann, Frank Provo, John Pickard
Book: Frank Provo, John Pickard
No productions

Where's Charley?
New York opening: St. James Theatre, October 11, 1948
792 performances
Musical comedy in 2 acts, 9 scenes
Music and lyrics: Frank Loesser
Book: George Abbott after Brandon Thomas's play, *Charley's Aunt*
Director: George Abbott
Choreographer: George Balanchine
Producers: Cy Feuer and Ernest H. Martin with Gwen Rickard
New York revivals:
    1. Broadway Theatre, January 29, 1951
    2. New York City Center, May 25, 1966
    3. Circle-in-the-Square Theatre, December 19, 1974
Other productions:
    1. Film, Warner Bros. 1952
    2. London, Palace Theatre, 1958
Complete recordings:
    1. 1952 film soundtrack (ECNAD 216)
    2. 1958 London production (Columbia, EMI, Monmouth Evergreen)

Guys and Dolls
New York opening: 46th Street Theatre, November 24, 1950
1,200 performances
Musical "fable" [comedy] in 2 acts, 17 scenes
Music and lyrics: Frank Loesser
Book: Jo Swerling and Abe Burrows after short stories by Damon Runyon
Director: George S. Kaufman
Choreographer: Michael Kidd
Producers: Cy Feuer and Ernest H. Martin
New York revivals:
    1. New York City Center, April 20, 1955
    2. New York City Center, April 28, 1965
    3. New York City Center, June 8, 1966
    4. Broadway Theatre, July 21, 1976
    5. Martin Beck Theatre, April 14, 1992

Other productions:

    1. London, Coliseum, May 23, 1953

    2. Film, MGM, 1955

    3. Bremen (Germany), Theater der Hansestadt, May 26, 1968

    4. Melbourne (Australia), Total Theatre, July 27, 1974

    5. London, National Theatre, March 9, 1982

Complete recordings:

    1. Original cast (Decca)

    2. 1951 studio production (RCA)

    3. 1955 film soundtrack (Decca)

    4. 1955 studio production, including film songs (Columbia)

    5. 1962 British studio production (World Record Club)

    6. 1976 revival (Motown)

    7. 1982 London revival (Chrysalis)

    8. 1992 revival (RCA Victor)

    9. 1996, stage score plus film songs and "Traveling Light" (Jay)

The Most Happy Fella
**New York opening: Imperial Theatre, May 3, 1956;
moved to Broadway Theatre, October 21, 1956
676 performances**

Musical in 3 acts, 11 scenes

Book, music, and lyrics: Frank Loesser, after Sidney Howard's play, *They Knew What They Wanted*

Director: Joseph Anthony

Choreographer: Dania Krupska

Producers: Kermit Bloomgarden and Lynn Loesser

New York revivals:

    1. New York City Center, February 10, 1959

    2. New York City Center, May 11, 1966

    3. Majestic Theatre, October 11, 1979

    4. New York State Theater, September 4, 1991

    5. Booth Theatre, February 13, 1992

    6. New York State Theater, March 4, 2006

Other productions:

    1. London, Coliseum, April 21, 1960

    2. Melbourne (Australia), Princess Theatre, June 9, 1961

Complete recordings:

    1. 1956 original cast (Columbia, 3 LP records)

    2. 1960 London cast (HMV)

    3. 1991 production, two-piano version (RCA Victor)

    4. 2000 studio recording, including many songs unused on stage (Jay)

Dream People
1956–57
Music and lyrics: Frank Loesser, based on Garson Kanin's play, *A Touch of the Moon*
Incomplete and unproduced

Greenwillow
New York opening: Alvin Theatre, March 8, 1960
97 performances
Musical comedy in 2 acts, 15 scenes
Music and lyrics: Frank Loesser
Book: Lesser Samuels and Frank Loesser, based on B. J. Chute's novel of the same name
Director: George Roy Hill
Choreographer: Joe Layton
Producer: Robert Willey with Frank Productions
Complete recording: 1960 original cast (RCA Victor, DRG)

How to Succeed in Business Without Really Trying
New York opening: 46th Street Theatre, October 14, 1961
1,417 performances
Musical comedy in 2 acts, 24 scenes
Music and lyrics: Frank Loesser
Book: Abe Burrows, Jack Weinstock, and Willie Gilbert, based on Shepherd Mead's handbook of the same name
Director: Abe Burrows
Producers: Cy Feuer and Ernest H. Martin with Frank Productions
New York revivals:
    1. New York City Center, April 20, 1966
    2. Richard Rodgers Theatre, March 23, 1995
Other productions:
    1. London, Shaftesbury Theatre, March 28, 1963
    2. Melbourne (Australia), Her Majesty's Theatre, August 16, 1963
    3. Paris [in French translation], Théâtre de Paris, 1964
    4. Vienna [in German translation], Theater an der Wien, 1965
    5. Film, United Artists, 1967
Complete recordings:
    1. 1961 original cast (RCA Victor)
    2. 1963 London cast (RCA Victor)
    3. 1964 French cast (Philips)
    4. 1965 Austrian cast (Ariola-Eurodisc)
    5. 1967 film soundtrack (United Artists)
    6. 1995 revival (RCA Victor)

Leocadia
1962

Fragments of music and lyrics: Frank Loesser, based on Jean Anouilh's play, *Time Remembered*
Incomplete and unproduced

Pleasures and Palaces
Detroit (tryout) opening: Fisher Theatre, March 11, 1965; closed April 10, 1965, without opening in New York

Musical comedy
Music and lyrics: Frank Loesser
Book: Sam Spewack and Frank Loesser, after Spewack's play, *Once There Was a Russian*
Director and choreographer: Bob Fosse
Producer: Allen B. Whitehead with Frank Productions
No revivals or complete recordings

Señor Discretion Himself
Washington, D.C., opening: Arena Stage/ Fichandler Theater, April 9, 2004

Musical comedy in 2 acts, 18 scenes
Music and lyrics: Frank Loesser
Book: Frank Loesser and Culture Clash, based on a short story by Budd Schulberg
Director: Charles Randolph-Wright
Choreographer: Doriana Sanchez
Loesser gave up work on the still incomplete show in March 1968. In 2000 Jo Sullivan Loesser engaged the services of Charles Randolph-Wright (an Arena Stage associate artist, writer, and director) and Culture Clash (consisting of Ric Salinas, Herbert Siguenza, and Richard Montoya) to develop Loesser's material for production.

The Song Lyrics of Frank Loesser
in Three Lists

This listing includes unused or unperformed lyrics and lyrics for which no music is
known to exist.

* = Loesser composed both music and lyrics

1. Independent Song Lyrics
[unattached to a film or show]

1929

Alone in Your Class
Let's Incorporate
Melancholy Me

1930–31

Box o' Candy
Doing the Dishes
Where the Grass Grows Green
Ticker Tape Tap
In Love with a Memory of You
It's You I Love (Waltz)
She's Exclusively Mine
I'll See You in the Morning
When Spring Comes Around Again
One Little Robin
Bluebird on My Wallpaper
Jig-Saw Puzzle
Hat Check Girl

1933–34

I've Got So Much to Forget
Spaghetti
Junk Man
The Old Oak Tree
Goo Goo G'da
I Wish I Were Twins
Stars on the Highway
Oh! What a Beautiful Baby You Turned
    Out to Be
Home Ties
Doesn't That Mean Anything to You?

1935

Sunday at Sundown
The Traffic Was Terrific
I Just Came Back to Haunt You (Boogy
    Boogy Boogy Boo!)

1936

A Tree in Tipperary
Chile Moonlight

1937
Here Comes Tomorrow (Give Me
    Another Kiss Tonight)
Kiss at Midnight
Striver's Row to Sugar Hill
Forevermore
Shim-sham Rumba
Dream Tonight

1938
Enchanted
Wallpaper Roses

1939
If I'd Never Been in Love Before
When You're Dressed in Blue
Fragrant Night
Bubbles in the Wine
I'm All A-Tremble over You
I Kinda Dream
Old Fashioned Love
Here Comes the Night
That Moonlight from Last Night
Night-Blooming Jasmine
No Sales Slip Necessary

1940
By the By

1941
Ahoy, Minnie

1942
*Praise the Lord and Pass the Ammuni-
    tion
The Moon Is Down
*Song of the Windshield Wiper

1943
*What Do You Do in the Infantry?
*Have I Stayed Away Too Long?
*You Haven't Got Cheeks Like Roses

1944
*Leave Us Face It (We're in Love)
*The One-Pip Wonder [Song of the
    Canadian Armored Corps]
*The Sad Bombardier
One Little WAC
*Salute to the Army Service Forces
Buy a Bond

1945
*Rodger Young
*Two Beautiful Things
Wave to Me, My Lady
*Port Battalions on Parade
[Animal songs offered to Paramount but
    unused]
*The Bee
*The Dog
*The Duck
*The Fish
*The Horse
*The Mouse
*The Owl
*The Seal
*The Worm

1947
*Bloop, Bleep!
*What Are You Doing New Year's Eve?
*Keep Your Eye on the Sky
*A Tune for Humming

1948
*The Last Thing I Want Is Your Pity
*The Feathery Feeling
*Down the Stairs, Out the Door Went
    My Baby

1940s [?]
And Then We Met
I Met You
April in April
Asking for Trouble
*The Delicatessen of My Dreams
Nostalgia

1950
Hoop-Dee-Doo
Meet Me at the College Bowl

1951
We're in Love with Those Wonderful
   Guys
Girls' School Alma Mater
*Three-Cornered Tune [based on "Fugue
   for Tinhorns"]

1952
*Stone Walls
Makes Me Feel Good All Over

1953
*No Swallerin' Place
*Benny to Helen to Chance
*Just Another Polka
*All Is Forgiven (and All Is Forgotten)

1954
*Crying Polka
*Lullaby?
*Warm and Willing/Aphro

1955
Don't Send Lucy to the Store

1957
Mozart's in Hiding, Not Dead

1958
*Piels beer commercial

1961
Analyst's Wife/Oh, What a Mis'rable
   Morning

1963
*Les Oeufs (Balls)

1964
The Boycott: A Waltz for Anybody—1964

1968
For God and Gideon

[Miscellaneous, undated, 1960s]
*Every Love
*I Could Have Told You
Helen to Ricky
Holiday for Jews?
*Lullaby?
A Man Can Be Talented and Also Be
   Nice
Lyrics for a Leading Man in an Uncon-
   vincing Operetta
My Opening Song
On the Other Side of the Room
On the Road to Romance
Song for Bobby [Fosse]
*Tell Me No Tall, Tall Tale
*That Was My Love I Gave You
*The Wind Blows in My Window
Yesterday's Love

2. Song Lyrics For Films
[production studio name; other
production information]

1935
Edgar A. Guest's Poetic Gems
[original lyrics written for music by Louis
   Herscher; a series of planned short sub-
   jects were never produced]
Ev'rybody's Ship Comes In (but Mine)
A Symphony in Green
Take Me Home to the Mountains
Indian Moon
Little Miss Mischief
Down the Lane to Yesterday
By a Silvery Stream
The Snowflakes
Don't Grow Any Older (My Little Boy
   Blue)
Here's to the Builder
Get under the Sun
A Real True Pal
Backseat Drivers

1936

Postal Inspector
[Universal]
Let's Have Bluebirds
Hot Towel

Yellowstone
[Universal]
Joggin' Along

The Man I Marry
[Universal]
Old Homestead
I Know I'm in Harlem

1937

Three Smart Girls
[Universal]
You're My Heart
Life Is Peaches and Cream
Since When
Heart of Harlem

The Golfers
[Universal, Walter Lantz cartoon]
Meany, Miny, Moe

Mysterious Crossing
[Universal]
The Railroad That Ran Through Our
   Land

Everybody Sing
[Universal, Walter Lantz cartoon]
Everybody Sings

The Duck Hunt
[Universal, Walter Lantz cartoon]
A-Hunting We Will Go

Walter Wanger's Vogues of 1938
[United Artists]
Lovely One

Fight for Your Lady
[RKO Radio]
Blame It on the Danube

The Hurricane
[United Artists]
The Moon of Manakoora

Blossoms on Broadway
[Paramount]
You Can't Tell a Man by His Hat
No Ring on Her Finger

1938

College Swing
[Paramount]
The Old School Bell
College Swing
What Did Romeo Say to Juliet?
How'dja Like to Love Me?
I Fall in Love with You Every Day
You're a Natural
Moments Like This
What a Rumba Does to Romance
Beans

Stolen Heaven
[Paramount]
Boys in the Band

Cocoanut Grove
[Paramount]
Says My Heart
Ten Easy Lessons

The Texans
[Paramount]
I'll Come to The Wedding

Give Me a Sailor
[Paramount]
Give Me a Sailor
I'm in Dreamland

Sing, You Sinners
[Paramount]
Small Fry

Freshman Year
[Universal]
Chasing You Around

Spawn of the North
[Paramount]
I Wish I Was the Willow
I Like Hump-Backed Salmon

Men with Wings
[Paramount]
Men with Wings

Thanks for the Memory
[Paramount]
Two Sleepy People

A Song Is Born
[Paramount Headliner Short]
Heart and Soul

1939
Zaza
[Paramount]
Zaza
Hello, My Darling
Forget Me
He Died of Love
I'm the Stupidest Girl in the Class
Street Song

St. Louis Blues
[Paramount]
Oh, You Mississippi
I Go for That
Junior
Blue Nightfall
The Song in My Heart Is a Rumba

Café Society
[Paramount]
Kiss Me with Your Eyes
Park Avenue Gimp

Some Like It Hot
[Paramount]
Some Like It Hot
The Lady's in Love with You
Whodunit?

The Gracie Allen Murder Case
[Paramount]
Snug as a Bug in a Rug

Heritage of the Desert
[Paramount]
Here's a Heart

Man about Town
[Paramount]
That Sentimental Sandwich
Fidgety Joe
Strange Enchantment
Man about Town
Petty Girl Routine
A Love Letter

Invitation to Happiness
[Paramount]
Invitation to Happiness

Beau Geste
[Paramount]
The Legionnaire's Song

Island of Lost Men
[Paramount]
Music on the Shore

The Star Maker
[Paramount]
Valse des Fleurs

Hawaiian Nights
[Universal]
Hawaii Sang Me to Sleep
Then I Wrote the Minuet in G
Hey, Good-Looking

$1,000 a Touchdown
[Paramount]
Fight On for Madison

Destry Rides Again
[Universal]
Little Joe, the Wrangler
You've Got That Look (That Leaves Me
    Weak)
The Boys in the Backroom

The Llano Kid
[Paramount]
El Huapango
Posada
Starry Eyes

The Great Victor Herbert
[Paramount]

Happy Day
Wonderful Dreams
You Are Beautiful

1940
All Women Have Secrets
[Paramount]
Rockabye Baby—Interruption

The Farmer's Daughter
[Paramount]
Jungle Jingle

Seventeen
[Paramount]
*Seventeen

Adventure in Diamonds
[Paramount]
The Whistler's Ditties
A Flea Flew in My Ear
Love in Bloom [special lyrics]

Johnny Apollo
[20th Century-Fox]
Dancing for Nickels and Dimes

Buck Benny Rides Again
[Paramount]
Say It (Over and Over Again)
My! My!
My Kind of Country
Drums in the Night
Roses round My Room

Typhoon
[Paramount]
Palms of Paradise

Those Were the Days
[Paramount]
Alpha Rho Song
Any Minute Now
Siwash Alma Mater
We're All Here at Siwash
Siwash Spring Song

The Quarterback
[Paramount]

Out with Your Chest (and Up with Your
    Chin)

Seven Sinners
[Universal]
The Man's in the Navy
I Fall Overboard
I've Been In Love Before

Dancing on a Dime
[Paramount]
Mañana
I Hear Music
Operatic prologue to "I Hear Music"
    reprise
Lovable Sort of Person
Dancing on a Dime
Debutante Number One

Youth Will Be Served
[20th Century-Fox]
With a Banjo on My Knee
Youth Will Be Served
Hot Catfish and Corn Dodgers

Moon over Burma
[Paramount]
Mexican Magic
Moon over Burma

Northwest Mounted Police
[Paramount]
The Tall Pines

1941
A Night at Earl Carroll's
[Paramount]
Li'l Boy Love
I Wanna Make with the Happy Times
I've Walked through Wonderland

Arizona Sketches
[Paramount short subject]
Prairieland Lullaby

Las Vegas Nights
[Paramount]
I Gotta Ride
Mary, Mary, Quite Contrary

Dolores
On Miami Shore prologue

Sis Hopkins
[Republic]
Look at You, Look at Me
That Ain't Hay (That's the U.S.A.)
Well! Well!
If You're in Love
Cracker Barrel County

There's Magic in Music
[Paramount]
The Stuttering Song
What Sort of Music Does the Public
   Like?

Caught in the Draft
[Paramount]
Love Me as I Am

Manpower
[Warner Bros.-First National]
He Lied and I Listened

Kiss the Boys Goodbye
[Paramount]
Kiss the Boys Goodbye
Find Yourself a Melody
Sand in My Shoes
I'll Never Let a Day Pass By
That's How I Got My Start
We've Met Somewhere Before

World Premiere
[Paramount]
Don't Cry, Little Cloud

Aloma of the South Seas
[Paramount]
The White Blossoms of Tah-ni

Hold Back the Dawn
[Paramount]
My Boy, My Boy

Sailors on Leave
[Republic]
Since You
Sentimental Folks

Henry Aldrich for President
[Paramount]
Johnny Jones

Birth of the Blues
[Paramount]
Memphis Blues [new lyrics]

Glamour Boy
[Paramount]
The Magic of Magnolias
Love Is Such an Old-Fashioned Thing

1942
Mr. Bug Goes to Town
[Paramount cartoon feature]
Katy-Did, Katy-Didn't
Boy, Oh Boy!
We're the Couple in the Castle
I'll Dance at Your Wedding (Honey Dear)

Reap the Wild Wind
[Paramount]
Sea Chanty

This Gun for Hire
[Paramount]
Now You See It, Now You Don't
I've Got You
I'm Amazed at You

Tortilla Flat
[MGM]
Ai-Paisano
Oh, How I Love a Wedding

True to the Army
[Paramount]
In the Army
Spangles on My Tights
Need I Speak?
Swing in Line
Jitterbug's Lullaby
Wacky for Khaki
Ophelia
We're Building Men

Beyond the Blue Horizon
[Paramount]

Malay Love Song
Pagan Lullaby

Sweater Girl
[Paramount]
Sweater Girl
I Said No
I Don't Want to Walk without You
What Gives Out Now?
Booker T. Washington Brigade

Priorities on Parade
[Paramount]
Johnny's Patter
Here Comes Katrinka
You're in Love with Someone Else
    (but I'm in Love with You)
Payday

The Forest Rangers
[Paramount]
Jingle, Jangle, Jingle
Tall Grows the Timber

Seven Days' Leave
[RKO Radio]
Please, Won't You Leave My Girl Alone?
You Speak My Language
A Touch of Texas
I Get the Neck of the Chicken
Can't Get Out of This Mood
Soft-Hearted
Puerto Rico
Baby

1943
Happy Go Lucky
[Paramount]
Sing a Tropical Song
Happy Go Lucky
Murder, He Says
Let's Get Lost
The Fuddy-Duddy Watchmaker
Jerry or Joe

Tornado
[Paramount]
There Goes My Dream

Army Show
[Warner Bros. two-reel concert film]
Hello, Mom

Thank Your Lucky Stars
[Warner Bros.]
Thank Your Lucky Stars
I'm Ridin' for a Fall
We're Staying Home Tonight (My Baby
    and Me)
I'm Goin' North
Love Isn't Born (It's Made)
No You, No Me
The Dreamer
Ice Cold Katy
How Sweet You Are
That's What You Jolly Well Get
They're Either Too Young or Too Old
Good Night, Good Neighbor
Closing medley

Riding High
[Paramount]
Music from Paradise

1944
See Here, Private Hargrove
[MGM]
In My Arms

The Road to Victory
[Warner Bros.]
*The Road to Victory

Christmas Holiday
[Universal]
*Spring Will Be a Little Late This Year

And the Angels Sing
[Paramount]
Shake Hands with Your Neighbor

1946
The Day before Spring
[MGM; unproduced]
It's Time for the Love Scene
Who Could Forget?
Bing Bang

My Sentimental Nature
You're So Reliable
Ibbedy Bibbedy Sibbedy Sab

Strange Triangle
[20th Century-Fox]
Your Kiss

1947
The Perils of Pauline
[Paramount]
*The Sewing Machine
*Rumble, Rumble, Rumble
*I Wish I Didn't Love You So
*Poppa, Don't Preach to Me
*The Firemen's Ball

Variety Girl
[Paramount]
*Your Heart Calling Mine
*Tallahassee
*He Can Waltz
*Impossible Things
*We French, We Get So Excited
*The French, They Get So Excited
*(I Must Have Been) Madly in Love
*I Want My Money Back

Lady from Lariat Loop
[Paramount; unproduced]
*Pindy Fendy
Batten Down Her Hatches

1948
On Our Merry Way
[United Artists]
*The Queen of the Hollywood Islands

1949
Neptune's Daughter
[MGM]
*I Love Those Men
*On a Slow Boat to China
*My Heart Beats Faster
*Baby, It's Cold Outside
*Neptune's Daughter

Roseanna McCoy
[RKO Radio]
*Roseanna

Red, Hot, and Blue
[Paramount]
*I Wake Up in the Morning Feeling Fine
*That's Loyalty
*Hamlet
*(Where Are You) Now That I Need You?

1950
Let's Dance
[Paramount]
*Can't Stop Talking
*Jack and the Beanstalk
*Oh, Them Dudes
*Why Fight the Feeling?
*The Hyacinth
*Tunnel of Love
*The Ming Toy Factory

1952
Hans Christian Andersen
[RKO Radio]
*The King's New Clothes
*The Inch Worm
*I'm Hans Christian Andersen
*Wonderful Copenhagen
*Street Voices
*Thumbelina
*The Ugly Duckling
*Anywhere I Wander
*No Two People
*The Shoe Song
Give Your Love to Me
Second Fantasy
So You Want to Be a Fireman?

1955
Guys and Dolls
[MGM]
*Pet Me, Poppa
*Adelaide
*A Woman in Love

1967
*How to Succeed in Business Without
Really Trying*
[United Artists]
[no new songs]

3. Song Lyrics for Stage Shows

1932–33
[Leonardo da Vinci]
operetta
Things Have Come to a Pretty Pass
You're a Bounder, You're a Blighter
I'm a Gentleman, a Scholar
I've Lived for This Moment
Here Comes a Patron of the Arts
Oh Heaven, Give Me Strength Tonight
Here's to It, Whatever It Is
One Word from You
Dirty Work at the Crossroads
I'd Love to Push the Plow with You
Love Is One of Those Things
Bravo
Unaccustomed as I Am to Public
    Speaking
Eggs
I Regard You with Suspicion
If That's What You're Looking For
When Isabella Likes a Fella
Abyssinia

1933
Hollywood Be Thy Name
vaudeville act
If I Can't Get the Man I Want
He Went Like This, So I Went Like That
My Football Hero!
Looking Out the Window at the Rain

1936
The Illustrators' Show
revue
If You Didn't Love Me
I Like to Go to Strange Places
I'm You

Bang—The Bell Rang!
Give Me Wild Trumpets
Finale

1944
Skirts
musical comedy(?)
Skirts
About Face!
revue
Dog Face
Gee, but It's Great
First Class Private Mary Brown
PX Parade
Why Do They Call a Private a Private?

Hi, Yank!
revue
Yank, Yank, Yank
The Saga of the Sack
My Gal and I
My Gal's Working at Lockheed
General Orders
Classification Blues
Little Red Rooftops
The Most Important Job

P.F.C. Mary Brown
revue
Something New Has Been Added
In Twenty-five Words or Less
New-Style Bonnet
Come On, Honey
Poor Lonely MP
Lost in a Cloud of Blue
The WAC Hymn

Okay, U.S.A.
revue
*A Trip round the USA
*Way Down Texas Way
*My Chicago
Miss America
*Tonight in San Francisco
*When He Comes Home
*You're OK, USA!

1945
It's the Goods
musical comedy
Civvy in a Fork Lift Truck
Is This by Chance Romance?
Heroes
What Might Have Been
All the Way
What a Way to Win a War
Let's Make It Forever
It's the Goods

1948
Where's Charley?
musical comedy
*The Year before Us
*Better Get Out of Here
*The New Ashmolean Marching Society
   and Students' Conservatory Band
*My Darling, My Darling
*Make a Miracle
*Serenade with Asides
*Lovelier Than Ever
*The Woman in His Room
*Pernambuco
*Where's Charley?
*Once in Love with Amy
*The Gossips
*At the Red Rose Cotillion
*Culture and Breeding
*Saunter Away
*Your Own College Band
*The Train That Brought You to Town
*Don't Introduce Me to That Angel

1950
Guys and Dolls
musical comedy
*Fugue for Tinhorns
*Follow the Fold
*The Oldest Established
*I'll Know
*A Bushel and a Peck
*Adelaide's Lament
*Guys and Dolls

*If I Were a Bell
*My Time of Day
*I've Never Been in Love Before
*Take Back Your Mink
*Adelaide's Second Lament
*More I Cannot Wish You
*Luck Be a Lady
*Sue Me
*Sit Down, You're Rockin' the Boat
*Adelaide Meets Sarah
*Marry the Man Today
*Shango
*Traveling Light
*Nathan's Problem
*It Feels Like Forever
*I Come A-Running

1956
The Most Happy Fella
musical
*Ooh! My Feet!
*I Know How It Is
*Seven Million Crumbs
*I Don't Know
*Maybe He's Kind of Crazy
*Somebody, Somewhere
*Prelude to "The Most Happy Fella"
*The Most Happy Fella
*A Long Time Ago
*Standing on the Corner
*Joey, Joey, Joey
*Soon You Gonna Leave Me, Joe
*Rosabella
*Abbondanza
*Plenty Bambini
*Sposalizio
*I Seen Her at the Station
*Benvenuta
*Aren't You Glad?
*No Home, No Job
*Don't Cry
*Fresno Beauties
*Cold and Dead
*Love and Kindness
*Happy to Make Your Acquaintance

*I Don't Like This Dame
*Big D
*How Beautiful the Days
*Young People
*Warm All Over
*Young People Gotta Dance
*I Like Ev'rybody
*I Love Him
*Like a Woman Loves a Man
*My Heart Is So Full of You
*Mamma, Mamma
*Goodbye, Darlin'
*I Like Ev'rybody [duet]
*Song of a Summer Night
*Please Let Me Tell You
*Tell Tony and Rosabella Goodbye for
    Me
*She's Gonna Come Home wit' Me
*Nobody's Ever Gonna Love You [trio]
*I Made a Fist
*Finale
*How's About Tonight?
*House and Garden
*Love Letter
*So Busy
*Is It Really Real?
*Wanting to Be Wanted
*Joe's Entrance
*Everybody Is Talking
*Nobody's Ever Gonna Love You [solo]
*I'm-a No Wanna
*Collar Incident
*Six o'Clock Train
*Marie and Doc
*Aren't You Glad? [tag]
*Mad Money
*Eyes Like a Stranger
*Such a Pretty Picture
*Doctors Don't Tell You Everything
*They're Throwing a Party Today
*Lovers' Quarrel
*I'll Buy Ev'rybody a Beer

1957

Dream People
musical
*Dream People [opening]
*Imagining
*Dream People [part II]
*At the Home Appliance Show
*We Harmonize
*Marshmallow Magic
*Won'tcha Settle for Me?
*Amateur Psychiatrist
*For the Fam'ly Album
*The Green-Eyed Monster
*Take Me Now

1960

Greenwillow
musical comedy
*A Day Borrowed from Heaven
*Dorrie's Wish
*A-Tangle, A-Dangle
*Amos Long Entrance
*The Music of Home
*Gideon Briggs, I Love You
*Summertime Love
*Blasphemy
*Walking Away Whistling
*The Sermon
*Could've Been a Ring
*Never Will I Marry
*Greenwillow Christmas
*Faraway Boy
*Clang Dang the Bell
*What a Blessing
*He Died Good
*Finale
*Riddleweed
*My Beauty
*All A-Tousle
*The Call
*A Head on Her Shoulders
*Buzz a Buzz
*Percussion Ballad
*Heart of Stone
*Down in the Barley

1961
How to Succeed in Business Without Really Trying
musical comedy
*How to Succeed In Business Without
   Really Trying
*Happy to Keep His Dinner Warm
*Coffee Break
*The Company Way
*A Secretary Is Not a Toy
*Been a Long Day
*Grand Old Ivy
*Paris Original
*Rosemary
*Finale, Act One
*Cinderella, Darling
*Love from a Heart of Gold
*I Believe in You
*Brotherhood of Man
*Status
*I Worry about You
*Organization Man
*Company Man
*Knit Pretty
*World Wide Wicket
*White-Collar World
*Bless This Day
*Lashes
*The Business Man's Shuffle
Bumper to Bumper
Reaction to Hedy
Marvelous Mind

1962
Leocadia
musical
Only the Rich
You Live in My Heart
I Am a Jolly Peasant
Speak to Me

1965
Pleasures and Palaces
musical comedy
*I Hear Bells

*My Lover Is a Scoundrel
*To Marry
*Hail, Majesty
*Thunder and Lightning
*To Your Health
*Neither the Time nor the Place
*I Desire You
*In Your Eyes
*Truly Loved
*Sins of Sura
*Hoorah for Jones
*Propaganda
*Foreigners
*Barabanchik
*What Is Life?
*Ah, to Be Home Again
*Pleasures and Palaces
*Tears of Joy
*Far, Far, Far Away
Catherine the Great
Potemkin's Solo
The Fruit
Peaceful Harbor
Partial Martial
Rodyina
At the Victory Ball
Kat
As a Man of High Importance

1965–68
Señor Discretion Himself
musical comedy
*Padre, I Have Sinned
*To See Her
*Pan Pan Pan
*Papa, Come Home
*Pancito's Song
*World Peace
*If You Love Me, You'll Forgive Me
*You Understand Me
*Heaven Smiles on Tepancingo
*I Love Him, I Think
*Compañeros
*Julio's First Song
*Mexico City

*I Only Know
*Hasta La Vista
*Don't Drink
*Goodbye Agitato
*I Cannot Let You Go
*The Wisdom of the Heart
*Traveling Carnival

*Got to Have a Somebody
*Hilario's Home-Made Ballad
*As Long as He Is Only a Dream
*Now I Love Her
*The Real Curse of Drink
*Martin (To the PTA)
*The Padre

Notes

Biographical Introduction

1. Susan Loesser, *Most Remarkable Fella*, 12.

2. He later received a diploma from DeWitt Clinton High School at the age of fifteen. He was subsequently admitted to City College of New York, but lasted only one semester there before again being expelled for a prank. See Susan Loesser, *Most Remarkable Fella*, 8.

3. Kimball and Nelson, *Complete Lyrics*, 4–16. Meyer's most famous song, for example, was "California, Here I Come," with lyrics by Buddy DeSylva and Al Jolson.

4. Susan Loesser, *Most Remarkable Fella*, 14.

5. According to Lynn Loesser, the critics gave a polite nod to the five Actman and Loesser songs, especially "Bang—The Bell Rang!" Susan Loesser, *Most Remarkable Fella*, 18–19. Ten other songwriters were listed among the credits, including Frederick Loewe (later famous as the composer of *Brigadoon, My Fair Lady*, and *Camelot*).

6. Ewen, *All the Years*, 264–65.

7. Wilk, *They're Playing Our Song*, 250.

8. Kimball and Nelson, *Complete Lyrics*, 92.

9. Ewen, *All the Years*, 429.

10. Susan Loesser, *Most Remarkable Fella*, 46–47.

11. Ewen, *All the Years*, 262.

12. *About Face*, Headquarters, Army Service Forces, Special Services Division, ASF [n.d.], 47. I was able to examine the "Blueprint Special" copy held in Special Collections, Hargrett Rare Book and Manuscript Library, University of Georgia, Athens.

13. Not exactly a freelance, Loesser was constrained by his contract with Paramount. But arrangements to do work with other studios were routinely made. Hemming, *Melody Lingers On*, 337–46; Kimball and Nelson, *Complete Lyrics*, xv. See also the listing of song lyrics in this volume's appendixes.

14. Hirschhorn, *Hollywood Musical*, 303; Harrison, *Songwriters*, 275.

15. Frommer and Frommer, *It Happened on Broadway*, 119–21; Taylor, *Jule*, 81–82.

16. Stanley Green, *Broadway Musicals Show by Show*, 138.

17. Susan Loesser, *Most Remarkable Fella*, 228–29.

18. Ibid., 124.

19. The adjectives are Brooks Atkinson's; see *New York Times*, October 3, 1939, p. 19.

20. Lynn Loesser also coproduced plays, including *The Carefree Heart*, *The Love Doctor*, and *High Fidelity*. Gänzl, *Encyclopedia of Musical Theater*, 884.

21. Susan Loesser, *Most Remarkable Fella*, 164–68. Stuart Ostrow notes in an unpublished memoir that when critics at the Philadelphia tryout performances used the word "opera," Loesser instantly sought to squelch the idea. In an interview with Murray Schumach for the *New York Times* given just days before the New York opening, Loesser again avoided the genre question: "It's a musical with music. I don't know what it is. If it's any good, if it makes people feel—oh hell. We'll see." April 29, 1956, section 2, p. 3.

22. Block, *Enchanted Evenings*, 314–15; Gänzl, *Encyclopedia of Musical Theater*, 1018. See chapters 4 and 7 for further discussion on this point.

23. Susan Loesser, *Most Remarkable Fella*, 240–45.

24. Ibid., 278.

25. Ibid., 283.

26. Ibid., 286.

CHAPTER 1. Juvenile Poet, Hollywood Lyricist, Wartime Songwriter

1. Susan Loesser, *Most Remarkable Fella*, 287.

2. Crawford, *America's Musical Life*, 300 and ff.

3. Susan Loesser, *Most Remarkable Fella*, xx.

4. Ibid., 5.

5. Mann, "Musicals of Frank Loesser," 27. Lehmann (1848–1929) sang in the first complete Wagner *Ring* cycles in both Bayreuth (1876) and New York (1889), as well as performing the role of Isolde in the New York premiere of *Tristan und Isolde* (1886).

6. H. Wiley Hitchcock and Stanley Sadie, eds., *New Grove Dictionary of American Music* (London: Macmillan, 1986), s.v. "Loesser, Arthur." In the 1920s Arthur also toured with such notables as Maud Powell, Mischa Elman, and Ernestine Schumann-Heink. During World War II he learned and taught the Japanese language for the U.S. Army. According to Nicolas Slonimsky, he was the first "American musician in uniform to play for a Japanese audience [after hostilities ended], appearing as soloist with the Nippon Philharmonic at its regular concerts in Tokyo in February 1946." See *Baker's Biographical Dictionary of Musicians*, 5th ed. (New York: G. Schirmer, 1958), 974.

7. Susan Loesser, *Most Remarkable Fella*, 10.

8. Arthur Loesser, "My Brother Frank," 218.

9. Telephone interview with Abba Bogin, April 25, 2006.

10. Frank Loesser to Vincent Persichetti, April 10, 1948. Vincent Persichetti Papers, New York Public Library for the Performing Arts.

11. Telephone interview with Abba Bogin, April 25, 2006.

12. Susan Loesser, *Most Remarkable Fella*, 17–18.

13. Arthur Loesser, "My Brother Frank," 218.

14. Oja, *Making Music Modern*, 369.

15. Ibid., 47, 59.

16. Ibid., 325. See also Don Rayno, *Paul Whiteman: Pioneer in American Music*, vol. 1, *1890–1930* (Lanham, Md.: Scarecrow Press, 2003), 72–86.

17. Stanley Green, *Broadway Musicals Show by Show*, 55–61; Kimball and Nelson, *Complete Lyrics*, xiv. According to Wilk (*They're Playing Our Song*, 244), Loesser served for a few months as the city editor for the *New Rochelle Register*.

18. Furia, *Poets of Tin Pan Alley*, 5.

19. Forte, *Listening to Classic American Popular Songs*, xi.

20. Furia, *Poets of Tin Pan Alley*, 94.

21. Arthur Loesser, "My Brother Frank," 219.

22. Leacock, *Nonsense Novels*, 57–59.

23. Kimball and Nelson, *Complete Lyrics*, 5.

24. Flora Rheta Schreiber and Vincent Persichetti, *William Schuman* (New York: G. Schirmer, 1954), 6. Steve Swayne has informed me about a handful of lyrics ascribed to Loesser in the William Schuman papers at the Library of Congress Music Division, Washington, D.C., which are listed in the appendix at the end of this volume. In 1933 Loesser and Jean Herbert cowrote a vaudeville act with songs for the former Ziegfeld Follies beauty Mary Nolan, entitled *Hollywood Be Thy Name*; see Kimball and Nelson, *Complete Lyrics*, 8.

25. Kimball and Nelson, *Complete Lyrics*, 3. Speak-O-Phone records were long-playing (33 rpm) aluminum discs requiring ultrasoft (wooden or fiber) needles. The New York Speak-O-Phone Recording Studio was located at 201 West Forty-ninth Street.

26. Schuman interview transcript, Yale Oral History, American Music Project, 44–45. The songs are preserved on a compact disc released in 1995, *Frank Sings Loesser: Rare and Unreleased Performances* (Koch International Classics 3-7241-1H1).

27. William Schuman Papers, Library of Congress Music Division.

28. Ibid.

29. The origins of the "Frankie and Johnny" ballad are obscure, but it appears to be linked to other ragtime songs from about 1900. A complete published version first appeared in 1912 (New York: Tell Taylor). Loesser may have been aware of revivals of it in the 1920s, especially a handful that were printed and discussed in the famous collection *The American Songbag*, compiled by Carl Sandburg in 1927 (New York: Harcourt, Brace). See James J. Fuld, *The Book of World-Famous Music: Classical, Popular, and Folk*, 3rd ed. (New York: Dover, 1985), 233–34.

30. Mildred Bailey recorded "Junk Man" with the Goodman band for Columbia in February 1934. "I Wish I Were Twins" was issued by Victor in May 1934 and was distributed in Australia, England, and Germany. See Brian Rust, *Jazz Records* (New Rochelle, N.Y.: Arlington House, 1978), 593, 1624.

31. Kimball and Nelson, *Complete Lyrics*, xix. Kantor and Maslon, *Broadway*, 18–26.

32. Bordman's *American Musical Comedy* provides an excellent survey of these forms of entertainment, 15–62.

33. Hirschhorn, *Hollywood Musical*, 11.

34. Altman, *Silent Film Sound*, 55–76.

35. Herbert's full score to accompany Thomas F. Dixon's *The Fall of a Nation* (1916) is lost. Henry Hadley (1871–1937), most famous as a conductor and staunch advocate

of American music, composed and conducted a fully synchronized score for the Vita-phone Company to accompany *When a Man Loves* in 1926.

36. Clifford McCarty, *Film Composers in America*, 2nd ed. (New York: Oxford University Press, 2000), 7.

37. McCarty, *Film Composers in America*, 9.

38. Sauer, "Photoplay Music," 198–99.

39. McCarty, *Film Composers in America*, 17.

40. Sanjek, *Pennies from Heaven*, 148.

41. McCarty, *Film Composers in America*, 4.

42. Bradley, *First Hollywood Musicals*, 271 and ff.

43. Hirschhorn, *Hollywood Musical*, 149, 161, 172, 218, 229, 284, 303.

44. Although Loesser's productivity is impressive, it is probably on a par with his fellow writers. For comparison, one of Loesser's occasional colleagues at Paramount was German expatriate composer Frederick Hollander (né Friedrich Hollaender). Hollander had studied with composer Engelbert Humperdinck and worked with director Max Reinhardt before founding his own Berlin cabaret in the 1920s. He wrote the music for "Falling in Love Again," famously sung by Marlene Dietrich in *The Blue Angel* (1930), and accompanied her in other shows. In Hollywood he worked on over 120 films between 1933 and 1953, serving most often as "music director," a job that included a variable combination of arranging, new composition, orchestration, compilation, management, and financial business as necessary. See McCarty, *Film Composers in America*, 3–4.

45. Hirschhorn, *Hollywood Musical*, 183.

46. Ibid. See also Susan Loesser, *Most Remarkable Fella*, 38.

47. Kimball and Nelson, *Complete Lyrics*, xv.

48. *The Stardust Road and Sometimes I Wonder: The Autobiographies of Hoagy Carmichael* (New York: Da Capo Press, 1999), 260.

49. *Frank Loesser Song Book* (1971), 10.

50. Susan Loesser, *Most Remarkable Fella*, 30.

51. He would use a similar joke, a clandestine love affair for a married couple, in a 1939 lyric, "A Love Letter." See Kimball and Nelson, *Complete Lyrics*, 47.

52. Kimball and Nelson, *Complete Lyrics*, 35.

53. Sanjek, *Pennies from Heaven*, 165–66.

54. Making useful comparisons among movie songwriters is difficult, since various individuals divided their time in different ways for a mixture of stage and film assignments. But even the most prolific movie tunesmiths (such as Ralph Rainger and Harry Warren) seldom worked on more than a half-dozen shows per year. Jule Styne's level of productivity—seven films in 1940, seventeen in 1941, and fourteen in 1942—most closely resembles Loesser's among the major writers of the period. See Hemming, *Melody Lingers On*, 357–59.

55. Crawford, *America's Musical Life*, 682–83.

56. See Charles K. Harris's "After the Ball" (1892), Shields and Evans's "In the Good Old Summertime" (1902), and George M. Cohan's "Over There" (1918).

57. Wilder, *American Popular Song*, 511.

58. Deanna Durbin, acting the role of a forlorn, deserted singer in a sleazy New

Orleans club, sang both this song and Berlin's "Always" as part of her act within the film *Christmas Holiday* (1944).

59. *Hi, Yank! The Army Show*, Blueprint Special No. 2, i.

60. Ibid., "Orchestrations," 2.

61. Loesser would certainly have known of Irving Berlin's earlier revue about military life, *Yip, Yip, Yaphank* (1918), which included "Oh, How I Hate to Get Up in the Morning." But there is no clear link between the earlier and later shows.

62. *The Movie Guide*, 668–69.

63. Personal communication with Prof. John T. LaSaine, Air Command and Staff College, Montgomery, Ala., August 10, 2005.

64. Crawford, *Civil War Songbook*, viii, x, 113–16.

65. Its contour also matches George Gershwin's 1919 song "Nobody but You."

CHAPTER 2. The First Broadway Hit

1. Loesser's sympathy for homely subjects and the life of the working stiff was honored in 1947, when he was awarded honorary membership in the Merchant Plumbers Association of Los Angeles "for his outstanding contribution to the plumbing industry by having composed the ode to the leaky faucet, 'Bloop, Bleep.'" Kimball and Nelson, *Complete Lyrics*, 134.

2. Spada, *Streisand*, 527.

3. *Charley's Aunt* was well known to Americans and had enjoyed many revivals in each decade since it first appeared on Broadway in 1893, a year following its English opening.

4. *The Movie Guide*, 103; Laufe, *Broadway's Greatest Musicals*, 111.

5. Frommer and Frommer, *It Happened on Broadway*, 119–21. Astonishingly, Feuer and Abbott's elimination of the central character of the play, Fancourt Babberley, went almost completely unremarked in the critical hubbub over the musical.

6. George Abbott, *Mister Abbott* (New York: Random House, 1963), 177–78.

7. Ibid.

8. Stanley Green, *Broadway Musicals Show by Show*, 116.

9. Despite a shared march tempo and the word "society" in their titles, "The New Ashmolean" bears no resemblance to the Gershwins' opening number for *Strike Up the Band* (1930), "Fletcher's American Cheese Choral Society." According to Ernest Havemann (writing in 1952), when Loesser was investigating the background of Oxford University in preparation for writing the musical, he encountered the name of its local museum, "Britain's oldest public museum," the Ashmolean, and was immediately struck by its euphonious ring. *Life*, December 8, 1952, 164–65.

10. Kimball and Nelson, *Complete Lyrics*, 138.

11. Ewen, *All the Years of American Popular Music*, 262.

12. Seaton, "Music and Dramatic Function," 18. It is not out of the question that Loesser and his parents attended a Metropolitan Opera performance of Donizetti's work, since it was a favorite of the reigning tenor of the day, Enrico Caruso. Stanley Sadie, ed., *New Grove Dictionary of Opera* (London: Macmillan, 1992), s.v. "Elisir d'amore, L.'"

13. Laufe, *Broadway's Greatest Musicals*, 110.

14. John Lardner, "An Old Ritual Plus Ray Bolger," *New York Star*, October 13, 1948.

15. *New York Theatre Critics' Reviews*, vol. 9, 1998.

16. Wilk, *They're Playing Our Song*, 249.

17. Ibid.

18. Ibid., 200.

19. Ibid.

20. This song form is sometimes called the "two-part" or "two-halves" thirty-two-measure form, in contrast with the more modern statement-restatement-contrast-return (AABA).

21. Swain, *Broadway Musical*, 15–49.

22. Mordden, *Beautiful Mornin'*, 248.

23. Brooks Atkinson, *New York Times*, October 12, 1948.

24. Vincent Canby, "Theatre: *Where's Charley?* Revived," *New York Times*, May 26, 1966, 57.

25. Music Theatre International's records can be consulted through its Web site, http://www.MTIshows.com/default_home.asp.

26. Bordman, *American Musical Comedy*, 163.

27. William G. King, "Composer for the Theater: Kurt Weill Talks about 'Practical Music,'" *New York Sun*, February 3, 1940.

28. Susan Loesser, *Most Remarkable Fella*, 147.

29. In an interview with Murray Schumach, Loesser claimed "I've always had a flair for concurrent speech in my songs—take 'Sue Me' and 'Baby, It's Cold Outside.'" *New York Times*, April 29, 1956, section 2, p. 3.

30. Prior to working on *The Most Happy Fella*, Loesser reportedly began to study Bach's music on his own and referred to his duet for Cleo and Marie, "I Don't Like This Dame," as "derivative of the time of Bach. . . . I use the form [a sort of two-part invention] because I like the sound of it and I don't think the form belongs in any special niche." Gilbert Milstein, "The Greater Loesser," *New York Times*, May 20, 1956, magazine section, 22.

31. Susan Loesser, *Most Remarkable Fella*, 129–30.

32. Ibid.

33. Charles Hamm, *Irving Berlin: Songs from the Melting Pot: The Formative Years, 1907–1914* (New York: Oxford University Press, 1997), 200, 213–15; Benjamin Sears and Bradford Conner, *Everybody Step: Irving Berlin's Music Box Revues and Other Songs from 1921–1925* (Boston: Oakton Recordings, 2004).

34. Their performance is included on the 1995 compact disc *Frank Sings Loesser* (Koch International Classics 3-7241-2 H1).

35. Ernest Havemann, "The Fine Art of the Hit Tune," *Life*, December 8, 1952, 170, 173.

36. The song was registered for copyright as an unpublished song in 1948, then published by Frank Music Corporation and copyrighted again on April 25, 1949. See Kimball and Nelson, *Complete Lyrics*, 148.

37. See Abe Burrows's *New York Times* obituary for Frank Loesser, August 10, 1969, partially reprinted in Kantor and Maslon, *Broadway*, 277.

38. Kimball and Nelson, *Complete Lyrics*, 59, 200–201.

CHAPTER 3. The Broadway Composer Arrives

1. Atkinson, *New York Times*, December 3, 1950, section 2, p. 1.

2. The designated licensing organization, Music Theatre International, approved 515 separate productions in 2005, a typical year.

3. Bordman, *American Musical Theatre*, 154–55.

4. Ibid., 175 and ff.

5. Garebian, *Making of Guys and Dolls*, 21.

6. Frommer and Frommer, *It Happened on Broadway*, 123–24.

7. Kimball and Nelson, *Complete Lyrics*, 159, 163.

8. Burrows, *Honest Abe*, 135, 142–43.

9. Laufe claims that as many as ten different writers were asked before Burrows was finally given the job; see *Broadway's Greatest Musicals*, 145.

10. Ibid., 147.

11. Garebian, *Making of Guys and Dolls*, 12–15.

12. *Guys and Dolls: The Stories of Damon Runyon*, introduction by William Kennedy, xv.

13. John Mosedale, *The Men Who Invented Broadway: Damon Runyon, Walter Winchell and Their World* (New York: Marek, 1981), 22–23. Runyon's fondness for many individuals in the criminal underworld is well documented. In his biography of Runyon, Jimmy Breslin notes, "His stories are based on Broadway and 50th Street in Manhattan, in front of an all-night delicatessen called Lindy's. He had the most admiration for Arthur Bieler of Tenth Avenue, an undertaker's delight, who in real life rarely missed when shooting at people he didn't like." *A Life of Damon Runyon* (New York: Ticknor and Fields, 1991), 17.

14. Runyon, *Romance in the Roaring Forties*, introduction by Tom Clark, 15.

15. Breslin, *A Life of Damon Runyon*, 16–17.

16. *Guys and Dolls: The Stories of Damon Runyon*, introduction by William Kennedy, xv.

17. On the subject of feet, however, "Ooh! My Feet!"—later used in the opening restaurant scene of *The Most Happy Fella*—was originally intended for a footsore Lt. Brannigan in *Guys and Dolls*, according to Abba Bogin. Quoted in Block, *Enchanted Evenings*, 377.

18. Burrows, *Honest Abe*, 138; Kantor and Maslon, *Broadway*, 74–75; Green and Laurie, *Show Biz*, 413.

19. Knapp, *American Musical*, 135.

20. Porter, *With an Air Debonair*, 28–29; Mordden, *Coming Up Roses*, 31.

21. Mann, "Musicals of Frank Loesser," 69.

22. H. Wiley Hitchcock with Kyle Gann, *Music in the United States: A Historical Introduction*, 4th ed. (Englewood Cliffs, N.J.: Prentice Hall, 2000), 244. Enthusiastic lobbying by critics called attention to the quality of the show and urged its re-revival in 1955. *Threepenny*'s long run, invested with the authoritative presence of Kurt Weill's widow, Lotte Lenya, launched the careers of hundreds of Broadway actors and returned over $3 million on an initial investment of $10,000. See also David Farneth's notes (pp. 11–12) for the compact disc recording, released in 2000, of *Kurt Weill's The Threepenny Opera: A Decca Broadway Original Cast Album* [1954] (UMG Records 012 159 463-2).

23. Mann, "Musicals of Frank Loesser," 69.

24. Hirsch, *Kurt Weill on Stage*, 57.

25. *George Bernard Shaw's Plays*, 486.

26. A film of *Major Barbara* with Robert Morley, Rex Harrison, and Wendy Hiller was pronounced "bracingly intelligent cinema," "uniformly marvelous, with the dry radiance of Hiller firing every scene," *The Movie Guide*, 411.

27. Knapp, *American Musical*, 136.

28. Burrows, *Honest Abe*, 150.

29. Ibid.

30. Ibid., 132. By this time, Kaufman was a show business icon, having helped to write or direct the Marx Brothers comedies *The Cocoanuts* (1925) and *Animal Crackers* (1928), as well as musicals with the Gershwins, Irving Berlin, and Richard Rodgers: *Of Thee I Sing* (1931), *Face the Music* (1932), and *I'd Rather Be Right* (1937).

31. Ibid., 152.

32. Stanley Green, *Broadway Musicals Show by Show*, 156, 166, 196, 206, 302. Burrows wrote the book for and directed *Can-Can* (1953), cowrote *Silk Stockings* (1955), and directed *What Makes Sammy Run?* (1964). He was often involved in revivals of *Guys and Dolls* and *How to Succeed in Business Without Really Trying*.

33. Stephen Banfield suggests a plausible connection between the "sleazy" street scene of *42nd Street* and *Guys and Dolls*; see David Nicholls, ed., *The Cambridge History of American Music* (Cambridge: Cambridge University Press, 1998), 334.

34. Brian Drutman, the third of three liner notes for *Guys and Dolls: A Decca Broadway Original Cast Album*, reissued on CD in 2000 (UMG Recordings 012 159 112-2); Kimball and Nelson, *Complete Lyrics*, 166–67.

35. Garebian, *Making of Guys and Dolls*, 21. Knapp has noted that the piece is "no more a fugue than a tinhorn is a real musical instrument; rather it is a 'tinhorn fugue,' a simple canon 'putting on airs.'" *American Musical*, 140.

36. Lindsay, "Recollections of Frank Loesser," 57.

37. Knapp, *American Musical*, 140.

38. *New Grove Dictionary of American Music*, s.v. "Mercer, Johnny."

39. Block, *Enchanted Evenings*, 207–9.

40. *New Grove Dictionary of American Music*, s.v. "Bliss, Peter Paul," "Sankey, Ira," and "Gospel." Lowell Mason, the dean of American hymn writers in the middle of the nineteenth century, wrote in a characteristically clear and simple style for congregational hymn singing.

41. In further illustration of this point, "The New Ashmolean Marching Society" number in *Where's Charley?* presents an entirely different mood with the same device.

42. Max Preeo, the second of three liner notes for *Guys and Dolls: A Decca Broadway Original Cast Album*.

43. Loesser had applied a similar Handelian expression in "The Gossips" ensemble of *Where's Charley?* Small choruses or ensembles found in *The Pirates of Penzance*, *HMS Pinafore*, *The Yeomen of the Guard*, and *The Mikado*, to name only a few among Gilbert and Sullivan's many works, also feature assorted characters frozen in place to perform a four-part a cappella piece in one stanza, generally referred to as a "madrigal."

44. Block, *Enchanted Evenings*, 209.

45. Knapp, *American Musical*, 140.

46. Block, *Enchanted Evenings*, 201.

47. The key of the original score is E major. The original cast members sang it in G, but subsequent published scores place the number in F major.

48. Other instances of New York dialect appear in tough guy and street urchin dialogue in such 1930s films as *Dead End* (1937), which stars Humphrey Bogart as a hardened criminal hiding out in his old neighborhood and befriending a group of adolescent gang members. The pair of comic gangsters featured in *Kiss Me, Kate* (1948) would have been known to the *Guys and Dolls* creators.

49. Engel, *Words with Music*, 64.

50. In 2000 Universal Classics Group issued a compact disc re-release of the original cast album of 1951, *Guys and Dolls: A Decca Broadway Original Cast Album* (UMG Recordings 012 159 112-2).

51. Engel, *Words with Music*, 225.

52. Susan Loesser, *Most Remarkable Fella*, 18.

53. According to Lynn Loesser, Frank first came across the opening lines, quoted as a popular Southern expression, in Truman Capote's collection of stories, *Other Voices, Other Rooms*; see Kimball and Nelson, *Complete Lyrics*, 159.

54. As Raymond Knapp observes, "Remarkably [Adelaide's] two 'onstage' numbers manage to combine apparent naiveté with what seems to be habitual cynicism, making her seem outwardly oblivious to the sexual innuendos and rampant double entendres that pervade her milieu. Both the name of the night club that she performs in (the 'Hot Box') and her first number there ('A Bushel and a Peck') wear their verbal play so openly that it can either pass unnoticed or be taken for granted by audiences and characters alike, almost as if it were merely a part of the scenery." *American Musical*, 141.

55. *The Jerome Kern Song Book*, 5–9.

56. Wilder, *American Popular Song*, 519.

57. Gibbs is quoted in Burrows, *Honest Abe*, 172.

58. Michael Buchler, "Modulation as a Dramatic Agent in Frank Loesser's Broadway Songs," unpublished lecture. Buchler notes that, while an upward modulation by half steps is a virtual cliché of intensification in popular songs, a descending modulation by a whole step is exceptional.

59. Block, *Enchanted Evenings*, 206.

60. Knapp, *The American Musical*, 137.

61. Phillip Gossett is quoted in Richard Taruskin, *The Oxford History of Western Music*, vol. 3 (New York: Oxford University Press, 2004), 9.

62. Laufe, *Broadway's Greatest Musicals*, 145.

63. Ibid., 143.

64. *Variety*, November 2, 1955, n.p.

65. Hirschhorn, *Hollywood Musical*, 349.

66. Burrows, *Honest Abe*, 203–5.

67. *New York World-Telegram* and *The Sun*, November 25, 1950.

68. Ibid.

69. *New York Herald Tribune*, November 25, 1950; *New York Post Home News*, November 26, 1950.

70. *New York World-Telegram* and *The Sun*, November 25, 1950.

71. *New York Times*, December 3, 1950.

72. Ibid.

73. Gänzl, *Encyclopedia of Musical Theater*, s.v. "Guys and Dolls."

74. *The Guys and Dolls Book*, 79–111.

75. Norton, *Chronology of American Musical Theater*, vol. 3, 33

76. Susan Loesser, *Most Remarkable Fella*, 118–19; Sennett, *Hollywood Musicals*, 291.

77. *Variety*, November 2, 1955.

78. Hirschhorn, *Hollywood Musical*, 349.

79. Hischak, *Film It with Music*, 136–37.

80. Mast, *Can't Help Singin'*, 318.

81. Matthew-Walker, *Broadway to Hollywood*, 102.

82. Mordden, *The Hollywood Musical*, 195.

83. Quoted in James Robert Parish and Michael R. Pitts, *The Great Hollywood Musical Pictures* (Metuchen, N.J.: Scarecrow Press, 1992), 278.

84. The letter remains in the Academy of Motion Picture Arts and Sciences' Margaret Herrick Library and is reprinted by kind permission of the writer's son, Charles Manley.

85. Hischak, *Film It with Music*, 137.

86. These revues included *Perfectly Frank* at the Helen Hayes Theater (1980), *More of Loesser* at the St. Regis-Sheraton Hotel (1982), and *I Hear Music . . . of Frank Loesser and Friends* at the Ballroom Theater (1984). See Norton, *Chronology of American Musical Theater*, vol. 3, 538.

87. The conversation between Loesser and Burrows is reported in Wilk, *They're Playing Our Song*, 258.

88. Mordden, *Coming Up Roses*, 35–36.

89. Garebian, *Making of Guys and Dolls*, 140–42.

90. Kimball and Nelson, *Complete Lyrics*, 157.

91. Ibid.

92. The unofficial estimates come from the Rodgers and Hammerstein Organization and Music Theatre International.

93. Burrows, *Honest Abe*, 341.

CHAPTER 4. Just Don't Call It Opera

1. Howard, *They Knew What They Wanted*, xiii.

2. Kantor and Maslon, *Broadway*, 277.

3. Mann, "The Musicals of Frank Loesser," 89.

4. Susan Loesser, *Most Remarkable Fella*, 141; Block, *Enchanted Evenings*, 215.

5. Block, *Enchanted Evenings*, 317.

6. According to Jo Sullivan Loesser, quoted in New York City Opera's *Playbill* (March 2006), 23.

7. Jo Sullivan Loesser, interview by Terry Gross, *Fresh Air*, National Public Radio, March 20, 2006.

8. Carol Oja, review of *Trouble in Tahiti*, by Leonard Bernstein (Opus Arte DVD), *American Music* 23 (Winter 2005): 526.

9. Before World War II, Broadway operas were rare. Gertrude Stein and Virgil Thomson's *Four Saints in Three Acts* (1934) chalked up only forty-eight performances. The now canonical *Porgy and Bess* (1935) enjoyed only 124 in its first Broadway outing. More closely contemporary with *The Most Happy Fella*, Marc Blitzstein's *Regina* (1949, revived in 1953, 1958, 1959) has usually been mounted as part of the New York City Opera's regular schedule, with no more than a half-dozen performances each time. Kurt Weill's *Street Scene* (1947) seems to be developing a place in the repertory of universities and regional companies; it appeared at the New York City Opera in 1978 and in the United Kingdom during the 1980s. Its first run lasted 148 performances at the Adelphi Theatre. *The Consul* (1950), with 269 performances, achieved the longest run of any of Gian Carlo Menotti's Broadway operas, but this was still fewer than half as many performances as *The Most Happy Fella*.

10. Susan Loesser, *Most Remarkable Fella*, 140.

11. Ibid., 141.

12. Gilbert Milstein, "The Greater Loesser," *New York Times*, May 20, 1956, magazine section, 22.

13. Howard, *They Knew What They Wanted*, 8.

14. Alan Gevinson notes that Joseph Breen of the Production Code censorship office insisted to the studio (RKO Radio) that the "sinners" be punished properly by the end of the film. Furthermore, when Italy entered the Second World War on the Axis side, director Garson Kanin was forced to obtain permission from the British Embassy so that Laughton, a Brit, could still play an Italian American onscreen. See *Within Our Gates*, 1025.

15. White, *Sidney Howard*, 166.

16. Murray Schumach, "Molding a Musical," *New York Times*, April 29, 1956, section 2, p. 3.

17. Loesser wrote a considerably longer opening scene for a larger group of waitresses, who comment on Rosabella's love letter ("Love Letter"), and a song for Rosabella about her dreams of a "House and Garden." Both numbers are included on a 1992 CD release, *An Evening with Frank Loesser: Frank Loesser Performs Songs from His Hit Shows* (DRG Records 5169).

18. Howard, *They Knew What They Wanted*, 94.

19. Susan Loesser, *Most Remarkable Fella*, 164. Susan Loesser seems to be suggesting that Frank understood "Abbondanza" would only be properly appreciated as part of the full show. In any case, she is clear that her father absolutely refused to license the song for any separate performances, even with the original cast members. Jo Sullivan Loesser later confirmed that Loesser always urged "saving the big songs" by withholding too frequent permissions for single performances. Sullivan Loesser, interview by Gross.

20. Schumach, "Molding a Musical."

21. Milstein, "The Greater Loesser."

22. The 2006 New York City Opera production reduced the number of acts to two by combining acts 2 and 3, making a few small cuts in the dialogue, and omitting the "Abbondanza" reprise, to entirely satisfactory effect.

23. Howard, *They Knew What They Wanted*, xiii–xiv.

24. See Arthur Gewirtz, "Historical Note," New York City Opera *Playbill*, March

2006; Eric Myers, "A Most Memorable Fella," New York City Opera 2005–2006 Souvenir Program, 22–23; Stanley Sadie and John Tyrrell, eds., *New Grove Dictionary of Music and Musicians* (New York: Grove's Dictionaries), s.v. "Weede [Wiedefeld], Robert").

25. Susan Loesser, *Most Remarkable Fella*, 147.

26. Myers, "A Most Memorable Fella," 22.

27. Susan Loesser, *Most Remarkable Fella*, 152–53. According to his original *Playbill* biography (1954), Lund's "superb physique" had helped him letter in six college sports: football, baseball, tennis, swimming, track, and boxing.

28. Hill, *Most Happy Fella* review, 438–39.

29. Block, "Frank Loesser's Sketchbook," 60–78.

30. *Allegro* means fast and lively, *pesante* heavy, and *lento* slowly.

31. Seaton, "Music and Dramatic Function," 56.

32. Jenness and Velsey, *Classic American Popular Song*, 110–11.

33. Ibid.

34. Block, "Frank Loesser's Sketchbook," 72.

35. Hill, *Most Happy Fella* review, 439.

36. Sullivan Loesser, interview by Gross.

37. Seaton, "Music and Dramatic Function," 63.

38. The Bizet motive is accompanied in most instances by a tremulous D-minor chord; the Loesser fragment is usually unharmonized.

39. Block, *Enchanted Evenings*, 220–23.

40. This accusation of genre mismatching was aimed also at Gershwin's *Porgy and Bess* (1935) for its recitatives and other "white" operatic elements (Knapp, *American Musical*, 196–97) and at Weill's *Street Scene* (1947) for the inclusion of such a lighthearted dance song as "Moon-Faced, Starry-Eyed" in the same show as the intense aria "Somehow I Never Could Believe." Gänzl, *Encyclopedia of Musical Theater*, s.v. "Street Scene."

41. The three-record set, filling 134 minutes, was produced for Columbia by Goddard Lieberson in May 1956, two weeks after the New York premiere, with the full regular cast: Susan Johnson as Cleo, Jo Sullivan as Rosabella, Lee Cass as the Postman, Robert Weede as Tony, Mona Paulee as Marie, Shorty Long as Herman, and Art Lund as Joe. Herbert Greene directed the orchestra and singers. Sony Broadway produced the compact disc reissue in 1991.

42. Kurt Weill, "Score for a Play," *New York Times*, January 5, 1947.

43. Block, *Enchanted Evenings*, 217.

44. Ibid., 219.

45. The Venetian origins of the barcarolle are well attested; see *New Grove Dictionary of Music and Musicians*, s.v. "barcarolle."

46. *Most Happy Fella*, vocal score, 166.

47. Porter, *With an Air Debonair*, 73, 307.

48. Fields and Fields, *From the Bowery to Broadway*, 206.

49. William Mahar, *Behind the Burnt Cork Mask* (Urbana: University of Illinois Press, 1999), especially chapters 3 and 4.

50. Milstein, "The Greater Loesser."

51. The critiques are quoted and summarized in the liner notes for the RCA Victor cast recording of the 1992 Broadway revival (BMG 09026-61294-2).

52. Blitzstein's *Regina* was recorded by the New York City Opera Company in 1958 by Columbia Records. Liner notes were contributed by Loesser, Lillian Hellman, and Leonard Bernstein.

53. Susan Loesser, *Most Remarkable Fella*, 123–24.

54. Loesser actually composed twelve songs but only eight were finally used, along with a short set of street cries for the movie chorus's market scene.

55. Both Petit and Jeanmaire had made their mark as principals in the Ballet de Paris's 1949 production of *Carmen*.

56. Berg, *Goldwyn*, 463–65. Both Loesser and Danny Kaye later reported receiving tumultuous receptions for their work in Denmark.

57. Ibid.; Kimball and Nelson, *Complete Lyrics*, 173.

58. Kimball and Nelson, *Complete Lyrics*, 170–71. The private recordings can be found on the 1995 compact disc *Frank Sings Loesser* (Koch 3-7241-2). John Coltrane's 1962 recording of "The Inch Worm" (reissued on the 1997 compact disc *John Coltrane Quartet*, GRP Records 215) is one of the more interesting renditions to spin off from this show.

59. Susan Loesser, *Most Remarkable Fella*, 127.

60. Gänzl, *Encyclopedia of Musical Theater*, 613.

CHAPTER 5. Another Way to Write a Broadway Hit

1. When earlier asked to musicalize another workplace play, *7 1/2 Cents*, Loesser firmly declined but passed it on to the young team of Richard Adler and Jerry Ross, who created *The Pajama Game* (1954), which racked up 1,063 performances, only 137 off the mark set about that time by *Guys and Dolls*. Stanley Green, *Broadway Musicals Show by Show*, 161.

2. Mead, *How to Succeed*, passim.

3. Quoted in Kimball and Nelson, *Complete Lyrics*, 215.

4. Garebian, *Making of Guys and Dolls*, 4.

5. Howard Taubman, *New York Times*, October 16, 1961.

6. Stuart Ostrow, unpublished (private) manuscript.

7. See Stanley Green, *Broadway Musicals Show by Show*, 196; Susan Loesser, *Most Remarkable Fella*, 197–98. Weinstock and Gilbert have received full credit in every production. Apparently it was Cy Feuer who made the decision to tap Robert Morse for the lead role, and Morse's talents helped to clinch the deal with Burrows (Kimball and Nelson, *Complete Lyrics*, 215). The part of Rosemary was played first by Bonnie Scott, who was succeeded by Michele Lee.

8. That the show's plans were carefully laid is confirmed by Maurice Zolotow's preview article in the *New York Times*, October 8, 1961, section 2, p. 3. He quotes Loesser: "We first choose the song areas. We lay out the spots where to place the ballads, the comedy songs, the patter songs, dance numbers, like that."

9. *The Movie Guide*, 27.

10. Burrows, *Honest Abe*, 333.

11. Ibid., 335.

12. Mast, *Can't Help Singin'*, 290. Engel, *Words with Music*, 225–26.

13. Walter Kerr, in *New York Theatre Critics' Reviews*, vol. 22, 226.

14. Burrows, *Honest Abe*, 339.

15. Altman, *Silent Film Sound*, 10; Denny Martin Flinn, *Musical! A Grand Tour: The Rise, Glory, and Fall of an American Institution* (New York: Schirmer Books, 1997), 302–3.

16. Seaton, "Music and Dramatic Function," 77–78.

17. Richard Watts Jr., in *New York Theatre Critics' Reviews*, vol. 22, 225–26.

18. Dizzy Gillespie's autobiography *To Be, or Not . . . to Bop* (New York: Doubleday, 1979) devotes a chapter to debunking the myths that had grown up surrounding modern jazz in the 1940s—and there was considerable misunderstanding to be addressed. Robert Walser includes an excerpt from this chapter in *Keeping Time: Readings in Jazz History* (New York: Oxford University Press, 1999), 155–70.

19. Hugh Hefner, for example, in the June 1957 issue of *Playboy* magazine, described himself as follows for his readers: "His dress is conservative and casual. He always wears loafers. . . . There is an electronic entertainment wall in his office, very much like the one featured in *Playboy*'s Penthouse apartment, that includes hi-fi, AM-FM radio, tape, and television, and will store up to 2,000 LPs. Brubeck, Kenton or Sinatra is usually on the turntable when Hefner is working. He is essentially an indoors man, though he discovered the pleasures of the ski slope last winter. He likes jazz, foreign films, Ivy League clothes, gin and tonic and pretty girls—the same sort of things that *Playboy* readers like—and his approach to life is as fresh, sophisticated, and yet admittedly sentimental as is the magazine." Quoted in Halberstam, *The Fifties*, 574–75.

20. Block, *Enchanted Evenings*, 246; Gänzl, *Encyclopedia of Musical Theater*, s.v. "West Side Story."

21. For an example, hear Bill Evans's rendition of "So What" with the Miles Davis Sextet, included in the 1987 *Smithsonian Collection of Classic Jazz*, selected and annotated by Martin Williams (CBS Special Products).

22. Susan Loesser, *Most Remarkable Fella*, 33, 36.

23. Kimball and Nelson, *Complete Lyrics*, 222; Burrows, *Honest Abe*, 334–35.

24. Block, *Enchanted Evenings*, 318–19. The other Tony Awards won by *How to Succeed* were best composer (Loesser), best authors of a musical (Burrows, Weinstock, and Gilbert), best featured actor in a musical (Reilly), best direction of a musical (Burrows), best conductor and musical director (Elliot Lawrence), and best producers of a musical (Feuer and Martin).

25. Walter Kerr, *New York Herald Tribune*, October 16, 1961.

26. Ibid.; Susan Loesser, *Most Remarkable Fella*, 202–3.

27. *New York Theatre Critics' Reviews*, vol. 22, 224–27.

28. Ibid.

29. *New York Daily News*, January 20, 1962, 1. This photo was reprinted in Burrows, *Honest Abe*, between pp. 312 and 313.

30. Burrows, *Honest Abe*, 338. Burrows's authority for the story was apparently Arthur Schlesinger Jr., a personal friend of his as well as an adviser to President Kennedy and a distinguished historian.

31. Gänzl, *Encyclopedia of Musical Theater*, s.v. "How to Succeed in Business Without Really Trying"; Hirschhorn, *Hollywood Musical*, 338.

32. John Simon in *New York* magazine, April 3, 1995, called the tunes "caged, corseted, teased and tormented into something unspontaneous, overblown, unmusical."

33. Vincent Canby, *New York Times*, March 24, 1995; Howard Kissel, *New York Daily News*, March 24, 1995.

34. *Wall Street Journal*, March 24, 1995.

35. *Variety*, April 2, 1995.

CHAPTER 6. The Unknown Loesser

1. The cast recording of the 1958 London production was digitally remastered and issued by EMI as a compact disc in 1995.

2. The music, unpublished, survives in a manuscript score. See Kimball and Nelson, *Complete Lyrics*, 197.

3. Kimball and Nelson, *Complete Lyrics*, 199–200.

4. Ibid., 197.

5. Bernstein, *Trouble in Tahiti*, 21–22. Apparently, however, it is unrelated to the most famous psycho-musical of the 1940s: Moss Hart, Kurt Weill, and Ira Gershwin's *Lady in the Dark* (1941), in which music appears only in the heroine Liza's dream states, to differentiate them from her everyday waking life.

6. Susan Loesser, *Most Remarkable Fella*, 179.

7. Taryn Benbow-Pfalzgraf, ed., *American Women Writers: A Critical Reference Guide*, 2nd ed. (Farmington Hills, Mich.: St. James Press, 2000), vol. 1, 204.

8. B. J. Chute, *Greenwillow* (New York: Dutton, 1956), 53 passim.

9. *Greenwillow: The Original Cast Album* (RCA Victor LOC 2001, 1960).

10. Chute, *Greenwillow*, 1.

11. Perhaps the closest match to *Greenwillow* in its folk theology would be Marc Connelly's Pulitzer Prize–winning play *Green Pastures* (1930), whose characters (southern rural black folk) reenact biblical stories as they sing harmonized spirituals and attend fish fries. See Errol Hill and James V. Hatch, *A History of African American Theatre* (Cambridge: Cambridge University Press, 2003), 308–10.

12. Ira Gershwin liked to quote the *Encyclopedia Britannica* on this subject, which defined "song" as a "joint art of words and music, two arts, under emotional pressure, coalescing into a third." *Lyrics on Several Occasions* (New York: Alfred A. Knopf, 1959), 362.

13. See *New Grove Dictionary of Music and Musicians*, s.v. "false relation," for a fuller explanation of this phenomenon.

14. Al Stillman and Robert Allen, "Home for the Holidays" (1954). Perry Como made his recording for RCA Victor.

15. Kimball and Nelson, *Complete Lyrics*, 206.

16. Ibid., 208.

17. Ibid.

18. Susan Loesser, *Most Remarkable Fella*, 180–81. Osborn wrote the stage play adaptation of *The World of Suzie Wong* and the screenplays for *The Yearling*, *East of Eden*, and *South Pacific*, among others. Loesser was also turned down by Albert Hackett and Frances Goodrich, most famous for their dramatization of the Anne Frank story..

19. Ibid., 182.

20. Ibid., 181, 188. Like Samuels, the director George Roy Hill also had never worked on a Broadway musical.

21. *New York Times*, June 15, 1959.

22. *Boston Record*, March 30, 1960.

23. *New York Times*, March 10, 1960.

24. Tynan is quoted in Susan Loesser, *Most Remarkable Fella*, 193.

25. Clive Barnes, "Failed Musical Gets Showing by Equity," *New York Times*, December 8, 1970; Brendan Gill, *New Yorker*, October 22, 1979; Kevin Kelly, *Boston Globe*, June 25, 1991.

26. Patricia Moyes translated Anouilh's original play into English in 1955. It was published in New York by Coward-McCann in 1958 and by Samuel French in 1959.

27. Brooks Atkinson called it "just about ideal" (*New York Times*, November 13, 1957); Robert Coleman deemed Hayes "nothing less than irresistible" (*New York Daily Mirror*, November 13, 1957); Burton "rises . . . to comic and caustic splendor . . . [with] superb . . . precision and power," according to Walter Kerr (*New York Herald Tribune*, November 13, 1957).

28. Kimball and Nelson, *Complete Lyrics*, 226.

29. *New York Times*, February 20, 1961.

30. Samuel Eliot Morison's *John Paul Jones: A Sailor's Biography* (Boston: Little, Brown, 1959), 360–65, confirms this bit of Jones's history.

31. Fosse had made his first big impression on Broadway at the age of twenty-six, with his "Steam Heat" choreography for *Pajama Game* (1954), written by Loesser protégés Richard Adler and Jerry Ross.

32. Susan Loesser, *Most Remarkable Fella*, 242.

33. A script is included in the Gwen Verdon Papers of the Library of Congress, Music and Performing Arts Division.

34. "In Your Eyes" is included in *The Frank Loesser Songbook* (1994), 89–91.

35. This article can be found in the archives of the Harvard Theatre Collection with the music materials for *Pleasures and Palaces*, part of the Gwen Verdon Collection.

36. It was "lesser Loesser," according to the *Detroit News*. The *Detroit Free Press* declared, "It's a Rolls-Royce of a show, a magnificent combination of artful scenery, lively choreography, and engaging people. But there's no gas in the Rolls-Royce tank." Susan Loesser, *Most Remarkable Fella*, 245.

37. Stewart, *Broadway Musicals*, 762.

38. Kimball and Nelson, *Complete Lyrics*, 229.

39. Ibid., 232.

40. Susan Loesser, *Most Remarkable Fella*, 98, 252, 285.

41. Loesser spent much time and effort over the story. Schulberg (b. 1914), the son of the onetime head of Paramount, then stood at the peak of his fame as the author of the novel *What Makes Sammy Run?* (1941) and the screenplay for the Academy Award–winning film *On the Waterfront* (1954). Suskin points out that, in 1952, Loesser, Burrows, Feuer, and Martin announced and then withdrew a musical version of a 1938 film about a French baker's wife, *La femme du boulanger* (Suskin, *Show Tunes*, 249).

42. Susan Loesser, *Most Remarkable Fella*, 275.

43. Ibid., 276–77.

44. Kimball and Nelson, *Complete Lyrics*, 243.

45. These lyrics differ in a few small respects from those printed in Kimball and Nelson, *Complete Lyrics*, 245.

46. Gänzl, *Encyclopedia of Musical Theater*, s.v. "Loesser, Frank [Henry]."

47. According to the Arena Stage program and publicity brochures, the show was scheduled in the Fichhandler Theater from April 9 through May 23, 2004. Charles Randolph-Wright directed. Doriana Sanchez served as choreographer, Brian Cimmet as musical director and vocal arranger, Thomas Lynch as set designer, Emilio Sosa as costume designer, Michael Gilliam as lighting designer, and Timothy Thompson as sound designer. The cast included Doreen Montalvo as the Curandera, John Bolton as Hilario, Shawn Elliott as Pancito, Ivan Hernandez as Martin, and Elena Shaddow as Lupita.

CHAPTER 7. The Legacy of Frank Loesser

1. Agnes de Mille was contracted for the choreography, and Lynn Riggs (author of *Green Grow the Lilacs*, the basis for *Oklahoma!*) was lined up for the book and lyrics. See Howard Pollack, *Aaron Copland: The Life and Work of An Uncommon Man* (New York: Henry Holt, 1999), 419.

2. Jimmy McHugh with Anne St. John, "Bring Him Along—He Plays!" unpublished autobiography, ca. 1967.

3. Leonard Bernstein, quoted in Engel, *American Musical Theater*, 154.

4. Ibid.

5. Ibid.

6. Guernsey, *Broadway Song and Story*, 392.

7. Wilk, *They're Playing Our Song*, 248.

8. Grant, *Rise and Fall*, 94–95.

9. Guernsey, *Broadway Song and Story*, 198.

10. She made this point most recently in her interview with Terry Gross on National Public Radio's *Fresh Air*, March 20, 2006.

11. The show, *Red, Hot, and Blue* (1949), which starred Betty Hutton and Victor Mature, bore no relationship to the 1936 Cole Porter musical of the same name. Film historian Clive Hirschhorn wryly declared of Loesser's performance, "As an actor he was a pretty good tunesmith!" (*Hollywood Musical*, 303). Loesser also supplied lyrics for the songs by Jimmy McHugh. See Susan Loesser, *Most Remarkable Fella*, 92–93.

12. Susan Loesser, *Most Remarkable Fella*, 108.

13. Preface to *The Frank Loesser Song Book* (1971), 5.

14. Wilk, *They're Playing Our Song*, 242.

15. Susan Loesser, *Most Remarkable Fella*, 70.

16. The letter to Abba Bogin begins, "Dear Abba, Your Carta arrived and it sure was Magna. I will not subscribe to one bit of it and you can come and get me here at Runnymede. . . . You are advised in addition, that Donald Walker who has been misharmonising [*sic*] me during my entire reign is already scheduled for the gallows or possibly, through my leniency, a life sentence in the Tower with no pencil sharpener." Don Walker Papers, Music Division, Library of Congress.

17. Kimball and Nelson, *Complete Lyrics*, 159.

18. Wilk, *They're Playing Our Song*, 246. A briefer version of the identical anecdote appears in Kimball and Nelson, *Complete Lyrics*, xv.

19. *The Frank Loesser Song Book* (1971), 5.

20. Rosenberg and Harburg, *Broadway Musical*, 144.

21. Ibid., 147.

22. Susan Loesser, *Most Remarkable Fella*, 154–55.

23. Abba Bogin, interview by author, April 25, 2006.

24. Walter Kerr, "A Sly, Scaled-Down, and Charming *Charley*," *New York Times*, December 26, 1974.

25. *New York Times*, December 20, 1974.

26. *New York Post*, December 20, 1974.

27. Ibid.

28. Crawford, *America's Musical Life*, 683, 737.

29. Susan Loesser, *Most Remarkable Fella*, 227.

30. Lane is quoted in Wilk, *They're Playing Our Song*, 245.

31. Stuart Ostrow, personal communication, December 10, 2003.

32. Lindsay, "Recollections of Frank Loesser," 29.

33. Ibid., 12.

34. Kimball and Nelson, *Complete Lyrics*, xiii.

35. *Weekly Variety*, September 9, 1969.

36. Mattfeld, *Variety Music Cavalcade*, xvii.

37. Harrison, *Songwriters*, 2.

38. Sanjek, *Pennies from Heaven*, 203.

39. Ibid., 166.

40. Ibid., 175.

41. The persistence of his songs can be followed week after week in 1948 and 1949 on the "Top Record of Talent and Tunes" lists of *Variety*; see Hischak, *Tin Pan Alley Song Encyclopedia*, 276, 291, 312, 390.

42. Susan Loesser, *Most Remarkable Fella*, 222.

43. Mattfeld, *Variety Music Cavalcade*, xvii.

44. Barrios, *Song in the Dark*, 408–9.

45. Sanjek, *Pennies from Heaven*, 152.

46. Mattfeld, *Variety Music Cavalcade*, xvii.

47. Sanjek, *Pennies from Heaven*, 158.

48. Mattfeld, *Variety Music Cavalcade*, xviii.

49. Taylor, *Jule*, 85.

50. Jo Sullivan Loesser, interview by Gross.

51. Their show *Magdalena* (1948), with music by Heitor Villa-Lobos, closed at the Ziegfeld Theatre after a three-month run. Bordman, *American Musical Theatre*, 658.

52. Susan Loesser, *Most Remarkable Fella*, 224.

53. Stanley Green, *Broadway Musicals Show by Show*, 158.

54. Kimball and Nelson, *Complete Lyrics*, xvii.

55. Frommer and Frommer, *It Happened on Broadway*, 249.

56. Ibid., 5–6.

57. Susan Loesser, *Most Remarkable Fella*, 225.

58. Frommer and Frommer, *It Happened on Broadway*, 135. Loesser is still held deeply in the hearts of those who went on to successful careers under his auspices. When Stuart Ostrow was awarded a Tony for producing *M. Butterfly* in 1989, twenty years after the death of Frank Loesser, the first words of gratitude he spoke recalled his old boss. Susan Loesser, *Most Remarkable Fella*, 290.

59. Quoted in Secrest, *Stephen Sondheim*, 157.

60. Frommer and Frommer, *It Happened on Broadway*, 250.

61. Whiting's 1987 testimonial was recorded and broadcast on Terry Gross's National Public Radio program *Fresh Air* on December 31, 2003. See also Comden, *Off Stage*, 323, and Susan Loesser, *Most Remarkable Fella*, 225–26.

62. Ostrow, unpublished (private) manuscript.

63. Lindsay, "Recollections of Frank Loesser," 48.

64. Susan Loesser, *Most Remarkable Fella*, 235.

65. Joseph Weiss, Frank Loesser Enterprises, personal communication, February 23, 2005.

66. Guernsey, *Broadway Song and Story*, 402–3.

67. Bogin, interview by author.

68. Lindsay, "Recollections of Frank Loesser," 49–50.

69. *The Frank Loesser Song Book* (1971), 9.

70. Kimball and Nelson, *Complete Lyrics*, xvi.

71. Susan Loesser, *Most Remarkable Fella*, 229.

72. Ibid., 228–29. See also the Web site for Music Theatre International and http://www.freddiegershon.com.

73. http://www.frankloesser.com, accessed on February 23, 2005.

74. Joseph Weiss, Frank Loesser Enterprises, personal communication, June 23, 2005.

75. According to the files at Frank Loesser Enterprises, Frank Music contracted with Dancer-Fitzgerald-Sample Inc., the advertising agency that represented General Mills, and hired Ed Doyle and Helen Ayres to provide the new lyrics for an undisclosed amount of money.

76. Sanjek, *Pennies from Heaven*, 467.

77. Susan Loesser, *Most Remarkable Fella*, 228.

78. Barrios, *Song in the Dark*, 387.

79. In 1922 a former postmaster general, Will H. Hays, had been appointed to "head a new organization set up by the film industry to regulate itself: the Motion Picture Producers and Distributors of America, Inc. (MPPDA), known in time simply as the Hays Office" (Barrios, *Song in the Dark*, 20). The office would step up its enforcement regulations in 1934 and become a close censor of the industry before restructuring in the 1970s. Joseph Breen retained the reins of command in the office from 1934 to 1954.

80. Barrios, *Song in the Dark*, 387.

81. Susan Loesser, *Most Remarkable Fella*, 231.

82. Berg, *Goldwyn*, 434.

83. In his unpublished manuscript, Stuart Ostrow tells of Loesser devising a prank and publicly insulting Edwin Lester, the founder and general manager of the Los Angeles Civic Light Opera Association, who took the liberty of trimming lines from *Guys and Dolls* in Lester's West Coast version of the show. Ostrow also reports that Loesser agreed to write a show for him, during the younger man's Army Air Force days, provided that Burrows, who was blacklisted at the time, was also hired. With signed agreements from Burrows and Loesser, Ostrow was elated until a week later he was called before a Senate subcommittee curious about his Ukrainian family background.

84. Lindsay, "Recollections of Frank Loesser," 14, 24.

85. Gottfried, *Broadway Musicals*, 265.

86. Susan Loesser, *Most Remarkable Fella*, 225–26.

87. Mast, "Musicals of Frank Loesser," 292.

88. The term "concept musical" generally refers to book shows that place less emphasis on telling a tautly constructed narrative than on presenting a series of loosely connected vignettes surrounding a situation, theme, or symbolic figures. Thus they tend to be more unified than a revue but less tightly knit than, say, *South Pacific* or *Sweeney Todd. Hair* (1968) and *Company* (1970) are commonly cited examples. Knapp, *American Musical*, 162. See also Stephen Banfield, *Sondheim's Broadway Musicals* (Ann Arbor: University of Michigan Press, 1993), 147–48.

89. Arthur Loesser, "My Brother Frank," 225.

90. Jacques Barzun, preface to *Men, Women, and Pianos: A Social History*, by Arthur Loesser (New York: Simon and Schuster, 1954), viii–ix.

91. Susan Loesser, *Most Remarkable Fella*, 167.

92. Hoagy Carmichael, *Sometimes I Wonder* (New York: Farrar, Straus and Giroux, 1965), 260.

93. Mast, *Can't Help Singin'*, 297–98.

94. Ibid.

95. *New Grove Dictionary of American Music*, s.v. Kern, Jerome David.

96. Bordman, *Jerome Kern*, 34. Mr. Wix, however, bears no relationship to Charley Wykeham of *Where's Charley?*

97. Stanley Green, *Broadway Musicals Show by Show*, 33, 50.

98. Ibid., 138.

99. Thus his term "generative," as opposed to "today's replicative musicals." Grant, *Rise and Fall*, 6.

100. *The Jerome Kern Song Book*, ix–xii.

101. Joseph Weiss, liner notes for *An Evening with Frank Loesser: Frank Loesser Performs Songs from His Hit Shows* (DRG Records 5169).

102. Ewen, *American Popular Songs*, 36.

103. Loesser's support for the work of Robert Wright and Chet Forrest, most of whose Broadway efforts involved adapting classical music to their books and lyrics, has already been cited.

104. Abba Bogin reports, "I remember being in his office one day when he was listening on the radio to an obscure Haydn string quartet, which he knew. He had an unbelievable retentive memory." Quoted in Kimball and Nelson, *Complete Lyrics*, xvi. Personal communications with Gregor Benko (a Cleveland pianist, biographer of Arthur Loesser, and founder of the International Piano Archive in 1965, who made Frank's acquaintance in the mid-1960s) also confirm Loesser's astonishing memory for old music and his capacity for explaining how popular songs might be related to classical works.

105. Gordon, *Mark the Music*, 338.

106. Frank Loesser, liner notes to Blitzstein's *Regina*, recorded in 1958 by the New York City Opera Company (Columbia 03S 202).

107. Bayrd Still, *Mirror for Gotham* (New York: Washington Square Press, 1956), 212–63.

108. Hamm, *Yesterdays*, 325; Kenney, *Recorded Music in American Life*, 67.

109. Kantor and Maslon, *Broadway*, x.

110. Grant, *Rise and Fall*, 6–7.

111. Letter dated August 18, 1965, William Schuman Papers, New York Public Library, Lincoln Center.

Bibliography

A substantial number of Loesser songs and scores, as well as several relevant manuscripts, books, photographs, business records, and scrapbooks are held at the offices of Frank Loesser Enterprises, 56 West Forty-fifth Street, New York, NY 10036-4206. The New York Public Library for the Performing Arts at Lincoln Center also houses a large body of Loesser sketches, manuscripts, videos, programs, reviews, and photographs.

Adler, Richard, with Lee Davis. *You Gotta Have Heart: An Autobiography.* New York: D. I. Fine, 1990.

Altman, Rick. *Silent Film Sound.* New York: Columbia University Press, 2004.

Barrios, Richard. *A Song in the Dark: The Birth of the Musical Film.* New York: Oxford University Press, 1995.

Benjamin, Ruth, and Arthur Rosenblatt. *Movie Song Catalog: Performers and Supporting Crew for the Songs Sung in 1,460 Musical and Nonmusical Films, 1928–1988.* Jefferson, N.C.: McFarland, 1993.

Berg, A. Scott. *Goldwyn: A Biography.* New York: Alfred A. Knopf, 1989.

Bernstein, Leonard. *Trouble in Tahiti.* Piano-vocal score. New York: G. Schirmer, 1953.

Blitzstein, Marc. "Notes on the Musical Theatre." *Theatre Arts* 34 (June 1950): 30–31.

———. *Regina.* Liner notes by Frank Loesser. Columbia Records LP recording 03S 202, 1958.

Block, Geoffrey. *Enchanted Evenings: The Broadway Musical from "Show Boat" to Sondheim.* New York: Oxford University Press, 1997.

———. "Frank Loesser's Sketchbook for *The Most Happy Fella.*" *Musical Quarterly* 73, no. 1 (1989): 60–78.

Bloom, Ken. *Hollywood Song: The Complete Film and Musicals Companion.* New York: Facts on File, 1995.

Bobbie, Walter. "Frank Loesser: A Survey of His Theatrical Writing." Unpublished typescript at Frank Loesser Enterprises, New York, 1985.

Bordman, Gerald. *American Musical Comedy: From Adonis to Dreamgirls.* New York: Oxford University Press, 1982.

———. *American Musical Theatre: A Chronicle.* 3rd ed. New York: Oxford University Press, 2001.

———. *American Operetta.* New York: Oxford University Press, 1981.

———. *Jerome Kern: His Life and Music.* New York: Oxford University Press, 1980.

Bradley, Edwin M. *The First Hollywood Musicals.* Jefferson, N.C.: McFarland, 1996.

Burrows, Abe. "Frank Loesser: 1910–1969." *New York Times,* August 10, 1969.

———. *Honest Abe: Is There Really No Business Like Show Business?* Boston: Little, Brown, 1980.

"Burrows Denies He Was Real Red." *New York Times,* November 13, 1952.

Canby, Vincent. "Theatre: 'Most Happy Fella' Revived." *New York Times,* May 12, 1966.

Citron, Stephen. *Jerry Herman: Poet of the Showtune.* New Haven, Conn.: Yale University Press, 2004.

———. *The Wordsmiths: Oscar Hammerstein II and Alan Jay Lerner.* New York: Oxford University Press, 1995.

Comden, Betty. *Off Stage.* New York: Simon and Schuster, 1995.

Craig, Warren. *Sweet and Lowdown: America's Popular Song Writers.* Metuchen, N.J.: Scarecrow Press, 1978.

Crawford, Richard. *America's Musical Life: A History.* New York: W. W. Norton, 2001.

———. *The Civil War Songbook.* New York: Dover, 1977.

Elon, Amos. *The Pity of It All: A History of the Jews in Germany, 1743–1933.* New York: Henry Holt, 2002.

Engel, Lehman. *The American Musical Theater.* New York: Macmillan, 1975.

———. *Words with Music: The Broadway Musical Libretto.* New York: Macmillan, 1972.

Everett, William A., and Paul R. Laird, eds. *The Cambridge Companion to the Musical.* Cambridge: Cambridge University Press, 2002.

Ewen, David. *All the Years of American Popular Music.* Englewood Cliffs, N.J.: Prentice-Hall, 1977.

———. *American Popular Songs from the American Revolutionary War to the Present.* New York: Random House, 1966.

———. "He Passes the Ammunition for Hits." *Theatre Arts* 60 (May 1956): 73–75.

Fields, Armond, and L. Marc Fields. *From the Bowery to Broadway: Lew Fields and The Roots of American Popular Theater.* New York: Oxford University Press, 1993.

Forte, Allen. *Listening to Classic American Popular Songs.* New Haven, Conn.: Yale University Press, 2001.

Frommer, Myrna Katz, and Harvey Frommer. *It Happened on Broadway: An Oral History of the Great White Way.* Madison: University of Wisconsin Press, 2004.

Furia, Philip. *Ira Gershwin: The Art of the Lyricist.* New York: Oxford University Press, 1996.

———. *Irving Berlin: A Life in Song.* New York: Schirmer Books, 1998.

———. *The Poets of Tin Pan Alley: A History of America's Great Lyricists.* New York: Oxford University Press, 1990.

Gänzl, Kurt. *The Encyclopedia of The Musical Theatre.* New York: Schirmer Books, 1994.

Garebian, Keith. *The Making of Guys and Dolls.* Oakville, Ont.: Mosaic Press, 2002.

Gevinson, Alan, ed. *Within Our Gates: Ethnicity in American Feature Films, 1911–1960*. American Film Institute Catalog. Berkeley: University of California Press, 1997.

Gordon, Eric. *Mark the Music: The Life and Work of Marc Blitzstein*. New York: St. Martin's Press, 1989.

Gottfried, Martin. *Broadway Musicals*. New York: Harry N. Abrams, 1979.

Gottlieb, Robert, and Robert Kimball, eds. *Reading Lyrics*. New York: Pantheon Books, 2000.

Grant, Mark N. *The Rise and Fall of the Broadway Musical*. Boston: Northeastern University Press, 2004.

Green, Abel, and Joe Laurie Jr. *Show Biz, from Vaude to Video*. New York: Henry Holt, 1951.

Green, Stanley. *Broadway Musicals Show by Show*. 5th ed. Revised and updated by Kay Green. Milwaukee: Hal Leonard, 1996.

The Guys and Dolls Book. London: Royal National Theatre and Nick Hern Books, 1997.

Guernsey, Otis, ed. *Broadway Song and Story: Playwrights/Lyricists/Composers Discuss Their Hits*. New York: Dodd and Mead, 1985.

Halberstam, David. *The Fifties*. New York: Villard Books, 1993.

Hamm, Charles. *Yesterdays: Popular Song in America*. New York: W. W. Norton, 1979.

Harrison, Nigel. *Songwriters: A Biographical Dictionary with Discographies*. Jefferson, N.C.: McFarland, 1998.

Hemming, Roy. *The Melody Lingers On: The Great Songwriters and Their Movie Musicals*. New York: Newmarket Press, 1986.

Hill, Richard S. Review, "Frank Loesser: *The Most Happy Fella*. Vocal Score and Libretto." *Music Library Association Notes* 14 (June 1957): 438–39.

Hirsch, Foster. *Kurt Weill on Stage: From Berlin to Broadway*. New York: Alfred A. Knopf, 2002.

Hirschhorn, Clive. *The Hollywood Musical*. 2nd ed. New York: Portland House, 1991.

Hischak, Thomas S. *The American Musical Film Song Encyclopedia*. Westport, Conn.: Greenwood Press, 1999.

———. *The American Musical Theatre Song Encyclopedia*. Westport, Conn.: Greenwood Press, 1995.

———. *Film It with Music: An Encyclopedic Guide to the American Movie Musical*. Westport, Conn.: Greenwood Press, 2001.

———. *Say It with Music: An Encyclopedic Guide to the American Musical Theatre*. Westport, Conn.: Greenwood Press, 1993.

———. *The Tin Pan Alley Song Encyclopedia*. Westport, Conn.: Greenwood Press, 2002.

Howard, Sidney. *They Knew What They Wanted*. New York: Doubleday, Page, 1925.

Jasen, David A. *Tin Pan Alley: An Encyclopedia of the Golden Age of American Song*. New York: Routledge, 2003.

Jenkins, Philip. *A History of the United States*. New York: St. Martin's Press, 1997.

Jenness, David, and Don Velsey. *Classic American Popular Song: The Second Half-Century, 1950–2000*. New York: Routledge, 2006.

Kantor, Michael, and Laurence Maslon. *Broadway: The American Musical*. New York: Bulfinch Press, 2004.

Kenney, William. *Recorded Music in American Life: The Phonograph and Popular Memory, 1890–1945*. New York: Oxford University Press, 1999.

Kern, Jerome. *The Jerome Kern Song Book: The Words and Music of 50 of His Best-Loved Songs*. Edited, with an introduction and text by Oscar Hammerstein II. Arrangements by Dr. Albert Sirmay. New York: Simon and Schuster and T. B. Harms, 1955.

Kimball, Robert, and Steve Nelson, eds. *The Complete Lyrics of Frank Loesser*. New York: Alfred A. Knopf, 2003.

Kirk, Elise. *American Opera*. Urbana: University of Illinois Press, 1998.

Knapp, Raymond. *The American Musical and the Formation of National Identity*. Princeton, N.J.: Princeton University Press, 2005.

Kowalke, Kim, ed. *A New Orpheus: Essays on Kurt Weill*. New Haven, Conn.: Yale University Press, 1986.

Laufe, Abe. *Broadway's Greatest Musicals*. 3rd ed. New York: Funk and Wagnalls, 1977.

Leacock, Stephen. *Nonsense Novels*. 9th ed. London: J. Lane, 1916.

Lehman, David. "The Man Who Rhymed 'Barbasol.'" *New York Times Book Review*, December 7, 2003.

Lindsay, Cynthia, comp. "Recollections of Frank Loesser." Unpublished typescript of forty-seven interviews at Frank Loesser Enterprises, New York, ca. 1970.

Loesser, Arthur. "My Brother Frank." *Music Library Association Notes* 7 (1949–50): 217–39.

Loesser, Frank. *The Best of Frank Loesser*. Eighty-five songs published by the Frank Music Corporation. New York: Bradley Publications, 1981.

———. *The Frank Loesser Song Book*. Preface by Richard Rodgers and introduction by Cynthia Lindsay. New York: Frank Music Corporation, 1971.

———. *The Frank Loesser Songbook*. Milwaukee: Hal Leonard, 1994.

———. *Guys and Dolls*. Vocal score. New York: Frank Music Corporation, 1950.

———. *How to Succeed in Business Without Really Trying*. Vocal score. New York: Frank Music Corporation, 1961.

———. "The Most Happy Fella." *Theatre Arts* (October 1958): 236–53.

———. *The Most Happy Fella*. Vocal score and libretto. New York: Frank Music Corporation, 1956.

———. *Where's Charley? A Musical Comedy in Two Acts*. Vocal score. New York: Frank Music Corporation, 1948.

Loesser, Frank, and George Abbott. *Where's Charley?* Libretto. London: Samuel French, 1948.

Loesser, Susan. *A Most Remarkable Fella: Frank Loesser and the Guys and Dolls in His Life: A Portrait by His Daughter*. 1993. Reprint, New York: Hal Leonard, 2000.

Mann, Martin Arthur. "The Musicals of Frank Loesser." Ph.D. diss., City University of New York, 1974.

Mast, Gerald. *Can't Help Singin': The American Musical on Stage and Screen*. Woodstock, N.Y.: Overlook Press, 1987.

Mattfeld, Julius. *Variety Music Cavalcade, 1620–1969: A Chronology of Vocal and Instrumental Music Popular in the United States*. 3rd ed. Englewood Cliffs, N.J.: Prentice-Hall, 1971.

Matthew-Walker, Robert. *Broadway to Hollywood: The Musical and the Cinema*. London: Sanctuary Publishing, 1996.

McCarty, Clifford. *Film Composers in America: A Filmography, 1911–1970.* 2nd ed. New York: Oxford University Press, 2000.

Mead, Shepherd. *How to Succeed in Business Without Really Trying: The Dastard's Guide to Fame and Fortune.* 1952. Reprint, New York: Simon and Schuster, 1995.

Meyer, Leonard. *Music, the Arts, and Ideas: Patterns and Predictions in Twentieth-Century Culture.* Chicago: University of Chicago Press, 1967.

Meyerson, Harold, and Ernie Harburg, with the assistance of Arthur Perlman. *Who Put the Rainbow in* The Wizard of Oz? *Yip Harburg, Lyricist.* Ann Arbor: University of Michigan Press, 1993.

Millstein, Gilbert. "The Greater Loesser." *New York Times Magazine,* May 20, 1956, 20, 22.

Mordden, Ethan. *Beautiful Mornin': The Broadway Musical in the 1940s.* New York: Oxford University Press, 1999.

———. *Better Foot Forward: The History of American Musical Theatre.* New York: Grossman Publishers, 1976.

———. *Coming Up Roses: The American Musical in the 1950s.* New York: Oxford University Press, 1998.

———. *The Hollywood Musical.* New York: St. Martin's Press. 1981.

The Movie Guide. Compiled by the editors of CineBooks. New York: Berkley Publishing Group, 1998.

Munden, Kenneth W., ed. *The American Film Institute Catalog of Motion Pictures Released in the United States: Feature Films, 1921–1930.* New York: R. R. Bowker, 1971.

New York Theatre Critics' Reviews. New York: Critics' Theatre Reviews, 1948–62.

Nicholls, David, ed. *The Cambridge History of American Music.* Cambridge: Cambridge University Press, 1998.

Norton, Richard C. *A Chronology of American Musical Theater.* 3 vols. New York: Oxford University Press, 2002.

Oja, Carol. *Making Music Modern: New York in the 1920s.* New York: Oxford University Press, 2000.

Porter, Susan. *With an Air Debonair: Musical Theatre in America, 1785–1815.* Washington, D.C.: Smithsonian Institution Press, 1991.

Rodgers, Richard. *Musical Stages: An Autobiography.* New York: Random House, 1975.

Romano, Anthony. "A Production History of Frank Loesser's *The Most Happy Fella.*" M.A. thesis, City University of New York, 2000.

Rosenberg, Bernard, and Ernest Harburg. *The Broadway Musical: Collaboration in Commerce and Art.* New York: New York University Press, 1993.

Runyon, Damon. *The Damon Runyon Omnibus.* 1944. Reprint, New York: American Reprint Company, 1976.

———. *Guys and Dolls: The Stories of Damon Runyon.* New York: Viking, 1992.

———. *Romance in the Roaring Forties and Other Stories.* New York: William Morrow, 1986.

Sanjek, Russell, updated by David Sanjek. *Pennies from Heaven: The American Popular Music Business in the Twentieth Century.* New York: Da Capo Press, 1996.

Sauer, Rodney. "Photoplay Music: A Reusable Repertory for Silent Film Scoring, 1914–1929." *American Music Research Center Journal* 8/9 (1998–99): 55–76.

Schumach, Murray. "Frank Loesser Hit Parade Habitué." *New York Times*, December 17, 1950.

Seaton, Gayle. "Music and Dramatic Function in Frank Loesser's Musicals." Doctoral treatise, Florida State University, 1985.

Secrest, Meryle. *Stephen Sondheim: A Life*. New York: Alfred A. Knopf, 1998.

Sennett, Ted. *Hollywood Musicals*. New York: Harry N. Abrams, 1981.

Shale, Richard. *Academy Awards: An Ungar Reference Index*. New York: Ungar, 1982.

Shaw, George Bernard. *George Bernard Shaw's Plays*. Edited and selected by Sandie Byrne. New York: W. W. Norton, 2002.

"Shows Out of Town: *Pleasures and Palaces*." *Variety*, March 17, 1965.

Smith, Cecil, and Glenn Litton. *Musical Comedy in America*. New York: Theatre Arts Books, 1981.

Sowell, Thomas. *Migrations and Cultures: A World View*. New York: Basic Books, 1996.

Spada, James. *Streisand: Her Life*. New York: Crown Publishers, 1995.

Spewack, Samuel. *The Prince and Mr. Jones*. New York: Dramatists Play Service, 1961.

Stewart, John. *Broadway Musicals, 1943–2004*. Jefferson, N.C.: McFarland, 2006.

Steyn, Mark. *Broadway Babies Say Goodnight: Musicals Then and Now*. New York: Routledge, 1999.

Suskin, Steven. *Show Tunes*. 3rd ed. New York: Oxford University Press, 2000.

Swain, Joseph P. *The Broadway Musical: A Critical and Musical Survey*. New York: Oxford University Press, 1990.

Swayne, Steve. *How Sondheim Found His Sound*. Ann Arbor: University of Michigan Press, 2005.

Taruskin, Richard. *The Oxford History of Western Music*. 6 vols. New York: Oxford University Press, 2005.

Taylor, Theodore. *Jule: The Story of Composer Jule Styne*. New York: Random House, 1979.

White, Sidney Howard. *Sidney Howard*. Boston: G. K. Hall, 1977.

Wilder, Alec. *American Popular Song: The Great Innovators, 1900–1950*. New York: Oxford University Press, 1972.

Wilk, Max. *They're Playing Our Song*. New York: Atheneum, 1973.

Woll, Allen. *The Hollywood Musical Goes to War*. Chicago: Nelson-Hall, 1983.

Selected Discography

Most recordings associated only with single musicals are listed in the Stage Works appendix.

An Evening with Frank Loesser: Frank Loesser Performs Songs from His Hit Shows. Liner notes by Joseph Weiss. CD recording. Digitally remastered from demonstration recordings. DRG Records 5169 (1992).

Frank Sings Loesser: Rare and Unreleased Performances. Liner notes by Steve Nelson. CD recording. Koch International Classics 3-724-2H1 (1995).

Greenwillow. Original cast album. Liner notes by B. J. Chute. LP recording. RCA Victor LOC 2001 (1960).

Hans Christian Andersen. Eight songs from the 1952 film, reissued with songs from *The Court Jester,* 1956 (another Danny Kaye vehicle). CD recording. Varese Sarabande VSD-5498 (1994).

I Hear Music. Archival compilation of songs with Loesser lyrics. CD recording. Pearl 7830 (1998).

Loesser by Loesser: A Salute to Frank Loesser, starring Jo Sullivan Loesser. CD recording. DRG Records 5170 (1992).

Where's Charley? CD recording. Digitally remastered from the 1958 original London cast recording. Angel 89058 (1993).

Permissions

For permission to reprint lyrics and/or music contained in this book, the publishers gratefully acknowledge the following corporations.

"Classification Blues"
by Frank Loesser
© 2003 Frank Loesser Enterprises
International Copyright Secured.
All Rights Reserved. Used by Permission.

"I'm a Gentleman"
by Frank Loesser
© 2003 Frank Loesser Enterprises
International Copyright Secured.
All Rights Reserved. Used by Permission.

"Marshmallow Magic"
by Frank Loesser
© 2003 Frank Loesser Enterprises
International Copyright Secured.
All Rights Reserved. Used by Permission.

"Poor Lonely MP"
by Frank Loesser
© 2003 Frank Loesser Enterprises
International Copyright Secured.
All Rights Reserved. Used by Permission.

"Saga of the Sack"
by Frank Loesser
© 2003 Frank Loesser Enterprises
International Copyright Secured.
All Rights Reserved. Used by Permission.

"You Live in My Heart"
by Frank Loesser
© 2003 Frank Loesser Enterprises
International Copyright Secured.
All Rights Reserved. Used by Permission.

Frank Music Corporation
Music and Lyrics

"Adelaide's Lament"
by Frank Loesser
© 1950 (Renewed) Frank Music Corp.
All Rights Reserved. Used by Permission.

"Benvenuta"
by Frank Loesser
© 1956 (Renewed) Frank Music Corp.
All Rights Reserved. Used by Permission.

"Brotherhood of Man"
by Frank Loesser
© 1961 (Renewed) Frank Music Corp.
All Rights Reserved. Used by Permission.

"A Bushel and a Peck"
by Frank Loesser

"The Ugly Duckling"
by Frank Loesser

"Walking Away Whistling"
by Frank Loesser

"Warm All Over"
by Frank Loesser

Lyrics Only

"Baby, It's Cold Outside"
by Frank Loesser

"Been a Long Day"
by Frank Loesser

"Clang Dang the Bell (Baptism of a Calf)"
by Frank Loesser

"Gold Medal Commercial"
by Frank Loesser

"I Believe in You"
by Frank Loesser

"I Wish I Were Twins"
Lyric by Edgar De Lange and Frank Loesser
Music by Joseph Meyer

"If I Were a Bell"
by Frank Loesser

© 1948, 1950 (Renewed) Frank Music Corp.
All Rights Reserved. Used by Permission.

Irving Berlin Music Company
Lyrics

"Blue Skies"
by Irving Berlin
© 1926, 1927 by Irving Berlin. Copyright Renewed.
International Copyright Secured.
All Rights Reserved. Reprinted by Permission.

Warner Bros. Publications U.S. Incorporated
Lyrics

"Heart and Soul"
from the Paramount Short Subject *A Song Is Born*
Words by Frank Loesser
Music by Hoagy Carmichael
© 1938 (Renewed 1965) by Famous Music LLC
International Copyright Secured. All Rights Reserved.

"I Wish I Didn't Love You So"
from the Paramount Picture *The Perils of Pauline*
Words and music by Frank Loesser
© 1947 (Renewed 1974) by Famous Music LLC
International Copyright Secured. All Rights Reserved.

"Seventeen"
from the Paramount Pictures film *Seventeen*
Words and music by Frank Loesser
© 1939 (Renewed 1966) by Paramount Music Corporation
International Copyright Secured. All Rights Reserved.

"Tallahassee"
by Frank Loesser
© 1947 (Renewed 1974) by Famous Music LLC
International Copyright Secured. All Rights Reserved.

"They're Either Too Young or Too Old"
Words by Frank Loesser
Music by Arthur Schwartz
© 1943 (Renewed) Warner Bros. Inc.
All Rights Reserved. Used by Permission of Alfred Publishing Co., Inc.

"Thou Swell"
Words by Lorenz Hart
Music by Richard Rodgers
© 1927 (Renewed) by Williamson Music and Warner Bros., Inc.
International Copyright Secured.
All Rights Reserved. Used by Permission.
© 1927 (Renewed) Warner Bros., Inc.
Rights for Extended Renewal Term in U.S. controlled by WB Music Corp.

Index

Italicized page numbers indicate illustrations (*i*), musical examples (*e*), and tables (*t*).